Religious Orders of the Catholic Reformation

John C. Olin, with his Bene Merenti medal in recognition of forty years of service at Fordham University.

Religious Orders of the Catholic Reformation

IN HONOR OF JOHN C. OLIN
ON HIS SEVENTY-FIFTH BIRTHDAY

Edited by
RICHARD L. DeMOLEN

Fordham University Press
New York
1994

Library of Congress Cataloging-in-Publication Data

Religious orders of the Catholic Reformation : essays in honor of John
C. Olin on his seventy-fifth birthday / edited by Richard L. DeMolen.
    p.   cm.
Includes bibliographical references and index.
ISBN 0–8232–1512–1 : $30.00
    1. Monasticism and religious orders—Europe—History—16th
century. 2. Counter-Reformation. I. DeMolen, Richard L. II. Olin,
John C.
BX2590.R45   93–23762
271'.0094'09031—dc20   CIP

PUBLICATION OF THIS BOOK WAS AIDED BY A GRANT
FROM THE HARRY J. SIEVERS, S.J. MEMORIAL PUBLISHING FUND

Printed in the United States of America

CONTENTS

Dedication

Roger Wines

"An historian must be old," Leopold von Ranke once remarked, not only because of the vast extent of the field of study, but also because historical scholarship is enriched by a lifetime of experience. Musicians and mathematicians bloom early, but historians get better with each passing decade. John C. Olin's career in history, which has produced so many studies, so many students, and so many friends, is a classic example of this thesis. His major publications in the field of the Catholic Reformation came only after the age of forty; and despite forty years of teaching at Fordham University, his youthful enthusiasm and mature insight continue to produce solid works of scholarship in the twilight of retirement.

I first met John in 1954 as a college student in his course on the Reformation, and was struck by his special qualities as a teacher. Fordham had several dynamic professors in the history department in those days: the colorful Sam Telfair, the intense Robert Remini, the encyclopedic Paul Levack, and the magisterial Ross Hoffman. But John's style of teaching seemed unique. While other professors taught the facts, he stood in respectful awe of the past, pointing out problems and mysteries and introducing his students to a sense of discovery. His mastery of the subject, founded in humility before the task, encouraged many of us to take up history as a career. Though my professional interests diverged from his, I have never lost my enthusiasm for the topics he had laid before us; and to this day, I am as eager to pick up a good book on Erasmus as one on Frederick the Great. Later on, I would study the Reformation in graduate school at Columbia University with the brilliant Garrett Mattingly, but what I had learned from John proved to be more enduring and far more inspirational.

As his reputation grew, John convinced colleagues in other institutions to devote their efforts to the Catholic Reformation and attracted many talented students to the graduate program at Fordham. In 1967, I helped John and Wilhelm Pauck of Union Theological Seminary to organize a conference on the 450th anniversary of Luther's Ninety-Five Theses, which brought together for the first time many leading Catholic and Protestant scholars of the Reformation era. It became clear to this group that more research on the Catholic Reformation was essential if we were to understand fully the events that troubled the sixteenth century at the very time that the Catholic Church itself was undergoing a process of renewal and revision of its post-Tridentine traditions, which required an honest examination of its own past, and a reconsideration of the events and issues that had produced the fatal division of Christendom. As an early advocate and catalyst, John played a significant part in developing today's renewed interest in the Catholic Reformation. Comments by others in this volume may explore that theme more fully; let me turn to the man himself.

John C. Olin, who was born in Buffalo, New York, on October 7, 1915, was educated at Canisius High School and Canisius College, where he graduated with a B.A. in history in 1937. He moved on from the Jesuits of Buffalo to the Jesuits of New York City as a graduate student in Modern European History at Fordham University from 1940 to 1942, earning his M.A. in 1941. During the war years, he served as a U.S. Navy officer in China and married his wife, Marian, in 1943. After the war he returned to Fordham to help teach the great rush of veterans in 1946. John also commenced his studies for the Ph.D. at Columbia University, began a family (Mary Beth, John, Margaret, and Thomas), and built a house for them with his own hands in a forest in Rockland County. By 1960, when he completed his dissertation at Columbia under Shepard Clough on "Christian Democrats and Foreign Policy in France, 1919–1950," John had become an important part of the History Department at Fordham.

In those days, latter-day Thomism still held sway in Fordham's Philosophy Department, and the standard history course for the B.A. was Medieval History. With its required Latin, Gothic architecture, and Jesuit atmosphere, Fordham was a natural vantage point from which to approach the era of the Catholic Reformation. Even before he completed formal requirements for the doctorate, John's interests had begun to shift from twentieth-century French history to Erasmus and the sixteenth century.

During the tumultuous years of the 1960s, John steadfastly busied himself with the events of an earlier era. He produced a series of articles and critical editions of sixteenth-century texts: *Christian Humanism and the Reformation: Selected Writings of Erasmus* (New York: Harper & Row, 1965); *A Reformation Debate: Sadoleto's Letter to the Genevans and Calvin's Reply* (New York: Harper & Row, 1966); and *The Catholic Reformation: Savonarola to Ignatius Loyola* (New York: Harper & Row, 1969).

Equally significant for his development as a scholar were two major conferences which he helped to organize at Fordham University. In 1967, a joint meeting of Catholic and Protestant scholars produced a collection of essays, *Luther, Erasmus, and the Reformation: A Catholic-Protestant Reappraisal* (New York: Fordham University Press, 1969), and in 1985, John chaired a symposium on Thomas More's *Utopia*, whose proceedings he edited as *Interpreting Thomas More's Utopia* (New York: Fordham University Press, 1989).

In order to complete his scholarship, John visited rare book collections in various European and American libraries. He also worked with Joseph F. O'Callaghan to edit a translation of *The Autobiography of St. Ignatius Loyola, with Related Documents* (New York: Harper & Row, 1974) and published various articles on Erasmus in *Six Essays on Erasmus and a Translation of Erasmus' Letter to Carondolet, 1523* (New York: Fordham University Press, 1979). In 1990, he summed up much of his earlier efforts in *Catholic Reform from Cardinal Ximenes to the Council of Trent, 1495–1563*, which, like so many of his recent books, was published by Fordham University Press. Among John's briefer works are a study on "The Idea of Pilgrimage in the Experience of Ignatius Loyola," which first appeared in *Church History* and is reprinted in *Catholic Reform*, and an article on Erasmus and St. Jerome in the *Erasmus of Rotterdam Society Yearbook* for 1987.

Alongside the progress and publication of his own studies, John witnessed the steady development of the whole field of research in the Catholic Reformation. He was invited to speak to many groups and to teach courses at the University of San Francisco, Princeton Theological Seminary, and Notre Dame University. He also served on the editorial board of the *Erasmus of Rotterdam*

Society Yearbook (1981 to 1992), and gave the seventh annual Erasmus Society Birthday Lecture at the Folger Shakespeare Library in 1986. His retirement from active teaching and service on the Faculty Senate at Fordham University in 1986 gave him the opportunity to travel more widely and to pursue an impressive program of research.

Over the last decades, John has worked on many aspects of sixteenth-century reform but most frequently on the prince of humanists, who was so central to the movement itself. Of all of Erasmus' works, none has occupied him for so long as that scholar's great edition of the *opera* of St. Jerome. He and Professor James F. Brady of Fordham's Classics Department collaborated on a volume on that work which was published by the University of Toronto Press in 1992 in the Collected Works of Erasmus series. Though separated by centuries, Erasmus and Jerome were kindred spirits, and I think that John was attracted to them because he too shares their spirit. Moreover, I believe that Erasmus would have been pleased with the results of these years of labor because he could not have found a better critic nor a truer friend, and neither could we.

Preface

To honor John C. Olin for his many contributions to the study of Catholic reform in the sixteenth century, I have assembled nine essays on Catholic religious orders of that period. The contributors chose the religious order of their preference, but they were asked to devote attention to the spirituality of the founder(s) as well as to the specific apostolate of their order. With the exceptions of the Discalced Carmelites (Spain) and the Visitandines (France), the orders of men and women discussed in this volume originated in Italy.

This collection of essays focuses on the religious communities that were founded between 1524, when the Theatines, whom Paul Hallett referred to as the "cradle of the Catholic Reformation," arose, and 1621, when the Piarists were recognized by the papacy as a religious order.[1] Although the rules of the Theatines, which was the first of the ten orders of clerics regular, and the Piarists differed, the apostolates of these communities of priests were the same: to reform the clergy and to evangelize the laity by preaching, teaching, performing good works, and administering the sacraments. Most of these orders were founded for reasons unrelated to the crisis posed by Protestantism, but they were soon enlisted by the hierarchy to counteract its effects. If the Council of Trent (1545–1563) can be considered as the architect of Catholic reform and renewal, and the papacy and the episcopate as its enforcers, surely the religious orders of men and women in the sixteenth and early seventeenth centuries—whether newly founded or reformed—ought to be considered as the initiators or disseminators of reform while serving as missionaries, teachers, preachers, catechists, and confessors.

Monuments to these religious orders, which contributed so much energy to Catholic renewal in the sixteenth century, were commissioned in the nineteenth century. Sculptors produced larger-than-life statues of the various founders and foundresses for the interior colonnade of St. Peter's Basilica in Rome. Some of these figures are readily recognizable images of well-known saints, but others are more obscure. Among the marble statues one can find likenesses of St. Antonio Maria Zaccaria, founder of the Barnabites and the Angelic Sisters of St. Paul; St. Angela Merici, foundress of the Ursulines; St. Filippo Neri, founder of the Oratorians; St. François de Sales, co-founder of the order of the Visitation; St. Gaetano da Thiene, co-founder of the Theatines; St. José de Calasanz, founder of the Piarists; St. Ignatius de Loyola, founder of the Jesuits; and St. Teresa de Avila, foundress of the Discalced Carmelites. The religious communities founded by these saints, together with the Capuchins whose founders have not been canonized, will be discussed in the following chapters.

Side by side with the sixteenth-century orders of clerics regular and the various religious congregations with or without simple vows labored the earlier orders of monks (Benedictines, Cistercians, and Carthusians), the canons regular (of the Lateran, Praemonstratensians, Crosiers, etc.), and the mendicant friars (Trinitarians, Franciscans, Dominicans, Servites, etc.). These communities complemented the later foundations (even if they were occasionally critical of individual members), because they promoted distinct apostolates and observed different traditions. Observant monks, friars, and nuns attempted to reform their orders throughout the sixteenth century, but, with the exceptions of the Discalced Carmelites and the Capuchins, their contributions will not be identified in this book.

The Capuchins, who were founded by Matteo da Bascio (d. 1552), a Franciscan Observant, and several collaborators about 1525, remained a branch of the Franciscan Observants until the seventeenth century. Bernardino d'Asti defended the Capuchins at the Council of Trent for their refusal to own property and their insistence upon begging as a livelihood. In 1574, Gregory XIII gave them permission to establish houses outside Italy. Friaries soon appeared in France, Spain, Switzerland, Bohemia, Bavaria, and Ireland. The Capuchins were given their independence from the Observants in 1619.

From some 18 members in 1529, the Capuchins grew to 17,000 members by 1625, located in 42 provinces throughout Europe. Their first martyr was the missionary Fidelis of Sigmaringen, who was killed by Calvinists in Switzerland in 1622. But the Capuchins were not satisfied with apostolic labors in Europe alone. The supreme monument to their missionary zeal was the

Congregation for the Propagation of the Faith. The Capuchin vicar general Girolamo da Narni suggested its creation to Gregory XV in 1622.[2] The first prefect of the Congregation was the Capuchin cardinal Antonio Barberini, the brother of Urban VIII. In Chapter 2, Elisabeth G. Gleason provides a detailed account of the origins of the Capuchin Friars.

Parallel to the formation of religious orders of men, there appeared communities of women who followed the Rules of the four ancient orders of the Church: those of St. Anthony, St. Basil, St. Augustine, and St. Benedict. All orders or congregations—whether of men or women—that were established after these four religious families had to be affiliated with one of them, even if they developed a distinctive constitution of their own.

In addition to the first orders of men and the second orders of contemplative women, third orders of lay people were established in the thirteenth century. By the sixteenth century the Franciscans, Dominicans, Augustinians, Servites, Mercedarians, Trinitarians, Carmelites, and Norbertines had established third-order communities of women throughout Europe. Congregations of sisters that were not directly related to one of the older orders of men also appeared in the sixteenth and early seventeenth centuries. These included the Angelic Sisters of St. Paul, the Ursulines, and the Visitandines—each of whom will be discussed in one of the following chapters.

The Company of the Virgins of St. Ursula of Brescia was founded by St. Angela Merici in 1535. Individual members chose their own spiritual directors and continued to live in separate homes without taking vows or wearing religious habits; but they combined their efforts to teach girls the elements of learning and to care for the poor. Archbishop Carlo Borromeo invited twelve Ursulines to Milan in 1568 and then pressured them into accepting the authority of a male spiritual adviser he would appoint, adopting enclosure, wearing a uniform habit, and professing solemn vows after a two-year novitiate. Moreover, he imposed his own rule on them, which was approved by Gregory XIII in 1582. Other bishops followed his example throughout Italy and in Avignon and Paris. For a detailed discussion of the early history of the Ursulines, see Chapter 4 by Charmarie J. Blaisdell.

In contrast with the active life of the Ursulines, the Discalced Carmelites were founded as a contemplative order by St. Teresa de Avila in 1562. She sought to observe the primitive rule with pristine fidelity. Although she traveled widely by mule-drawn cart, St. Teresa kept in touch through correspondence with the sixteen convents she had established. The nuns of her order devoted themselves to the recitation of the Divine Office in choir, prayer, and sacrifice for the spread of the faith, the extirpation of heresy, and the sanctification of priests. Chapter 6, by Jodi Bilinkoff, offers additional information on the influence of the Discalced Carmelites in Spain.

The Order of the Visitation of the Virgin Mary, on the other hand, combined the active and the contemplative life. Founded by St. François de Sales and St. Jeanne de Chantal in 1610 as a congregation of sisters with simple vows who cared for the poor and the sick outside its convents, the order accepted candidates who were virgins or widows, young or old, healthy or infirm. Both co-founders kept in contact with the various convents of the order through frequent letters. In 1615, the archbishop of Lyons, Denis-Simon de Marquemont, imposed enclosure on the convent in Lyons and required that these sisters profess solemn vows. Paul V favored the archbishop's innovations and approved the Visitation order in 1618 on condition that all its members embrace enclosure and profess solemn vows. He was, in effect, enforcing the decrees of the Council of Trent, but at the expense of suppressing innovation. Wendy M. Wright discusses the spirituality of the Visitandines in Chapter 8.

In the opening decades of the sixteenth century, the Catholic Church strengthened its resolve to imitate the life of Christ by activating a network of new religious orders of men which, together with the episcopate, the secular clergy, and a lay apostolate, would promote spiritual renewal through self-denial and service to humankind. Encouraged in these efforts by the papacy, especially Paul III, Gregory XIII, and Sixtus V, the various religious orders—some of them newly reformed—joined forces with the Council of Trent to renew the Church and to counter the advances of Protestantism by extinguishing abuses, clarifying doctrine, and serving as models of Christian virtue.

Nine of the orders of clerics regular were established in Italy between 1524 and 1617 as alternatives to the forms of service offered by monks, canons, and friars. These orders of priests adopted the cassocks of the secular clergy and became indistinguishable from them in appearance. Eventually they admitted lay brothers who performed menial tasks in their houses. The ministries of the clerics regular were located in the towns and cities of Italy and were centered in hospitals, orphanages, schools, and homes for wayward adolescent girls. They also engaged in the administering of the sacraments and in the preaching of the gospel. Less emphasis was placed on the traditional monastic, canonical, and mendicant practices of fasting and abstinence, the Divine Office in choir, and contemplation. The clerics regular gave greater emphasis to mental prayer, spiritual reading, and the Holy Eucharist in the Forty Hours' Devotion.

The first of the orders of clerics regular was founded in Rome in 1524 by St. Gaetano da Thiene and Giovanni Pietro Carafa (later Paul IV), who adopted the cross of Christ as the emblem of the Theatines. In a letter, dated 1526–1527, they declared that their rule of life was based on the Acts of the Apostles, but it can also be viewed as an extension of the observances maintained by the Oratory of Divine Love, which St. Gaetano had helped to establish in Rome about 1515. Concerning the unlikely combination of Thiene and Carafa, James Brodrick, s.J., has noted: "His [Carafa's] partnership with Cajetan [Thiene], one of the sweetest and most lovable of the saints, was the strangest imaginable, that of an eagle with a nightingale."[3]

The Theatines dedicated themselves to the reform of clergy and the fostering of lay spirituality within and without the already existing confraternities. Although Thiene and Carafa opposed monastic enclosure, they advocated community life that provided for periods of study, meditation, and penitential practices in the daily schedule. The word "Theatine" soon became a synonym for reform. The best-known expression of the spirituality of the Theatines in the sixteenth century can be found in *Spiritual Combat*, probably composed by the Theatine Lorenzo Scupoli, who recommended daily communion for the laity. Kenneth J. Jorgensen, s.J., compares and contrasts the contributions of the cofounders in Chapter 1.

St. Antonio Maria Zaccaria founded the third order of Clerics Regular of St. Paul in 1533 and the Angelic Sisters of St. Paul in 1535. Like the Praemonstratensians and the Bridgettines before them, these congregations of men and women combined their ministries. They worked among the poor and the afflicted in Mi-

lan until ecclesiastical authorities intervened. For further information on the first centenary of the Barnabites, see Chapter 3 by
the editor.

Toward the end of 1536, nine companions of Ignatius de Loyola, en route to Venice from Paris, visited the tomb of Erasmus
of Rotterdam, who had died in July at Basel and was buried there
in the cathedral: Diego Laínez, Simón Rodrigues, Alfonso Salmerón, St. Francis Xavier, Claude Le Jay, Paschase Bröet, Jean
Codure, Nicholas Bobadilla, and Bl. Pierre Favre all paid their
respects to this internationally known priest-scholar, who had left
the cloister of his monastery at Steyn in 1493 to pursue a scholarly
life in the world while maintaining the apostolic spirit of the order
of Canons Regular of St. Augustine. Through the printed word,
Erasmus reached thousands of readers and helped to reform the
religious life of the cleric and the layman as well.[4]

United in their desire to serve Christ, these admirers of Erasmus helped to establish the Society of Jesus, which was founded
in Rome as the fifth order of clerics regular by St. Ignatius de
Loyola in 1540. It soon became the largest of these orders. The
Society's importance to Catholic reform, especially its promotion
of the goals of Trent, warrants additional space in this Preface.
Loyola completed the first draft of his Constitution in 1550, which
was confirmed by a General Congregation of the order after his
death in 1558. He made the instruction of children one of the
principal parts of the Jesuit apostolate in Section 4 of the
Constitution.

As a result of his innovative spirit, Loyola was twice brought
before the Inquisition in Spain, accused with his companions of
heresy ("a secret Lutheran sect") in Paris, and investigated later
in Rome. Melchior Cano (d. 1560), a Spanish Dominican from the
University of Salamanca, denounced Loyola's *Spiritual Exercises* as
heretical, but Paul III authorized its publication and it soon became
a spiritual classic, the first composed by a layman for the laity.
The purpose of the *Exercises* was "to seek and find the Divine
Will in the laying out of one's life" and, once "elected," to fulfill
one's vocation through perfection. Loyola saw self-conquest and
self-denial as indispensable prerequisites for an active, enduring
love of Christ. He himself practiced acts of mortification while
superior general of the order.

Alongside their network of papally approved seminaries, the

Society of Jesus established schools (referred to as colleges) for boys, who were between the ages of ten and fourteen. Jesuits also wrote textbooks and catechisms for students. St. Peter Canisius (1521–1597), for example, authored three catechisms between 1555 and 1558, which went through numerous editions in many languages for students inside and outside Jesuit-staffed schools. These catechisms reflected Tridentine doctrine. In addition to Canisius, three other Jesuits, namely Le Jay, Laínez, and Salmerón, influenced Catholic reform by participating directly in the deliberations at Trent. See Chapter 5 on the Jesuits by John W. O'Malley, s.j., for further contributions.

The last of the orders of clerics regular that appeared in Italy were the Piarists or the Clerics Regular of the Mother of God of the Pious Schools. They were founded in Rome by St. José de Calasanz (1557–1648) in 1617. He had earlier established the first free school for poor boys in 1597 at Santa Dorotea in Trastevere (Rome) and sought financial assistance for it from wealthy patrons. In 1602, Clement VIII authorized the followers of Calasanz to live a common life but without professing formal vows. Between 1614 and 1617 the community was joined to the Leonardini or Clerics Regular of the Mother of God who had been founded by St. Giovanni Leonardi in 1574. Paul V separated them in 1617. In 1621, Gregory XV recognized the Piarists as a religious order with solemn vows and approved their Constitution in 1622. In spite of their founder's Spanish origin, the Piarists maintained a distinctly Italian focus, except for small houses in Moravia and Poland, until the later seventeenth century. Chapter 9, by Paul F. Grendler, details their educational activities in Italy.

Perhaps the two most influential leaders of Catholic reform in the sixteenth century who were not popes were Borromeo and Neri. St. Carlo Borromeo (1538–1584), the aristocratic and austere cardinal-archbishop of Milan, tried to impose greater control over the lives of members of religious orders by enforcing the decrees of the Council of Trent. St. Filippo Neri (1515–1595), the unpretentious and playful apostle of Rome, resisted ecclesiastical attempts to force him to adopt an apostolate that was associated with the traditional activities of monks, canons regular, friars, and clerics regular. Neri gave vent to an indigenous spirituality among the secular clergy with whom he had a special affinity. The fact that Borromeo was canonized in 1610 and Neri in 1622 gave added

weight to their respective positions and enshrined their reputations in the religious orders that they founded or influenced. In
Chapter 7 John Patrick Donnelly, s.j., underscores those qualities
of Neri that ensured his success as the founder of the Oratorians.

As preachers, teachers, catechists, missionaries, and servants of
the poor and the afflicted, these religious orders—in deference to
the wishes of cardinal protectors who had been appointed by the
papacy—disseminated the decrees of the Council of Trent and
sought renewal within the framework of its teachings. Those
houses that opposed Tridentine reforms were suppressed by the
papacy and episcopate. At the same time, religious communities
that promoted reform and renewal under their direction were re-
warded with preferments. In the words of John C. Olin, the
Catholic reformers "sought the revival of religion, that is the reform of the individual Christian in a Church renewed and rededi-
cated to its spiritual tasks."[5] Moreover, it was the religious orders
of the sixteenth century that strove to preserve the unity of the
Church after the initial success of the Protestant Reformation. It
is the unity of their purpose rather than individual differences
which should be kept in mind when reading the following collection of essays.

RICHARD L. DeMOLEN
Bethlehem, Pennsylvania

NOTES

1. Paul H. Hallett, *Catholic Reformer: A Life of St. Cajetan of Thiene*
(Westminster, Md.: Newman, 1959), p. 76.

2. Cuthbert of Brighton, o.s.f.c. [Lawrence A. Hess], *The Capuchins:
A Contribution to the History of the Counter-Reformation*, 2 vols. (Port
Washington, N.Y.: Kennikat, 1971), II:355n9. Originally published in
1928.

3. James Brodrick, s.j., *The Progress of the Jesuits (1556–79)* (Chicago:
Loyola University Press, 1986), p. 3. Originally published in 1940.

4. Richard L. DeMolen, "Erasmus' Commitment to the Canons
Regular of St. Augustine," *Renaissance Quarterly*, 26 (1973), 437–43.

5. John C. Olin, *Catholic Reform from Cardinal Ximenes to the Council of Trent, 1495–1563* (New York: Fordham University Press, 1990), p. 37.

ACKNOWLEDGMENT

I am indebted to the following individuals or religious communities for supplying information on specific religious orders of priests, brothers, and sisters in the preparation of this volume: Sister Sheila Campbell, o.s.u., secretary of the Ursuline Provincialate (Bronx, New York); the Company of Mary (Tustin, California); the Rev. Italo Dell'Oro, c.r.s., of the Somascan Fathers and Brothers (Suncook, New Hampshire); the Franciscan Sisters of Mary Immaculate (Amarillo, Texas); Professor Nelson H. Minnich of The Catholic University of America, Brother Stephen de la Rosa, o.h., provincial of the Hospitaller Brothers of St. John of God (Los Angeles, California); the Rev. Halbert Weidner, c.o., of the Oratorians in Rock Hill, South Carolina; and the Rev. Donald Wiest, O.F.M. Cap., of St. Bonaventure Monastery (Detroit, Michigan).

Religious Orders of the Catholic Reformation

St. Gaetano Thiene by an anonymous seventeenth-century artist. Theatine Generalate, Rome.

1

The Theatines

Kenneth J. Jorgensen, S.J.

Spirituality and Biographies of the Co-Founders

The Roman Oratory of Divine Love provided the impetus that convinced four of its members to establish a new religious community in 1524. Of the four, Gaetano Thiene[1] and Gian Pietro Carafa,[2] because of their individual accomplishments and their overall influence on the group, have rightly become identified as the co-founders of this first community of clerics regular, the Theatines. This community reflected the lives of the founders in many ways but did so particularly in a tenuous combination of Thiene's piety and Carafa's commitment to ecclesiastical reform. Although Thiene and Carafa came from similar Italian backgrounds and traditional clerical training, each had a distinctive vision of the group, particularly its basic service to the Catholic Church. Moreover, each had arrived at his decision in 1524 by different paths.

Gaetano Thiene's entire adult life was one of sacramental piety and benevolent service. Born at Vicenza in 1480, he was the offspring of a noble family. Little is known of his youth except that his father died in 1482 and his mother, Maria Porto, saw to his rearing, especially his religious training. He completed a legal education at the University of Padua in 1504 by graduating *in utroque iure*, that is, in both civil and canon law, and the same year received tonsure. In the beginning of 1507, he went to Rome where he received a position as a protonotary apostolic. His circle of friends brought him into contact with the Roman Oratory of Divine Love, a confraternity, founded sometime between 1514 and 1517, which was modeled on the prototype in Genoa and committed to providing care for the incurably sick.[3] The spiritual renewal this facilitated prompted Thiene to request ordination to the priesthood in September 1516; henceforth, Gaetano Thiene identified himself with the values and activities of the Oratory of Divine Love.

From 1518 to 1523, Gaetano Thiene undertook an extended trip to Vicenza, Verona, and Venice,[4] and in each city he supported the founding of Oratories and the establishment of hospitals for incurables. In January 1519 at Vicenza he joined the Compagnia di San Girolamo della Carità and transformed it with the addition of features from the Roman Oratory, especially the encouragement of more frequent confession and communion. Moreover, he used his own funds to support the hospital of the Misericordia (which the confraternity had administered since 1506). Gian Domenico Zanninelli, a confrère at Vicenza, advised Thiene to moderate his generosity, to which he responded: "I will never cease to donate to the needy until on behalf of Christ I become so poor myself that I cannot obtain my own burial place except by begging."[5] Having already provided food and medicine to the sick of the Misericordia, he convinced the brothers of San Girolamo to overcome any loathing and to re-establish their institution exclusively for the incurably sick. When they agreed, he then left his family estates and began to reside at the hospital. During his time in Vicenza, Thiene also made a six-month excursion to Verona. In July 1519, he entered Verona's Confraternità Segrega del Sanctissimo Corpo di Cristo where, as he had done with others, he encouraged the members to practice more frequent communion and to accept the care of a hospital for incurables.

After leaving Verona and Vicenza, Thiene traveled to Venice where he founded another Oratory of Divine Love in 1521 and helped to establish (during Lent 1522) another hospital.[6] The project grew rapidly, supported by the nobility and the Venetian government. (Eighty patients lived at the hospital in 1524; by April 1525, the number had reached 150.[7]) This hospital served, moreover, as a focus for evangelizing the poor. The state of religion in Venice, in particular, had discouraged Thiene; at the beginning of 1523, writing to his friend Paolo Giustiniano, he lamented: "This magnificent city—how can one help weeping over you? Certainly, there is no one here who seeks Christ crucified." He complained that he could not discover even one member of the nobility who despised honor for the love of Christ. "Christ waits; no one is moved. I do not say that there are no people here of good will, but all remained . . . embarrassed to be seen going to confession and communion."[8] Thiene believed that Christians in Venice, instead of being restrained out of fear for the adverse judgments of neighbors, should declare their beliefs by their participation in the sacraments. They should thereby "with great glory instead of embarrassment approach the priest [to partake of communion] as famished individuals seeking to be fed."[9]

Gaetano thought that the laity's reluctance to participate in confession and communion resulted from insufficient courage to live out their beliefs in public; their religious practice was so lax that the clergy had to minister diligently to the laity. He realized that alone he could accomplish little, but with similarly minded clergymen he could improve religious and sacramental habits. The discouraging circumstances of the Venetian church must have contributed in part to Thiene's resolution, formalized upon his return to Rome in 1523, to create a community of idealistic priests who could transform such negligent attitudes and habits among lay Christians.

By contrast, the Theatine co-founder, Gian Pietro Carafa, scion of a wealthy and influential Neapolitan family, concentrated on a career within the hierarchy of the Church. His first episcopal see of Chieti became the basis for the commonly used name *Teatino*. Although personally pious and devoted to his church office, Carafa had never experienced poverty and sacrifice; nor had he, prior to 1522, identified himself with works of charity. Educated from the age of fourteen in ecclesiastical and diplomatic circles that prepared him to move easily among the elite, Carafa went to Rome in 1494, where he resided at the Orsini palace with his paternal uncle, Cardinal Oliviero Carafa, a canonist and theologian, who was *papabile* in five conclaves. Oliviero supported the arts and attracted "a group of intellectuals noted for their devotion to scriptural studies and to the antique."[10] He was an early patron of printing and supported scholars and artists such as Bramante and Filippino Lippi. Oliviero, however, combined his appreciation for the arts with rigorous doctrinal and institutional standards for the Church. Gian Pietro, educated within this artistic yet strict environment for thirteen years, became known for "his astonishing memory, which enabled him to quote with ease from Scripture and the works of Thomas Aquinas."[11] He continued his intellectual interests during his travels as a papal diplomat, and in

England in 1514 he met Erasmus, with whom he subsequently corresponded sporadically. According to Erasmus, Carafa was "a man of consummate learning."[12] While writing to Leo X in 1515, Erasmus declared that "[Carafa] adds . . . such integrity, such holiness of life, such modesty, such friendliness seasoned with an admirable dignity, that he . . . offers . . . a finished model, whence all may draw their pattern for every virtue."[13] Later Erasmus asked Carafa for "literary and learned help."[14] Within this environment young Gian Pietro was exposed to currents of reform in the Catholic world; he took from it tools useful for his life, but unfortunately he seemed to leave behind certain underlying principles of Renaissance learning. Those values combined a respect for humanistic and classical scholarship with the traditional piety of the Church.

By the time Carafa joined the Roman Oratory of Divine Love in 1522–1523 at the age of forty-six, he had achieved prominence and held two ecclesiastical positions. He was bishop of Chieti and archbishop of Brindisi. His association with the Oratory seems to have changed his life. This confraternity included both laymen and priests, but was overwhelmingly lay. Internally, as a *disciplinati* company, its devotional life centered on the communal, the liturgical, and the penitential, specifically calling for the regular use of the discipline in imitation of Christ's scourging; these associations of personal piety emphasized penance through self-flagellation.[15] Besides giving alms and visiting sick brothers, members of the Oratory cared for the genteel poor and the syphilitic. Their desire for self-sanctification branched out toward the governance of hospitals devoted to the chronically sick. Even though this Roman group left few records of its daily life, it can be assumed that while he was a member, Carafa performed the regular duties of a brother-member with his habitual dutifulness. He probably even shared in such common penances as anonymity, fasting, and taking the discipline. Unfortunately, he does not disclose in anything extant why he joined or what he thought of this pious lay group that intentionally limited clerical membership and influence. Gian Pietro Carafa apparently approved of the Oratory's public works of charity, such as the Roman Hospital for Incurables, Arcispedale di S. Giacomo, since he was selected by the Hospitals for Incurables to represent their interests at the Roman curia.[16]

Although groomed for high ecclesiastical office, Carafa shared in the egalitarian lay nature of the confraternity. This experience, however, did not broaden his view of reform. It would seem that he did not value this species of lay piety or incorporate any of its ideals into his later policies. The influence of the Oratory—positive in light of his rejecting aspects of his past, perhaps negative in his attitude toward lay piety—fostered his desire to join with others in some form of brotherhood of priests.

By 1524 Gaetano Thiene and Gian Pietro Carafa had independently reached a similar decision: to establish a congregation of Roman Catholic priests who would embrace the responsibilities of the clerical state devoutly and austerely. Either could have initiated his own community, but Carafa approached Thiene and asked to be allowed to join the group gathering around him. Thiene, concerned that Carafa's wealth, influence, and double bishoprics would prevent his full participation in a poor community of simple priests, refused. According to the early chroniclers, Carafa fell to his knees, warning Thiene that if he continued to refuse Carafa's request, he would be held responsible for the bishop's soul on the day of judgment. Thiene then knelt down and, embracing Carafa with affection, promised: "I will never abandon you!" This dramatic confrontation led to the agreement by which these two reformers founded their community of regular clerics.[17]

Of the two reformers Carafa is more problematic than Thiene because his life and attitudes are not as consistent. In many respects, in fact, there seem to have been two Carafas: the early one up to 1527 and perhaps to 1536 (when he became cardinal and relocated permanently to Rome) and the later Carafa who appears clearly after 1542 and especially after 1555 when he was elected pope. Although there are continuities, there was great change in his outlook and in the severity of his actions. Carafa's privileged lineage and career had prepared him to encourage priests and bishops in their duties and to pursue policies that strengthened ecclesiastical and moral discipline; his many positions with curial responsibilities kept his focus on the central government of the Church.

As Pope Paul IV, Carafa was notorious for actions that contradicted the concerns and efforts of the early Theatines and their confraternal forebears. In 1555, for example, he ordered (in *Cum nimis absurdum*) that Jews must live in ghettos, must sell their real property to Christians, and must limit their commercial activity with Christians to the sale of secondhand clothing.[18] For Rome and other papal cities, these restrictions entailed the rapid formation of Jewish ghettos and compromised earlier tolerance.

In January 1559, Paul IV promulgated the Roman Index of Prohibited Books.[19] This action was the fruition of efforts (since 1543) as master inquisitor to destroy pernicious literature anywhere in Catholic lands. The Index forbade the ownership and reading of all books by Protestant writers, such as Calvin, Luther, and Cranmer, and even included their writings on subjects other than theology or religion.[20] It also condemned 330 anonymous books, editions of the vernacular Bible, and books dealing with matters such as divination, magic, and astrology. In addition, the Inquisition and its Index condemned Talmudic and rabbinical literature.[21] A number of texts by Catholic writers in good standing (or who had died in good standing) were also prohibited. All of Erasmus was included, even his editions of such patristic writers as Cyprian, Jerome, and Augustine on the grounds that they had become contaminated by his comments and notes. As a final ironic touch, Paul IV put some of his own efforts on the Index by prohibiting the report of the 1537 reform commission (the *Consilium*), of which he had been a member.[22] The Roman Index of Paul IV shows the extent to which he thought the Catholic Church should censor literature. The cultural repression tragically put him in opposition to much of what was meant by the word Renaissance.

Paul IV believed that the Vatican curia, above all, was responsible not only for abuses in the Church, but also for the lack of ecclesiastical discipline and proper order within the hierarchy. He thought that the pope and the bishops must be models of Christian pastors—serving dutifully in an exemplary fashion. This entailed primarily the enforcement of all aspects of Canon Law, a topic he often referred to, and he wanted to begin this enforcement with a reform of the Roman curia itself. As Pastor puts it, "For sixty years . . . this had been talked of; he was going at last to carry it out, energetically, and without respect of persons, as one chosen by God for the purpose. . . ."[23] At the same time, he intended to rid the Church of such abuses as simony and absenteeism. "He looked upon [these financially inspired abuses] as mere inventions of the devil."[24] Paul IV issued decrees to effect these reforms and submitted their enforcement to his favorite and most trusted institution, the Inquisition.[25] These efforts as pope echo his earlier concerns, as evidenced, for instance, in his contribution to the founding of the Roman Inquisition in 1542, the *Concilium de emendanda ecclesia* of 1537, of which he was an important member, and his own 1532 "Memorial to Pope Clement VII" on church reform in Venice. All these endeavors at reform reflect a preoccupation with the institution of the Catholic Church and a ferocious desire to reform its civil service, its clergy, and its hierarchy, by extirpating financial abuses, moral failures, and heresy.

Gaetano Thiene, on the other hand, had emerged from, and thereby embodied the spirituality of, the Oratories of Divine Love; he never ceased to perform the biblical works of mercy, especially caring for the sick and the dying. He embodied their ideals of humility, poverty, penance, and practical charity. The Oratory's influence can also be seen in his abiding exhortation to the laity to continue their selfless caring for the sick and the improverished. In 1541, more than twenty years after his visit to Vicenza, Thiene maintained contact as evidenced by his letter of encouragement to the Compagnia di San Girolamo. He told them that God had selected them to perform an important work, "that of having care and management over ulcerated and unhealthy people; and also of applying themselves to other works of the spirit and virtue, which you exercise in your holy oratory and company, all the deeds of true mercy both spiritual and corporal."[26] As a priest, Thiene set an example of this type of behavior. Many of the earliest members of the Theatines also emerged from this environment. Carafa, while ostensibly influenced by the same confraternal tradition, seemed preoccupied with the institutional concerns of the Church. Although both traditions were incorporated into the Theatines, the union was not always harmonious, especially during the changing circumstances after 1524. Two headstrong and dedicated personalities led not so much to explicit conflicts as to a community not clearly focused on the future. Its strength rested on a dynamic ideal rooted in the piety and activities of the various Oratories of Divine Love and committed to sacramental ministry.

HISTORY OF THE THEATINES

The manuscript *Acta capitulorum generalium Congregationis Clericorum Regularium* traces the origins of the Theatines and chronicles their early history.[27] At its beginning, the *ACG* portrays the founding ceremonies, which occurred on September 14, 1524, the Feast of the Exaltation of the Cross, in St. Peter's Basilica in the presence of the papal delegate, notaries, and witnesses from the Roman Oratory.[28] The four founding members are listed as the reverend fathers" . . . Gian Pietro Carafa of Naples, Bishop of Chieti, . . . Gaetano da Thiene, Protonotary Apostolic, and Doctor of both laws from Vicenza, . . . Bonifacio de' Colli, cleric of Alessandria, and . . . Paolo de Consiglieri, cleric of Rome. . . ."[29] Gathering early in the morning, they heard Mass celebrated at the altar in the chapel of St. Andrew, and, after receiving communion, they processed to the main altar of St. Peter's.

The apostolic letter *Exponi nobis*, of June 24, publicly read during the ceremony, contained much that the community had requested on May 3, 1524, during their audience with Pope Clement VII:[30] the faculty to pronounce in public the vows of religion; the permission to live in whatever modest place they chose; the privilege of being placed under the immediate and special protection of the apostolic see; the right each year to elect a superior, who could serve up to a total of three years; the permission to admit priests or laymen to profession (provided they had completed a year of probation); the faculty, whether by statute or constitution, to make provisions suitable and conducive to their particular way of life; and special recognition that they were forming a new type of religious community for men, that of regular clerics.[31] The four (Carafa, followed by Thiene, de' Colli, and Consiglieri) then pronounced their public professions of poverty, chastity, and obedience. They also promised obedience to the one whom they would elect superior and to his successors. According to the *ACG*, this founding ceremony in St. Peter's concluded by incorporating the Theatines' first congregation, which thereby inaugurated a government for the nascent community. They "unanimously and harmoniously" selected Bishop Carafa, who had resigned his bishopric, as their first superior.[32]

Although for almost a century the Theatines had no official constitution, about two years after the community's establishment, Gian Pietro Carafa did compose a letter containing a selective description of the practices developing within the Theatine community of Rome; this text became their initial rule.[33] Its composition reflected the papal authority given to the community by which they could prepare "some rules and constitutions to begin in an orderly and uniform way to live as clerics and religious. . . ."[34] In this partial picture, Carafa presented a distinctive understanding of their vows and described some communal activities within the new group; its own yearly meetings, called general chapters or congregations, would presumably explicate and expand this sketch as new issues arose. Even though his synopsis contained practices derived from the Oratory of Divine Love, the Theatine community's own inner life centered not on patterns of piety, penitential austerities, or specific ministries, but on the practice of the three vows.

Carafa saw the vows of chastity and obedience as reflections of traditional ecclesiastical principles. For instance, he cautioned members to preserve chastity "by safeguarding not only bodily purity, but also the senses and speech, and as far as possible by purity of thought and desire, and also by frugality with food and sobriety."[35] Carafa hoped to instill careful discipline in all aspects of Theatine activity—thought, desire, speech, and senses. In fact, any dealings with women should be judged by the superior; the individual's judgment could not be trusted in a matter of such importance and delicacy both as to virtue and in regard to public reputations. Likewise, in discussing the vow of obedience, Carafa appears similarly vigilant: "Obedience is owed first of all to the Superior and the Elders, as to the Vicar and ministers of God. . . ."[36] The Theatines are reminded that they owe their obedience to the superior of the community just as to the pope. By analogy, the members of the community should also obey one another, serving one another in charity, "in such a way however that all may be done in due order, as the Apostle says, and that no one may usurp [for himself] either the office of Superior or of another or the authority to command."[37] Although describing a different and more communal interpretation that could modify the traditional view, Carafa's appraisal of obedience nevertheless returns in the end to the hierarchical pattern.

Unlike his interpretations of chastity and obedience, however, Carafa's delineation of Theatine poverty was distinctive. To be poor in a religious community had always signified that members could not own private property. While Carafa presupposed this basic tenet, he also insisted that "all [members] may live in and of the community, not by begging, because the Canons forbid this, but by the gifts of the faithful freely offered."[38] He required that the Theatines, contrary to the mendicant tradition, refrain from begging; they were instead to await the spontaneous, free-will offerings of the faithful. Nevertheless, he did tolerate the acceptance of tithes and first fruits "where it is just, as servants without recompense of the altar and the Gospel."[39] The Theatines could accept these relatively small, tax-like gifts along with free-will benefactions; but the retention of solicited funds or possessions was prohibited.[40] This demanding interpretation of the vow of poverty apparently dictated that the Theatines wait with confidence and prayers for their good works and preaching of the gospel to induce the faithful to be magnanimous.

Gian Pietro Carafa's handling of the vows reflects a propensity for the practical. His views do not express biblical teachings or theology as much as they do a concern that each member should embrace specific and cautionary practices. He emphasized the need to protect the vowed life—whether from contacts with women, usurpation of authority, or begging. Instead of persuading the members by spiritual teachings, he reinforced the vows by specific usages.

Carafa's letter also manifested a preoccupation with communal activities: the training of novices, the Divine Office and administration of the sacraments, the community's habit, daily prayer, fasting, and table reading. For Carafa, the most important of these, the heart of the Theatine communal ideal and activity, was the proper recitation of the Divine Office in choir.[41]

Carafa explained that the entire liturgical life of the community—the celebration of Mass and recitation of the Divine Office—was governed by specific regulations. Besides conforming to the standards established in "the genuine and ancient rubrics of the Missal and the Roman Breviary . . . ,"[42] their liturgical practices should also follow a community guidebook that contained "very brief and simple rules that have been handed down, where you are advised even when you should include or omit some Proper of the Saints."[43] Their style of communal recitation of the Office done without singing would become identified as distinctively Theatine. Other clerics knew about it and even imitated it. In the summer of 1537, for example, Alvise Priuli, on a diplomatic mission in the diocese of Liège with Reginald Pole and Gian Matteo Giberti, wrote a description of their pious practices.

In the morning, after spending time in private prayer, "we would gather in a small domestic chapel, and together we chant the hours [matins] '*more Theatinico*' without song."[44] This communal chanting without singing streamlined the praying of the Divine Office for active priests such as the Theatines and fulfilled their duties carefully yet expeditiously.

Carafa's description of the Theatines' apparel reflected a surprisingly tolerant attitude: "No color of dress or specific habit is prescribed among us; nor is any prohibited. . . ."[45] Carafa's letter expressed concern that the appearance of the community members be appropriate to that of "respectable clerics and . . . not contrary to the Sacred Canons or inconsistent with common usage of the city or diocese in which we may happen to be staying."[46] In October 1524 an unknown author in Rome described the early Theatines as they visited the hospitals "with a black soutane, white socks, black cloak with a very high collar, a priest's biretta, [and] a large tonsure, and everywhere they go, they do so on horseback and with a groom. . . ."[47] The members of the Theatine community wanted to appear outfitted as respectable clerics—not as members of a specific religious community.

It is interesting that Carafa did not refer at all to the most important goal of the new community, its specific apostolate, but that omission is understandable. Because of their continuing involvement with the Oratories of Divine Love (first in Rome, later in Venice and Naples) and their regular performance of basic priestly duties, the Theatines implicitly recognized and practiced their specific ministry: they were a group of priests living in community—bound together by mutual commitments to chastity, obedience, and a distinctive poverty.

For the first eighty years of the community, Carafa's letter, the annually elected superior, and the meetings of the congregations governed the Theatines. The very quantity of this legislation proved unwieldy, and the General Congregation in 1585 decided to compile and systematize it into a constitution. The Theatines finished this project in 1603, approved it at their General Congregation in that year, and then published the *Constitutiones Congregationis Clericorum Regularium* (Rome, 1604).[48] This compilation contained the regulations in Carafa's letter, the subsequent decisions of superiors and general congregations, and applicable directives from the Church.

The sack of Rome by the army of the Holy Roman Emperor Charles V on May 6, 1527, did violence to the nascent Theatine community. Initially, during the ensuing occupation, members of the community helped the victims of the marauding soldiers. This ministry did not protect them, however. Caracciolo reported that German soldiers pillaged their residence. Even after a thorough search and an impromptu sermon by Thiene explaining the Theatine's severe poverty, the soldiers were not satisfied and tortured him in an attempt to extract information on the whereabouts of any valuables.[49] (For the sake of modesty, Castaldo even demurred from a full description of the circumstances of this torture.[50]) Realizing that if Thiene had known anything he would have spoken, the soldiers departed. (The Theatines considered Gaetano's survival miraculous.) Later the Theatines were taken to the Vatican and held for ransom. Eventually they were released and immediately hurried to the Tiber and fled the city by boat. With the help of the Venetian ambassador, Domenico Venier, they were directed to ships on the coast, bound for Venice.

In June 1527 the Venetian ships transported the company of Theatines from the fury of Rome to a haven in Venice where they found sanctuary with a circle of friends.[51] "And the procurators for the Hospital for Incurables went to meet them, and, with the consent of the brothers of the *Caritade*, provided the fourteen with temporary shelter at San Clemente."[52] The Theatines came to interpret their selection of Venice as providential; indeed, they realized a new beginning—almost a second founding—in their adopted city. The resettled members found the courage to recreate their distinctive manner of living; Venice became the primary site of Theatine activity until the General Congregation established a second base at Naples in 1533 and a third at Rome in 1557. During the same time there were also several failed attempts to expand the community elsewhere. For instance, a settlement in Salò in 1542 faltered due to a lack of housing, and a return to Rome proposed by Ignatius de Loyola in 1548 also came to nothing.[53] An earlier unsuccessful venture at Verona suggests some reasons for these failures.

The Theatines avoided depending for their support on any one individual or group. The Carafan prohibition against begging contributed to their limited sojourn in Verona. Bishop Gian Matteo Giberti had administered this diocese from Rome for four years (including the period of his imprisonment during the Sack of 1527) and had only recently taken up actual residence. He proposed various reforms there and sought out the Theatines to be his assistants in these efforts.[54] As a result, Bonifacio de' Colli and a group of seven other Theatines went to Verona in November 1528 and spent almost a year there.[55] The eight Theatines must have included almost all the current membership except for the three other founding members; this mission may have been preparing the way for the entire community's eventual resettlement in Verona. The large Theatine community lacked both food and necessities "since the Veronese were not aware of the strictness of the vow that forbade them to beg or to make known their wants."[56] Fortunately, a local nobleman, Girolamo Giusti, sent his servants periodically with food, which allowed them to survive the winter. Their precarious financial predicament evidently did not interfere with their ministry, however: "When they found no supplies, they gave thanks nevertheless, happy to feel the inconvenience and suffering of the poverty they had vowed."[57] In addition to their privation, the location of their residence near the square in front of the church created a further, unfortunate predicament. It exposed them to the popular spectacles, loud noise, and disorderly conduct that regularly accompanied festivals; since the Theatines believed that this atmosphere interfered with their communal life and piety, they resolved to leave Verona.[58]

Besides the self-imposed ideological restrictions in their ministries, the Theatine community and its development were circumscribed by their limited ability to attract novices. They did expand but only gradually; as a group with such high ideals, their numbers were never very impressive. Moreover, rather than training their own seminarians, they admitted almost exclusively priests who were attracted to their devotional piety and strictness. At the time of their flight from Rome, the total membership was twelve.[59] By 1550, there were only twenty-seven members living; fifteen members, including Gaetano Thiene, eleven other priests, one subdeacon, and two lay brothers, had died. The aggregate number of Theatines in 1550, living or deceased, was thirty-four priests and eight brothers.[60] There were eight new members at Rome between 1524 and 1527, but this rate was not sustained in Venice and Naples. (If that growth had been maintained, the community would have comprised between seventy and eighty individuals in 1550.) In fact, only one or two new members, on the average, joined every year; unfortunately many also quit, and thirty-five percent of the membership had died.[61] Although in existence twice as long, the Theatines in the 1550s had less than a twentieth as many members as the Jesuits;[62] due to their elevated standards, as Francesco Andreu has noted, the Theatines prided themselves throughout their history as being *selecti inter electos,* the chosen among the elect.[63]

Some idea about the ongoing ministry of the Theatines can be gleaned from their activities in Naples, where Clement VII had ordered them to found a house in 1533. Gaetano Thiene and Giovanni Marinoni began the mission there, and subsequent efforts appear fairly consistent with the Theatine mission elsewhere. Reflecting the order's special commitment, Thiene preached on the need for frequent communion, and he also gave spiritual direction to a convent of Dominican nuns. Marinoni, in his turn, guided the founding of a school for boys, where he provided spiritual direction to its students. What is especially notable, given Theatine traditions, is that they worked and even lived for a while at a hospital for incurables. They were constantly busy in preaching, in hearing confessions, and in exhorting the laity to receive the sacraments more frequently and to undertake charitable works for the sick and the distressed. Following their basic principles, moreover, they led retired and unobtrusive lives; they did not preach in the open air as the Capuchins and the early Jesuits did. They developed their own particular way of being wholehearted priests as they responded to the needs and opportunities they encountered.[64]

Between 1531 and 1534, the Theatines in Venice assisted in the founding of another Italian religious community, the Somascans (or Somaschi).[65] Their founder, Girolamo Emiliani, had visited with the Theatines and sought their advice about how to serve God and to care for the great numbers of orphans that he encountered.[66] Moreover, Emiliani had belonged to the Venetian Oratory of Divine Love, and his community's ministry was influenced by his benevolent activity there. Both Carafa (by means of spiritual direction) and Thiene (by drafting a rule for the enterprise) helped Emiliani reach his decision to found a community of regular clerics, specifically committed to the needs of orphans, which later also provided education.[67] Emiliani selected the city of Somasca, near Bergamo, as his headquarters and established there the first of many Somascan orphanages. The two groups' special relationship, originating in shared roots in the Oratory, was further strengthened when (for a period of eight years, from 1547 to 1555) they were administratively united.[68] Castaldo explains that the Theatines, at the command of Pope Paul III, "received into their care and administration the Fathers of the Congregation of Somasca, and all their works. . . ."[69] The Theatines hoped to use some of the Somascans in their pastoral efforts, while the Somascans could avail themselves of Theatine spiritual guidance and leadership. Apparently, the two groups labored to make the union effective, but a difference in spirit and in self-definition ultimately undermined it. The Theatines did not want to work in orphanages or at rearing the young; the Somascans found the pastoral ministry beyond their resources. The divergent purposes of the two communities convinced the members to separate, and Pope Paul IV ratified a separation in December 1555. The Theatines—unlike the Somascans—emphasized the spiritual and institutional rather than the altruistic aspects of their predecessor confraternity, the Roman Oratory of Divine Love.

Unlike their contact with the Somascans, the Theatines' relationship with the Jesuits involved early disagreements that later partisan accounts sharpened.[70] The Theatines and the Jesuits came from backgrounds separated by location, language, and culture. The Theatines were the inheritors of Italian piety and the linear outgrowth of its lay confraternities. Moving exclusively between Italian cities, they performed parochial duties and ministered in the hospitals for incurables. In contrast, when Ignatius de Loyola and his followers (four of whom were Spanish) arrived in Italy, they could not initially have been familiar with the traditions of the widespread, existing confraternities, many of which guarded their very existence with secrecy. Moreover, they were not involved with—and maybe not even aware of—the network of individuals, lay and clerical, associated with the Oratories of Divine Love. Loyola and the Jesuits were outsiders in the Italian world from which the Theatines emanated, so it is not startling that the two founders and their respective orders misunderstood each other. This applies particularly to the relationship between Loyola and Carafa. The animosity between these two religious leaders was real enough and reflected at least a different point of view about the nature of religious life. This contrast, moreover, became explicit after Loyola's death when Carafa, as Pope Paul IV, required the Jesuit constitutions to be modified to correspond to features in the Theatine tradition.[71]

Gian Pietro Carafa's rising prominence overshadowed the work of the Theatines in the 1540s and 1550s. The best-known and most controversial of the community members, Carafa received numerous honors and commissions in the institutional church, and his influence expanded beyond the community as he accepted wider pastoral responsibilities and contributed to the formation of church policy (especially on matters related to reform). As he gained influence and power, however, Carafa became increasingly rigid and authoritarian, with a reputation for being "a rigorist, moralist, autocrat, ecclesiastical disciplinarian, a man utterly opposed to any change in practice, doctrine, or discipline that might be interpreted as a concession to 'the Lutherans.'"[72] As a result no one would have predicted that he was destined to become Pope Paul IV and thus bring the Theatine name into the central administration of the Catholic Church.

During his papacy Paul IV favored the Theatine community in various ways and asserted a previously unknown degree of control over their activities.[73] Originally all members had been required to attend each congregation, but gradually a system of representational vicars had developed. By reducing the autonomy of the superior, the annual congregations had managed to keep the direction of the community under regular oversight of the complete membership. During his papacy, in contrast to earlier practice, Paul IV assumed the leadership of the community and suspended the annual meetings of the General Congregation.[74] In Rome since 1536 Carafa had been absent from the group's life, then centered in Venice and Naples, but after his election he resumed involvement and imposed his authority. The *Acta* of the General Congregations indicate that the community members willingly abstained from their Congregations during Carafa's papacy and submitted the order's leadership to their co-founder.[75] The election of one of their members was a great honor, especially for an order so recently formed, and the members showed their respect for Carafa by accepting him as superior, protector, and "very loving father." Consequently, the Theatines for those four years became tied to the papacy. Carafa's assumption of the governance of the Theatines created an anomalous situation, one which foreshadowed and precipitated lasting problems for the community, especially in the popular consciousness.

The founding Theatines had made no provision for members of their community to become bishops; in fact, quite the contrary seemed part of the original program. The rule called for a strict vow of poverty. This ideal conflicted with the demands of the episcopal office which—at that time—dictated an imposing style of life. The Theatines, in contrast, were humble and poor priests. During his first year, the Theatine pope selected one member to join him in the episcopate and transferred another, thereby identifying this community with the hierarchy. Henceforth, the Theatines became more involved with the episcopate and with the central government of the Church. Specifically, in 1555 Paul IV named Bernardino Scotti, who had joined the community in 1525, bishop of Trani in Apulia, and made him a cardinal as well. The pope attempted to do the same for Paolo Consiglieri (the pope's *maestro di camera*) and one of the four founding Theatines, but he persistently refused the honor. He also selected Thomas Goldwell, the only English Theatine, to be bishop of Oxford.[76] Paul IV began a new relationship between the Theatines and the episcopate.[77]

Paul IV's opinions compromised his entire pontificate. Carafa refused to yield on anything he considered correct and necessary for the Catholic Church, and he used his full authority to justify his own personal opinions. Many of Carafa's contemporaries as well as later scholars viewed him negatively and his papacy as disastrous. The initiation of the Roman Index, the institution of the Roman ghetto, and the failure of the war with Spain colored subsequent appraisals of the Theatines. While Carafa was pope, the efforts of the community were engulfed by his drastic actions; to others he became their only experience of the Theatines, and they interpreted his policies as reflections of the community. Moreover, no one in the Theatine family confronted him or tried to moderate his actions especially since Thiene, the co-founder, had died in 1547; the community and its pope had become indistinguishable. Consequently, for the remainder of the sixteenth century, the Theatines inherited the legacy of the Theatine pope and felt duty-bound to defend him. Henceforth, the name Theatine became associated with the person of Gian Pietro Carafa. Ironically, his policies as pope contrasted sharply with the charitable practices of the first Theatines.

By the 1620s the order reached a certain plateau of prominence. The limited sphere of their corporate ministries suggested that they would never be a decisive force in the Catholic Church. As an organization founded in Italy, the Theatines continued to be almost exclusively Italian in membership and in geography. At the death of Paul IV, the community had residences in Venice, Naples, and Rome. Subsequently, the order initiated ones in Padua (1565), Cremona (1565), Piacenza (1569), and Milan (1570), followed by settlements in Genoa (1575), Lecce (1584), Verona (1591), Florence (1592), Bologna (1599), and two other houses in Naples.[78] Their expansion was quite restricted, however, probably a total of fifteen communities—all in Italy—by the year 1600. During these years of European religious turmoil and colonial expansion, they never undertook ventures outside Italy, whether to dispute with Protestants in Germany or to attempt the conversion of the native populations in the Americas or the Far East. The Theatines concentrated on the religious needs of Italy and the individual piety of their own members. Only in the seventeenth century did they establish communities in Austria, Germany, Spain, Portugal, and Poland.[79]

The Theatines' basically conservative policy may be explained in part by the relatively small growth of the community between 1524 and 1600; their size (in synergy with their own interests) may have precluded bold steps or vast initiatives. Evidence indicates that there had been a cumulative sum of 352 members by 1588, and 392 more would join by 1600.[80] Including Carafa, Branson enumerates seventeen among this group as bishops before 1600.[81] The number during their first century (1524–1624) would total forty-five. Because the community membership likewise was predominantly Italian and provided priests and bishops for Italian sees, its focus of attention remained regional and dealt with a population already at least nominally Catholic.

The Roman Oratory of Divine Love and its Theatine heir were reformers with limited goals. The original aspirations of these priests were not to remedy the abuses of the constitutional Church but to care for the suffering poor and the sick of society by the labors of the confraternal brothers and priests whose own lives

had already been reformed. The Theatines sought further sanctification by performing the works of mercy while living in an
approved community that occupied a middle ground between
monasticism and modern clerical practice. With the introduction
by Bishop Carafa of ecclesiastical reform as a component of the
Theatine charism, the community found itself transformed—in
contrast to the personal piety of his co-founder—to meet needs
other than those of the sick. It seems significant that of the two
founders—Gaetano Thiene and Gian Pietro Carafa—the former,
representing the traditional works of mercy, was canonized,
whereas the latter, enforcer of church practice and discipline, was
reviled at his death.

BIBLIOGRAPHIC ESSAY

The early scholarship about the Theatines can be divided into
three basic areas: defensive and apologetic work about the papacy
of Paul IV; hagiography on Gaetano Thiene, emphasizing his influence on the community's identity; and chronicles of the community's early activities and successes. These areas grew out of
the needs of the Theatines; accordingly, their own members
produced the most significant writings. For the most part, only
incidental references to the community occur in the writings of
modern historians specializing in aspects of the sixteenth century.
Some recent scholarship, however, has begun to explore the gene-
sis of the community and to interpret Carafa's role in the community, at the same time providing the necessary integration of the
Theatine model of religious reform and religious life into the
wider themes of the Catholic Reform and the Counter
Reformation.

The fundamental tool for studying the Theatine community is
the eighteenth-century bibliography of Antonio F. Vezzosi, *I scrittori de' Chierici Regolari detti Teatini*, 2 vols. (Rome: Congregazione
de Propaganda Fide, 1780; Fascimile edition. Farnborough: Gregg,
1966). Vezzosi provides lists and summaries of contents of everything he knew written by the Theatines; unfortunately, he does
not record the works of any other writers on Theatine history.

The earliest biographies of the founding members were, quite
naturally, compiled by Theatines themselves. The first was a life

of Paul IV prepared by an admirer and apologist: Antonio Caracciolo, *De vita Pauli quarti Pont. Max. collectanea historica* (Cologne: Kincki, 1612). The published version constitutes only a small part of a much larger manuscript collection prepared by Caracciolo, *Vita e gesti di Giovan Pietro Carafa cioè di Paolo IV. P. M.* This manuscript material remains an important source of information even if partisan and uncritical. For a listing of the contents of the *Vita e gesti*, see George Duruy, *Le Cardinal Carlo Carafa (1519– 1561): Étude sur le pontificat de Paul IV* (Paris, 1882), pp. xxi–xxvi. Because it used many original papers that are now lost, the Caracciolo collection serves as the basis of most research on Carafa. Soon after followed Giovanni Battista Castaldo's *Vita del Sanctissimo Pontefice Paolo Quarto, Fondatore della Religione de[i] Chierici Regolari* (Rome: Mascardi, 1615). The two Theatines present Carafa in a positive light, defending his actions, and recognizing little darkness in his character. These *Vitae* from the seventeenth century have survived, but neither has been published critically.

There are few modern biographies of Paul IV or thorough studies of his papacy. His own writings are scattered, and few have been reproduced in modern editions. The only extensive source of his writings is Gennaro Maria Monti, *Ricerche su papa Paolo IV* (Benevento: Cooperativa Tipografi Chiostro S. Sofia, 1923, repr. Turin: Bottega d'Erasmo, 1980). Aside from Antonio Veny-Ballester, *Paolo IV, cofundador de la clerecia religiosa, 1476– 1559* (Palma de Mallorca: Istituto de Estudios Balearicos, 1976), most modern studies touch only particular aspects of his papacy: for example, René Ancel on ecclesiastical reform policy in *Paul IV et le Concile* (Louvain: Bureaux de la Revue, 1907); Kenneth R. Stow on papal legislation toward the Jews in *Catholic Thought and Papal Jewry Policy, 1555–1593*, Moreshet Series, Studies in Jewish History, Literature, and Thought 5 (New York: Jewish Theological Seminary of America, 1977); Massimo Firpo on the Inquisitional process against Cardinal Morone in *Il processo inquisitoriale del cardinal Giovanni Morone*, 5 vols. (Rome: Istituto storico italiano per l'età moderna e contemporanea, 1981–1989); and Tullio Torriani on the papal war with Spain and on Carafa's nephews, Cardinal Carlo and Duke Giovanni, who betrayed Paul IV, in *Una tragedia nel cinquecento romano: Paolo IV e i suoi nepoti* (Rome: Fratelli Palombi, 1951). These historians rarely searched his earlier active life for pattern or development.

For the life and writings of Gaetano Thiene many biographies exist, but the principal early ones came from within the order. Antonio Caracciolo included his *Vita Caietani Thienaei* (pp. 172–260) when he published *De Vita Pauli IV. Pont. Max. Collectanea historica*. The *Acta sanctorum Aug.* (Anvers, 1735), 2:240–324, reproduced Caracciolo's *Vita* with a commentary by J. Pien. Castaldo also wrote a biography of Thiene, *Vita del B. Gaetano Tiene, fondatore della Religione de[i] Chierici Regolari* (Rome: Mascardi, 1616). Both these studies are primarily hagiographic.

The foundation of critical studies was the publication of Thiene's letters with extensive commentary in *Le Lettere di San Gaetano da Thiene*, ed. Francesco Andreu, Studi e Testi 177 (Vatican City: Biblioteca Apostolica Vaticana, 1954). Other modern studies and biographies include Pio Paschini, *S. Gaetano Thiene, Gian Pietro Carafa, e le origini dei chierici regolari teatini* (Rome: Scuola Tipografica Pio X, 1926); P. Chiminelli, *S. Gaetano Thiene: Cuore della riforma cattolica* (Vicenza: Soc. an. Tipografica fra cattolici vicentini editrice, 1948); Paul H. Hallett, *Catholic Reformer: A Life of St. Cajetan of Thiene* (Westminster, Md.: Newman, 1959); and Gabriel Llompart, *Gaetano da Thiene, 1480–1547: Estudios sobre un reformador religioso* (Wiesbaden: Steiner, 1969). Gaetano Thiene's life, unlike Carafa's, is relatively uncontroversial, and these recent investigations—even when objective and critical—generally accept him as admirable and holy.

Early histories of the community follow in the tradition of the *Vitae*. Giovanni Battista del Tufo's *Historia della Religione de' Padri Chierici Regolari, in cui si contiene la fondatione e progresso di lei infino a quest' anno MDCIX* (Rome, 1609) and *Supplimento alla Historia della Religione de' Padri Chierici Regolari* (Rome, 1616) as well as Giuseppe Silos's *Historiae Clericorum Regularium a Congregatione condita*, 3 vols. (Rome, 1650–1666), though providing histories of the community, follow in the tradition of not seeing a dark side to Carafa.

Modern history of the order really began with Ludwig Pastor's discussion (in Volume 10 of his *The History of the Popes, from the Close of the Middle Ages*, 4th ed. trans. R. F. Kerr [London: Paul, Trench, Trubner, 1938]) of the founding of the Roman Oratory and its connection to the Theatines and the beginnings of the Catholic reform. Scholarship in English was advanced in 1941 by Paul A. Kunkel, "The Theatines in the History of Catholic Reform before the Establishment of Lutheranism" (Ph.D. Diss., Catholic University of America, 1941), a study limited by a lack of original sources and a dependence on extensive and at times flawed secondary material. In 1946, the Theatines began the publication of *Regnum Dei*. In addition to historical studies of various periods, events, and individuals in the community's history, *Regnum Dei* has also provided critical editions of writings by Theatines (such as Blessed Paolo Burali in 1976 and Saint Giuseppe Maria Tomasi in 1986) and, most recently, articles investigating Theatine art and architecture.

The Theatine Archive at their Generalate, adjacent to S. Andrea della Valle in Rome, houses extensive manuscript material, such as *Acta capitulorum Generalium Congregationis Clericorum Regularium* and *Elenchus professorum Congregationis Clericorum Regularium*. Extant copies of the canonization processes of the Theatine blesseds and saints, records of individual houses, and missionary reports from throughout their history are essential for any further study of the order. Of primary importance is the fact that the Theatine archival records have been intact since their founding in 1524.

Notes

1. For the life and writings of Gaetano Thiene, consult Antonio Caracciolo, *Vita Caietani Thienaei* (pp. 172–260), published with *De Vita Pauli IV. Pont. Max. Collectanea historica* (Cologne: Kincki, 1612); Gianbattista Castaldo, *Vita del B. Gaetano Tiene, fondatore della religione de[i] Chierici Regolari* (Rome: Mascardi, 1616); *Acta sanctorum Aug.* (Anvers, 1735), 2:240–324, which reproduced Caracciolo's *Vita* with a commentary by J. Pien; Pio Paschini, *S. Gaetano Thiene, Gian Pietro Carafa, e le origini dei Chierici Regolari Teatini* (Rome, 1926); P. Chiminelli, *S. Gaetano Thiene: Cuore della riforma cattolica* (Vicenza: Soc. an. Tipografica fra cattolici vicentini editrice, 1948); *Le Lettere di San Gaetano da Thiene*, ed. Francesco Andreu, Studi e Testi 177 (Vatican City: Biblioteca Apostolica Vaticana, 1954); and Gabriel Llompart, *Gaetano da Thiene, 1480–1547: Estudios sobre un reformador religioso* (Wiesbaden: Steiner, 1969).

2. For the life and writings of Gian Pietro Carafa (Pope Paul IV), consult: Antonio Caracciolo, *De vita Pauli IV. Pont. Max. Collectanea historica*, pp. 1–171; Gianbattista Castaldo, *Vita del sanctissimo Pontefice Paolo IV, fondatore della Religione de[i] Chierici Regolari* (Rome: Mascardi, 1615); Gennaro Maria Monti, *Ricerche su Papa Paolo IV Carafa* (Bene-

vento: Cooperativa Tipografi Chiostro S. Sofia, 1923; repr. Turin: Bottega d'Erasmo, 1980); idem, "Papa Paolo IV, Profilo," in *Studi sulla riforma cattolica e sul papato nei secoli XVI–XVII* (Trani: Vecchi, 1941), pp. 45–88; Francesco Andreu, "Carafa, Gian Pietro," *Dizionario degli istituti di perfezione*, vol. 2 (Rome: Edizioni Paoline, 1975), cols. 256–61; and Antonio Veny-Ballester, *Paolo IV, cofundador de la clerecia religiosa (1476–1559)* (Palma de Mallorca: Istituto de Estudios Balearicos, 1976); and Alberto Aubert, "Alle origini della Controriforma: Studi e problemi su Paolo IV," *Rivista di storia e letteratura religiosa*, 22 (1986), 303–55.

3. For the Oratory of Divine Love, consult P. Tacchi Venturi, *Storia della Compagnia di Gesù in Italia* I, part 2, 3rd ed. (Rome: La Civiltà Cattolica, 1950), pp. 25–37, with the documents of the Genoese Oratory; Antonia Cistellini, *Figure della riforma pretridentina* (Brescia: Morcellina, 1948), with the documents of the Roman and Brescian Oratories, pp. 269–88; Alfredo Bianconi, *L'opera delle Compagnie del Divino Amore nella riforma cattolica* (Città di Castello: Lapi, 1914); Pio Paschini, *La beneficenza in Italia e le "Compagnie del Divino Amore" nei primi decenni del Cinquecento* (Rome: Editrice F.I.U.C., 1925); idem, *Tre ricerche sulla storia della Chiesa nel Cinquecento* (Rome: Edizioni Liturgiche, 1945); Cassiano da Langasco Carpaneto, *Gli ospedali degli incurabili* (Genoa: Pesce, 1938); and Kenneth J. Jorgensen, "The Oratories of Divine Love and the Theatines: Confraternal Piety and the Making of a Religious Community" Ph.D. diss., Columbia University, 1989.

4. He had gone back to his native Vicenza to console his mother at the death of his brother, Gianbattista; in August his mother also died, leaving him the responsibility of putting her financial affairs in order.

5. Caracciolo, *Vita Caietani Thienaei*, p. 188.

6. P. Paschini, *Tre ricerche*, pp. 65–67; Silvio Tramontin, "Lo Spirito, le attività, gli sviluppi dell'Oratorio del Divino Amore nella Venezia del Cinquecento," *Studi Veneziani*, 14 (1972), 111–36; idem, "I Teatini e l'Oratorio del Divino Amore a Venezia," *Regnum Dei*, 29 (1973), 53–76.

7. Marino Sanuto, *I diarii*, vol. 36 (Venice, 1893), col. 103, and ibid., vol. 38 (Venice, 1893), col. 141.

8. *Le Lettere di San Gaetano*, ed. Andreu, p. 56.

9. Ibid., pp. 56–57.

10. Gail L. Geiger, *Filippino Lippi's Carafa Chapel: Renaissance Art in Rome*, Sixteenth-Century Essays and Studies 5 (Kirksville, Mo.: Sixteenth-Century Journal Publications, 1986), p. 33.

11. D. S. Chambers, "Paul IV," in *Contemporaries of Erasmus: A Biographical Register of the Renaissance and Reformation*, ed. Peter Bietenholz, 3 vols. (Toronto and Buffalo: University of Toronto Press, 1985–1987), 3:56–57.

12. *The Correspondence of Erasmus. II. 1501–1514*, trans. R. A. B. My-

nors and D. F. S. Thomson (Toronto: University of Toronto Press, 1974), p. 278.

13. *The Correspondence of Erasmus.* III. *1514–1516*, trans. R. A. B. Mynors and D. F. S. Thomson (Toronto: University of Toronto Press, 1976), p. 107.

14. Ibid., pp. 209–10.

15. Consult Ronald Weissman, *Ritual Brotherhood in Renaissance Florence* (New York: Academic, 1982), pp. 48–50, esp. n. 23 for bibliography. The *disciplinati* are also known as flagellant (from *flagellum*, Latin for "whip") confraternities.

16. Brian Pullan, *Rich and Poor in Renaissance Venice: The Social Institutions of a Catholic State, to 1620* (Cambridge, Mass.: Harvard University Press, 1971), p. 258.

17. Caracciolo, *Vita Caietani Thienaei*, p. 192, and Castaldo, *Vita del B. Gaetano Tiene*, pp. 25–27. One aspect of Carafa's willingness to adhere to Thiene's plans was the requisite renunciation of his two sees.

In their decision to create a community of priests there was no accompanying desire by Thiene and Carafa to augment it with a female branch. Only after their deaths did a Neapolitan woman, Orsola Benincasa (1547–1618), decide to found a community of female Theatines (*Teatine*). Eventually these female religious did come under the direction of members of the Theatine community, and they now devote themselves to educational and missionary activities.

18. Based on Kenneth Stow, *Catholic Thought and Papal Jewry Policy, 1555–1593*, Moreshet Series, Studies in Jewish History, Literature, and Thought 5 (New York: Jewish Theological Seminary of America, 1977), p. 3. Summarized also in Salo W. Baron, *A Social and Religious History of the Jews*, 2nd ed. rev and enl. (New York: Columbia University Press, 1952–1969), 14:35.

19. Consult George H. Putnam, *The Censorship of the Church of Rome*, 2 vols. (New York: Knickerbocker, 1906), 1:168–76; and Ludwig Pastor, *The History of the Popes from the Close of the Middle Ages* XIV, ed. Ralph F. Kerr (St. Louis: B. Herder, 1936), pp. 276–82.

20. Putnam, *Censorship of the Church of Rome*, 1:172.

21. Baron, *Social and Religious History of the Jews*, 14:33.

22. Putnam, *Censorship of the Church of Rome*, 1:169.

23. See Pastor, *History of the Popes*, 14:185. This comment ("for sixty years") is dated from 1556 and so would refer to the year 1496, the same time, coincidentally, that his uncle, Oliviero Carafa, was appointed by Alexander IV to a reform commission to correct the same abuses.

24. Pastor, *History of the Popes*, 14:197.

25. Ibid., 14:203.

26. *Le Lettere di San Gaetano*, ed. Andreu, p. 92.

27. Rome, Archivio Generalizio dei Teatini, Volume I (1524–1624), listed as MS. 6; hereafter cited as *ACG*. Although this Latin document contains a summary of each annual assembly, it was clearly compiled later (perhaps in the 1560s) following an examination of the community archives in various Italian cities (which are accordingly cited); however, the material on the founding itself was dependent on an earlier and now lost contemporaneous chronicle.

28. Based on *ACG*, s.v. "Anno 1524," entitled "Congregationis Clericorum Regularium institutio et primum capitulum. Romae." No reason is offered for the selection of this feast for the founding of the community. Undoubtedly, the discovery of Christ's cross and its subsequent veneration (which beliefs formed the motivation for this feast) must have seemed an appropriate date for a group of priests who sought to follow Christ penitentially.

29. *ACG*, s.v. "Anno 1524."

30. This document is published in *Bullarum diplomatum et privilegiorum Sanctorum Romanorum Pontificum*, Turin ed., ed. Francisco Gaude, 25 vols. (Rome, 1857–1872), 6:73–74.

31. Concerning this title, its history, and the various subsequent and comparable religious communities (such as the Barnabites, the Somascans, the Jesuits, and the Camillans), see: F. Claeys-Boùùaert, "Clercs réguliers," *Dictionnaire de droit canonique*, vol. 3 (1942), cols. 872–75; Francesco Andreu, "I Chierici Regolari," *Regnum Dei*, 30 (1974), 55–78; idem, "Chierici Regolari," *Dizionario degli istituti di perfezione*, vol. 2 (Rome: Edizioni Paoline, 1975), cols. 897–909.

32. *ACG*, s.v. "Anno, 1524."

33. The first publication of the Latin text occurred in Giuseppe Silos, *Historiae Clericorum Regularium a congregatione condita* I (Rome, 1650), pp. 73–75. A copy is included in Paul A. Kunkel, "The Theatines in the History of Catholic Reform before the Establishment of Lutheranism," Ph.D. Diss., Catholic University of America, 1941, pp. 166–68. Another copy, incomplete and with minor grammatical variances, is included in Francesco Andreu, "La regola dei Chierici Regolari nella lettera di Bonifacio de' Colli a Gian Matteo Giberti," *Regnum Dei*, 2 (1946), 51–53 and hereafter cited as "La regola." John Olin in *The Catholic Reformation* (New York: Harper & Row, 1969; repr. New York: Fordham University Press, 1992), pp. 128–32, translates the Silos text, which is hereafter cited as "Theatine Rule of 1526."

Silos, *Historiae Clericorum Regularium*, p. 73, and Andreu, "La regola," p. 42, attribute the text to Carafa even though it was included in a letter from de' Colli to Giberti. The sources and arguments are found in "La regola," pp. 41–44; but the original motivation behind the letter is not explained. On the basis of Caracciolo, *Vita D. Caietani* (Pisa,

1738), p. 52, Andreu, "La regola," pp. 41–42, believes that the text was written between 1525 and 1526 and de' Colli included it in a letter to Bishop Giberti of Verona as a friend of the community.

34. Antonio Caracciolo, *Vita di Papa Paolo IV*, MS. cit. II.4, cited in Andreu, "La regola," p.42*n*12.

35. Olin, "Theatine Rule of 1526," p. 130. Kunkel, "Theatines," pp. 166–67.

36. Olin, "Theatine Rule of 1526," p. 130. Kunkel, "Theatines," p. 167.

37. Olin, "Theatine Rule of 1526," p. 130. Kunkel, "Theatines," p. 167.

38. Olin, "Theatine Rule of 1526," p. 130. Kunkel, "Theatines," p. 166.

39. Olin, "Theatine Rule of 1526," p. 130. Kunkel, "Theatines," p. 166. Carafa's exception, rather than the severe prohibition itself, corresponded to the principle expressed in 1 Corinthians 9:13–14.

40. This prohibition on possessions extended to the holding of benefices, ecclesiastical positions that guaranteed in return for pastoral services a fixed amount of property or money. Even though Carafa admitted that Canon Law did not forbid religious groups such as the Theatines from holding these annual ecclesiastical revenues in common, ". . . nevertheless we care little about having them for many reasons, having been taught by experience itself." See Kunkel, "Theatines," p. 166.

41. For a discussion (in Latin) of the role of choir in Theatine life, consult Francesco Andreu, "De obligatione chori in Ordine Clericorum Regularium," *Regnum Dei*, 10 (1954), 83–96.

42. Olin, "Theatine Rule of 1526," p. 131. Kunkel, "Theatines," p. 168.

43. Olin, "Theatine Rule of 1526," p. 131. Kunkel, Theatines," p. 168.

44. ". . . nella qual'hora convenimo in una Chiesivola domestica, ed insieme cantiamo le ore *more Theatinico* senza canto." This is in a letter, to one Ludovico Beccadelli, included in the *Epistolarum Reginaldi Poli S.R.E. Cardinalis et aliorum ad ipsum Collectio* II, ed. A. M. Quirini, (Brescia, 1745), p. 104.

45. Olin, "Theatine Rule of 1526," p. 131; Kunkel, "Theatines," p. 168.

46. Olin, "Theatine Rule of 1526," p. 131; Kunkel, "Theatines," p. 168.

47. Marino Sanuto, *I diarii*, vol. 37 (Venice, 1893), col. 90.

48. The "Constitutions of the Congregation of Clerks Regular" was approved by Pope Clement VIII on July 28, 1603. This document was soon followed by Antonio Caracciolo's edition of the constitutions but now accompanied by notes: *Constitutiones Clericorum Regularium, et ad eas ab antiquitate firmandas, Antonii Caraccioli clerici regularis notae* (Rome, 1610). For an examination of the first document, see Kunkel, "Theatines," pp. 77–111.

49. ". . . compressis scilicet artubus [sic] inter arcarum [sic] labra,

totoque corpore funibus in altum sublato." Caracciolo, *Vita Caietani Thienaei*, p. 206.

50. Castaldo, *Vita del B. Gaetano Tiene*, p. 68, writes: "All'hora coloro . . . legano il mansueto Agnello con modi crudelissimi e brutti, da tacersi per modestia, e sollevandolo in alto gli danno varij tormenti."

51. Their arrival is recorded by Sanuto, *I diarii*, vol. 45 (Venice, 1896), col. 343.

52. Ibid. I understand the *Caritade* to refer to the Venetian Oratory of Divine Love (founded by Thiene) because of the reference to the hospital for incurables.

53. For the situation in Salò, see *Le Lettere di San Gaetano*, ed. Andreu, pp. 128–30; for Rome, Antonio Veny-Ballester, "S. Ignacio de Loyola y el retorno de los Clerigos Regulares a Roma," *Regnum Dei*, 9 (1953), 18–25.

54. The presence of the Theatines definitely fit within the reform goals of Bishop Giberti. See Adriano Prosperi, *Tra evangelismo e controriforma: G. M. Giberti (1495–1543)*, Uomini e Dottrine 16 (Rome: Storia e Letteratura, 1969), p. 198.

55. Caracciolo, *Vita Bonifacii a Colle* (Cologne, 1612), p. 270 (misnumbered as 280); the General Congregation (*ACG*, s.v. "Anno 1528") in 1528 selected de' Colli as the superior of the new residence in Verona.

56. Paul H. Hallett, *Catholic Reformer: A Life of St. Cajetan of Thiene* (Westminister, Md.: Newman, 1959), p. 106.

57. Ibid.

58. Caracciolo, *Vita Bonifacii a Colle*, pp. 270–71 (misnumbered as 280–81), describes the inappropriate location and its noise as decisive in their departure.

59. As if to symbolize their more secure location, on June 26, 1527, shortly after their arrival in Venice, the community members welcomed a novice, Matteo (called Antonio) of Serravalle (he died in February 1529); their second novice, Bartolomeo, a priest of Verona, entered on September 15, 1528 (he died in December 1533). On December 9, 1528, Giovanni Marinoni also would join the community and soon become a leader in the community's history. See Paschini, *Thiene, . . . Carafa, e le origini . . . Teatini*, pp. 64–65.

60. Francesco Andreu, "Appunti per una statistica generale dell'Ordine Teatino," *Regnum Dei*, 30 (1974), 80.

61. One explanation for this mortality rate, which seems high, is that novices may have been older when they joined the Theatines. Individuals, for example, who entered in their twenties in 1530 would have been between forty and fifty in 1550; but if they had been in their forties in 1530, this proportion becomes more understandable given the overall

mortality rate. Perhaps the austerity of the community did not appeal to younger novices.

62. The number of Jesuits at the death of Ignatius in 1556 (sixteen years after the founding of the community) was about 1,000, most of whom still remained in the Society of Jesus' training program. Ignatius of Loyola, *The Constitutions of the Society of Jesus*, trans. George E. Ganss (St. Louis: Institute of Jesuit Sources, 1970), p. 232n2.

63. Andreu, "Appunti per una statistica generale dell' Ordine Teatino," 83.

64. Stefano Casati, "Le trattative per l'unione tra Somaschi e Teatini (1546–1547)," *Somascha*, 10. No. 2 (August 1985), 78–79. On Marinoni, see *Regnum Dei*, 18 (1962), particularly Cleto Linari, "Il Beato Giovanni Marinoni (Profilo)," 7–46; Francesco Andreu, "Lettere e scritti del B. Giovanni Marinoni," 47–121; and Gabriel Llompart, "San Paolo Maggiore de Nápoles una iglesia de la primera reforma católica," 173–95.

65. Pio Bianchini, s.v. "Chierici Regolari Somaschi," *Dizionario degli istituti di perfezione*, vol. 2 (Rome: Edizioni Paoline, 1975), cols. 75–78. Also, Luigi Zambarelli, "S. Gaetano Thiene e S. Girolamo Emiliani," *Rivista della Congregazione di Somasca* (November, 1925), 189ff.

66. For Girolamo Emiliani, see G. Landini, *San Girolamo Emiliani dalle testimonianze processuali, dai biografi, dai documenti editi ed inediti fino ad oggi* (Rome: Ordine dei chierici regolari somaschi, 1947); C. Pellegrini, *San Girolamo Miani, Profilo* (Casale Monferrato: n.p., 1962); *Vita del clarissimo signor Girolamo Miani gentil huomo venetiano (di autore anonimo)*, ed. C. Pellegrini (Manchester, N.H.: Somascan Publishers, 1970), translated as *Life of Jerome Emiliani, Most Distinguished Venetian Nobleman* (Manchester, N.H.: Somascan Publishers, 1973).

67. For a fuller description, see C. Pellegrini, "San Gaetano Thiene, Giampietro Carafa, e San Girolamo Miani, I Teatini e la Compagnia dei Servi dei Poveri," *Somascha*, 13 (May 1988), 58–77.

68. See the *ACG*, s.v. "1547, 1555." For background consult: Casati, "Le trattative per l'unione tra Somaschi e Teatini," 69–90.

69. *Vita del SS. P. Paolo IV* (Rome, 1615), p. 144.

70. In his *Vita del B. Gaetano Tiene*, for example, Castaldo relates an encounter between Ignatius and Thiene in which Ignatius asked to join the Theatines. Castaldo's account, of dubious authenticity, generated a controversy between the two groups during the seventeenth century. For further details and other incidents, see Kenneth Jorgensen, "Oratories of Divine Love and the Theatines," passim.

71. The Jesuit John W. O'Malley offers this interpretation; "The antipathy between Ignatius and Carafa is as well known and well documented as explanations of it are obscure. Carafa's rabid anti-Spanish sentiments had something to do with it. Perhaps more important were

two fundamentally different visions of how 'the reform of the Church' was to take place, as a recent study by Peter Quinn has argued." "The Jesuits, St. Ignatius, and the Counter Reformation: Some Recent Studies and Their Implications for Today," *Studies in the Spirituality of Jesuits*, 14, No. 1 (January 1982), 19–20. The Quinn article is "Ignatius Loyola and Gian Pietro Carafa: Catholic Reformers at Odds," *Catholic Historical Review*, 67, No. 3 (1981), 386–400.

72. O'Malley, "The Jesuits, St. Ignatius, and the Counter Reformation," 19–20.

73. For more details, see Kenneth J. Jorgensen, "Theatine Identity and the Impact of the Papacy of Pope Paul IV," *The Proceedings of the Sixteenth Annual Conference of the Middle Atlantic Historical Association of Catholic Colleges and Universities*, 5 (1990), 38–42.

74. *ACG*. s.v. "Anno 1560."

75. *ACG*, s.v. "Anno 1555."

76. Bishop Thomas Goldwell and Cardinal Bernardino Scotti performed one particular service for the Catholic Church: they attended the final sessions of the Council of Trent, which occurred after the death of Paul IV. But they appear to have had little influence on the course of the Council. See Cleto Linari, "Contributo dell' Ordine Teatino al Concilio di Trento," *Regnum Dei*, 4 (1948), 203–29.

77. In his discussion of this aspect of the Theatines, Ludwig von Pastor explains: "Thus the Theatine Order was not so much a seminary for priests, as at first might have been supposed, as a seminary of bishops who rendered weighty service to the cause of Catholic reform." *History of the Popes* 10:418.

78. Andreu, "Chierici Regolari Teatini," cols. 989–90.

79. In addition to Italy, today Theatines work in Spain, the United States (Colorado), Argentina, Mexico, and Brazil. In 1973 the order had 42 houses and 191 members, of whom 134 were priests. Andreu, "Appunti per una statistica generale," 83.

80. Ibid., 80–81. The cumulative membership from 1524 to 1600 included 639 priests and 105 lay brothers.

81. Charles N. Branson, "Les Évêques théatins (1505–1858)," *Regnum Dei*, 40 (1984), 148–52. About 2.6 per cent of the cumulative priest membership had been selected for the episcopate by 1600. This percentage would increase in the later history of the community; of the entire 4,400 priests who had entered by 1850, 203 are known to have become bishops—4.6 per cent of the total. This figure is based on a correlation between the statistics provided by Andreu ("Appunti per una statistica generale," 82–83) and those from Branson (p. 202).

Fra Matteo da Bascio by Mich. van Lothom. Reproduced from Father Cuthbert [Hess], O.S.F.C., *The Capuchins* I (New York: Longmans, Green, 1929).

2

The Capuchin Order in the Sixteenth Century

Elisabeth G. Gleason

Foundation and History

FOR ALL THE DRAMATIC SUCCESS that awaited them, the Capuchins began in obscurity. The early history of the Capuchin order is not as carefully explored or as well known as that of the Society of Jesus, for example, whose founder Ignatius de Loyola was one of the commanding figures of the sixteenth-century Catholic church. No such leader is associated with the beginning of the Capuchins. Unlike the Jesuits, the first Capuchins were neither innovators nor members of an association with sharply delineated characteristics. Their gradual separation from Franciscan Observants and the forging of their own identity followed complex, at times tortuous paths which preclude the possibility of a simple summary. By mid-century they had become a new and vital branch of the Franciscan family and were to play a key role in the history of early modern Catholicism in Europe and the non-European world.

The background of the Capuchins is the turbulent history of the Franciscan order which almost from its inception was wracked by internal tensions.[1] The principal disagreements among its members concerned the thorny issue of how the Rule of St. Francis should be observed in their communities. The rule, magnificent in its idealism and simplicity, demanded a degree of commitment and asceticism that made its literal observance most difficult for friars of a less heroic cast than that of their founder. The Franciscan order was torn between accommodation to practical necessities and repeated demands that absolute poverty be observed in accordance with the will of St. Francis. Time after time movements for reform arose, the most complex and notorious among which was that of the Spiritual Franciscans.

In the sixteenth century, too, the familiar issues of strict observance and the nature of Franciscan poverty reappeared. Pope Leo X tried to deal with them by issuing the bull *Ite vos* of May 29, 1517, which united all friars desiring to strictly observe the Rule of St. Francis into the Order of the Observants, henceforth separated from the Conventuals. The ways of the former, however, failed to satisfy the most zealous friars, for whose sake the general of the Observants, Francisco Quiñones, agreed to institute at least five houses in each Spanish province as havens where men could live according to the strictest Franciscan ideals. This legislation was extended to Italy in 1526, only to be opposed immediately by the more conservative Observants who feared a split in their order between the majority and those whom they regarded as an overzealous minority.

But the internal history of the Franciscans alone is not sufficient for our understanding of the first Capuchins. They were founded at a time and place that were deeply affected by European political and religious developments. Central Italy had been crisscrossed by French and imperial armies since the late fifteenth century. The struggles of their masters, Francis I of France and Emperor Charles V, culminated in the terrible sack of Rome in May 1527, which not only shocked Italians profoundly but also increased their apocalyptic mood. The Marches were an area of particular political turbulence. Wandering prophets called for repentance and conversion, blaming luxury and sin among the clergy and laity for bringing God's punishment on Italy. News of a mighty heretic who had arisen in Germany contributed to widespread fear that terrible events were about to happen, since God was chastising the Church. Accounts of the birth of monsters were taken as evidence of impending cataclysms which threatened all of Christendom.[2] Many thought that only by prayer, fasting, and steadfast faith could the evils about to beset society be held at bay.

The beginning of the Capuchin order must be set against this background. Early in 1525 an Observant Franciscan friar, Matteo da Bascio, secretly left the house of his order in Montefalcone in the Marches. Dissatisfied with the comfort it offered to members of the community while the mass of the people suffered hunger and poverty, Matteo resolved to observe the Rule of St. Francis literally after hearing an interior voice urging him to do so.[3] As a sign of his discipleship, he clothed himself in what he took to have been the original habit of the Franciscans, a garment made of coarse cloth onto which a pointed hood had been sewn. In emulation of the first friars he wore a beard. Pope Clement VII must have been impressed by Matteo because he orally gave him permission to wear his habit and beard, observe the Rule of St. Francis literally, and preach.

It seems that Matteo had no thought or intention of founding an order at this time or even in November, when he was joined by two brothers, Observants both. Ludovico and Raffaele Tenaglia of Fossombrone had the same desire to follow the rule of St. Francis literally, which they found not possible within their community. Their departure from it was bitterly resented by their superior, Giovanni Pili of Fano, who prevailed upon the pope to excommunicate them together with Matteo as apostates on March 8, 1526. To avoid persecution and harassment, the three Franciscans fled to the Camaldolese hermitage of Cupramontana belonging to the Congregation of Monte Corona, itself reformed by Paolo Giustiniani.[4] He not only received them kindly, but also persuaded them to regularize their status by appealing to Cardinal Lorenzo Pucci, the grand penitentiary. Pucci granted them absolution and the permission to lead eremitical lives provided they observed the Franciscan rule and placed themselves under the authority of the bishop of the place where they resided. Matteo continued to move about as an itinerant preacher but joined the two brothers in Camerino, which was hit hard by the recurrence of the plague in the cataclysmic year 1527. Soon a fourth Observant Franciscan became associated with them, Paolo da Chioggia.[5] Their fearless assistance to the sick brought them the good will of Caterina Cibo, duchess of Camerino and second cousin of Pope Clement VII, who became their first protectress.

At this point the question might be asked: Who was the founder of the Capuchins? Although Matteo da Bascio was an admired and venerable figure, he showed no interest in leading a new congregation. While his idealism and example inspired the early Capuchins, in a juridical sense he was not their organizer.[6] That role fell to the more ambitious and practical Ludovico da Fossombrone. With the support of Caterina Cibo he persuaded the pope to issue the bull *Religionis zelus* of July 3, 1528, which is considered the "Magna Carta" of the Capuchin order and its juridical foundation.[7] The bull gave permission to Ludovico and his brother Raffaelo to live as hermits observing the Rule of St. Francis as far as human frailty permitted, to wear their distinctive habit and beard, and, most important, to receive both clerics and laymen into their company. They were given the same privileges as those granted to the Camaldolese. Curiously enough, neither the name of Matteo da Bascio nor even that of the new congregation itself is mentioned.

One can legitimately wonder whether the bull points to any new elements in the nascent order. A recent work argues persuasively that the only innovation of the early Capuchins mentioned in the bull was their beard, and that "the real difference between the Capuchin reform and other previous reforms of the strict observance is to be sought in the manner in which the Capuchins posed and resolved the problem of harmonizing the contemplative life with the apostolic life, and in their survival down to the present as a third autonomous family of the first Franciscan order."[8]

As soon as the papal approval of a new and strict Franciscan congregation became known, zealous friars sought to join. Barely a year after the bull of Clement VII, there were over thirty "friars minor of the eremitical life," as they called themselves. Predictably, they elected the austere Matteo da Bascio as their first superior. But he was unprepared for holding this office, as can be seen in his quick and sudden resignation from it. Ludovico da Fossombrone took his place as the effective leader of the small group of friars. The name "cappucciati" was applied to them for the first time in a document of 1534, but the more common "cappuccini" prevailed, given them on account of their pointed hood.[9]

The friars grew in reputation and numbers beyond the Marches, where they had begun. As they steadily attracted new recruits, including a group of Calabrian Observants in 1529, the general of the Observant order, Paolo Pisotti, became worried about its fragmentation. He pressured the vacillating Clement VII to rescind all permissions granted to Ludovico da Fossombrone and his little band of friars, who were told to return to their original convents. Technically, this would have spelled the end of the Capuchins, since most of their members were, as a matter of fact, former Observants. The brief contains a preamble which must be among the more ironic products of the papal chancery.

The Capuchins are accused of causing scandal not by any kind of abuse, but by their zeal:

> The friars calling themselves Capuchins withdraw from the houses of the Observance and dwell in various places where they live a life so exceedingly austere and rigid that it is hardly human, and thus greatly disturb the minds of other members of the Order who in consequence doubt whether they themselves are equally living up to the obligations of the Rule: thus many are scandalised.[10]

The indecisive pope did not enforce these regulations, however, leaving the matter in the hands of two cardinals who sought to find a solution. At issue was whether and how the Capuchins could continue to exist alongside the Observants. When the pope died in 1534, the question was still open.[11]

Meanwhile, the new association grew in numbers, and the reputation of the Capuchins attracted to the fledgling order men of considerable renown. Among them was the famous preacher Bernardino Ochino of Siena, its future general. Even Giovanni Pili of Fano, who had been so ill disposed toward the Tenaglia brothers in 1526, now joined their group of friars, to whom "he was another Saul become Paul."[12] Pope Paul III, the successor of Clement VII, at first sought to stem the exodus of Observants to the Capuchins. At the beginning of his pontificate the Capuchins consisted of about five hundred friars who were committed to leading the austere life envisioned by St. Francis. The politically astute pontiff did not intend to disband them. He was also open to arguments in favor of the Capuchins advanced by Vittoria Colonna, who urged him not to treat the friars simply as a temporary splinter group of Franciscans or order them to return to Observant houses.

The poet Vittoria Colonna, widow of the marquis of Pescara, belonged to the highest Roman nobility.[13] She participated in Italian intellectual and religious circles concerned with reform of the Church. Vittoria became the second protectress of the Capuchins, honored by them as a "most beloved mother."[14] She used her considerable influence with Paul III to support the new order's right to exist, and to defend it against its detractors or enemies.[15] This was no easy task, since Cardinal Quiñones, protector of the Franciscans, himself an Observant and a man trusted by Paul III, tried to convince the pope that the Capuchins were troublemakers who posed a danger for the established branches of the Franciscans by depriving them of ascetic and zealous friars.[16] In an unusually outspoken letter to Paul III, Vittoria Colonna went to the heart of the matter: if the Capuchins are accused of causing scandal by their way of life, she wrote, then one can argue that "no one should do any good lest he offend those who do evil."[17] We have here a clear example of the struggle between the spirit of prophecy and that of order, so characteristic of the history of Catholicism.

While the battle to sway the pope for or against the Capuchins continued at his court and involved other personalities as well, more unsettling disputes took place within the new order itself. Ludovico da Fossombrone (who, in accordance with Capuchin practice, dropped his family name and retained only that of his place of origin), its vicar general, was at their center. From the time he began guiding the Capuchins in 1529, his style of leadership showed markedly autocratic tendencies. A disturbing rift developed between friars who agreed with Ludovico's insistence on manual labor and others who gave priority to apostolic work and studies.[18] Ludovico's initial inaction concerning the calling of a general chapter turned into his actual attempts to prevent its convocation. Even the general of the Conventual Franciscans, under whose legal protection the Capuchins were at this time, in vain urged Ludovico to agree to the convocation.[19] Once again, Vittoria Colonna came to the rescue of the Capuchins. Her brother Ascanio had Ludovico detained in one of the Colonna castles until he relented and agreed to convoke the chapter. Vittoria herself then prevailed on the pope to reinforce Ludovico's ostensible willingness in this matter by ordering him to proceed to the convocation without further delay.[20]

The general chapter finally met in November 1535. It soon elected a new superior, to Ludovico's extreme displeasure. Bernardino d'Asti, as vicar general, proceeded in consultation with other friars to draft rules for governing the order. Ludovico contested the validity of Bernardino's election, and attempted to put all sorts of obstacles in his path. Despite this, the pope on April 29, 1536, not only affirmed the election of Bernardino, but declared that all who refused him obedience were not to be considered as Capuchins and had no right to wear their habit.[21] Ironically, among them was Matteo da Bascio, the originator of the Capuchin ideal, who returned to the Observant Franciscans, and gave up the habit with the pointed hood which he had introduced among his first followers. Ludovico refused obedience to Bernardino d'Asti and his successors.

In August, Paul III issued a bull confirming the provisions of *Religionis zelus* of 1528, and transferred to the vicar general, Bernardino d'Asti, all the privileges originally granted to Ludovico and Raffaello da Fossombrone. The Capuchins were placed under the jurisdiction of the Conventual Franciscans rather than under that of the Observants.[22] They were therefore legally not independent, since their vicar general had to be confirmed upon election by the general of the Conventuals. In another papal bull issued less than half a year later, an attempt was made to put a stop to continuing frictions between Capuchins and Observants. Each group was forbidden to accept members of the other without written permission of both superiors. More important, to pacify the Observants, the pope forbade the Capuchins under pain of excommunication to expand north of the Alps.[23]

In October 1536, the obstreperous Ludovico was expelled from the order, to which internal tranquillity was restored. He never made peace with the Capuchins, but persisted in his defiance and died as a hermit years later. Again, the question of who was the founder of the Capuchins might be posed. The names of Matteo da Bascio and Ludovico da Fossombrone should rightly be mentioned, but that of Bernardino d'Asti, whom Vittoria Colonna determinedly supported, must be joined to theirs.[24] His good judgment, devotion to the Franciscan ideal, and organizational ability employed without arrogance, contributed to shape the Capuchin order decisively in 1536, when the constitution was issued. Slightly revised in 1552, it has remained the fundamental document regulating the order's organization and government.

Six years after the new order had overcome the difficulties created by Ludovico da Fossombrone, at a time when it was growing[25] and developing with remarkable success in Italy, it experienced the worst crisis of its early history. Its vicar general, Bernardino Ochino of Siena, successor of Bernardino d'Asti, fled in August 1542 from Italy to Switzerland, where he declared his adherence to Protestantism.[26] The shock caused by this event, of course, transcended Capuchin communities. Ochino had been a most sought-after preacher of such fame that cities vied with one another to attract him especially for Lenten or Advent sermons.

His flight was a terrible blow not only to his order, but also to
the so-called *spirituali*, men and women who championed reform
of the individual Christian and of the Church.[27]

A former Observant Franciscan, Ochino joined the Capuchins
in 1534. The next year, when Bernardino d'Asti was elected vicar
general, Ochino became an official of the order. An observer who
was not among his admirers noted that "Everything about Ochino
contributed to make the admiration of the multitude overstep
all human bounds. . . ."[28] Singled out for special mention were
Ochino's pale and thin face, long beard, and reputation for holiness. His imposing appearance, passionate sermons, and Christocentric theology drew people from all social classes to hear him.
Befriended and protected by great ladies like Vittoria Colonna
and by cardinals like Gasparo Contarini, Ochino was admired by
writers, poets, religious thinkers, and earnest friars. When he was
elected vicar general of the Capuchins in 1538 and again in 1541,
he appeared to embody the ideals of St. Francis to perfection.

Ochino's apostasy predictably strengthened the position of critics and enemies of the Capuchins. The friars were accused of
everything from having created a seedbed of heresy to spreading
Lutheran ideas through their sermons and attacking the Church
while ostensibly championing reform. They were depicted as introducing corrosive strife into both branches of the Franciscan
order by their pretense of strict asceticism and "holier than thou"
attitudes, through which other friars fell into disrepute with the
general population. Even the pope seemed to join the enemies of
the Capuchins. Paul III received the news of Ochino's apostasy
while traveling from Perugia to Rome. On seeing a Capuchin
friary near the road, he is reported to have said: "Soon there will
be no Capuchins or Capuchin houses!"[29]

The pope may have given serious thought to abolishing the
new order,[30] but Vittoria Colonna continued to be its advocate,
and Cardinal Sanseverino prevailed upon Paul III and the other
cardinals not to act hastily. His advice was to examine the superiors of Capuchin houses so as to determine whether heresy was
a problem in the order. The subsequent inquiry did not turn up
evidence of widespread disaffection, and the pope was reminded
by one of the friars that even among the apostles there had been
a traitor. Paul III relented, put the scandal of Ochino's apostasy
behind him, and appointed a new protector of the Capuchins. In

Cardinal Rodolfo Pio Carpi they found a man sympathetic to their cause. The next year, in May 1543, Francesco da Jesi as vicar general and the revered Bernardino d'Asti as first definitor assumed leadership of the Capuchins, and devoted themselves to rebuilding the order's reputation as well as encouraging its shaken members.[31] The pope forbade the friars to preach for the time being, however, and lifted the ban only in 1544 when he was convinced that the majority were doctrinally orthodox.

After the death of Paul III in November 1549, tensions between Capuchins and Observants surfaced once again. Pope Julius III upheld the decrees of his predecessor which prohibited Capuchins from accepting Observants into their communities, or establishing themselves in Northern Europe. Pope Paul IV seems to have conceived the idea of uniting the Capuchins with the Conventuals, presumably so that the former could act as a leaven to reform and revitalize their lax brethren. This union never took place, and successive popes were more favorably disposed to the idea of accepting the Capuchins as a third branch of the Franciscans and a distinctive order. When the Council of Trent discussed reform of the regular clergy during its final session, the Capuchins were praised as strict followers of St. Francis, and their right not to hold any common property as an order was confirmed. Several council fathers declared that the Capuchins not only needed no reform, but should be encouraged to continue their mode of life and allowed to wear their distinctive habit.[32] Although they tried to observe the Council's decrees pertaining to regulars, the Capuchins found that their practice of giving every member a vote in affairs of their order contradicted Tridentine norms restricting the franchise to priests. But Pope Pius V supported their egalitarian ways, and all Capuchins, whether priests, deacons, or lay brothers were henceforth allowed to participate in elections as they had from the beginning.

The first movement of the Capuchins beyond the borders of Italy occurred in an unusual way: they began to minister to Catholic armies engaged in the many and bitter conflicts of the sixteenth century. Matteo da Bascio, by now only a former Capuchin, accompanied the imperial soldiers fighting against the Protestants at the battle of Mühlberg in 1546. Members of the order were chaplains on board ship during the expedition of Emperor Charles V to Tunis in 1535 and were present on other vessels serving in conflicts with the Turks in the Mediterranean.[33] Pope Pius V called Capuchins to the ministry on papal ships when the Holy League was formed which was victorious in the great naval battle of Lepanto in 1571. Capuchins were in the armies of Don John of Austria in the Netherlands, among the contingents fighting the Turks in Hungary, and as chaplains to the Catholic forces in the Empire.[34] Thus, they became a familiar sight among Catholic soldiers and sailors, even though they were still technically confined to Italy.

The year 1574 was of prime importance for the Capuchin order. On May 6 Pope Gregory XIII lifted the prohibition of Paul III that prevented the friars from expanding outside Italy. Now they were granted freedom to cross the Alps, to establish themselves in France "and in all the world, and to found and build there houses, places, secured settlements and provinces, according to their custom."[35] This permission marks the beginning of the second period in early Capuchin history, which saw rapid growth in membership and remarkably swift expansion of the order throughout Europe and in the non-European world.

A few dates will illustrate this process. Capuchins established their first branches in the following countries or areas: France, 1574; Spain, 1577–1578; Switzerland, 1581; Tyrol, 1593; Bohemia, 1599; Bavaria, 1600; Rhineland, 1611; Ireland, 1615.[36] When the first century of its existence came to a close, the order had 16,967 members, 1,260 houses, and 42 provinces.[37] Though the seventeenth century was the "golden age" of the Capuchins, its solid foundations were laid during the last quarter of the sixteenth. From that time until the French Revolution the order's activity was one of the most important ways in which the early modern Catholic Church spread its message in Catholic areas to the masses of the population in town and country, and to the poor and neglected. Capuchins shaped and guided the religious devotions of ordinary Europeans, preached in Protestant areas when possible, and after 1600 embarked upon missionary work in Africa, Asia, and the Americas.

The first century of Capuchin history closed with the bull *Alias felicis recordationis* of Pope Paul V, issued on January 28, 1619,[38] which granted their order full independence within the Franciscan family. The Capuchins no longer had to obtain confirmation of their elected vicar general by the superior of the Conventuals, as they had been required to do for the preceding ninety-one years. From here on they were free of legally binding ties to either the Observants or the Conventuals, and had their own identity as the third branch of the Franciscans in fact and in law.

In 1538, with the bull *Cum monasterium* of Pope Paul III, the female branch of the Capuchins received its charter of foundation. The organization of Capuchin nuns was the result of the activities of Maria Lorenza Longo, an influential, well-connected Neapolitan lady and admirer of the charitable work done by members of the Confraternity of Divine Love in hospitals for the so-called "incurables," mostly victims of syphilis. Maria Lorenza Longo founded the first hospital for incurables in Naples, and in 1535 established an adjoining convent for Franciscan Tertiaries. Pope Paul in the same year appointed her its superior for life, putting the convent under the spiritual direction of Capuchin friars. His bull overrode their express prohibition against involvement with the direction of nuns. The first house of Capuchin sisters adopted the strict rule of the Poor Clares which stressed poverty and prayer, and the female Capuchines in the sixteenth century remained strictly cloistered, austere nuns who soon became part of the second order of St. Francis.[39]

The Constitutions of the Capuchin Order

After the papal approval of the Capuchins, their first chapter took place in Albacina in the hermitage of S. Maria dell' Acquarella. In April 1529, the friars of the new congregation met to elect their superior and to decide by what rules they would be governed. As has been mentioned, Matteo da Bascio was elected vicar general but relinquished his post almost immediately, to be succeeded by Ludovico da Fossombrone, under whose name the so-called Constitution of Albacina was issued. There is some question whether these regulations should be called a constitution at all, since they are random prescriptions rather than fully formulated and systematic legislation.[40] They lack a firm principle of organization and seem to be a draft or collection of jottings rather than a logical whole like the Rule of St. Benedict, for example.

To begin with, the friars were enjoined to observe the canonical hours and the Franciscan custom of saying only one Mass so as to guard against people flocking to their houses and offering alms in return for Masses.[41] Scourging was a part of Capuchin devotions. Prayer and contemplation were envisioned as a state rather than as actions performed at certain hours only. A series of specific prescriptions regulated what could be begged or eaten. The friars were to wear their characteristic simple habit with the pointed hood and a belt made of rough cord. Their mission was to go about preaching the gospel. They were prohibited from owning anything, including books, and from writing letters "to themselves or to others"; nor could they "send or receive them without the permission of their superiors."[42] This provision was directed against exploring one's interior state through the keeping of a journal or diary, and thus paying undue attention to oneself. A motley series of prohibitions follows which leaves the modern reader wondering whether their purpose was to virtually prevent members from leading not an austere but a cheerful life. It is as if someone collected pieces that never quite coalesced to form an harmonious whole. If indeed Ludovico da Fossombrone was the author of these rules, they clearly show the great gulf between his mind and that of a systematic monastic legislator.

The definite constitution of the Capuchins was issued by the chapter general which met in Rome in 1536. Though bearing the imprint of Bernardino d'Asti's ideas, it reflects the thought of many of his companions as well, and has remained the basic document spelling out the spirit and organization of the order despite emendations and additions in 1552, 1575, 1608, 1643, and further changes in the twentieth century.

> No book written by a member of the order, no treatise concerning Capuchin spiritual life over the centuries can be compared with the constitution of 1536 if one wants to elucidate the authentic ideals of the friars, or understand the intentions of those who initiated the [Capuchin] reform, or express the values which are found in the imitation of Christ and St. Francis,

maintains a recent writer.[43] This constitution expresses the distinctive spirituality of the Capuchins and shows how they saw their mission.[44]

The lengthy document, comprising a prologue and twelve chapters, was written in Italian and printed in Naples in 1537. It is much more carefully and logically arranged than the prescriptions of 1529. From the beginning, the order's Christocentric orientation is stressed. The Rule of St. Francis, to be observed literally, is called the core of the gospel. The friars are prohibited from studying and reading "impertinent and vain" writings which would distract them from Sacred Scripture. The Constitution echoes the mistrust of human learning expressed by St. Francis, and enjoins the friars to adhere strictly to his vision of what the mission of his followers should be. "If we are sons of St. Francis, let us do the works of St. Francis"[45] is the simple summary of what the order is all about.

Unlike other mendicants, the Capuchins freely put themselves under obedience to the ordinaries in whose dioceses they resided, renouncing any and all exemptions. Above all, they declare their obedience to the pope. In order to ensure that members of their order will live up to its ideals, rigorous selection among postulants is necessary, as is the weeding out of unsuitable novices and the training of the promising ones.[46] All friars must lead an austere life devoid of any comfort. The theme of the *imitatio Christi* appears again and again: the ideal friar is a follower of Christ and St. Francis.

No new rituals or liturgical practices are prescribed for the Capuchins. Rather, they are to follow the common rites of the Catholic Church, including the saying of canonical hours and the celebration of Mass. The prohibition against accepting payment for Masses or allowing burials in their churches is a clear attempt at preventing the kinds of abuses which the Protestant reformers attacked with particular sharpness.

Prayer is seen as central to the lives of the friars. Mental prayer is considered especially important since it establishes personal contact with God. It has to be cultivated in silence. Although the friars are allowed to leave their houses for good reason, communal life is the norm. In their houses austerity must be observed in all things from food and drink to clothing and bedding. Holy poverty must reign among them, and they must embrace it gladly just as St. Francis did. More than a life of poverty, theirs must also be a life of penance. Like the rules of many late medieval Italian confraternities, the Capuchin Constitution makes scourging mandatory. It was to be done on Mondays, Wednesdays, and Fridays, and every day during Holy Week.[47] The reason for this practice is made clear: it, too, is rooted in the imitation of Christ: "While scourging themselves, the friars with a devout heart should think of sweet Jesus, the Son of God, bound to a pillar, and should make an effort to feel a small part of His most distressing pain."[48]

As "pilgrims on earth and citizens of heaven"[49] Capuchins were forbidden to erect large or sumptuous churches or to build spacious houses. Everything associated with them had to be simple, even minimal, like their tiny cells. Their houses were to be near towns and cities, so that they could minister to the people. Those who wished to follow an eremitical vocation were to be accommodated, but the majority of the friars combined action with contemplation. Apostolic work among the laity excluded the hearing of confessions except in unusual circumstances, so that friars would not become too enmeshed in the lives of others. The spiritual direction of confraternities, secular clergy, and especially convents of nuns was strictly forbidden.[50] Their main activity was to be preaching the word of God.

A series of regulations laid down the manner in which the order was to be governed, beginning with triennial general chapters at which the vicar general of the Capuchins was elected. Great pains were taken to ensure that voting was free and without taint of corruption.[51] Under the vicar general were the superiors of provinces, and in each province the Capuchin houses with guardians at their head. Friars were either priests or lay brothers. A cardinal protector, appointed by the pope, had the responsibility of supervising the entire order.[52]

Provisions dealing with the choice, training, and supervision of preachers were an important part of the constitution, since spreading the word of God was the primary form that the apostolate of the Capuchins assumed. Just as the friars were forbidden to read frivolous books, so they were not to preach in accordance with the rules of human eloquence or to use stories, fiction, or poetry. Their sermons, like their churches, were to be extremely simple, stripped of artifice. They were to use above all the New Testament, and to preach Christ to the people. Yet they were not conceived as some kind of primitive fundamentalists. The Constitution mentions the necessity of studying Scripture and theology for friars who want to be efficacious in their apostolate.

Above all, the Capuchins were to be imitators of both Mary and Martha: "When as a result of work among the laity [the friars] feel a slackening of the spirit, they should return to solitude and remain there until, filled again with God, the impetus moves them to spread divine grace in the world."[53] Here the specificity of the order emerges clearly: its members were to live a mixed life with action and contemplation as its two poles. How to apportion their time between them was left up to the individual. The framers of the Constitution show remarkable respect for each person's spiritual development, giving friars a certain degree of freedom to follow their own path, which in some cases might lead them to be missionaries to infidels or heathens, even to become martyrs.[54]

The Constitution of 1536 laid down the principles of the Capuchin order with great clarity. The friars had two models after whom to pattern themselves: Christ and St. Francis. The Franciscan rule without glosses or interpretations was their basic charter. Like their founder, they were devoted to absolute poverty as a means of coming closer to Christ. Lady Poverty was their bride, as she had been of St. Francis, and their life was to be uncompromisingly austere. No friar was to have any personal property, and the order was not to possess anything in its own name.

But in spite of a core of common ideals, the Capuchins were not all stamped from the same mold. A fruitful tension between action and contemplation shaped each friar's existence, and had to be resolved on an individual basis. The overarching mission of all members of the order was the spreading of God's word among the mass of men and women. Catholics were to be strengthened in their faith, heretics converted, and pagans taught. To this the Capuchins devoted themselves first in Italy, then in other European countries, and finally in mission lands, not as undisciplined wandering preachers, but as Franciscans under holy obedience to their superiors and ultimately to the pope. Their subordination to the leadership of the Church and their acceptance of its magisterium distinguished them from their predecessors the Spiritual Franciscans with whom otherwise they had obvious similarities.[55]

ACTIVITY AND SPIRITUALITY

Given the primacy of preaching in the apostolic work of the order, the Capuchin friars became a common sight in European towns as well as in the countryside. From the beginning of their activity in Italy their sermons were geared to the level of comprehension they expected of their audiences. That they were closely attuned to the people can be seen in their use of simple, unadorned, even popular language to explain the meaning of the gospels.[56] The common people, in turn, reacted to their style of preaching with enthusiasm. Descriptions abound of the great crowds who flocked to hear famous Capuchin preachers, not only the notorious Bernardino Ochino, but others like Giovanni da Fano, Francesco da Soriano, Giuseppe da Leonessa, or Anselmo Marzati, preacher to the pope who became cardinal in 1604.

The piety and devotional style of the Capuchins were entirely Franciscan. They were not innovators but, in their best examples, men who were perceived as living models for the Christian people. Capuchin religiosity was rooted in Catholic ritual, practice, and tradition and in Franciscan thought going back to the late Middle Ages. For instance, the friars strengthened lay confraternities that had existed in Italian cities for decades, sometimes centuries, or founded new ones following established procedures, such as the Confraternity of the Most Precious Blood in Florence in 1575. After the Council of Trent they promoted with special fervor the veneration of Mary and the *Quarant' ore*, or Forty Hours' Devotion to the Eucharist, which was exhibited to the faithful in beautifully wrought monstrances. Capuchins were engaged from their earliest days in social work, giving assistance to the sick and dying, to prisoners, condemned criminals, Christian captives of the Moslems, especially in North Africa, and galley slaves. A whole new field of their apostolic activity was their ministry in the armies of Catholic princes and among the sailors of Catholic fleets. Another aspect of their work was the protection, sheltering, and teaching of children, orphans, and abandoned or imperiled young men and women in cities. Finally, their preaching in Protestant or religiously mixed areas of Europe should be mentioned, such as in Switzerland, where they assisted the efforts of St. Francis de Sales to convert Protestants to Catholicism, or in France, where they organized missions among the Huguenots.[57]

The Constitution of 1536 recognized that the Capuchins needed both fervor and education to achieve success in their apostolic work:

> In order that they, while preaching to others, should not [themselves] become castaways, they should withdraw from time to time

from the multitude to ascend with the most sweet Savior the mount of prayer and contemplation, and strive there to become inflamed like the seraphim with divine love, so that they can warm others by their flame.[58]

Ardor alone was not enough, however; preachers had to study Sacred Scripture if they wanted to be efficacious.[59] In keeping with the decrees of the Council of Trent, the Capuchins in 1575 adopted a program of studies for those of their members who aspired to become preachers. Since not every province could have a *studium generale*, as many were established as could be staffed, among them in Naples, Rieti, Rome, and Bologna. Friars were trained in philosophy and theology, primarily that of St. Bonaventure. From the early seventeenth century on, the works of St. Lorenzo da Brindisi, a noted Capuchin theologian who died in 1619, acquired particular authority within the order.

Though the ministry of the Capuchins in general was directed to the common people of Europe, their order also produced a remarkable number of spiritual writers who addressed themselves not only to ordinary Christians, but in a special way to ardent souls seeking closer union with God. Only a few of the most important sixteenth-century works of this kind will be mentioned here: Giovanni da Fano's *The Art of Union [with God]* of 1536 was the beginning of a long series of treatises on prayer, meditation, and the nature of spiritual life. They bear titles like *The Mirror of Prayer* by Bernardino da Balbano, published in 1564, which instructs the reader in techniques of contemplative prayer, or *The Way in Which the Spiritual Person Should Pray* by Silvestro da Rossano in 1574. *The Compendium of One Hundred Meditations* by Cristoforo da Verrucchio of 1592 is a guide to spiritual reflection suffused by Franciscan piety. Mattia Bellintani da Salò is still regarded as a master in the literature of spirituality, and his *Practice of Mental Prayer* has remained a classic.[60]

Two Capuchin authors at the end of the sixteenth and the beginning of the seventeenth century had a profound impact on French Catholicism: the Englishman Benet of Canfield with his *Rule of Perfection*, and Laurent de Paris, author of *The Palace of Divine Love*. Their works also played an important role in the history of Jansenism.[61]

The list of Capuchin saints and *beati* belonging to the first century of the order is lengthy. Among them we find the humble

Roman lay brother Felice da Cantalice, the Swiss martyr Fidelis of Sigmaringen, the preachers Benedetto da Urbino and Giuseppe da Leonessa, and the theologian Lorenzo da Brindisi. A relatively recent work illuminates the lives of many Capuchin saints and is a good point of departure for readers wishing to familiarize themselves with that topic.[62]

In retrospect, the history of the Capuchins between their foundation in 1528 and their achievement of complete autonomy in 1619 is a story of growth and success. They continue to exist as the third branch of the Franciscans alongside the Conventuals and Observants, with houses all over the world.[63] A wealth of primary sources offers ample documentation for the activities of the Capuchin order during the last 465 years, and an extensive secondary literature has contributed valuable studies of almost every aspect of Capuchin history. Yet a lay historian reading and reflecting about the Capuchins cannot but be struck by the fact that despite the rich collections of primary and secondary sources there is very little interpretive work that comes up to the highest standards of modern historical scholarship. The explanation for this would require an essay on trends in historiography during the last 150 years.

The Capuchins began as an Italian order, and their origins and early history must be studied in the context of sixteenth-century Italian religious history. But since the unification of Italy in the nineteenth century, the split between so-called lay culture and Catholic scholarship has relegated the study of religious orders definitely to the latter. Every movement of criticism and dissent and every heretic about whom anything is known has received serious scholarly attention from lay historians. But the history of Catholic orders has remained a family affair, as it were, cultivated within the various institutes established by the orders and staffed by their members. Learned and thoughtful articles reach a limited readership since they are too frequently published in periodicals that are in the nature of house organs. It is as if a whole side of religious life barely existed—yet the new orders of the sixteenth century must be integrated into the history of the Church as well as of Italian culture and thought in their entirety.

That task is yet to be done. In the case of the Capuchins, a number of questions remain unanswered. Among them is the problem of reform thought: Why was the Franciscan ideal in all its austerity so attractive precisely at a time when Protestant ideas

were spread throughout the peninsula? Were there possible connections between what we might call Franciscan fundamentalism
and Protestant calls for purification of the Church and a return to
biblical theology? What were the connections between sixteenth-
century Italian evangelism and the thought of the first generation
of Capuchins? Who were the first Capuchins—what was their
social and educational background? Why did their preaching find
such a resounding echo in Italian society? And why did the Capuchins play such an important role in European diplomacy, from
Mattia da Salò, to the intermediaries in the conversion of Henri
IV of France, and culminating with Père Joseph, the *éminence grise*
behind Cardinal Richelieu?

At a time of great religious turmoil and innovation, the Capuchins upheld an ancient form of piety and devotion. How can we
explain their success first in Italy and then in Europe as a whole?
Fr. Cuthbert ends his readable and affectionate history of the
Capuchins with this thought:

> Not without reason were the most convinced friends and uphold-
> ers of the nascent [Capuchin] Reform found amongst the devout
> humanists of the time. It was in fact the imperious religious instinct
> of the Catholic humanist movement which moulded and gave char-
> acter to the Capuchin Reform from the days of Vittoria Colonna
> till the time of Yves of Paris. That is the outstanding feature of
> their history; and for that the history of the Capuchins deserves
> more attention than has hitherto been given it in the study of the
> Catholic Reformation.[64]

These words were written in 1929. But the integration of Capuchin history with that of humanism in all its varieties, with the
religious history of sixteenth-century Italy, and with the history
of Italian and European popular piety still awaits modern historians who are familiar with the techniques and issues of current
history and historiography. Recent works by anthropologists, so-
ciologists, and psychologists offer a wealth of suggestions that
might contribute to make future studies of the early Capuchins a
more central part of sixteenth-century history than they have been
until now.

BIBLIOGRAPHY

NOTE: Readers are reminded that European Capuchin authors,
who figure prominently in the lists below, use their name in reli-

gion coupled with their place of origin. Accordingly, the works of Édouard d'Alençon, for example, are catalogued by libraries under E, not under D or A.

It may also be worth observing that less commonly available Capuchin and other Franciscan works are often held in the specialized libraries of St. Bonaventure University, St. Bonaventure, New York, and Holy Name College, Washington D.C., among others.

Periodicals

Bibliographia Franciscana, each volume of which covers the publications of several years, includes both periodical literature and books. The bibliographies covering the years 1929–1937 were included in the periodical *Collectanea Franciscana* at irregular intervals from 1931 to 1942. Thereafter the Bibliographia became an independent publication, each volume cumulating several years' publications. In all, 15 volumes, covering the literature down to 1985, have appeared to date.

Collectanea Franciscana, published by the Capuchin Historical Institute in Rome, is valuable for the source material it includes. Since its inception in 1931 it has included articles on all aspects of Franciscan and especially Capuchin history. An index for the years 1931–1970, edited by Claudius van de Laar, has been published (Rome: Institutum Historicum Fratrum Minorum Capuccinorum, 1972).

Other important periodicals are *Miscellanea Franciscana* (1886—) and *Laurentianum* (1960—), with bibliographical information. Other sources of bibliographical information are *Rivista di Storia della Chiesa in Italia* (1947—), *Rivista di Storia e Letteratura Religiosa* (1965—), *Études Franciscaines* (1899–1977), and *Revue d'histoire écclésiastique* (1900—); the last-named includes a section on religious orders in the bibliography at the end of each issue.

The "Index Bibliographicus," pp. xvii–xxvii in *Lexicon capuccinum* (see the next section), is useful.

Encyclopedias

Especially useful for the male and female branches of the Capuchins, their history and foundations, the personalities associated with them, and works written by members of the order are the eight volumes of the *Dizionario degli istituti di perfezione* (Rome: Edizioni Paoline, 1974–1988). Each article includes bibliography.

Lexicon capuccinum: *Promptuarium historico-bibliographicum Ordinis Fratrum Minorum Capuccinorum* (1525–1950) (Rome: Bibliotheca Collegii Internationalis S. Laurentii Brundusini, 1951) contains short articles on Capuchin history and personalities.

Helpful encyclopedias are *Dictionnaire de théologie catholique*, 15 vols. (Paris: Letouzey et Ané, 1926–1950); *Lexikon für Theologie und Kirche*, 11 vols. (Freiburg: Herder, 1957–1965); *The New Catholic Encyclopedia*, 15 vols. (New York: McGraw-Hill, 1967); *Dictionnaire d'histoire et de géographie écclésiastiques*, 22 vols. to date (Paris: Letouzey et Ané, 1912—); *Dictionnaire de spiritualité*, 12 vols. to date (Paris: Beauchesne, 1932—).

History of the Capuchins

Lazaro de Aspurz, O.F.M.Cap., *Franciscan History: The Three Orders of St. Francis of Assisi*, trans. by Patricia Ross from the Spanish original of 1979 (Chicago: Franciscan Herald Press, 1982), situates Capuchin history within the larger Franciscan framework. Since its author is a Capuchin, the Capuchins receive quite substantial treatment. Useful are the bibliography of the three Franciscan orders, pp. xxvii–xxxvii, and the summary of Capuchin history on pp. 195–225 based largely on the much fuller Latin work of Melchior a Pobladura on the Capuchins (see below).

Father Cuthbert, o.s.f.c., *The Capuchins: A Contribution to the History of the Counter-Reformation*, 2 vols. (New York and Toronto: Longmans, Green, 1929), remains a fine first book to read specifically on the Capuchins, containing not only valuable information but many suggestions for further research.

Melchior a Pobladura, O.F.M.Cap., *Historia generalis Ordinis Fratrum Minorum Capuccinorum*, 3 parts in 4 vols. (Rome: Institutum Historicum Ordinis Fratrum Minorum Capuccinorum, 1947–1951) is a general and somewhat summary history of the order. Each section is preceded by a good bibliography.

———. "Cappuccini," *Dizionario degli istituti di perfezione*, vol. 2 (Rome: Edizione Paoline, 1975), cols. pp. 203–52.

———. "La 'Severa riprensione' di fra Matteo da Bascio (1495?–1552)," *Archivio italiano per la storia della pietà*, 3 (1961), 281–309.

Miscellanea Melchior de Pobladura, 2 vols. (Rome: Istituto Storico

Cappuccino, 1964) is a collection of 41 essays honoring Fr. Melchior on his 60th birthday and contains several pieces on the early Capuchins. Particularly useful is Optatus de Veghel, "Le fond franciscain de la réforme capucine," in Volume I, pp. 11–59.

A recent and useful first orientation is *The Capuchin Reform: Essays in Commemoration of Its 450th Anniversary, 1528–1978*, trans. Ignatius McCormick, O.F.M.Cap., from the *Analecta Ordinis Minorum Capuccinorum*, 94 (1978) (Pittsburgh: North American Capuchin Conference, 1983).

Servus Gieben, "L'historiographie capucine, aujourd'hui et demain," *Collectanea Franciscana*, 48 (1978), 435–49.

Le origini della riforma cappuccina: Atti del convegno di studi storici, Camerino, 18–21 settembre 1978 (Ancona: Curia Provinciale Frati Cappuccini, 1979).

Édouard d'Alençon, *Tribulationes Ordinis Fratrum Minorum Capuccinorum (1534–1541)* (Rome: Curia Generalitia O.F.M.Cap., 1914), and *De primordiis Ordinis Fratrum Minorum Capuccinorum (1525–34)* (Rome: Curia Generalitia O.F.M.Cap., 1921) should still be consulted. These volumes are the first modern historical works on the origin of the Capuchins written by the archivist of the order.

Duncan Nimmo, *Reform and Division in the Medieval Franciscan Order from Saint Francis to the Formation of the Capuchins* (Rome: Capuchin Historical Institute, 1987) gives full treatment to the background against which the Capuchins arose.

Thaddeus McVicar, *The Franciscan Spirituals and the Capuchin Reform*, ed. Charles McCarron (St. Bonaventure, N.Y.: The Franciscan Institute, 1986).

Theophil Graf, *Zur Entstehung des Kapuzinerordens: Quellenkritische Studien* (Olten and Freiburg: Walter, 1940). Written by a Capuchin author, this work gives a different interpretation of the first Capuchins from that of Melchior a Pobladura, who disagreed strongly with Graf.

Callisto Urbanelli, *Storia dei Cappuccini delle Marche*, 3 vols. in 4 (Ancona: Curia provinciale FF. Cappuccini, 1978–1984).

———. "L'apporto dei cappuccini alla riforma cattolica del secolo xvi," in *Eremiti e pastori della riforma cattolica nell'Italia del 1500: Atti del VII Convegno del Centro di studi avellaniti, Fonte Avellana, 31 agosto - 2 settembre 1983* (Arezzo: Camaldoli, 1983).

Le origini dei cappuccini veneti: Studi per il 450o di fondazione (1535–1985) (Venice: Curia Provinciale Frati Cappuccini, 1988).

Costanzo Cargnoni, "La tradizione dei compagni di San Francesco, modello dei primi Cappuccini: Nuovi studi e fonti, specie su un codice assisano," *Collectanea Francescana*, 52 (1982), 5–106.

"La vita dei frati cappuccini ripensata nel 450o anniversario della loro riforma," *L'Italia Francescana*, 53 (1978), 513–679, is a group of lectures given at the national Capuchin convention in 1978, on the present-day significance of the Capuchins' work. Stanislao da Campagnola, "L'esperienza dei primi decenni di vita cappuccina in alcuni studi recenti," *Laurentianum*, 4 (1963), 497–516.

Mariano d'Alatri, "Reformationis capuccinae implantatio per Italiam saeculo xvi," *Analecta Ordinis Fratrum Minorum Capuccinorum*, 94 (1978), 325–35.

———. "Bernardino d'Asti padre della riforma cappuccina," in *Santi e santità nell'Ordine cappuccino. I. Il cinque- e il seicento*, ed. Mariano d'Alatri (Rome: Istituto storico dei Cappuccini, 1980), 21–31.

Arsenio d'Ascoli, *La predicazione dei cappuccini nel Cinquecento in Italia* (Loreto [Ancona]: Libreria "S. Francesco d'Assisi," 1956).

Isidro de Villapadierna, "The Capuchins—Hermits and Preachers," *Greyfriars Review*, 2 (1988), 93–113. This is the best up-to-date bibliographical orientation for anyone approaching the early history of the Capuchins. The bibliography on pp. 106–13 is informative about recent publications.

Sources

Father Cuthbert [Hess], O.F.M.C., "Of the Sources of Early Capuchin History," *The Capuchins* II, pp. 431–41 is still the best starting-point. The fullest collection of sources is the recently completed *I frati cappuccini: Documenti e testimonianze del primo secolo*, ed. Costanzo Cargnoni (Perugia: Edizioni Frate Indovino, 1988–1993). This massive collection comprising more than 11,000 pages and an index volume opens up a wealth of material on every aspect of early Capuchin history. The editorial standards are very high, and the criteria for inclusion of documents allow for an immensely rich mass of material which awaits the researcher.

Monumenta historica Ordinis Minorum Capuccinorum, 23 vols.,

1937–1993 (Vols. 1–3, Assisi: Collegio San Lorenzo da Brindisi; vols. 4–23, Rome: Institutum Historicum Ord. Fr. Min. Cap.), is an indispensable collection of early accounts of the order and much other useful material.

Dionigi da Genova, O.F.M.Cap., *Bibliotheca scriptorum Ordinis Minorum S. Francisci Capuccinorum*, rev. and enl. Bernardo a Bononia (Venice: Coleti, 1747) is still important as a record of the writings of earlier Capuchin authors.

NOTES

1. A good treatment of these topics is Duncan Nimmo, *Reform and Division in the Medieval Franciscan Order from Saint Francis to the Formation of the Capuchins* (Rome: Capuchin Historical Institute, 1987).

2. Ottavia Niccoli, *Prophecy and the People in Renaissance Italy* (Princeton: Princeton University Press, 1990).

3. Fr. Cuthbert, o.s.f.c., *The Capuchins: A Contribution to the History of the Counter-Reformation*, 2 vols. (New York and Toronto: Longmans, Green, 1929), I:20.

4. For a biographical sketch see Jean Leclerq, *Un humaniste ermite: Le bienheureux Paul Giustiniani (1476–1528)* (Rome: Edizioni Camaldoli, 1951).

5. Fr. Cuthbert, *Capuchins*, 1:44n32.

6. Callisto Urbanelli, "How the Order Sprang Up and Took Roots," *The Capuchin Reform: Essays in Commemoration of Its 450th Anniversary, 1528–1978*, trans. Ignatius McCormick, O.F.M. Cap. (Pittsburgh: North American Capuchin Conference, 1983), p. 17.

7. Isidro da Villapadierna, "Bulla 'Religionis zelus,'" *Collectanea Franciscana*, 48 (1978), 243–48; Stanislao Santachiara, "La bolla 'Religionis zelus,'" in *Le origini della riforma cappuccina: Atti del convegno di studi storici, Camerino, 18–21 settembre 1978* (Ancona: Curia Provinciale Frati Cappuccini, 1979), pp. 261–80.

8. *I frati cappuccini: Documenti e testimonianze del primo secolo* I, ed. Costanzo Cargnoni (Perugia: Edizioni Frate Indovino, 1988), p. 21.

9. Ibid., p. 22.

10. Quoted from Fr. Cuthbert, *Capuchins*, 1:82.

11. *I frati cappucini*, p. 24n25.

12. Fr. Cuthbert, *Capuchins*, 1:81.

13. For a sketch of her life and full bibliography, see G. Patrizi, "Vittoria Colonna," *Dizionario biografico degli italiani*, vol. 27 (Rome: Istituto della Enciclopedia Italiana, 1982), cols. 448–57.

14. Melchior a Pobladura, *Historia generalis Ordinis Fratrum Minorum Capuccinorum* I (Rome: Institutum Historicum Ordinis Fratrum Minorum Cappucinorum, 1947), p. 38.

15. Pietro Tacchi Venturi, "Vittoria Colonna e la riforma cappuccina," *Collectanea Franciscana*, 1 (1931), 28–58; idem, "Vittoria Colonna fautrice della riforma cattolica secondo alcune sue lettere inedite," *Studi e documenti di storia del diritto*, 22 (1901), 149–79.

16. Ludwig von Pastor, *Geschichte der Päpste. V. Geschichte Pauls III. (1534–1549)* (Freiburg: Herder, 1956), p. 367.

17. Fr. Cuthbert, *Capuchins*, 1:101, and 2:441–47 (text of Vittoria's letter).

18. Urbanelli, "How the Order Sprang Up," p. 33.

19. Giorgio Abate, "Conferme dei vicari generali cappuccini date dai maestri generali conventuali (1528–1619)," *Collectanea Franciscana*, 33 (1963), 428.

20. Fr. Cuthbert, *Capuchins*, 1:91–92; *I frati cappuccini*, ed. Cargnoni, p. 28.

21. The Latin text of this brief, *Cum sicut nobis*, is printed with an Italian translation in *I frati cappuccini*, pp. 75–79.

22. The bull *Exponi nobis* of August 25, 1536, is among the most important documents of the Capuchin order. The text with Italian translation is in ibid., pp. 80–93.

23. *Dudum siquidem* of January 5, 1537: text and Italian translation in ibid., pp. 94–97.

24. *Historia generalis*, pp. 53–54, discusses the question of who the founder is. Melchior a Pobladura argues against Theophil Graf (*Zur Entstehung des Kapuzinerordens* [Olten and Freiburg: Walter, 1940]), who in his opinion attributed disproportionate importance to Bernardino d'Asti. See also Constantius Cargnoni, O.F.M.Cap., "Bernardine of Asti: Principal Promoter of the Capuchin Reform," in *Capuchin Reform*, pp. 97–114.

25. In 1538 there were already about 700 Capuchins divided into twelve provinces in Italy: Melchiore da Pobladura, "Cappuccini," *Dizionario degli istituti di perfezione*, vol. 2 (Rome: Edizioni Paoline, 1975), col. 204.

26. Fr. Cuthbert, *Capuchins*, 1:121–38, summarizes the events, and gives a somewhat unsympathetic view of Ochino.

27. Gigliola Fragnito, "Gli 'spirituali' e la fuga di Bernardino Ochino," *Rivista Storica Italiana*, 84 (1972), 777–813. Bernardino Ochino, *Seven Dialogues*, ed. and trans. Rita Belladonna (Ottawa and Toronto: Dovehouse, 1987) has an excellent introduction to Ochino and a useful bibliography.

28. Quoted from Ochino, *Seven Dialogues*, ed. Belladonna, p. xii.

29. Quoted by Fr. Cuthbert, *Capuchins*, 1:138.

30. *Historia generalis*, p. 80: "Paulus III qui Perusiae ochinianam fugam didicerat, de extinguenda sodalitate capuccina serio deliberaverat."

31. Fr. Cuthbert, *Capuchins*, 1:142–43.

32. *Historia generalis*, p. 58.

33. Ibid., pp. 292–97.

34. *I frati cappuccini*, ed. Cargnoni, p. 38.

35. Bull *Ex nostri pastoralis officii*, the text and Italian translation of which are in ibid., pp. 118–21. The passage quoted is found on p. 120.

36. Melchior a Pobladura, "Cappuccini," p. 204.

37 Ibid., p. 205. These figures are based on a census of 1625. The rapid growth of the Capuchins can be seen by comparing these figures with those of 1608, when the order had 10,708 members, 808 houses, and 35 provinces, and of 1618, when there were 14,846 friars, 1,030 houses, and 40 provinces. See *I frati cappuccini*, ed. Cargnoni, pp. 48–50.

38. The text and Italian translation are in *I frati cappucini*, pp. 134–38.

39. Felice da Mareto, "Cappuccine," *Dizionario degli istituti di perfezione*, 2:184–92, with bibliography.

40. Fedele Elizondo, "Las constituciones capuchinas de 1529: En el 450° aniversario de su redacción en Albacina," *Laurentianum*, 20 (1979), 389–440. For a full bibliography of literature on the Constitution of Albacina, see Isidro de Villapadierna, "The Capuchins—Hermits and Preachers," *Greyfriars Review*, 2 (1988), 110n33.

41. Text in *I frati cappuccini*, ed. Cargnoni, pp. 179–225.

42. Ibid., p. 203.

43. Fedele Elizondo, "Las constituciones capuchinas de 1536," *Estudios Franciscanos*, 83 (1982), 148, quoted in ibid., p. 229. For recent editions of the Constitution, see Villapadierna, "Capuchins—Hermits and Preachers," 112n53.

44. The original text with the additions and changes from 1552 to 1643 is in *I frati cappuccini*, ed. Cargnoni, pp. 249–464.

45. Ibid., p. 263.

46. Ibid., pp. 269–83.

47. Ibid., p. 329.

48. Ibid., p. 330.

49. Ibid., p. 344.

50. Ibid., p. 440.

51. Chapters 7 and 8 (ibid., pp. 363–406) deal with elections and the various officials of the order.

52. *Historia generalis*, section III: "De constitutione seu structura ordinis," pp. 123–62.

53. Ibid., p. 413.

54. Ibid., p. 450.

55. Thaddeus McVicar, *The Franciscan Spirituals and the Capuchin Reform*, ed. by Charles McCarron (St. Bonaventure, N.Y.: The Franciscan Institute, 1986).

56. Arsenio d' Ascoli, *La predicazione dei cappuccini nel Cinquecento in Italia* (Loreto [Ancona]: Libreria "S. Francesco d'Assisi," 1956). A detailed review of the Franciscan preaching tradition is found in Anscar Zawart, "The History of Franciscan Preaching and of Franciscan Preachers (1209–1927): A Bio-Bibliographical Study," *The Franciscan Educational Conference*, 9 (1927), 242–587.

57. *Historia generalis*, section IV: "De actione apostolica," pp. 245–335.

58. *I frati cappuccini*, ed. Carcagnoni, p. 420.

59. Ibid., pp. 423–30.

60. *Historia generalis*, pp. 189–200: "De magistris vitae spiritualis," and the attractive survey by Fr. Cuthbert, *Capuchins*, 2:397–428.

61. Henri Bremond, *Histoire littéraire du sentiment religieux en France depuis la fin des guerres de religion* I–III (Paris: Bloud et Gay, 1916–1921).

62. *Santi e santità nell'Ordine cappuccino. I. Il cinque- e il seicento*, ed. Mariano d'Alatri (Rome: Istituto storico dei Cappuccini, 1980).

63. See the statistical table in Melchior a Pobladura, "Cappuccini," p. 246, for the distribution of Capuchin houses and personnel in 1970.

64. Fr. Cuthbert, *Capuchins*, 2:429–30.

St. Antonio Maria Zaccaria by Alessandro Mochetti. Reproduced from *Epistolae ad . . . Pium Septimum . . . pro causa beatificationis et canonizationis . . . Antonii M. Zaccariae . . .* (Rome: Sacred Congregation of Rites, 1806).

3

The First Centenary of the Barnabites
(1533–1633)

Richard L. DeMolen

In 1806, Alessandro Mochetti of Rome produced a portrait engraving of the Venerable Antonio Maria Zaccaria (1502–1539) of Cremona to accompany the cause of his canonization.[1] Zaccaria, whose canonization did not occur until May 27, 1897, is holding a crucifix in his right hand and is pointing with his left index finger at the corpus of Christ crucified. He is garbed in the nineteenth-century habit and biretta of the Barnabites. In the center lower portion of the engraving are two objects conspicuous by their pivotal position: a spray of lilies and a knotted penitential cord. These three symbols—crucifix, lilies, and penitential cord—summarized the spirituality of Zaccaria and breathed life into the two religious congregations—the Clerics Regular of St. Paul (the Barnabites) and the Angelic Sisters of St. Paul—and the lay sodality—the Married Couples of St. Paul—that he founded. Zaccaria employed the figure of Christ crucified as the major image in his letters and sermons. Through purity (lilies) and self-denial (penitential cord), he called his followers to a life of religious perfection.

ZACCARIA'S SPIRITUALITY

Writing to the Mother Prioress, Domenica Battista da Sesto, at St. Paul's Convent in Milan, on May 26, 1537, Zaccaria described to the Angelics his spirituality, which had been influenced earlier by two Dominican priests, Marcello of Cremona and Battista

Carioni da Crema (ca. 1460–1530). He urged his followers to display "great and noble generosity of spirit toward the Crucified one, toward our own suffering and humiliations, and toward the redemption and perfection of our neighbors."[2] Zaccaria insisted that his followers imitate the crucified Christ by performing acts of penance and humiliation, by observing chastity, and by devoting their apostolate to the spiritual renewal of their neighbors. The spirituality of Zaccaria influenced not only his followers but the entire Church through his contribution to the Forty Hours' Devotion, which quickly spread throughout Europe and became one of the most popular religious observances in modern times.

Zaccaria's blueprint for holiness can be found in his sermon on the third commandment, which was delivered shortly after his 1528 ordination to a group of laypersons, the *Amicizie*, in the parish church of St. Vitale. It was a call to holiness by a nobleman to fellow nobles—an attempt to energize the laity in Cremona and to promote lay involvement in the reform of the Church in the early sixteenth century. If his listeners wanted to be sanctified, he insisted that they must "imitate Christ. Imitate God. Be merciful, particularly on holy days more than on any other day. Feed the hungry. Give drink to the thirsty. Clothe the naked. Welcome the stranger. Visit the sick. Free the imprisoned"—works of mercy enjoined by Christ in Matthew 25:35–36.[3] Zaccaria also exhorted his fellow nobles to heed the words of St. Paul: "in everything let charity urge you on."[4] As a test of their love of God, they must show love of neighbor. But,

> if all I have said so far fails to convince you that love of God is effected and manifested by love of neighbor, be at least convinced by this: that for this very reason God became man. May the word of Christ also convince you: "This is my commandment: that you love one another"; "if you have love for one another, then all will know that you are my disciples." . . . Throughout the whole of Scripture, my dearest, you will find that God has your neighbor as the means of reaching His Majesty.[5]

It seems clear from such passages as well as from his other writings that Zaccaria was influenced not only by Scripture but by such works as the *Imitation of Christ*, the product of the *Devotio Moderna* in the fifteenth century, where we read the following:

"Be not ashamed to serve others for the love of Jesus Christ. . . . Charity is to be had toward all" (1.7–8). He turned to the monastic fathers as well. In referring to the ladder of perfection by St. John Climacus, which called for the renunciation of the world on the first rung and proceeded to faith, hope, and charity on the thirtieth, Zaccaria outlined a gradual progression toward human sanctity. He asked his audience in Cremona: "In conclusion, do you want to climb to perfection? Do you want to make some progress in the spiritual life? Do you want to love God, to be dear to Him, and to be a good child of His? Then, love your neighbor, orient yourself toward your neighbor, acquire a benevolent disposition toward your neighbor, excluding all malevolence."[6]

ANTONIO MARIA ZACCARIA

Antonio Maria Zaccaria was born in 1502 into the noble Cremonese family of Zaccaria, which had developed a thriving woolen business in the fifteenth century. Following the death of his father, Lazzaro, in 1503 and his uncle Pasquale in 1504, the business began to wane and its profits decreased. Antonio was raised by his mother, Antonietta Pescaroli, and tutored at home before attending public high school in Cremona. At eighteen, he began studies at the University of Padua in philosophy, but probably also in medicine because these two disciplines were closely linked as natural philosophy in the sixteenth century.[7] There is no documentary evidence that Antonio actually earned the degree of doctor of medicine at Padua—the register for 1524 which records the degrees that were awarded is incomplete—and on his return to Cremona he was described as a "student" in a legal document dated October 1524. Nonetheless, his name does appear in the 1525 register of physicians in Cremona where he applied for a license to practice medicine. His career as a physician must have been short-lived because an early Angelic nun, Paola Antonia (Giulia) Sfondrati, who was an aunt of Pope Gregory XIV's, has recorded in a ca.-1584 manuscript that "afterward [after leaving Padua] he [Zaccaria] did not pursue the [medical] profession."[8] Instead, he seems to have engaged in legal matters between 1528 and 1531, in 1533, and again between 1538 and 1539, which may indicate that he also studied law at Padua. In any case, according to documents found in the state archives of Cremona, Zaccaria arranged for the legitimatization, adoption, and marriage of Lucia Stroppi, a natural daughter of Giovanni Stroppi's, and took over the financial affairs of Veronica Panevini, widowed sister-in-law of Giovanni Stroppi, by removing the restrictions found in Giovanni's will regarding his minor son, Gian Francesco.

After his return to Cremona from Padua in 1524 and before his ordination in 1528, Zaccaria engaged in an active lay apostolate among the poor while living at home with his mother. He organized a group of nobles whom he styled *Amicizie*. Zaccaria was counseled in his endeavors by the Dominican priest Marcello of Cremona, who encouraged his apostolic efforts in and around the parish church of St. Vitale as well as his study of the Epistles of St. Paul and the works of the Church Fathers and St. Thomas Aquinas. Later Zaccaria extended his apostolate to the hospitals of Cremona, which points to his abiding interest in medical care.

Zaccaria organized the *Amicizie* about 1526. It was during this period that he also met the self-styled "Fra" Bono Lizari, who supported his charitable activities and later participated in the Barnabite ministries as a layman—occasionally serving as a mediator between church officials and those Barnabites who were accused of excessive public penances. "Fra" Bono combined an independent lifestyle with a conspicuous attire: a white cassock, over which hung a large crucifix, and boots.[9]

Zaccaria was ordained to the priesthood in 1528 and celebrated his first Mass without the customary solemnity in the church of St. Vitale. He later resigned the benefice that was given to him by his family in the church of St. George and assigned it to his relative Marc Zaccaria.

In 1530 Countess Ludovica Torelli introduced Zaccaria to Battista Carioni da Crema, the Dominican friar who would transform his life and assist him in drafting the Barnabite constitution. Zaccaria, Torelli, and Carioni later combined their efforts to establish the Barnabites and the Angelic Sisters of St. Paul. Fra Carioni directed the reforming energies of Zaccaria until his death in December 1533. Indebted to Sebastiano Maggi, O.P., for his own spiritual formation, Carioni left his friary in Milan in 1527 and preached religious reform throughout Lombardy and Venetia. His sermons and published writings were also clearly influenced by Eastern monasticism—the works of Johannes Cassianus (ca. 360–

435), St. John Climacus (ca. 579–ca. 649), and St. Isaac of Monte Luco (d. ca. 550); by Italian writers on asceticism and morality: St. Bonaventura (ca. 1221–1274), St. Caterina of Siena (ca. 1347–1380), Blessed Bartolomeo da Bragança (ca. 1200–1270), and St. Antonino of Florence (1389–1459); and by the Church Fathers, especially St. Jerome and St. Augustine. In his revision of the Barnabite constitution drafted by Carioni, Zaccaria inserted the works of Carioni among the list of recommended authors on the spiritual life, namely, *The Way of Open Truth* (1523), *On Self-Knowledge and Self-Mastery* (1531), *Divine Philosophy* (1531), and *Interior Mirror* (edited and published posthumously by Countess Ludovica Torelli in 1540).[10]

Carioni condemned the pursuit of Renaissance classical letters in *The Way of Open Truth* if such study interfered with the acquisition of Christian knowledge. He reasoned:

> Some people study those things which appeal to their curiosity and sense of beauty; for instance, the polished and elegant works of Petrarch and Dante, the finely imaginative poetry of Vergil, and thus they engage in a superficial type of learning. When they open the Bible, which combines profoundly stirring ideas with general unconcern for delicate style, they are unable to study it; they find it repelling and so they remain wholly deprived of things divine.[11]

The revised constitution by Zaccaria recommended to the Barnabites the study of both Scripture and the Church Fathers, but "first and foremost, let them delight even more in reading those books which deal with moral instruction, formation, and perfection, and the true imitation of Christ."[12] This attitude toward secular learning had been expressed earlier by St. Jerome, who recalled (in mid-Lent 374) a dream in which he was dragged before a heavenly tribunal and accused of being a Ciceronian rather than a Christian. Although he vowed for the future not to read or possess pagan literature, he never abandoned classical studies per se.[13] He simply gave precedence to biblical studies. Like St. Jerome, Carioni underscored the importance of Sacred Scripture as a source of and asceticism as a path to divine truth.

About 1527, in Milan, Carioni met the Countess of Guastalla (near Cremona), Ludovica Torelli (1499–1569), who had been twice widowed. Torelli had entered into two brief marriages. At 17, she married a Cremonese nobleman, Ludovico Stanga, who died in 1517, the same year as her marriage. In 1526, she married Count Antonio Martinengo of Brescia, who was killed the following year. Carioni with permission of his superiors took up residence in Torelli's palace at Guastalla in 1528 and served as her confessor and spiritual adviser until his death at the age of seventy-three. Under his influence, Torelli soon transformed her opulent and secular lifestyle into evangelical service to the less fortunate. To signify her interior transformation, she chose the name of Paola and promoted good works among a group of fourteen laywomen in 1530.[14]

Since Countess Torelli had lived in Cremona for some six months after her first marriage in 1517, she may have met Zaccaria and his mother at this time, but there is no documentation on the matter. He had certainly made her acquaintance by 1529. Zaccaria also must have met Carioni in Milan after he had been introduced to Countess Torelli. One thing is certain: Carioni never met Zaccaria in Cremona. Zaccaria did not make up his mind to accept Torelli's offer of a chaplaincy until 1530, following the death of his predecessor, Pietro Orsi, in the autumn of 1529.

Zaccaria became so devoted to the seventy-year-old Fra Carioni that he referred to him as "our divine Father" in his correspondence. Writing to Carioni in a letter of May 31, 1530, Zaccaria exhorted him: "Please! dear Father, do not abandon me, and be my patron saint with God."[15] But not everyone shared Zaccaria's perception of Carioni as a saint. In 1530, Fra Angelo da Faenza, the Dominican provincial superior, ordered Carioni to leave the residence of the countess of Guastalla even though Clement VII had issued a decree on July 10, 1530, exempting Guastalla from both episcopal and Dominican jurisdiction, and both the vicar general and the Inquisitor of Milan upheld the exemplary behavior and virtues of the countess, sending favorable reports concerning the charitable activities of Carioni and Torelli on August 4, 1530. Such testimonials as these also did not convince Bishop Gian Pietro Carafa, co-founder of the Theatines, who served as an adviser to the Inquisition, that Carioni's continued residence at Guastalla was proper. In a letter dated March 9, 1532, the bishop—apparently unaware of the cenobitic community, which included Zaccaria, that had been established by the countess in 1528—condemned Carioni's lifestyle outside his friary:

It was a great scandal . . . to see a religious of your age and renown, after so many years of religious profession, jump from your
monastery to live alone in the house of a widow of noble rank,
young, beautiful, twice married, independent, wealthy, exceed-
ingly sharp-witted, dreadfully capable of good and evil, mostly on
account of her fragile sex and unreliable age. Not only that, but
you took her triumphantly all over a city like Milan for everybody
to see.

Carafa called into question Carioni's judgment and pointed out
to him that his priestly state was compromised by conduct which
was opposed "not only by the Scriptures and the teaching of the
Fathers and all church laws and religious rules, but natural honesty
itself."[16] Many years later, as Paul IV, Carafa issued a bull (on
August 3, 1558) that suspended "vagrant monks . . . from the
performance of any ecclesiastical duties and especially those of a
priest."[17] It was, no doubt, aimed at friars like Carioni who had
developed a spiritual relationship with a young laywoman outside
the cloister of his friary.

Carafa's letter of condemnation was followed by a papal brief
ordering Carioni to return to his friary in Milan. Dated November 8, 1533, the directive was withheld from the friar because of
a serious illness by the countess herself. Instead, she directed Zaccaria to draft an appeal to this directive and to hand deliver it to
the provincial superior in Mantua, but neither the superior nor
his vicar would receive him.

When Zaccaria was a student at Padua, he met Serafino Aceti
da Fermo (1496–1540), who was to become a canon regular of
the Lateran congregation as well as a traveling preacher. In 1530,
both Zaccaria and Aceti joined the Oratory of Eternal Wisdom
in Milan where Aceti became a friend of Virginia Negri's (1508–
1555)and later encouraged her to join the Angelics (by whom she
was given the name of Angelica Paola Antonia). In 1541, Aceti
wrote a defense of Carioni against his Roman detractors. It was
in the form of an *apologia*, addressed to Giulia Picenarda, and
supported Carioni's orthodoxy. At the request of Torelli, he also
wrote the *Interior Mirror* in order to assist her in the reform of a
convent of nuns in Vicenza. Aceti's spiritual writings influenced
such major figures of the Catholic Reformation as St. Filippo Neri
(1515–1595) and St. Teresa de Avila (1515–1582).[18]

Zaccaria based what survives of his literary works (twelve let-

ters, six sermons, and the constitution of the Barnabites) on a
careful reading of the Old and New Testaments, citing the former
116 times and the latter 242 times—with 93 specific references to
St. Paul. He also referred to St. Augustine and St. John Climacus
twice and to St. Bernard and St. Gregory the Great once. In his
sermon on the third commandment, Zaccaria reminded his listeners that holiness is increased by the frequent reception of communion and recalled that St. Augustine exhorted Christians to
receive the Eucharist at least once a week.[19]

CLERICS REGULAR OF ST. PAUL

Giambattista (Melchior) Soresina (1514–1601), one of the nine
members of the Barnabite Congregation in 1534—most of whom
were from aristocratic backgrounds—has left us a memoir in
which he described the first community house, named after St.
Paul: "The beginning of our Congregation was in the year 1533
in Saint Caterina's [dei Fabbri] by Porta Ticinese [Milan], and the
Superior was Antonio Maria Zaccaria, a gentleman from Cremona and an only son. . . ."[20] The three Barnabite co-founders
were both noble and professional men. Zaccaria was a physician
by training, Giacomo Antonio Morigia (1497–1546) was an architect, and Bartolomeo Ferrari (1499–1544) was a notary. Their fellow noblemen objected to their unconventional actions and
maintained that their public penances were socially unacceptable
and brought ridicule and disgrace to their families.

　　Under Zaccaria's spiritual direction, the original group of Barnabites began to live a common life but took no formal vows.
Their inspiration came from the *Amicizie* in Cremona, but the
foundation itself can be traced to the Oratory of Eternal Wisdom
in Milan. Late in 1530, Carioni, Zaccaria, and Torelli joined the
Milanese Oratory. It was here that Zaccaria met the two co-
founders of the Barnabites, Morigia and Ferrari, neither of whom
was a priest at the time, and Countess Torelli met Negri, a leading
member of the nascent Angelics. In cooperation with the others,
Zaccaria assembled the Clerics Regular of St. Paul, the Angelic
Sisters of St. Paul, and the Married Couples of St. Paul about
1531. The married members of the *Amicizie* were directed to join
the Married Couples of St. Paul; single men to join the Clerics

Regular of St. Paul; and maidens and widows to join the Angelic Sisters of St. Paul.[21] The three persons most responsible for these foundations were Zaccaria, Carioni, and Torelli, but the environment that nurtured the origins of the Barnabites and the Angelics was the Oratory of Eternal Wisdom.

Lay oratories were an important seedbed of sixteenth-century reform. The first of the major Italian confraternities, the Oratory of Divine Love, was founded in Genoa by a layman, Ettore Vernazza, under the inspiration of a laywoman, St. Caterina of Genoa (1447–1510) in 1497. Vernazza established a second oratory in Rome about 1517, and others followed. About 1500, another laywoman, St. Jeanne of France (1464–1505) inspired Gian Antonio Bellotti (d. 1528), an Augustinian friar, to establish the Oratory of Eternal Wisdom in Milan at the Augustinian convent of St. Martha where Mother Arcangela Panigarola (d. 1525) was prioress. The Oratory promoted personal sanctification and corporal works of charity. It was open to all social classes, to both men and women, lay and religious.[22]

Sometime after meeting Morigia and Ferrari at the Oratory of Eternal Wisdom in 1530, Zaccaria conceived the idea of establishing a congregation of clerics which would combine the active and the monastic life. In a letter to Ferrari and Morigia of January 4, 1531, he referred to his intention to found such a community and indicated that he had experienced personal misgivings for some time: "Oftentimes I am deeply annoyed at my grievous irresolution, which holds sway and for long has held sway over my soul."[23] But, shaking off his tepidity, he continued:

One must contemplate over and over again, ponder, and ruminate when something important is to be decided upon. But once the thing has been thought over and one has received proper counsel, one should not hesitate to carry out what has been decided upon. The reason is that in the ways of God what is required above all else is promptness and expeditiousness.[24]

In order to eliminate any procrastination which might be lingering in the minds of his co-founders, Zaccaria concluded his letter with persuasive eloquence: "Come, come, Brothers: If up to now we have known any irresolution, let us cast it off together with all negligence and let us run like madmen not only toward God but toward our neighbor as well. It is our neighbor alone who can receive what we cannot give to God, who does not need anything from us."[25]

Having overcome indecisiveness, the two priest-founders, Zaccaria and Ferrari (who was ordained on March 31, 1532) sent a petition to Clement VII in 1532, requesting permission to profess the three religious vows before the archbishop of Milan (or his vicar general) and to begin common life somewhere in the archdiocese "in order to devote themselves more vigorously and unrestrictedly to God's gracious purposes and to probe more deeply matters pertaining to God."[26] Clement VII, perhaps at the bequest of Ferrari's brother, Basilio, who was a papal notary, responded favorably and granted their petition on February 18, 1533, in a brief entitled *Vota per quae vos*.[27] Zaccaria and Ferrari took possession of the first house of the Congregation on September 29, 1533, located near the church of St. Caterina dei Fabbri. Since this house could accommodate only two people, the Congregation acquired two other houses nearby. Zaccaria, Torelli, and Ferrari paid for these residences from their own resources.

It was at this time that Zaccaria asked Carioni to prepare a written constitution for the Congregation. The Dominican friar complied and produced a Latin text before the end of 1533. It was based on the Rule of St. Augustine and sketched a life suitable for hermits.[28] Carioni also requested permission from his superiors to join the Barnabites, but he died before permission was granted. Following Carioni's death, Zaccaria rewrote his constitution and produced a version which would be suitable for a more active life. It was designed as a guide to the religious life, not as a set of prescriptions.

In Chapter 18 of his constitution, Zaccaria identifies eight characteristics needed by anyone who wished to reform religious life in the sixteenth century. To begin with, a reformer must be realistic in choosing the right time and place for his reforming efforts. Second, he must be an individual with vision and courage who is also able to overcome pressures from hypocritical Christians bent on opposing reform by influencing the decisions of civil and religious authorities. Third, the reformer needs the quality of perseverance in adversity. Fourth, the individual must possess humility and display compassion and tolerance for individual differences. Fifth, an ideal reformer must be selfless and devote his energies to the glory of God and the salvation of souls. Sixth, he must be straightforward in his contacts with others. The seventh characteristic is the desire for perfection. Finally, the religious reformer must become totally dependent on God's help.[29] Zaccaria justified the foundation of new religious orders in the Church because of their charitable orientation. Quoting from St. Gregory the Great, he argued that modern-day saints were responsible for advocating change, but that they did so out of love of God and in response to the gospel. He also criticized the older religious orders for their accumulation of wealth.[30]

Lastly, the author of the revised Barnabite constitution recommended the use of seven steps to achieve the perfection of Barnabite novices: "to learn to restrain . . . all their desires so that they would be saddened if something should be done in accordance with their wishes"; "to confess well"; "to open their hearts completely to their [Novice] Master"; "[to acquire] the knowledge and the value of the interior man"; "[to acquire] the manner of preserving, of increasing the novitiate fervor"; "to have real love and desire for complete perfection"; and [to observe] "silence and all of the other exterior formalities." In his letter of November 3, 1538, Zaccaria observed that his written constitution could not be effective unless it was internalized.[31] The founder of the Barnabites wanted to produce novices who were both internally and externally dedicated to the spiritual life.[32]

The earliest Barnabites chose St. Paul as their chief patron and decided to adopt as their religious habit a dark brown cassock and round hat. They referred to themselves publicly as clerics regular and privately as children of St. Paul. In a bull (*Dudum felicis recordationis*) of July 24, 1535, Paul III recognized them as Clerics Regular of St. Paul and acknowledged their special devotion to St. Paul. In the bull *Pastoralis officii cura* of December 25, 1543, he also authorized them to build a church in St. Paul's honor and gave them permission to profess solemn vows. The Angelic Sisters later built St. Paul's Church in Milan; it was dedicated in 1552. The formal name of Clerics Regular of St. Paul Decapitated was approved by Julius III's bull of February 22, 1550 (*Rationi congruit*), and confirmed in the Barnabite Constitution of 1579. They were popularly referred to as Barnabites in the 1540s and thereafter because of their association with the Church of St. Barnabas, the motherhouse in Milan, which they acquired in 1545 and which remained their only canonical foundation until 1557. Julius III's bull (*Ad hoc nos Deus praetulit*) of August 11, 1550, confirmed their status as a religious order. In 1552, the Barnabites agreed to abandon the idea of apostolic poverty and to accept ownership of property, thus ensuring their self-sufficiency. During the lifetime of the founder, the Barnabites had accepted monthly donations from Countess Torelli and given whatever was left at the end of each month to the poor.

Although Zaccaria professed temporary vows and served as the first superior of the Barnabites between 1533 and 1536, he declined to take solemn vows, which were not approved for his Order until after his death. He spent most of his life as the founder of the Barnabites and the Angelics living on the estate of the countess of Guastalla. His death occurred in 1539 at his birthplace in Cremona, witnessed by his mother.[33]

Soon after they had received their religious habits on June 10, 1534, the Barnabites were accused, on October 5, 1534, of heresy and public disorder because of their outward display of penance and acts of mortification in the piazza and streets of Milan. Despite failing to find evidence against the Barnabites, the Republic of Venice later accused them of betraying state secrets by means of the confessional and expelled them on February 21, 1551.

Moreover, the writings of their spiritual adviser, Carioni, including the original Barnabite constitution, were censured and eventually placed on the Venetian Index of Forbidden Books in 1554.[34] Paolo Melso (1500–1559), who was superior general of the Barnabites at the time, was jailed and later placed under house arrest in Rome by orders of the Inquisition. Carioni's *Opera* remained on the Tridentine Index of Prohibited Books (1564) until 1900, that is, three years after the canonization of Zaccaria, because it was considered "partly scandalous, partly heretical, partly unreliable in matters of faith, and was to be totally shunned by all the faithful."[35]

Before the formal approval of the Barnabites in 1533 and the Angelics in 1535, these two religious groups met together in the same location for spiritual conferences, prayer, and chapters of self-accusation. They soon aroused the indignation of church and civic officials because they intermingled the sexes and performed public acts of penance at various open-air missions in the streets of Milan. Their behavior was all the more shocking to these officials because it was known that these priests and nuns had been members of the nobility who adhered to the notion of "noblesse oblige." In a demonstration of their devotion to Christ crucified and their contempt of the world, the Barnabites and Angelics painted their faces, wore heavy ropes around their necks, flogged themselves, carried large wooden crosses, and confessed their sins openly—forms of asceticism and mortification that were recommended by Carioni in *The Way of Open Truth*. As an expression of their vow of poverty, they would also beg for donations in the market place on behalf of the pregnant unwed girls of Saint Valeria. Moreover, on Fridays, the Barnabites and the Angelics would gather in the Cathedral of Milan and offer prayers with bowed heads and outstretched arms as the bells of the cathedral tolled. In 1532, Gian Marco Burigozzo, a Milanese merchant, recorded an entry in his diary describing the Friday afternoon devotions of a group of men and women whom he believed were led by Countess Torelli: ". . . by certain men who were considered to have a great degree of sanctity, and also women. . . . They have obtained permission to have the Ave Maria rung for a long time on Fridays at the hour when Christ died."[36]

Since the Barnabites had violated standards of public devotion, the Inquisition requested a formal trial on October 5, 1534. The Barnabites and Angelics stood accused of disorder and heresy. Zaccaria responded on October 4, 1534, with an impassioned defense of their behavior, reminding them that "anybody who tries to live in devotion to Christ is certain to be attacked" (2 Tim 3:12).[37] He urged his followers not to forsake their vocations and to take comfort from the holy mission that they had undertaken:

> Here we are, fools for the sake of Christ, who can boast about our sufferings, because those whom the world thinks common and contemptible are the ones that God has chosen to show up those who are everything. Let us not lose sight of Jesus, who endured the cross, disregarding the shamefulness of it, and we shall prove that we are servants of God by great fortitude in times of suffering, prepared for honor or disgrace, taken for imposters while we are genuine.[38]

Following the death of Carioni on December 31, 1533, Zaccaria became the sole spiritual leader of the Barnabites and Angelics, and it was his leadership and strength of character that persuaded his followers to remain true to their vocations. The trial that was conducted by Senator Francesco Casati, representing the civil authorities, Giovanni M. Tosi, representing the archbishop of Milan (Cardinal Ippolito II d'Este), and Melchiorre Crivelli, representing the tribunal of the Inquisition, found no incriminating evidence against the Barnabites and the Angelics. As a result, the inquiry was concluded but without rendering a formal verdict in their favor. Having failed to obtain the necessary exoneration, the Barnabites felt it necessary to ask for papal protection. In 1535, Paul III responded, exempting the Barnabites from the authority of the archbishop of Milan and placing them under papal jurisdiction. The papal bull went even further, praising their religious purposes and approving their common life, religious habit, and status as clerics regular. Moreover, they were given permission to profess the three vows and to appoint a religious superior for three years. Nevertheless, rumors of their misconduct persisted, and the Barnabites in 1537 requested a second investigation of the charges that they had fomented the thirteenth-century heresy of the Beghards and Beguines by promoting intense devotion to the Eucharist and to the passion of Christ. Once again, they were found innocent. Even more disconcerting than these charges of heresy were two attempts—the first at the urging of the archbishop of Genoa, Geronimo Sauli—to unite the Barnabites with the Jesuits in 1552 and 1559.[39] The proposed 1559 merger may have been a final effort by Carafa (as Paul IV) to discredit Carioni, who played a major role in drafting the first constitution of the Barnabites. Paul IV believed that "bad books" were the real source of heresy.[40]

Until 1552, the earliest Barnabites followed a religious life that was based on the general chapter system of governance. Since the Barnabite Congregation consisted of only one house (St. Barnabas in Milan), and never exceeded forty priests during its first twenty years, it was determined that the Congregation would meet regularly to deal with its religious and social concerns. Decisions made by the general chapter were termed "orders" and could be modified or changed by future chapters. The Barnabites emphasized the full participation of each cleric in the administration of the Congregation.

In reaction to the accusation of heresy and sedition by the Republic of Venice (1551), the Barnabites set aside the constitution that had been composed by Zaccaria from a draft by Carioni in

1533 and revised again by a general chapter in 1548, and drew up a new one that would not be associated with the heretical works of Carioni. It was sanctioned by the apostolic visitor, Bishop Leonardo Marini, on November 22, 1552, and approved by the papacy in 1553. Moreover, Julius III appointed Cardinal Alvarez de Toledo as their protector and overseer. The 1552 Constitution was the first authorized constitution of any of the orders of clerics regular, necessitated by accusations of heresy and by the desire to impose a uniform set of regulations on them. The Theatines did not find it necessary to obtain papal approval for their rule, which had been drafted by Carafa in 1526, and lived a common life without a formal constitution from 1524 to 1604.

But the 1552 Constitution soon required revision for four reasons. First, the dependent houses of the Congregation—termed missions—which had been under the control of the superior at St. Barnabas, began to exercise autonomy after 1576 in direct violation of the 1552 Constitution. Moreover, the superior at St. Barnabas (after 1576) began to function as a superior general—an office which was not recognized by the 1552 Constitution. A third innovation was the office of visitor which replaced that of the mayor who had been entrusted with the oversight of the rule at the motherhouse itself. Finally, additional growth in the number of religious houses made it imperative that a new constitution be drawn up and ratified.[41] Beginning in 1570, three Barnabites undertook the task of preparing a new constitution. They were encouraged to do so by the archbishop of Milan, Cardinal Carlo Borromeo (1538–1584), who wanted to establish a national congregation in place of one that was centralized in Milan. He also wished to protect the Barnabites from the possibility of future charges of heresy and disorderly conduct because of their association with Carioni. Melchior Cano (ca. 1509–1560), the Spanish Dominican theologian, went so far as to state that Carioni was the actual founder of the Barnabites, and no doubt he reflected a widespread suspicion in the sixteenth century.[42]

Cardinal Borromeo had earlier attempted to unite the Barnabites with the reformed priests of Tortona in 1565 and the Humiliati, a group of monks who followed the Rule of St. Benedict, in 1567 and 1570, but all three efforts failed, largely due to the persistence of St. Alessandro Sauli (1534–1592), who was the Barnabite superior general between 1567 and 1573. Sauli quickly perceived the incongruities in the lifestyles of the Humiliati and the Barnabites. To begin with, the Humiliati were primarily lay brothers, who were devoted to commercial enterprises, whereas the Barnabites were engaged in the priestly ministries and would have lost their clerical focus. Second, the Humiliati were seven times larger than the Barnabites and would have overwhelmed them.[43]

Since Borromeo had been entrusted by the papacy with "the examination, correction, amendment, and ratification of the new Constitutions and their application by commanding their observance," he directed that a general chapter of the order undertake the task.[44] The chosen committee, headed by Gian Pietro Besozzi, superior general of the Barnabites, produced an elaborate version in Italian. Expressing dissatisfaction with its length, Cardinal Borromeo directed his former secretary, now a Barnabite novice, Carlo Bascapè (1550–1615), to prepare a shorter version in 1578. Bascapè complied and drafted a Latin text that stripped away most of the committee's detailed commentary and shortened its length considerably. This version was later amended by Borromeo himself and ratified by the Barnabites on March 24, 1579, in Milan. Pope Gregory XIII gave his approval in the bull *Cum sicut accepimus* on November 7, 1579. In order to suppress any copies of the earlier version of the constitution, which might fuel further debate, Borromeo sent copies of the 1579 Constitution to every Barnabite community with an accompanying letter exhorting them to follow its wise counsel. He also reminded the Barnabites of his intention to visit them personally in community, but judiciously expressed hope that their voluntary observance of the new Constitution would make such a visit unnecessary—a skillful carrot-and-stick ploy![45]

At the insistence of the Council of Trent, the 1579 Constitution devised a hierarchical system of authority, which was distinct from the local chapter system that was found both in the original constitution by Zaccaria and in that of 1552. The 1579 Constitution was divided into four books, which in turn were subdivided into various chapters. Book I is concerned with the qualifications of novices, the novitiate itself, the profession of vows, dismissal from the order, and the education of professed clerics. Book II discusses the vows of obedience (which is given first place), chastity, and poverty (underscoring the personal renunciation of goods), confession and communion, the Divine Office, mental prayer, fasting and other forms of mortification, the rule of silence, and the disavowal of personal honors or higher office (which became in practice their fourth vow). The chapter of faults—in which professed members were enjoined to disclose their personal and moral faults—occupies a prominent place in the Constitution, but does not approach in intensity the public admission of faults characteristic of the earliest Barnabites. Book III concentrates on the pastoral ministries of the Barnabite priests outside their community, such as confession, preaching, visiting the sick, and the pursuance of theological studies. Book IV identifies the administrative network of the order, the duties of the general chapter, superior general, procurator general, and visitors, as well as the administration of community property.[46]

Although the Barnabites had established only one canonically independent house before 1557, twenty years earlier in May 1537, they were invited by Cardinal Niccolò Ridolfi, bishop of Vicenza, to work in his diocese toward the reform of two convents that had been founded earlier by relatives of St. Gaetano da Thiene. Zaccaria personally accompanied the Angelics' co-founder, Torelli, and Angelica Paola Antonia Negri, the Barnabite Francesco di Lecco, and Fra Bono, and established a temporary foundation.[47] After two months in Vicenza, Zaccaria withdrew and appointed the Barnabite co-founder, Ferrari, as superior of the mission. These Barnabites and Angelics introduced the Forty Hours' Devotion and organized a branch of the Married Couples of St. Paul. In effect, Zaccaria saw the three communities that he founded— the Barnabites, the Angelics, and the Married Couples—as linked together in a common spiritual apostolate. Just as all three groups had been named after St. Paul and had worked together as a unit in Milan, the founder wanted the same arrangement in Vicenza. To offset his absence, Zaccaria sent words of encouragement from Cremona to his co-founder Ferrari on October 8, 1538. He reminded him that nothing can stop an apostle of Christ, "neither the world above nor the world below."[48] Likewise, on June 11, 1539, shortly before his death, Zaccaria wrote a disciplinary letter to Battista Soresina in Milan from Guastalla, informing the Barnabite priest that he must obey co-founder Morigia, who was the religious superior, with humility and faith. Moreover, he advised him to see Christ ("the Shepherd of his soul") in Father Morigia.[49]

Soresina in turn described Zaccaria as a man who wore a wholly jubilant and cheerful smile.

Bolstered by their success in Vicenza, the followers of Zaccaria attracted the attention of other prelates. Bishop Gian Matteo Giberti (1495–1543), co-author of the *Consilium de emendanda ecclesia* (1537), invited the Barnabites and the Angelics to Verona in 1539, following the death of their founder. Here they worked in the hospitals of the Misericordia and the Pietà for the care of orphans and the sick. This invitation was followed by a similar one from the patriarch of Venice in 1544. Directed by Dionigi da Sesto and Gerolamo Marta, the Barnabites and the Angelics enlisted the support of Venetian aristocrats in the care of the underprivileged. They enriched their own effectiveness by gaining the enthusiastic commitment of a wider group of lay supporters.[50]

The first permanent foundations outside Milan were in Pavia (1557), Cremona (1570), Monza and Casale Monferrato (1571), Rome (1575), Vercelli (1576), Pisa (1595), and Bologna and Novara (1599). The Barnabites also established temporary missions in Malta (1582–1583) and the Valtellina (1583–1584), where they were sent by Gregory XIII to halt the spread of Protestantism and encouraged by Cardinal Borromeo, who made a pastoral visit. At the same time, the Barnabites declined invitations to establish houses in Portugal and Ireland in 1555.[51]

The Clerics Regular of St. Paul consisted of clerics only until 1554, when lay brothers were admitted. According to statistics provided by Andrea M. Erba, C.R.S.P., the Barnabites remained small in number throughout the sixteenth century. In 1576 they consisted of 45 priests, 21 brothers, and 15 clerics.[52] The Jesuits, according to J. C. H. Aveling, were far more successful in their recruitment efforts. From about 100 members in 1550, they grew to 700 members by 1556, and, according to Martin P. Harney, S.J., to 3,500 by 1565.[53]

Lacking the international membership of the Jesuits, the Barnabites continued to serve the dioceses of the Italian peninsula where most of their vocations originated. Relying on this limited area for future growth, the Barnabites consisted of 322 members, including novices, in 1608. Enlarging their horizons in the course of the seventeenth century, they grew to 633 members, which included 175 lay brothers, by 1635. The slow but steady increase in vocations after 1576 was due in part to the support of Cardinal Borromeo, who quarreled with the Jesuits in his archdiocese. In contrast to his misgivings about the Jesuits, he had effusive praise for the Barnabites; in a letter of August 6, 1567, he wrote: "You know what a great service the Lord receives in the Church from St. Barnabas' priests and how I protect them in view of their sinless life and their blessed practice."[54] In return, the Barnabites promoted Borromeo's canonization as early as the mid-1580s.[55] The Barnabites also obtained support from such influential leaders as Pius V, Filippo Neri, and Cardinal Roberto Bellarmino. Neri even entertained the notion of uniting his Oratory with the Barnabites, although in the end, he declined, observing with characteristic tact and humility: "It is a good thing to change from an evil life to a good one; but to change from a good state [the Oratory] to a better one [the Barnabites] is a thing to be long and well considered."[56]

Borromeo's pervasive presence inspired his Barnabite confidant and confessor, St. Alessandro Sauli, to follow his example as an episcopal reformer and to undertake reform in the dioceses of Aleria (Corsica) and Pavia. To encourage a new spirit of reform among the clergy of his diocese, Sauli wrote the *Doctrine of the Roman Catechism* (Pavia, 1581), which sets forth the official teachings of the Catholic Church. He also gained the admiration of St. Filippo Neri and St. François de Sales, who recommended the 1581 *Catechismo Romano* to the clergy of his diocese of Geneva.[57] Moreover, the Barnabite bishop, Carlo Bascapè, emulated Borromeo's reform efforts in Novara and wrote a biography of the saint (Ingolstadt, 1592) which is still read today in several twentieth-century editions.[58] Innocent XI referred to Bascapè as "a new St. Carlo."

As superior general of the Barnabites between 1591 and 1602, Agostino Tornielli (1543–1622) broadened the apostolic work of the order when he approved the appointment of a Barnabite to a prison chaplaincy in Bologna in 1599. Similar appointments followed in Leghorn and Naples. Cosimo Dossena (1548–1620), who served as the superior general between 1602 and 1611, approved the opening of new houses in Bologna (1600), Asti (1602), Spoleto (1604), Acqui and Lodi (1605), Perugia (1607), and Naples and Genoa (1609), and introduced still another undertaking when he approved the establishment of the first tuition-free day school (named after its benefactor Msgr. Giovanni B. Arcimboldi) in 1608, following Paul V's sanction in 1605. It was the beginning of an apostolate that would increase in succeeding years and produce a wealth of new vocations for the Order. The Barnabites were reluctant at this time to open tuition-bearing schools because they thought that instruction for money was too worldly; but they eventually overcame these objections. *Collegi* (or residential high schools) were subsequently founded in Savoy (1614), France (1620), Austria (1626), and Bohemia (1627). By the first quarter of the seventeenth century, the Barnabites assumed an international status. They were no longer content to limit their activities to the Italian peninsula and to the three provinces of Lombardy, Romagna, and Piedmont that had been established in 1608.

The first permanent foundation outside Italy was in Lescar (France) in 1610. Other houses and *collegi* were founded in Annecy (1614), Thonon-les-Baines (1615), Montargis (1620), Paris (1629), Étampes (1629), and Dax (1631). Two houses were opened in Austria, at Vienna (1626) and Mistelbach (1633).

The Barnabites also served the Counter-Reformation by establishing a mission to the Calvinists in Béarn at the request of Henry IV and Paul V in 1608 under the direction of a convert to Catholicism, Fortunato Colom. Invited to Savoy by St. François de Sales (1567–1622), who styled himself a Barnabite in spirit, to halt the spread of Calvinism in his diocese in the opening decade of the seventeenth century, the Barnabites soon won his support and affection. On April 12, 1615, St. François described the Barnabites as "Our . . . really good people, sweeter than you can tell, very helpful and kind, more than is customary in their country."[59]

In 1615, the Barnabites attempted to unite with the Doctrinaires of France (Pères de la Doctrine Chrétienne) but the plan failed. Whereas in 1623, the Barnabites merged successfully with the Fathers of Our Lady of the Annunciation (of Pescia), led by their founder, Antonio Pagni. Strengthened by additional manpower, the Barnabites exhibited heroic charity during the pestilence that struck Italy between 1630 and 1631, when they assisted in the care of plague victims in Pescia, Milan, Cremona, and Pavia. The heroism of those who served the plague victims was later immortalized by Alessandro Manzoni in his historical novel *I promessi sposi* (*The Betrothed*) in 1827. Some Barnabites also volunteered as chaplains to leprosy colonies in Piedmont, Emilia, and Tuscany.

ANGELIC SISTERS OF ST. PAUL

In a letter of May 26, 1537, Zaccaria wrote to the Mother Prioress et al., referring to Torelli as "divina Paola," at St. Paul's Convent in Milan, and urging the Angelics to be true apostles and missionaries to the world. They were to be activists and not confined to their convent cells: "My dear little daughters, raise your banners because Christ Crucified is about to send you to announce his enlivening tidings of spiritual renewal everywhere."[60]

Some ten months before the formal recognition of the Ursulines, the Angelic Sisters of St. Paul were approved as a religious order in a papal bull of January 15, 1535, by Paul III with the legal assistance of Bartolomeo Ferrari's brother, Basilio. They were called Angelics because they promoted the reception of daily communion, which they called "the Bread of Angels." Their rule was based on that of St. Augustine, and their habit was modeled after the Dominican nuns from whom the earliest Angelics received their religious formation. Zaccaria dictated the original rule of the Angelics and insisted that communion be "most frequent, almost daily and if every nun could not [receive], at least the greatest part of the Community should."[61]

Although Countess Torelli played a role in the founding of the Angelics, she never served as its religious superior. Like Jeanne of France, the wife of Louis XII, who founded the Franciscan Annunciades, Torelli professed vows in the order but chose to promote the work of the Angelics from outside the convent.[62] At Carioni's suggestion, about 1530 Countess Torelli had earlier organized a group of laywomen who devoted themselves to prayer and charitable work in the neighborhood of St. Ambrose's Basilica in Milan. These women dressed in plain garb and begged from door to door on behalf of the poor.

The first convent of the Angelics was named after St. Paul and was located in Milan. Angelica Domenica Battista da Sesto became the first superior in 1536. The formal name of the Angelic Sisters of St. Paul was approved by Paul III on August 6, 1545. In contrast to other orders of nuns, who chose the title of sister, the Angelics were individually given the title "Angelica." In 1549, the Angelics established a second convent, named after St. Martha, in Cremona, the birthplace of their principal founder. Cardinal Francesco Sfondrati welcomed them to the city, reminding them that four of his own sisters were members of their convent in Milan. A prioress served as the head of each convent for a three-year term, but actual power was exercised by the community in the form of chapters in which solemnly professed members had the right to cast a vote.

As initiators of an active apostolate, the Angelics gave religious instruction, organized groups of charitable women, reformed convents, and cared for the sick and orphans in cooperation with the Barnabites in Vicenza, Verona, Venice, Brescia, and Ferrara. Together, these two congregations offered vocational instruction to orphans which would permit them to learn a trade or skill. The Angelics were particularly concerned about the wholesale exploitation of adolescent girls by houses of prostitution.[63]

In October 1539, Countess Torelli sold her estate at Guastalla to the Spanish governor of Milan, Ferrante Gonzaga, so that she could devote her energies to the religious life. Since Torelli had been financially linked to the Spanish governor, both the Barnabites and the Angelics were accused of being spies for Spain. Torelli intended to use the 22,280 gold coins she obtained from the sale of her estate to further the work of the Barnabites and the Angelics. She employed Zaccaria to handle the sale of her property and to deal with her relatives and tenants, many of whom opposed the sale—a task to which Zaccaria was committed at the time of his death in Cremona on July 5, 1539.

The Angelics were eventually banished from the Republic of Venice in 1551, having been accused, along with the Barnabites, of heresy and sedition. But some of the responsibility for incurring expulsion from Venice was directed at Angelica Paola Antonia Negri, who had alienated most of the governors of the Santi Giovanni e Paolo Hospital because she took absolute positions on many matters. Several of the governors complained to the Senate that Angelica Negri was shown "excessive deference." She was also charged with exercising authority over priests, interpreting Scripture, assuming control of the Barnabites, Angelics, and Married Couples, and pretending to know "the secrets of the heart." Moreover, they expressed displeasure with the Angelics because they worked too closely with their all-male counterpart, the Barnabites, as well as with the Married Couples of St. Paul.[64]

Following an apostolic visitation by Bishop Leonardo Marini in 1552, Angelica Negri was enclosed in the monastery of the Poor Clares in Milan and the Angelics were cloistered and required to observe the rules of enclosure. Countess Torelli did not feel obliged to conform to the bishop's decree and withdrew from the Angelics. Thereafter she founded an institute of laywomen who did not take vows but lived in community and wore common dress. She also established a boarding school for girls from impoverished noble families in Milan, the Regio Collegio di Maria Vergine della Guastalla. After graduation at the age of twenty, these girls were given dowries so that they could marry or enter a convent. Before establishing her institute and *collegio*, Countess Torelli wisely obtained the patronage of the king of Spain, who guaranteed her exemption from the obligations of enclosure that would soon be mandated by the Council of Trent in 1563 and at the insistence of Cardinal Borromeo, who was a member of the commission that executed its decrees.[65] In Milan, she led the life of a pious laywoman, retaining the name of Paola Maria, until her death in 1569. Although formally disassociated from the enclosed Angelics, she remained in touch with some of the sisters in Cremona through correspondence. Along with Angelica Negri, the principal leaders of the Angelics after Torelli's withdrawal were Paola Antonia Sfondrati, who gave her patrimony to the order in an attempt to offset the economic distress caused by the withdrawal of Torelli's funding, and Bianca Martinengo, a daughter of Torelli's second husband.[66]

The Angelics founded a third cloistered community in Monza with the support of the Carcano sisters. Clement VIII gave his approval in 1595. The Barnabite priest and superior general (1586 to 1593), Carlo Bascapè, drew up a new constitution for the Angelics at the request of Cardinal Borromeo. It was formally approved by Urban VIII in 1625. Their apostolate was now restricted to the educational and spiritual needs of girls and young women who came to them as day students or took up residence in their convents. After enclosure, the Angelics were divided into two categories: choir nuns, who held the major offices and recited the Divine Office in chapel, and the lay sisters, who performed menial tasks. Such division was also a reflection of the social backgrounds of the individual Angelics. The choir nuns came from aristocratic or upper-middle-class families, which provided dowries, whereas the less affluent lay sisters came from the lower classes. Nevertheless, such distinctions between members of the order would have been opposed by both Zaccaria, whose own constitution insisted on equality and "fraternity," and Torelli whose concept of community life excluded any hierarchies.[67]

MARRIED COUPLES OF ST. PAUL

In his extant correspondence, Zaccaria not only addressed letters to the Barnabites and the Angelics, but composed a letter for members of the third organization which he founded, the Married Couples of St. Paul ("Maritati devoti di S. Paolo") in Milan about 1531.[68] Shortly after his return to Cremona from Padua in 1524, Zaccaria had organized a group of *Amicizie* to whom he preached sermons on the Decalogue, following his ordination in 1528. His sermons on the Ten Commandments, the first five of which have survived, focus on the love of God in the first three commandments and the love of neighbor in the others.

Like the Barnabites and the Angelics, the Married Couples of St. Paul were enjoined to "continuous growth" toward perfection and "to becoming great saints." In a letter to Bernardo Omodei and Laura Rossi, dated June 20, 1539,[69] Zaccaria discussed the importance of taking gradual steps toward the goal of perfection under the direction of an experienced spiritual adviser. He recommended, for example, avoiding gossip at the outset, then, in turn, idle talk, and finally concentrating only on conversations which will help others.[70] He also promoted the frequent reception of the Eucharist, mental prayer, and the reading of Scripture. In an earlier letter (July 28, 1531), to a Cremonese lawyer named Carlo Magni, Zaccaria exhorted Magni to follow the highest Christian standards by observing constant prayer (in the form of conversations with Christ), focusing attention on one's dominant weakness and refraining from self-indulgence.[71] The members of the Married Couples attended the community meetings of the Barnabites and the Angelics and together strove to achieve religious perfection. Married couples were likewise expected to sanctify the married state by observing voluntary abstinence from sexual intercourse at certain intervals and to work toward the reform of society and the spiritual growth of family members.[72] Following the founder's death in 1539, Gian Battista Soresina took over the direction of the Married Couples.

In order to promote frequent reception of the Eucharist among lay people along with his own devotion to Christ crucified, Zaccaria adopted the Forty Hours' Devotion—a three-day period of prayer before the Blessed Sacrament in commemoration of the forty hours that Christ was entombed after His death on the cross. It had been introduced in Milan by the founder of the Oratory of Eternal Wisdom, Gian Antonio Bellotti, sometime before 1528. Bellotti limited the observance of the Forty Hours of exposition of the Blessed Sacrament, which was confined to the tabernacle, to the feasts of Christmas, Easter, Pentecost, and the Ascension.

Zaccaria enlarged the scope of this devotion to include sermons on Christ's passion and the Sorrowful Mother,[73] expositions of the Blessed Sacrament outside the tabernacle, and solemn processions of the Eucharist without covering in various churches in Milan over a three-day period. He began this devotion in May 1537. Subsequently, Paul III on August 29, 1537, granted a special indulgence in Milan for those who participated.[74] Zaccaria was aided in the spread of the Forty Hours' Devotion by Giuseppe da Ferno, a Capuchin friar, who helped to introduce this devotion throughout northern and central Italy, following Zaccaria's death in 1539.[75]

Zaccaria was motivated to adopt and extend the Forty Hours' Devotion because of the common practice of keeping the Eucharist in a sacristy cupboard or in some inaccessible niche in the church. The ceremony that Zaccaria instituted included the exposition of the Blessed Sacrament on the high altar, the use of lighted processional candles, incense, and flowers, and involved, once again, the participation of laypeople as well as priests and religious.[76]

CONCLUSION

Of the three religious organizations that St. Antonio Maria Zaccaria founded in the 1530s, only the Clerics Regular of St. Paul would survive intact to witness his 1897 canonization in Rome.

Deprived of their active ministry after 1552, the Angelic Sisters of St. Paul were forced to abandon their unique work among unwed mothers, foundlings, and orphans in order to serve the needs of girls from aristocratic families. Enclosure symbolized their encapsulation. At the same time, the original band of Angelics, who had rejected their upper-class lifestyle, were subjected to harsh criticisms from conservative civic and religious officials because they were regarded as harbingers of dangerous innovations—as sixteenth-century Beguines, if you will. While their founder was alive, the Angelics were protected by his impeccable character and learning. Following his death in 1539, however, the Angelics were at the mercy of the local ordinaries in Milan and Venice, who could and would disband their charitable activities outside the convent. As head of the Consulta in Pius IV's curia, Carlo Borromeo enforced the Tridentine decision to sever the common ministries exercised by the Barnabites, Angelics, and Married Couples of St. Paul between 1531 and 1552 by compelling all women religious to become cloistered. Following Trent's decrees of enclosure, the tripartite division of Zaccaria's reform was forever fractured. Despite Borromeo's change of mind about the orthodoxy of the Barnabites after the 1560s, he, nevertheless, sought to abrogate their independence by attempting to merge them with the reformed priests of Tortona in 1565 and, when that failed, with the Humiliati monks in 1567 and 1570. Following these abortive efforts, Borromeo insisted on a thorough revision of the 1552 Constitution and personally supervised its final format and contents. Gone from the 1579 Constitution was any mention of the collaborative efforts of the Barnabites, Angelics, and Married Couples which had enriched the spirituality of Zaccaria's earliest followers. Henceforth, the Barnabites would work in the world alone, pursuing a variety of activities, but somewhat limited by the restrictions which had been imposed on them, including the recitation of the Divine Office in choir. In deference to Borromeo, they would abandon the habit of the original congregation and adopt the black cassock and four-sided biretta of the Milanese clergy. By the early seventeenth century, the Barnabites had been so identified with Borromeo that in the streets of Milan they were referred to by some as "St. Carlo's priests."[77] St. Carlo Borromeo was officially designated by the Barnabites as a patron of the order in 1615, but in fact he had served as their second founder. Some Barnabites also maintained that the "real" founder of the Order was Morigia, who had given form and direction to the Barnabites while serving as superior general between 1536 and 1542. In 1619 a general chapter silenced the critics and decided that all three co-founders would be recognized as equals.[78] As a result Gian Antonio Gabuzio's 1618 history of the order was not published at the time of its completion because the general chapter did not want to antagonize those Barnabites who did not wish to give primacy of place to Zaccaria.

It was only in the nineteenth century that the Barnabites actively sought to resurrect the contributions of their principal founder and to promote his canonization in a group effort; and it was not until the twentieth century that the Barnabites perceived the importance of the part played by Carioni in the formation of their spirituality. Is it any wonder then that Zaccaria's body was buried alongside Carioni's in an unmarked grave in the cloister of St. Paul's Church in Milan and that it was not recovered until May 1871?[79] In the minds of some sixteenth-century clerics, Zaccaria was as responsible as Carioni for the excess fervor of the early Barnabites and Angelics in Milan and Venice which resulted in the formal accusations of heresy in 1534 and 1551.

The Barnabites, the Angelics, and the Married Couples of St. Paul owed their origins indirectly to the *Amicizie* in Cremona and the nurturing environment of the Oratory of Eternal Wisdom. It was Carioni who persuaded both Zaccaria and Countess Torelli to join the Oratory of Eternal Wisdom where each of them succeeded in recruiting the first members of their respective congregations. The Oratory also inspired the Forty Hours' Devotion, which was later extended and enriched by Zaccaria. But St. Antonio Maria Zaccaria's indebtedness to Carioni and the Oratory of Eternal Wisdom should not obscure his major contribution to spiritual renewal in the sixteenth century, which he identified in his sermon on the third commandment: "to convert one's self to God both intrinsically and extrinsically."[80] Zaccaria was the first Catholic reformer to advocate a tripartite reformation program, involving the combined strengths and experiences of priests, religious women, and lay people—united in intertwined apostolates—in order to effect a transformation of self and neighbor "in the ways of God."[81]

SELECT BIBLIOGRAPHY

The Barnabites

Barnabite scholars have written a number of histories of their order, beginning with Gian Antonio Gabuzio (1551–1627), who completed the first history of the Barnabites in 1618. Because Gabuzio maintained that Zaccaria was the principal founder of the Barnabites rather than merely one of three co-founders, his work was not published until 1852 when the Barnabites were actively promoting Zaccaria's canonization. See Gabuzio, *Historia Congregationis Clericorum Regularium Sancti Paulli ab eius primordiis ad initium saeculi XVII [1618]* . . . (Rome: Salviucci, 1852). The only history of the order that appeared in the seventeenth century was written by Anacleto Secco [Secchi], *De Clericorum Regularium S. Pauli Congregatione, et parentibus synopsis* (Milan: Vigono, 1682).

The eighteenth century witnessed the appearance of Francesco Luigi Barelli's documented history of the Barnabites between 1533 and 1633 in two large folio volumes, *Memorie dell'origine, fondazione, avanzamenti, successi, ed uomini illustri in lettere e in santità della Congregazione de' Chierici Regolari di S. Paolo* . . . , (Bologna: Pisarri, 1703, 1707). This study was followed by Pietro Grazioli's biographical sketches of ten Barnabites, *Praestantium virorum qui in Congreg[atione] S. Paulli vulgo Barnabitarum* . . . (Bologna: Longhi, 1751). In the nineteenth century, Barnabites published still other works on the writings and lives of fellow members of their Congregation: Luigi M. Ungarelli, *Bibliotheca scriptorum e Congregatione Clerr. Regg. S. Paulli* (Rome: Salviucci, 1836), and Giuseppe M. Colombo, *Profili biografici di insigni Barnabiti*, 2 vols. (Crema: Campanini, 1870).

The first half of the twentieth century brought a wealth of new materials. Clearly the most important is the trilogy written by Orazio M. Premoli, C.R.S.P., *Storia dei Barnabiti nel Cinquecento . . . nel Seicento . . . dal 1700 al 1825*, 3 vols. (Rome: Desclée, Industria Tipografica Romana, and Società Tipografica A. Manuzio, 1913–1925). Albert M. Dubois, C.R.S.P., produced a sketch of the Congregation that underscores its expansion in *Les Barna-bites, Clercs Réguliers de Saint-Paul, 1533* (Paris: Letouzey et Ané, 1924). Carla Bascapè wrote a short monograph on *I Barnabiti e la Controriforma in Lombardia* (Milan: Liber Accademia Editoriale, 1931), which highlights the contributions of St. Alessandro Sauli and Carlo Bascapè.

To mark the four-hundredth anniversary of the Order, Luigi M. Levati, C.R.S.P., et al. produced biographical sketches of all the Barnabites who died before 1933, *Menologio dei Barnabiti*, 12 vols. (Genoa: Scuola Tipografica Derelitti, 1932–1938); Giuseppe M. Boffito, C.R.S.P., et al. compiled the excellent four-volume bibliography of works by Barnabite authors, *Scrittori Barnabiti . . . (1533–1933) . . .* (Florence: Olschki, 1933–1937); and Angelo M. Confalonieri, C.R.S.P. et al. composed a series of essays, *La Congregazione dei Chierici Regolari di S. Paolo detti Barnabiti nel IV centenario della fondazione, 1533–1933* (Genoa: Artigianelli, 1933).

The second half of the twentieth century produced works by Romano Contrisciani, *Perfil historico de los Barnabitas* (Palencia: Editorial Barnabita, 1968); Salvatore M. De Ruggiero, C.R.S.P., and Virginio M. Colciago, C.R.S.P., *Menologio dei Barnabiti dal 1539 al 1976* (Rome: Padri Barnabiti, 1977); Antonio M. Gentili, C.R.S.P., *The Barnabites: A Historical Profile*, trans. Santa Zanchetta and Anthony M. Bianco (Youngstown, N.Y.: The North American Voice of Fatima [1980]); Anthony M. Bianco, C.R.S.P,. "The Beginning of the Barnabite Order," unpublished essay in the Barnabite Fathers Seminary in Youngstown, New York, ca. 1980, and Vittorio M. Michelini, C.R.S.P., *I Barnabiti: Chierici Regolari di S. Paolo . . .* (Milan: Nuove Edizioni Duomo, 1983).

The four major participants in the formation and early development of the Barnabites and the Angelics were St. Antonio Maria Zaccaria, Battista Carioni da Crema, Ludovica Torelli, and St. Carlo Borromeo. Each of these individuals will be given separate bibliographical entries below.

St. Antonio Maria Zaccaria

As was not the case with Borromeo and Torelli, there were no published biographies of Zaccaria in the sixteenth and the seventeenth centuries. Francesco Luigi Barelli, C.R.S.P., wrote the first published biography, *Vita e detti notabili del Venerabile Padre Antonio Maria Zaccaria* . . . (Bologna: Pisarri, 1706). Alfonso M. Croce, C.R.S.P., published a second life in 1719, *Detti sacri del Ven. Padre Antonio Maria Zaccaria* . . . (Milan: Malatesta). In the nineteenth century the Barnabites launched a concerted effort to achieve Zaccaria's canonization, beginning with *Epistolae ad . . . Pium Septimum . . . pro causa beatificationis et canonizationis . . . Antonii M. Zaccariae* . . . (Rome: Sacra Rituum Congregatio, 1806). This work was followed by the documents prescribed by the Sacred Congregation of Rites in 1821, 1824, 1831, and 1833. During this process, Mariano M. Alpruni, C.R.S.P., published *Vita del Venerabile Antonio Maria Zaccaria* . . . (Rome: Poggiolo, 1815).

Perhaps the classic biography of Zaccaria is by Alessandro M. Teppa, C.R.S.P., who published the first edition of his work in 1853: *Vita del Venerabile Antonio Maria Zaccaria* . . . (Moncalieri: Collegio Carlo Alberto). The seventh edition of Teppa's biography appeared posthumously in the year of Zaccaria's canonization (Milan: Clerc, 1897).

Preceding Zaccaria's canonization, two popular biographies appeared in French and German respectively: Albert M. Dubois, C.R.S.P., *Le bienheureux Antoine Maria Zaccaria* . . . (Tournay: Casterman [1895]) and an anonymous Barnabite published *Leben des seligen Antonius Maria Zaccaria* . . . (Vienna: Barnabiten-Collegiums St. Michael, 1891).

The official 1897 biography of St. Antonio was written by Francesco Tranquillino Moltedo, C.R.S.P.. This magisterial work of 600 pages was entitled *Vita di S. Antonio Maria Zaccaria, Fondatore de' Barnabiti e delle Angeliche* (Florence: Ricci, 1897). Two popular sketches were written by Guy Chastel (alias Paul Granotier): *Saint Antoine-Marie Zaccaria Barnabite* (Paris: Grasset, 1930) and Andrea M. Erba, C.R.S.P., *St. Anthony M. Zaccaria*, trans. Louis Parnell (Youngstown, N.Y.: The North American Voice of Fatima, 1975). Two recent accounts of the saint are by the superior general, Giuseppe M. Bassotti, C.R.S.P., *S. Antonio M. Zaccaria e Cremona* (Cremona: Padri Barnabiti, 1989) and *450° anniversario della morte di S. Antonio M. Zaccaria* (Rome: Padri Barnabiti, 1990).

Two Barnabites have produced monographs on Zaccaria's promotion of the Forty Hours' Devotion. See Cardinal Giuseppe M. Granniello's pamphlet, *L'Orazione delle XL Ore e il B[eato]*

*Antonmaria Zaccaria . . . al XIII Congresso Eucaristico Milano-Set-
tembre-1895* (Rome: Tipografia Vaticana, 1895) and Louis Peter
M. Bonardi, "The Origin of the Forty-Hours Devotion and Its
Modern Founder," unpublished M.A. thesis, Niagara University, 1961.

Finally, the letters, sermons, and constitution by Zaccaria were
edited most recently by Virginio M. Colciago, c.r.s.p., *S. Antonio
Maria Zaccaria . . . Gli scritti* (Rome: Padri Barnabiti, 1975) and
serve as the framework for my comments on the founder. Antonio M. Gentili, c.r.s.p., assessed the importance of Zaccaria's
writings in *I Barnabiti: Manuale di storia e spiritualità dell'Ordine dei
Chierici Regolari di S. Paolo Decollato* (Rome: Padri Barnabiti,
1967).

Battista Carioni da Crema

Orazio M. Premoli, c.r.s.p., published a biographical sketch of
Carioni, "S. Gaetano Thiene e Fra Battista da Crema" in *Rivista
di scienze storiche* (Pavia: Artigianelli, 1910). He also published a
collection of related documents in *Fra' Battista da Crema: Secondo
documenti inediti . . .* (Saronno: Orfanatrofio, 1909). Luigi Boglioli
wrote an interpretive summary of Carioni's impact on the sixteenth century in *Battista da Crema: Nuovi studi sopra la sua vita, i
suoi scritti, la sua dottrina* (Torino: Società Editrice Internazionale,
1952).

Ludovica Torelli

Paolo Morigia authored a twenty-one-page biographical sketch of
Countess Torelli: *Vita essemplare e beato fine dell'ill. Lodovia Torella
Contessa di Guastalla* (Bergamo: Comino Ventura, 1592). It was
followed by two substantial works by Carlo G. Rosignoli, s.j.,
*Vita e virtù della Contessa di Guastalla Lodovica Torella nominata poi
Paola Maria . . .* (Milan: Marelli, 1686); and by Aldo Zagni, *La
Contessa di Guastalla* (Reggiolo: Biblioteca Maldotti di Guastalla,
1987). Zagni tends to exaggerate the part played by Countess
Torelli in the founding of the Angelics. Unfortunately, there is
no published history of the Order. For a description of the earliest
unpublished manuscript history of the Angelics, which was composed about 1552, see *Angelica Anonima: Memorie*, ed. Giuseppe

M. Cagni, C.R.S.P., Quaderni di storia e spiritualità Barnabitica 2 (Florence: Padri Barnabiti, 1979).

St. Carlo Borromeo

Two Barnabite superior generals promoted the canonization of Borromeo in the sixteenth century. Gian Pietro Besozzi praised his spirituality even before his death in 1584 in *Lettere spirituali sopra alcune feste et sacri tempi dell'anno* (Milan: Pontio, 1578) and Carlo Bascapè launched the canonization process in *Della morte dell'Illustrissimo Sig. Cardinale S. Prassede* (Milan: Tino, 1584). This twenty-two page pamphlet was reprinted simultaneously in Rome by Antonio Blado, in Piacenza by Giovanni Bazzacchi, in Venice by Giolitti, and in Brescia by Vincenzo Sabbio. In 1592, Bascapè completed a full-scale biography of Borromeo, *De vita et rebus gestis Caroli . . . Cardinalis . . . libri septem* (Ingolstadt: Sartor), which has been reprinted many times. See also the biography of Bascapè by Innocenzo M. Chiesa, C.R.S.P., *Vita di Carlo Bascapè: Barnabita e vescovo di Novara (1550–1615)* (Milan: Ghisolfi, 1636). A third edition, revised and expanded by Sergio M. Pagano, C.R.S.P., was published in Florence by Olschki in 1993. For two assessments of the influence of Borromeo on the Barnabites, see Giuseppe M. Bassotti, C.R.S.P., *San Carlo e i Barnabiti: Lettera ai Confratelli* (Rome: Don Bosco, 1984) and Andrea M. Erba, C.R.S.P., *S. Carlo Borromeo e i Barnabiti* (Saronno: Monti, 1965).

NOTES

The author wishes to thank the Very Reverend Anthony M. Bianco, C.R.S.P., who is the North American provincial superior of the Barnabites in Youngstown, New York, and the Reverend Giuseppe M. Cagni, C.R.S.P., who is the editor of *Barnabiti Studi* (Rome, 1984—) at the Barnabite Library Generalate in Rome, for their assistance in the preparation of this essay. I am likewise grateful to the National Endowment for the Humanities for a 1990 Travel to Collections Grant that enabled me to work in the library and archives of the Barnabites in Rome, now located at St. Carlo ai Catinari (Piazza Benedetto Cairoli).

1. Reproduced in *Epistolae ad . . . Pium Septimum . . . pro causa beatificationis et canonizationis . . . Antonii M. Zaccariae . . .* (Rome: Sacra Rituum Congregatio, 1806) as the frontispiece.

2. ". . . grandezza e nobile larghezza d'animo verso il Crocifisso, e verso le pene ed obbrobri di noi stessi, e verso il guadagno e perfezione consumata del prossimo. . . ." Zaccaria to Battista da Sesto and others, May 26, 1537, in *S. Antonio Maria Zaccaria . . . Gli scritti* (Rome: Edizioni dei Padri Barnabiti, 1975), p. 52. Hereafter referred to as *Gli scritti*. Because of the relative inaccessibility of Zaccaria's writings, I am reproducing the original Italian text.

3. "Imita Cristo, imita Dio, sii misericordioso, e *maxime* in giorno di festa più che negli altri; ciba il famelico, abbevera il sitibondo, vesti l'ignudo, raccogli il pellegrino, visita l'infermo, libera il carcerato. . . ." Ibid., p. 149.

4. ". . . in tutto la carità ti muova." Ibid.

5. ". . . se non ti paiono sufficienti queste cose a farti credere che l'amore del prossimo causi l'amor di Dio e lo mostri, te lo faccia credere almeno questo: Dio essersi fatto uomo per questo; Cristo aver detto: 'Questo è il mio comandamento: che vi amiate insieme' . . . 'In questo conosceranno che siete miei discepoli. . . . E per tutta la Scrittura, Carissimo, discorri che Dio pone il prossimo come mezzo per andare alla sua Maestà.'" Ibid., p. 166.

6. "Perciò vuoi tu ascendere alla perfezione? Vuoi tu acquistare qualche spirito? Vuoi tu amare Dio ed essergli caro e suo buon figliuolo? Ama il prossimo, ordina te verso il prossimo, componi il tuo animo in beneficare il prossimo e non offenderlo." Ibid., pp. 166–67.

7. Gian Antonio Gabuzio, C.R.S.P., asserts that Zaccaria began his university studies at the University of Pavia before transferring to Padua. See his *Historia Congregationis Clericorum Regularium Sancti Paulli ab eius primordiis ad initium saeculi XVII* [1618] . . . (Rome: Salviucci, 1852), p. 32. Zaccaria's notebook from the University of Padua contains aphorisms from the works of Hippocrates, Galen, and Averroës. See Vittorio M. Michelini, C.R.S.P., *I Barnabiti: Chierici Regolari di S. Paolo alle radici della Congregazione, 1533–1983* (Milan: Nuove Edizioni Duomo, 1983), p. 75. Superior General Giuseppe M. Bassotti, C.R.S.P., questions Zaccaria's presence at the University of Pavia and insists that he practiced medicine in Cremona after leaving the University of Padua in 1524. See his *S. Antonio M. Zaccaria e Cremona* (Cremona: Padri Barnabiti, 1989), pp. 18–19.

8. "Ma poi non seguí l'arte," in Paola Antonia Sfondrati (1530–1603), "Dell'origine e progressi del Monastero di S. Paolo," unpublished manuscript history of the Angelics in the Archivio Generalizio dei Barnabiti, Rome, L c 7.

9. See Bassotti, *S. Antonio M. Zaccaria e Cremona*, p. 22. The only biographical sketch of Lizari is the forty-two-page pamphlet-essay by Domenico Bergamaschi, *Vita di Fra Bono eremita istitutore delle SS. Quaran-*

tore (Monza: Artigianelli, 1908). Cf. Orazio M. Premoli, C.R.S.P., *A proposito di una recente biografia di "Fra Bono"* (Pavia: Artigianelli, 1909), a twelve-page pamphlet.

10. See Michelini, *I Barnabiti*, pp. 46–54.

11. Carioni, *Via de aperta verità* (1523), trans. Anthony M. Bianco, C.R.S.P., in "The Beginning of the Barnabite Order," unpublished essay, in the Barnabite Seminary (Youngstown, N.Y., ca. 1980), p. 34.

12. ". . . Ma particolarmente e in specialità si dilettino di più a leggere quei libri che trattano della instruzione e informazione dei buoni costumi, della perfezione della vita, della vera imitazione di Cristo. . . ." Zaccaria, *Gli scritti*, p. 239.

13. Eugene F. Rice, Jr., *Saint Jerome in the Renaissance* (Baltimore: The Johns Hopkins University Press, 1985), p. 3.

14. See Carlo G. Rosignoli, S.J., *Vita e virtù della Contessa di Guastalla Lodovica Torella nominata poi Paola Maria . . .* (Milan: Marelli, 1686).

15. "Deh! Caro Padre, non mi abbandonate, e siate il mio santo presso Dio. . . ." Zaccaria, *Gli scritti*, p. 29.

16. Ibid., p. 351.

17. Ludwig von Pastor, *The History of the Popes* XIV, ed. Ralph F. Kerr, repr. ed. (Liechtenstein: Nendeln, 1969), pp. 217–18. This work was first published between 1891 and 1924.

18. See Gabriele Feyles, *Serafino da Fermo . . . (1496–1540): La vita, le opere, la dottrina spirituale* (Torino: Società Editrice Internazionale, 1942) and Michelini, *I Barnabiti*, pp. 57–60.

19. Zaccaria, *Gli scritti*, p. 149.

20. Soresina, "Cronachetta C," in Archivio Generalizio dei Barnabiti in Rome. Quoted in an unpublished lecture, "February 18, 1533: The Official Birthday of the Barnabite Order," by Anthony M. Bianco, C.R.S.P., to a provincial chapter on January 13, 1983 in Youngstown, New York.

21. Bassotti, *S. Antonio M. Zaccaria e Cremona*, p. 22.

22. See Roberto Rusconi, "Confraternite, compagnie e devozioni," *Storia d'Italia*, ed. Giulio Einaudi, *Annali*, 9 (1986), 469–506.

23. ". . . tanto che molte volte ho occasione di ammirazione grande, considerando una tanta irrisoluzione che regna, e già molti anni è regnata nell'anima mia." Zaccaria, *Gli scritti*, p. 31. For biographical sketches of Ferrari and Morigia, see Innocenzo Gobio, *Vita dei Venerabili Padri Bartolomeo Ferrari e Giacomo Antonio Morigia . . .* (Milan: Besozzi, 1858).

24. "Perché l'uomo deve ben pensare e ripensare, trutinare e ritrutinare, quando ha da fare qualche effetto di importanza; ma, pensato che l'ha, ovvero consigliato[si], non deve farci poi dimora all'esecuzione: perché nella via di Dio la potissima cosa che si ricerca è la prestezza e sollecitudine." Zaccaria, *Gli scritti*, p. 33.

25. "Su, su, Fratelli! Se finora in noi è stata alcuna irrisoluzione gettia-mola via, insieme con la negligenza: e corriamo come matti non solo a Dio, ma ancora verso il prossimo, il quale è il mezzo che riceve quello che non possiamo dare a Dio, non avendo egli bisogno dei nostri beni." Ibid., pp. 35–36.

26. The Latin reads: "Professionem trium votorum substantialium religionis in manibus Archiepiscopi Mediolanensis seu eius in spirituali-bus Vicarii Generalis emittere in loco Mediolanensis civitatis seu Diocesis . . . morari et permanere ut liberius divinis beneplacitis insistere et quae Dei sunt perquirere possint." Quoted by Bianco in "February 18, 1533: The Official Birthday of the Barnabite Order."

27. For copies of all the papal briefs and bulls related to the Barnabite Order, see *Constitutiones Clericorum Regularium S. Pauli Decollati libris quatuor* (Naples: Tizzano, 1829), pp. 3–70.

28. Orazio M. Premoli, c.r.s.p., *Storia dei Barnabiti nel Cinquecento . . . nel Seicento . . . dal 1700 al 1825*, 3 vols. (Rome: Desclée, Industria Tipografica Romana, and Società Tipografica A. Manuzio, 1913–1925), I: 416–17.

29. "Qualità' del riformatore dei buoni costumi e quali coadiutori debba eleggersi o non ritrovandone farsene dei nuovi." Zaccaria, *Gli scritti*, pp. 288–98.

30. Ibid., pp. 281–82.

31. Ibid., p. 62.

32. Ibid., pp. 255–68.

33. In the absence of documentation, Premoli maintains that Zaccaria did not profess canonical vows in his religious order because of the obligations to maintain his ancestral estate. See Premoli, *Storia dei Barnabiti nel Cinquecento*, p. 40. It seems more reasonable to conclude—in light of Zaccaria's correspondence—that he professed simple vows and postponed until a later time his decision to take solemn vows.

34. See *Index de Venise* (1549) [and] *Venise et Milan* (1554), ed. J. M. De Bujanda (Sherbrooke: Éditions de l'Université de Sherbrooke, 1987), III, p. 233.

35. "' . . . parte scandalosa, parte eretica, parte sospetta riguardo alla fede e perciò da abbandonare e sfuggire da tutti i cristiani.'" *Visita Canonica di Mons. Marini*, in the Archivio Generalizo dei Barnabiti, Rome. Quoted by Michelini, *I Barnabiti*, p. 51.

36. Burigozzo, "Cronica Milanese di Gianmarco Burigozzo Merzaro dal 1500 al 1544," *Archivio Storico Italiano* III (1842), p. 509.

37. "'Et omnes qui pie volunt vivere in Christo Jesu, persecutionem patientur. . . .'" Zaccaria, *Gli scritti*, pp. 208–209.

38. ". . . 'Nos stulti propter Christum'"; Paraphrase of 1 Cor. 4:10, Rom. 5:3, 1 Cor. 1:26, Heb. 12:1, and 2 Cor. 6:4. Zaccaria,"Esortazione

alla confidenza in Dio e all'imitazione di Gesù Crocifisso." Zaccaria, *Gli scritti*, pp. 205–10. A translation appears in Bianco, "Beginning of the Barnabite Order," p. 22.

39. Pastor, *History of the Popes* XIV, p. 277.

40. Ibid., pp. 278–83.

41. See Anthony M. Bianco, c.r.s.p., "The Spirit of the Barnabite Rules," *Barnabite Messenger*, 17, No. 3 (September 1979), 1–2, 4; and ibid., No. 4 (December 1979), 3–4; Premoli, "Le costituzioni di S. Antonio M. Zaccaria," *Storia dei Barnabiti nel Cinquecento*, pp. 422–55.

42. Cano identified Carioni as the founder of the Barnabites in his *De locis theologicis* (posthumously published in 1563): "Paulus item tertius ordinem quem in Italia frater Baptista Cremensis instituit, litteris suis probasse dicitur: at nuper & ordo ille à Veneris [Venetiis] est edicto publico explosus [expulsus], & Baptistae doctrina, cui illius ordinis homines inhaerebant, Romae est condemnata." See Cano, *Opera* 5.5 (Cologne: Brickmann, 1605), p. 282. Cano's *De locis theologicis* was placed on the Lisbon Index in 1624. Zaccaria himself refers to Carioni as "our divine Father" (*nostro divin Padre*) in a letter to Morigia and Battista Soresina, dated November 3, 1538. See Zaccaria, *Gli scritti*, p. 65.

43. See Francesco T. Moltedo, c.r.s.p., *Vita di S. Alessandro Sauli* (Naples: D'Auria, 1904).

44. Andrea M. Erba, c.r.s.p., "The Barnabites Throughout History," trans. Maria Luisa Russo, unpublished 1979 essay in the Barnabite Library in Rome, pp. 1–2.

45. Giuseppe M. Bassotti, c.r.s.p., *San Carlo e i Barnabiti: Lettera ai Confratelli* (Rome: Don Bosco, 1984), pp. 66–75, and Premoli, *Storia dei Barnabiti nel Cinquecento*, pp. 282–87.

46. See *Constitutiones Clericorum Regularium Sancti Pauli Decollati . . .* [1579], 6th ed. (Rome: Augustiniana, 1946).

47. See Giuseppe M. Cagni, c.r.s.p., "In missione col s. fondatore," in *S. Antonio M. Zaccaria nel 450° della Morte . . .* , ed. Giuseppe M. Cagni, c.r.s.p. (Rome: Padri Barnabiti, 1989), pp. 121–32.

48. ". . . né demonio, né creatura alcuna. . . ." Zaccaria, *Gli scritti*, p. 55.

49. ". . . Pastore dell'anima vostra. . . ." Ibid., p. 77.

50. See Brian Pullan, *Rich and Poor in Renaissance Venice* (Cambridge, Mass.: Harvard University Press, 1971), pp. 382–86, and Christopher F. Black, *Italian Confraternities in the Sixteenth Century* (Cambridge: Cambridge University Press, 1989), pp. 36, 209–10.

51. Pastor, *History of the Popes* XIV, p. 245.

52. Erba, "Barnabites Throughout History," p. 52.

53. J. C. H. Aveling, *The Jesuits* (New York: Stein & Day, 1982),

p. 106, and Martin P. Harney, s.j., *The Jesuits in History* (New York: American Press, 1941), p. 122.

54. Erba, "Barnabites Throughout History," p. 8.

55. See Carlo Bascapè, *Della morte dell'illustrissimo Sig. Cardinale S. Prassede* (Milan: Tini, 1584).

56. V. J. Matthews, *St. Philip Neri: Apostle of Rome and Founder of the Oratory* (London: Burns, Oates, & Washbourne; repr. Rockford, Ill.: Tan Books, 1984), pp. 56–57. See Premoli, *Storia dei Barnabiti nel Cinquecento*, p. 270n1.

57. See Domenico Frigerio, *Alessandro Sauli: Vescovo e santo* . . . (Milan: Edizione "La Voce," 1992), which commemorates the 400th anniversary of his death.

58. Bascapè, *De vita et rebus gestis Caroli* . . . *Cardinalis* . . . *libri septem* (Ingolstadt: Sartor, 1592).

59. Erba, "Barnabites Throughout History," p. 5.

60. "0 Figliuole care, spiegate le vostre bandiere, che presto il Crocifisso vi manderà ad annunziare la vivezza spirituale e lo spirito vivo dappertutto." Zaccaria, *Gli scritti*, p. 50.

61. Giuseppe M. Miniero, c.r.s.p., *Il culto al SS. sacramento promosso dal Beato Antonio M. Zaccaria* (Naples: Accademia Reale, 1892), p. 7. This passage has been translated by Louis Peter Bonardi, c.r.s.p., in "The Origin of the Forty-Hours Devotion and Its Modern Founder," M.A. Thesis, Niagara University, 1961, pp. 51–52.

62. Premoli, *Storia dei Barnabiti nel Cinquecento*, p. 32n2.

63. See Adriano Prosperi, "Clerics and Laymen in the Work of Carlo Borromeo," in *San Carlo Borromeo: Catholic Reform and Ecclesiastical Politics in the Second Half of the Sixteenth Century*, edd. John M. Headley and John B. Tomaro (Washington, D.C.: Folger Shakespeare Library, 1988), pp. 126–27.

64. See Andrea M. Erba, c.r.s.p., *L'angelica Paola Antonia Negri da Castellanza* (Castellanza, 1984) and Paola Antonia Negri et al., *Lettere spirituali, 1538–1551*, edd. A. M. Erba and Antonio M. Gentili, c.r.s.p. (Rome: Padri Barnabiti, 1985). Concerning the question of Negri's authorship of these letters, see Giuseppe M. Cagni's article, "Negri o Besozzi? . . . ," *Barnabiti Studi*, 6 (1989), 177–217. Massimo Firpo not only questions Negri's authorship but also attacks her moral character in an article entitled "Paola Antonia Negri: Da 'Divina Madre Maestra' a 'Spirito Diabolico,'" ibid., 7 (1990), 7–66.

65. See Session 25, Chapter 5 of *The Canons and Decrees of the Council of Trent* II, trans. Theodore A. Buckley (London: Routledge, 1851), pp. 218–19.

66. See Aldo Zagni, *La Contessa di Guastalla* (Reggiolo: Biblioteca Maldotti di Guastalla, 1987).

67. Zaccaria uses the phrase "Repubblica Cristiana" in his constitution. See *Gli scritti*, p. 242.

68. For the only history of the Married Couples of St. Paul, see Andrea Spinelli, *Verso la "perfezione" insieme—Attualità di un' esperienza: I "Maritati di S. Paolo"* (Milan: Ancora, 1989).

69. Zaccaria, *Gli scritti*, pp. 80–85, 106.

70. Ibid., p. 106.

71. Ibid., p. 39.

72. Ibid., pp. 80–83.

73. Ibid., pp. 239, 240, and 247.

74. See Bonardi, "Origin of the Forty-Hours Devotion," p. 52.

75. Father Cuthbert [Hess], o.s.f.c., *The Capuchins: A Contribution to the History of the Counter-Reformation* I (Port Washington, n.y.: Kennikat, 1971), pp. 162–63. This book was published originally in 1928.

76. See Bonardi, "Origin of the Forty-Hours Devotion," pp. 34–53.

77. Erba, "Barnabites Throughout History," p. 8.

78. See *Storia dei Barnabiti nel Seicento* . . . , pp. 80–83.

79. Andrea M. Erba, c.r.s.p., *St. Anthony M. Zaccaria*, trans. Louise Parnell (Youngstown, n.y.: The North American Voice of Fatima, 1975), p. 36.

80. "Santificazione vuol dire convertirsi a Dio intrinsecamente ed estrinsecamente." Zaccaria, *Gli scritti*, p. 148.

81. ". . . nella via di Dio. . . ." Ibid., p. 200.

St. Angela Merici in 1540 by Moretto. Basilica of
St. Angela in Desenzano.

4

Angela Merici and the Ursulines

Charmarie J. Blaisdell

ON NOVEMBER 25, 1535, on the Feast of St. Catherine, in a small, borrowed house in the Piazza del Duomo in Brescia twenty-eight young women, accustomed to meeting with their spiritual leader for prayer and direction, received a set of principles to govern their lives, took the name Company of St. Ursula, and signed their names in a book. Thus each acknowledged her acceptance of a life as a consecrated virgin and bride of Christ, living in the world and serving God. Their foundress, Angela Merici, lived only five more years during which she formulated a Rule (*Regola*), Testament (*Testamento*), and Counsels (*Ricordi*) to guide the members of this new Company of religious women in following an active apostolate devoted to piety, charity, and Christian education.

The Ursuline ideal resonated with the mood of sixteenth-century spiritual renewal, and by the end of the century congregations of Ursulines existed in every major Italian city and had spread to France.[1] Then the powerful post-Tridentine resurgence of secular and ecclesiastical authority and of lay and clerical fears about uncloistered communities of women subverted the ideal and transformed the Company into an order of cloistered nuns living according to a modified Augustinian rule that hardly resembled the original Company or recalled its simple Brescian origins.[2] In both ideal and form the Ursulines were shaped and reshaped by the turbulent and conflicting currents of Early Modern religious and social life. What were the circumstances under which a woman created the first rule for an active apostolate for women? What was the social and religious context for this novel experiment? What exactly happened to subvert the original ideal?

The history of the Ursulines in Early Modern Europe can be conveniently divided into four periods. The first, during Angela Merici's lifetime and until her death, was closely connected to her personal spiritual life and the vitality of religious renewal in Italy in the first half of the sixteenth century. The second, following the death of the foundress, was marked by a period of strife and upheaval and was generally ignored in Ursuline histories until the twentieth century. It overlaps with the third period, marked by the mood of the Tridentine reform and its decrees promulgated to impose restrictions on religious orders in general and on new, uncloistered religious communities of women in particular. The fourth phase includes the exceptional growth of the Ursulines first as congregations and later as an order in Italy and France, as their ideals of Christian piety, service, and education appealed to the renewed spirituality and the desire for new forms of religious life for women. The first three phases of the development and growth of the Ursulines will be emphasized here and will demonstrate how clearly Angela Merici and her Company of Ursulines resonated with the spiritual needs of sixteenth-century women who were attracted to all phases of religious reform in Italy, especially to innovative means of following a vocation of active Christian service.

The early development of the Company of Ursulines was intimately related to both the life of the foundress and the religious and social conditions in Italy.[3] There is very little precise historical information about the early life or spiritual development of Angela Merici.[4] The few known facts may have been embellished by her friends and followers and biographers who sought her canonization. Unlike Caterina of Siena or Teresa de Avila, Angela could not write, although she could probably read.[5] The facts of her early life, even the exact dates of her birth (between 1470 and 1475), are imprecise. She dictated the *Regola*,[6] *Testamento*,[7] and *Ricordi*[8] to her friend, spiritual director, and first chancellor of the Company, Gabriel Cozzano, whose own writings help clarify our understanding of the original ideal.[9] Official documents of the Company exist, but many were destroyed and are only dimly revealed through seventeenth-and early eighteenth-century biographies.[10] Thus, knowledge about Angela depends on the perceptions of her amanuensis, Cozzano, and four friends—prominent citizens of Brescia, all male—who in 1568, twenty-eight years after her death, were encouraged by the women of Angela's Company to record their recollections in order to initiate the canonization process.[11]

Several other kinds of sources help clarify the origins of the ideal: her membership in the Franciscan Tertiaries; her close association with the Compagnia di Ss. Trinitas, a lay confraternity in Brescia; her friendship with Giacomo Chizzola, founder of schools to educate children and adults; the *Regola, Testamento,* and *Ricordi,* and, finally, the anniversaries and images she chose for the foundation of her Company and the frescoes commissioned for the Oratory where the nascent Company met.

ANGELA MERICI'S EARLY LIFE

Angela was born in Desenzano in the Lake District of northern Italy to a prosperous peasant, Giovanni Merici. Her mother belonged to the prominent Bianacosi family from nearby Salò, which had traditionally produced local ecclesiastics and magistrates.[12] The accounts of Angela's friends and biographers depict a close family circle. The father read "The Lives of the Saints" to the children, and Angela played religious games with her sister in the woods.[13] A catastrophe, possibly the plague, broke up the family, and Angela spent her adolescent years in the household of her maternal uncle in Salò where she performed menial household tasks[14] and may have learned to read.[15] The experience of the loss of her family may have initiated the development of Angela's spiritual life. The canonization testimonies agree that it was during this period of adolescence that Angela developed a spiritual life that was nourished by fasting, prayer, contemplation, curtailed sleep, holy visions, and frequent confession and participation in the celebration of the Eucharist.[16] Several witnesses vividly described her account of a vision of a heavenly procession of virgins accompanied by music. In one version her sister appeared in radiant glory and delivered assurances of her salvation.[17] In another version (recounted by Father Francesco Landini of Brescia, who was eager to establish Angela's authenticity with Carlo Borromeo), the sister told Angela she would found a Company of consecrated virgins in Brescia.[18] In the *Rule, Counsels,* and *Legacy,* Angela (or Cozzano) went to great lengths to express unshakable confidence that she was the mere instrument of God's will in the foundation of the Company.[19] Yet others recalled that Angela voiced a deep and traditional suspicion of visions as a source of the devil's work, not God's.[20]

About 1510 she returned to Desenzano where she adopted a life devoted to contemplation and acts of charity that included donning sack cloth and accompanying dead bodies of the poor to burial and wearing sack cloth.[21] Modern scholars speculate that she began teaching and catechizing children at this time, but contemporary accounts were remarkably silent about this point.[22]

The death of parents and siblings, the uprooting from home followed by her austere daily practices, and the experience of visions suggest that this was a formative period in Angela's life.[23] Sometime before 1515 at Salò or Desenzano she joined the Franciscan Tertiaries, who provided an appropriate focus for her spiritual needs.[24]

The popular Franciscan Third Order or Tertiaries offered pious men and women the opportunity to renounce comfort and wealth in exchange for a life balanced by contemplation, asceticism, and charitable work. Women found it an attractive alternative to traditional cloistered life, which suffered from serious economic and spiritual difficulties during this troubled period.[25] Angela's connections with the Tertiaries is one of the best-documented facts of her life. The witnesses' depositions for the canonization process all emphasize the fact that as a young woman she devoted herself to fasting, prayer, and contemplation, and point out that she asked for admission to the Franciscan Tertiaries so that she could attend to confession and Mass more frequently than was normally allowed to laypeople.[26]

The popularity of the Tertiaries and, later, the Ursulines belongs to that part of the complex religious revival in the late Middle Ages that drew women to lay religious groups of holy women such as the Beguines in Northern Europe and the *beatas* in Spain.[27] There were few precedents for women for an organized vocation that offered a life of respectability and the satisfaction of doing useful, charitable work in the community.[28]

Until she founded her own Company, Angela took her obligations to the Tertiaries seriously, using the name "Suor Angela Terziara," wearing the habit of the order, and accepting the directives of her Franciscan superior.[29] This affiliation with the

Tertiaries, who followed a life of penitential asceticism, charitable activities, and prayer, had a marked influence on Angela and her formulation of the idea of a new kind of apostolate for women.

THE BRESCIAN CONTEXT FOR ANGELA'S VISION

In 1516, when Angela was about forty years old, her Franciscan superior sent her on a mission to Brescia to console Caterina Patengola, who had recently lost her husband and two sons. The impact of this experience is unmistakable. At the time the city was in political turmoil caused by rebellions of the nobility and the upheavals following the French military campaigns of Louis XII. For several years Brescia's fate was uncertain as it passed from French to Spanish control.[30] Like most north Italian cities, it was filled with religious tensions related to the corruption of the clergy, the degeneration of monastic life, and popular, often radical, movements to reform the Church.[31] Clerical absenteeism and lack of religious instruction had created a favorable atmosphere for the spread of heretical and reform ideas through popular preachers such as the Carmelite Pallavicino and secret presses that disseminated the ideas of reform. The city council repeatedly attempted to reform the convents and monasteries and petitioned regularly for the return of the absentee bishop.[32] Economic and social problems, including prostitution and syphilis, demanded amelioration and gave rise to a spirit of philanthropy. As was common in urban areas since the late Middle Ages, laypeople had formed confraternities to honor the Virgin, a saint, or the Eucharist, to engage in pious and charitable work, such as helping the poor and the sick, and to reaffirm Christian values. Members of these societies placed special emphasis on the love of Christ through the celebration of the holy sacrifice of the Mass and service to the poor.[33] Angela's special mission to the Patengola widow thrust her into the midst of this political, social, and religious turmoil that was quite different from her peaceful existence in the Lake country. It also placed her in the circle of Brescian elites intimately connected with the recently founded Compagnia del Divino Amore.

Caterina Patengola and her nephew Girolamo were well-connected upper-class Brescians linked through friendship and patronage not only to the Franciscan Tertiaries but also to some of the leaders for a lay apostolate in Brescia. Their circle included people whose names were associated with the foundation of the Compagnia del Divino Amore and the Compagnia di Ss. Trinitas, the latter of which managed the hospital for the *incurabili*, or syphilitics.[34] Men and women longing to combine devotional expression with charitable activity were drawn to the Company of Divine Love and the Hospital for the *incurabili*, as the latter became the focus for the work of several other charitable societies. Bartolomeo Stella was one of at least five prominent Brescians who had joined the Compagnia in Rome, founded a hospital in Brescia in 1520, and helped promote the movement to create *conservatori*: refuges and orphanages for girls.[35] Angela may have belonged to the circle of women who participated in the work with the *incurabili*, especially nursing sick women, but the secrecy required of the members of the Company of Divine Love prevents our knowing the extent of her involvement with the day-to-day work.[36] Through the Patengola circle she became friends with the Countess Laura Gambara, who, with Elizabeth Prato and several other widows, supported the Conservatorio delle Convertite della Carità, an institution founded in response to the social and political upheavals to protect, assist, and teach young girls and penitent prostitutes.[37] Although no direct evidence places Angela among the helpers at the Conservatorio or the hospital for the *incurabili*, her friendship with the women of the Patengola circle, who valued these institutions as stressing the values of a Christian life, frequent Confession and communion, and good works, contributed significantly to the formation and realization of her ideas for an active apostolate for women. The young widow Elizabeth Prato, for example, became Angela's disciple, assistant, and, finally, in 1572, mother-general of the Company of St. Ursula.

After a few months with the Patengolas, Angela took lodging in the household of Antonio Romano, a wealthy merchant and Patengola associate, who accompanied her on several pilgrimages and was a key witness in the canonization process. The depositions of Romano and other friends agree on Angela's works of charity during this period: counseling or comforting strangers, drawing up wills, arranging marriages, bringing peace among members of quarreling families and civic factions.[38] They claimed that the fact that people throughout the region came to her door to ask for prayers indicated she had a reputation for holiness, and that priests and members of religious orders came to speak with her about Scripture suggested she possessed unusual knowledge or insight.[39] One witness claimed that she "converted souls" and "caused them to change their lives."[40] Contemporaries recognized qualities in Angela that were typical of a late medieval *beata* or holy woman: prayer, contemplation, frequent communion, fasting, wearing of a hair shirt, and charitable activity. No one identified her work at this time with a specific charitable group or spoke of activities related to teaching.

Pilgrimages to Mantua, to the tomb of the Dominican Tertiary and *beata* Osanna Andreasi, to Jerusalem, Rome, and a Franciscan shrine at Varallo extended her experiences beyond northern Italy and represented another side of her spiritual life.[41] Her traveling companion, Antonio Romano, who later described these pilgrimages in detail, noted that on the return voyage by way of Venice and Rome, the patriarch and pope, having learned of her reputation for lay leadership in Brescia, urged her to remain in their respective cities to organize lay groups for charitable work. But, as Romano pointed out, she felt called back to Brescia to fulfill the promise of her childhood vision and, perhaps, it might be conjectured, to work independently and without too much involvement with secular or ecclesiastical authorities, something that is clearly reflected in the original organization of her Company.

In 1532, her Company of women of all ages and classes, dedicated to virginity, piety, and charity, took shape. Some, like Elizabeth Prato, had already dedicated themselves to the work with *incurabili*; others were the daughters of women who performed charitable service at the hospital.[42] At the time the Company began to gather, Angela was sharing an ascetic and contemplative life with one of her spiritual daughters, Barbara Fontana, in a small room connected with the Church of St. Afra.[43] She must already have shifted her spiritual focus to her own Company of St. Ursula by then, because she petitioned to be relieved of the obligation to be buried as a Tertiary. In the first formal gathering of her spiritual daughters in 1535, as with Ignatius de Loyola and his followers at Montmartre the previous year, there was no official ecclesiastical ceremony or immediate formal ecclesiastical approval of the Company; nine months later, however, in August 1536, the Company of virgins received episcopal approval, an event that has been interpreted to show that she had no immediate plan to extend the Company beyond the diocese.[44]

Angela's membership in the Franciscan Tertiaries and her associations with participants of the Oratory of Divine Love and with widows dedicated to the work both at the *incurabili* and at foundations for penitent girls appear to have been the obvious sources of inspiration for her Company. Equally revealing, however, were the symbols she chose to represent her Company: the dates of its foundation, the patron saints, the decorations of the Oratory where the group met regularly.[45]

ANGELA'S VISION FOR HER COMPANY

It is generally agreed that Angela carefully chose November 25 to gather her Company. It was not only the anniversary of her return from her pilgrimage to Jerusalem, but also the feast of St. Catherine of Alexandria, a consecrated virgin and mystical spouse of Christ who, according to legend, had received a ring from His own hand.[46] The choice of St. Ursula as patroness signified the ideal of a virgin of the early Church who consecrated her life to God and remained in the world to lead other virgins to Him. A cult, which exalted her virginity and transformed her into a patroness of education, was popular in northern Italy at the time.[47] It is unknown whether Angela herself or, perhaps, one of the wealthy women from the Patengola circle such as Elizabeth Prato commissioned the frescoes that adorned the walls of the oratory where the Company first held its meetings.[48] Art for didactic and propaganda purposes usually adorned the walls of confraternity meeting halls.[49] A detailed seventeenth-century document describes a large crucifix painted on the wall surrounded by weeping angels, the three Marys, and St. John, symbols of Christ's Passion, and representations of St. Elizabeth of Hungary, who cared for the poor and the outcast, and of Sts. Paula and Eustochia, who symbolized ideal widowhood.[50] Angela's vision for her company is apparent in these symbolic frescoes. This was not to be a typical late-medieval lay organization dedicated to pious good works. It was to be exclusively female, and the young women were to be consecrated virgins and spouses of Christ dedicated to

Christian education, frequent prayer and confession, and daily celebration of the Mass—but without public or solemn vows.[51]

THE PRIMITIVE RULE

The Primitive Rule provides further insight into early Ursuline spirituality. The earliest version of the Rule disappeared, and the so-called Primitive Rule belongs to a period of internal struggles in the Company during the five years after Angela's death. The brevity and simplicity of even this amended Rule, consisting of a preface and twelve short chapters, is nevertheless significant.[52] Angela left the Rule informal to facilitate change, and it circulated in handwritten form until 1569, perhaps avoiding public censure and criticism but also making it liable to misinterpretation and unsolicited change.[53] She did not intend it to be complete, and before her death she added further instructions for the day-to-day management of the Company in the *Testamento*[54] and *Ricordi*.[55] Moreover, in the final version of the *Testamento* she acknowledged that change might be necessary and gave explicit permission to alter the Rule at a later time.[56]

The Rule, like that of the Franciscan Tertiaries, was remarkable for its simplicity, flexibility, and practicality: virginity, fasting, prayer (both vocal and mental), frequent confession, daily attendance at Mass, and obedience to all superiors. The basis of the Company was holy virginity.[57] Anyone desiring to enter had to be a virgin, at least twelve years old, be entering of her own free will, be unencumbered by monastic vows or promises of marriage, and have the permission of her parents or guardians. The women were to assume an attitude of poverty, rather than to accept poverty as an absolute. Thus, dress should be simple and modest, of black or brown serge or linen with no pleats or frills. Clothes that the women wore at the time they presented themselves for entrance could be kept until they wore out. Underlying the Rule was the assumption that each virgin would live a life of prayer and contemplation at home and practice the apostolate within her family and community.

The influence of the Tertiaries on the organization and mission of Angela's Company appears in the practical rules for contemplative life that were combined with an active apostolate of charity.

Fasting and vocal and mental prayer recall the Franciscan ideal that was popular among pious Catholics in the sixteenth century. The commands for frequent confession, daily participation in Mass, simple dress, and warnings against the corrupting influences of dancing and public spectacles were themes that the Tertiaries and Angela's Rule and Counsels for the Ursulines shared.[58] Like the Tertiaries, members of the Company owed obedience first to the Ten Commandments; second to the Church; third to the bishop, priest, and spiritual director; fourth to the governors of the Company; fifth to parents and superiors at home; and finally to the civil authorities.[59] The prescribed discipline was strict in regard to both their outward and their spiritual lives. Angela distrusted the youth and spiritual immaturity of her daughters, and feared their being corrupted by heretical preaching and confessors who might not take the spiritual discipline of young women seriously. Although she never wished to withdraw her Company from the world, she felt compelled to protect it from the world's corrupting influences. Thus, she cautioned the matrons to supervise their charges carefully and created an administrative structure that ensured that the young women were well-supervised in their spiritual lives, their families, and their teaching apostolate.[60]

Governance of the Company was less important than its spiritual life, a principle that Carlo Borromeo and others distrusted and later reversed. Instructions appear at the end of the Primitive Rule in one, brief chapter. Angela placed the management of the Company in the hands of "four of the most capable of the virgins" (called mistresses or guides), at least four matrons who were widows (called matrons or widow-governors), and "four men of experience and tried virtue" to act as "fathers and helpers," that is, spiritual guides and business managers, all to be elected by the entire Company. Fearful of outside corruption, Angela was especially wary of having the temporal business of the Company go outside the closed group and at the end of her life reminded the members to guard the handling of issues of property, gifts, and charity and keep them within the Company.[61] Special care was taken to give the Company, whose members were dispersed throughout the town, cohesion through demand for absolute obedience to the Rule and superiors, the common vocation, and the monthly celebration of the Eucharist together with an "experienced and prudent priest" who was also the confessor and spiritual director for the Company. Angela's advice regarding the careful choice of spiritual director revealed her distrust of the corrupting influence of outsiders (especially confessors) and her fear of heresy.[62]

The Primitive Rule said nothing about a mother-general, no doubt because it was assumed that Angela would function as the administrator. Although in August 1536 Lorenzo Muzio, vicar-general of Brescia, recognized Angela as the foundress, formal elections for mother-general were not held until March 1537, when a bequest of money required the Company to acquire legal status (like that of a confraternity) and a recognized head to accept the funds.[63]

The election of Angela as mother-general of the Company acknowledged her previously accepted role and clarified procedures that had been omitted from the Rule. The mother-general would be mother and treasurer for life, and, at her death, the virgins would elect her successor. The Company, which had grown to 76 virgins, also elected four mature virgins to be the Mistresses of the younger virgins, and the widows to be matron-governors and to oversee the day-to-day work of the Company. In 1537, the Company agreed that in the future anything done by the matron-governors would be considered as decided and done by the entire Company, a move that had important and unforeseen consequences. At the time of the elections, the Company did not proceed to choose the four male advisers because "the matter had not been sufficiently prepared," and, in fact, this procedure was delayed for many years.[64]

As the Company attracted more members, Angela created another group of supervisors called *colonelle*, or district leaders, not mentioned in the Primitive Rule. Each had to oversee the day-to-day work in an area of Brescia to which she was assigned. They were to be mature women and virgins, and, unlike the matron-governors (who were not bound by vows), actual members of the Company. By the time of Angela's death in 1540, the *colonelle* had become important to the everyday functioning of the Company, as her words of advice to them in the *Ricordi* reveal.

THE URSULINE VOCATION

Angela was neither an articulate reformer nor a studious theoretician of religious life, and one must read between the lines of the

Rule and her other dictated words to discern her attitudes toward traditional religious institutions at the time. Nowhere did she openly criticize contemporary convent life, which would have been easy to do.[65] Yet, in her own choice of a religious vocation and the foundation of the Ursuline Company, she demonstrated her belief that there were alternative and, perhaps, better ways than the traditional cloister for women wishing to dedicate themselves to a spiritual life. The discipline she laid down for her daughters was strict in regard to both their outward life and their spiritual life. Although her followers did not live a life in common, she emphasized the importance of community in their lives through insistence on regular meetings for confessions and celebration of the Mass together. Although she never wished to withdraw her Company from the world, she tried to ensure its protection from corrupting influences.

There was certainly no lack of traditional religious houses in sixteenth-century Brescia. In addition to the prominent and powerful S. Salvatore/S. Giulia, there were four other Benedictine houses, two of the Poor Clares, two of the Augustinians, one Dominican, one Carmelite, and a number of small convents following different rules. One estimate places the number of women in these religious houses at 3,000.[66] The rising cost of marriage dowries in the sixteenth century had increased the population in female religious houses enormously, with the entrance of many young girls who lacked a vocation for the cloistered spiritual life. What kind of women found Angela's Company appealing?

Like that of the Tertiaries and confraternities, the social diversity of the Company at its foundation was striking. It offered a practical alternative to young women who wished to follow a religious vocation but could not afford the inflated dowry expected by the traditional religious orders, or who found cloistered life unappealing.[67] One of the earliest registers of the Company lists the names of nine girls who were domestic servants and indicates that quite young, adolescent girls (perhaps orphans) sought membership in the Company. Although some women from wealthy prominent families were listed among the members, the majority lacked riches, as Carlo Borromeo observed when he visited the diocese of Brescia in 1580.[68] Many young women had fathers who were tradesmen: bakers, weavers, drapers, and goldsmiths.

Despite the social diversity, elite women dominated and held the supervisory positions. The matrons were aristocratic widows elected by the Company to protect the virgins and provide leadership and stability.[69] In her *Testamento*, Angela named these women individually, unlike the *Ricordi* written for the less distinguished women who became *colonelle*. Addressing them as her "dearest sisters" and "honored mothers," she spoke of their governing the Company, entrusted them to manage the financial affairs without outside help and to alter the Rule if it became necessary. The matrons were capable and, often, powerful women who, like so many Italian and French female aristocrats, seem to have been drawn to the new religious orders that stressed spiritual renewal and an active apostolate.

Although there were no instructions for the teaching apostolate in the Rule, there is little doubt that the virgins taught Christian doctrine to children both in their homes and in orphanages. The *Testamento* and *Ricordi*, for example, were quite explicit about the importance of the teaching vocation and about the methods the matron-governors and *colonelle* were to use with the virgins to instill in them examples of pedagogy, discipline, and love to use with their young students.[70] The educational thrust of the Ursulines connects Angela with other movements to reform society through Christian education, especially the Schools for Christian Doctrine, formally established in Milan in November 1536 by Castellino da Castello to teach the catechism to boys.[71] But Angela seems to have begun such a mission with her Company of virgins even before the introduction of the Schools of Christian Doctrine in Brescia, and by 1566 it was reported to Borromeo that "all the hospitals and all the schools of Christian doctrine for girls are staffed by the Ursulines."[72] Angela, Castellino, and Borromeo shared a similar aim: to reform the laity by teaching and by pious example.

DIVISION AND UPHEAVAL

Angela's death meant the loss to her Company of her personal vision and charismatic leadership. The clash of strong personalities among her successors and changed attitudes toward the religious life among clergy and laity fueled destructive strife within the

Company. The difference between the spirit of early Catholic reform and the spirit of Trent is reflected in some of the changes in the Company itself: a trend toward identifying with traditional religious communities through the requirement of a habit, greater control over the members by altering the structure of governance, stabilization of the Ursulines in community life, movement toward male control, and a bid for papal approval.

As the Company, which had grown to 150 members,[73] experienced a decline, local clergy and parents talked of the need to cloister the young women and impose a common mode of dress to bring the Company into line with more traditional religious orders.[74] Even before Angela's death a concern arose with regard to the financial stability of a Company with so little structure, and an attempt was made to put it on firmer ground by guaranteeing its members the right to expect a dowry from their families as if they were marrying or entering a convent.[75] Many of the young women succumbed to the pressures of their parents who demanded that their daughters leave the Company, enter a convent, or marry.[76] Not only did these parents express fears for their daughters' chastity, but they also objected to their mixing with working-class women.[77] Some accused the foundress of thinking she was above St. Benedict, St. Francis, and St. Clare by founding the Company in the first place.[78] Some clergy not only objected to the dangerous innovation of an active apostolate of uncloistered women, but spoke with contempt of such women and even suggested that Angela was damned for creating it in the first place.[79]

Some change was inevitable; the Company had been held together by a simple rule and the charismatic leadership of a laywoman. Though she had elaborated on her ideals for the benefit of her followers in the *Ricordi* and *Testamento*, and recognized that the Rule might have to be revised to fit the times, the Company had depended too much on her inspiration and leadership and her collaboration with Cozzano. Thus, a bitter struggle developed between the new mother-general, Lucrezia Lodrone, who recognized the need for change to save the Company from destruction, and Cozzano, who honored the foundress's memory by attempting to keep things the same and, perhaps, resented the leadership of the new and imperious mother-general.[80]

In an effort to avoid conflict, Angela had set aside the principle of election, and prior to her death named Lucrezia Lodrone, the widow of a Brescian aristocrat, to succeed her as mother-general.[81] Lodrone had been among the first matron-governors of the Company, a woman of wealth and position who appears to have possessed the ability to guide the Company through the difficult years ahead, but not without antagonizing Cozzano and some of the other matron-governors. She abrogated the provisions for democratic decision-making in the government of the Company which included shared power among the mother-general, matron-governors, *colonelle*, and the secretary-chancellor of the Company, Cozzano. The latter fought the changes on two fronts: first, he addressed the *Epistola confortatoria*, a letter of comfort during their troubled times and justification for their vocation;[82] second, in the *Risposta contro quelli persuadono la clausura alle vergini di Sant' Orsola*, he offered arguments against the clergy and other officials who advocated cloistering the Company. But the criticism continued.[83] Lodrone, perhaps fearing more serious attacks on the Company, acted to impose some standard attire to make the Company resemble a religious order by requiring the members to wear a black leather cincture.[84] In keeping with the flexibility of the early days of the Company, a standard form of dress had never been imposed. Cozzano regarded Lodrone's move as another threat and a further attempt to breach the Rule and modify the spirit of the Company. With the backing of several of the matron-governors he appealed her decision to the local ecclesiastical authorities—a succession of vicars-general who governed the diocese in the absence of a bishop.[85] In the meantime, Lodrone had built support for her proposal. In December 1545, she issued a definitive order that all Ursulines should henceforth wear a black leather cincture as an exterior sign of consecration, under pain of expulsion from the Company.[86] Furthermore, she petitioned for papal approval of the Company, which Angela herself may have done before her death.[87]

The issue became more complicated and the quarrel more heated.[88] Cozzano and other leaders of the Company not only objected to the order requiring the cincture but also to the high-handed way that Lodrone had made the decision. She, on the other hand, claimed that the decision regarding the cincture had been made "by a majority of the Company and the matron-governors."[89] Both Cozzano and Ginevra Luzzago, one of the matrons and leaders (and Lucrezia's successor), openly opposed her and enlisted the support of the vicar-general of Brescia, Gian-pietro Ferretti, who warned Lodrone to leave the sisters in peace. When she ignored him, he excommunicated her and some of her supporters among the matrons, and, in the spring of 1546, named Ginevra Luzzago mother-general in her place.[90]

On April 14, 1546, Pope Paul III promulgated the bull *Regimini universalis ecclesiae* that gave papal approval to the Company and to Lodrone's leadership.[91] This exacerbated the schism within the Company as it confirmed the revised Rule on dress and declared that all parts of it must be observed "in perpetuity." It absolved members of the Company from any excommunication they might have incurred in the recent struggles and granted the matron-governors the right to establish new rules without consulting the bishop and the power to inflict penalties on anyone who opposed them. The bull named the bishop of Verona and the archdeacon and the archpriest of Brescia (all known allies of Lodrone's) as "executors" and gave all three together and each one singly the right to publish the bull at will and to inflict penalties on those who did not obey the Rule. One of the executors, Aurelio Du-ranti, an archdeacon of Brescia and a Lodrone partisan with papal connections, published the bull with a document of his own, *Processo fulminato et esecutoriale della bolla*, which forbade anyone to disobey the bull and threatened the recalcitrants with censure and penalties. He specifically threatened Gianpietro Ferretti, the representative of the absentee bishop of Brescia, with excommunication if he took action against the bull or any of the documents connected with it. Finally, on April 20, 1546, four days after the promulgation of the bull, Lodrone and Duranti published a decree requiring all Ursulines to wear the cincture under pain of expulsion and created a register of members who, by signing their names, signified their acceptance of the new rules.[92] Those whose names were not inscribed in the new register would not be recognized as members of the Company. The names of Ginevra Luzzago, two other matron-governors, and Cozzano are missing from the book.[93]

These struggles led to profound changes in the original character of the Company. Decision-making became less democratic; a recognizable Ursuline costume was established, giving the Company and its members a special identity. The Company remained independent of the local bishop and effectively under the power of the archpriest and archdeacon of Brescia, who bore the titles "apostolic conservators" until 1580 when Carlo Borromeo placed the Company firmly under the jurisdiction of the bishop of Brescia. Angela had purposely left the Rule informal, had spoken in the *Testamento* to the matron-governors about the possibility of changes in the Rule,[94] and had created the Company with only the approval of an absentee bishop. Her intent seems to have been a small, local Company easily managed by group decisions. The bull recognized the Company as an institution of papal privilege which would lead to significant change including greater possibility for expansion outside the diocese of Brescia.[95] Whatever interpretation is put on the facts of the controversy—and there are differing interpretations—it remains clear that the events following Angela's death resulted in the development of the Company of St. Ursula in a way that ran counter to many of the foundress's basic ideas, including the requirement of a habit and rituals for acceptance (such as public vows) that helped transform the Company into a religious order. The issue appears to have been a matter not simply of the cincture, but of who would control the Company, as the power struggle that persisted reveals.

The state of upheaval continued for some time and divided the Company into two factions claiming legitimacy and pursuing official recognition.[96] The sources, even the official registers, reveal very little about what happened. Ginevra Luzzago remained in opposition to the cincture and the leadership of Lucrezia Lodrone, who dominated the Company as mother-general under the banner of papal approval. Her death in 1555 precipitated a new dispute over the election of a mother-general and reinforced the division between the factions, one which had supported and elected Ginevra Luzzago, and the other which chose Veronica Buzzi, an ally of Lodrone's and another leader of the cincture faction. The dispute dragged on for three years, during which time we catch occasional glimpses of the exchange of polemics and appeals to authorities in Venice and Rome, with each side claiming canonical legitimacy. Not until the death of Ginevra Luzzago in 1558 did the bitter quarrel begin to be resolved. In 1559, Veronica Buzzi's agreeing to step aside in favor of a compromise leader, Bianca Porcelaga, allowed the Company to reunite.

What brought about the reconciliation and reunification is unclear.[97] Some early sources credit the choice of Francesco Cabrini d'Alfinello, founder of the Congregation of the Fathers of Peace, as confessor in 1559–1560, and spiritual director in 1563, with helping to end the schism.[98] The election of Domenico Bollani to the bishopric of Brescia in 1559 gave the diocese not only its first resident bishop in many years, but also a leader who believed in reform at the parish level, including measures directed at the secular clergy and provisions for strict supervision of the religious activities of the laity, especially charitable confraternities.[99] It is significant that Gabriel Cozzano was no longer connected with the Company, and the Congregation of the Fathers of Peace joined Cabrini in giving spiritual direction to the Company.

RECONCILIATION AND CONSOLIDATION

With reconciliation accomplished, the Company entered a phase of rapid expansion of numbers and consolidation of leadership marked by the institution of a narrower, more defined governing structure, the gradual addition of clearly defined rules for entering the Company, the institution of ritual and vows at the conclusion of a novitiate, and the initiation of the process for Angela's canonization. For the first time the sources cite the charitable and educational activities of the Ursulines in the hospitals for women and in the schools of Christian Doctrine for children.[100] The Rule was revised for clarity's sake and amended to provide for three stages of admission to the Company: age twelve when one presented oneself for entrance (*presentazione*), age fifteen when one was accepted into the Company (*accettazione*), and age eighteen to twenty when one was finally accepted and signed the register (*recezione*).[101] The acceptance of new members was marked by a ceremony resembling the medieval ritual for the consecration of virgins.[102] The informal vow of consecration, which in the Primitive Rule was made in private and "carried in one's heart," was replaced by a formal public vow of consecration, at the request of the virgins themselves, according to Francesco Cabrini, who appears to have supported the idea and may even have initiated it.[103] The revised Rule was prepared for publication by Damian Turlino as a part of the process to establish the legal status that the Commune required of all confraternities, enabling them to receive property and to stabilize financial arrangements including

the receipt of dowries.[104] Finally, in 1572, the Company elected
Elizabeth Prato, Angela's old friend and one of the original Ursulines, mother-general, who immediately initiated reform and
strengthened the rules of governance. The number of *colonelle* was
increased from four to seven. The powers and functions of the
matron-governors, the mistresses of the virgins, and the *colonelle*
were clarified. Especially important was the greater role given to
the virgin-mistresses to oversee the behavior of the virgins in their
homes and to ascertain whether they taught Christian doctrine
and performed only those works of piety that had received the
approval of the father-confessor, the matron-governors, or the
colonelle.[105] Thus, the informal administration of the Company
during Angela's lifetime was revised, the loose ends of organization were tied together, and the Company was definitively transformed from a charismatically led group into an organized
institution.

Under Prato's leadership the Company regained local popularity and won recognition among bishops in neighboring dioceses,
Venice and Milan, for example.[106] Although many of the women
lived at home, those who were without families or who worked
in the Pietà for young girls or the Hospital for women lived a
life in common.[107] The movement toward community life which
began almost imperceptibly, and often for practical reasons, was
accelerated by the influence of Carlo Borromeo, the decree on
regulars of the last session of the Council of Trent, and social
pressure.

CARLO BORROMEO AND THE URSULINES

Not long after his appointment to the bishopric of Milan, the
reputation of the Ursulines captured the interest of Carlo Borromeo. By December 1566, he had obtained a copy of the Rule,
which he adapted and published for use in the diocese of Milan.[108]

Although Borromeo took some sections from the Brescian
Rule verbatim, he also made substantive changes. He removed
Angela's numerous quotes from Scripture, which were a source
of her inspiration and ideal, and the gentle, didactic passages of
instruction to her daughters. Fasts and vigils, which Angela considered essential to a full Christian life, were markedly reduced in

number. Provision was made for maidens "who might wish to make a public vow of virginity"—a matter that had been under consideration in Brescia and was introduced the following year at the maidens' request, it was said.[109]

Borromeo's reluctance to give the laity a role in church business was manifested in his tailoring of the Primitive Rule for use in his diocese. The Milanese version had a long and explicit section on internal governance, and instead of dividing the Company into districts under *colonelle*, it established separate Companies. A prior-general appointed by Borromeo replaced the mother-general, and sub-priors managed the separate Companies. The virgins had no role in governance, and the leadership of widowed and unmarried women of Angela's Company was now subordinated to male leadership, as Borromeo hand-picked Gaspare Belinzaghi, a priest of the Church of the Holy Sepulcher, future leader of the Oblates of St. Ambrose, and the prior-general of the Schools of Christian Doctrine, to be the first prior-general of the Company of St. Ursula in Milan. The Company not only became male-controlled but also increasingly dominated by women living in community. As the council of matron-governors lost importance, the Company of St. Anne, composed of widows who lived in a community according to a rule, became the day-to-day supervisors of the virgins living at home, as an alternative, according to Borromeo, to joining an impoverished cloistered order.[110]

This period probably marks the formal alliance of the Ursulines with the Schools of Christian Doctrine in Milan, as the administration of one group was merged with the other.[111] Borromeo, in effect, adapted what amounted to a lay confraternity of women for the work of teaching women and girls Christian doctrine and legitimized its activities through revising its rule and placing it under clerical control and leadership. Since the superiors of the Company of Ursulines were also the superiors of the Christian Doctrine Schools and the Oblates of St. Ambrose, the Ursulines were the natural candidates to teach the catechism to girls and young women on Sundays and feast days.[112] By 1576, in fact, Borromeo declared it the duty of bishops in the archdiocese to found a Company of St. Ursula in each of their dioceses for this purpose.[113] He regularized several charitable institutions connected with the Ursulines: St. Sophia, to provide protection to orphaned girls without suitable homes; and Santo Spirito and St.

Marcellina, to support Ursulines who lacked families or were sick, aged, and in need of care. By 1585, a new rule for the Ursulines in Milan had been drawn up, "For Ursulines Wishing to Live in Community," that included simple vows, ceremonies for reception, and instructions for community life.[114] Thus, another step was taken toward transforming the Ursulines into an order.

Borromeo's influence facilitated the transition of the Company into an order. From February 1580 until November 1582 he carried out an apostolic visitation at Brescia in the company of Girolomo Rabbia, an enthusiastic supporter of the Ursulines in Milan, and Carlo Agostini, superior-general of the Schools of Christian Doctrine. According to Borromeo's report, he met with the superiors of the Company of St. Ursula, presided over the acceptance of twenty-three maidens on November 25, 1580, promised to initiate the canonization process, and revised the Rule. The extent of participation of the female leaders in the revision of the Rule is unclear. The modifications followed the spirit of the Milanese Rules of 1567, 1569, and 1577, as Angela's spiritual legacy was replaced with Borromeo's juridical approach.[115] Quotations from Scripture were reduced, especially in the prologue. Theological interjections, scriptural references regarding confession that ran counter to current orthodoxy, and Angela's exhortation to "confess, confess often, confess well," were removed.[116] Fasting was severely limited. The chapter on obedience was so completely modified as to change its spirit. In the Primitive Rule, Angela had encouraged her followers to listen to the prompting of the Holy Spirit. In the mood of the decrees of Trent, Borromeo steered the Ursulines away from such potentially dangerous, unsupervised devotions. Finally, as he had in Milan, Borromeo expanded the last chapter of the Primitive Rule dealing with governance, to clarify lines of authority and structure. The qualifications for mother-general became narrower and were marked by a preference for a consecrated virgin over a widow who was at least forty years old and had been a member of the Company for at least ten years. Furthermore, her powers were restricted. The bishop of Brescia was given authority over the Company *and* the power to appoint the superior-general, a position that had been filled by the priests of the Company of Peace since the time of Francesco Cabrini. The revised Brescian Rule suggests, too, that the popularity of the Ursulines and the fact that they had spread throughout the diocese had created problems of maintaining uniformity which bothered Borromeo.[117] The final chapter dictated that new groups of Ursulines in the diocese of Brescia should defer to the authority of the Company within the city and that through regular visits the superiors of the Company of Brescia were to guide the activities of the provincial groups.[118]

EXPANSION AND TRANSFORMATION

The combination of Borromeo's energetic leadership and women's desire for an active apostolate contributed to the popularity and expansion of the movement in northern Italian cities, especially in Milan. The Company spread especially during the eighteen years of Borromeo's administration of the archdiocese. By the end of the sixteenth century the Ursuline congregations existed throughout Italy, and had spread to the papal city of Avignon, and to France. Independent Companies were set up by the bishop at Avignon, by the Somascan Fathers at Cremona, and by the city councils at Parma and Piacenza. Companies were founded in small villages by matron-governors whose country villas were in the vicinity.[119] Though the Rules varied from one locale to another, in most cases they were based on those of Brescia or Milan for virgins living with their families.[120] Similar groups associated in the popular mind with the Ursulines and going under different names such as *Dimesse*, *Beate*, and *Vergini* sprang up, introducing further diversity. In cities such as Venice and Rome, the Companies attracted aristocratic and noble-women. In Naples in 1609, the Company included both women and men, the latter forming a kind of Third Order.[121]

Papal approval added prestige to the movement and promoted its spread. The Brescian foundations attached the approval by Pope Paul III to the Rule. Borromeo obtained a brief from Gregory XIII. Ferrara received one from Sixtus V; and Bologna and Naples, from Paul V.[122] Diversity accompanied the expansion of the Ursulines, including the use of different versions of the Rule, and ranged from women living with their families, to living in unenclosed communities, to forming cloistered communities. The weight of Borromeo's approval, the need for teachers, and confusion surrounding the interpretation and implementation of the

Tridentine decree on regulars allowed the spread of uncloistered Ursuline communities in Italy until the seventeenth century.[123] Although the Rule of 1582, "For Women Wishing to Live in a Community," drawn up under Borromeo's supervision, encouraged the development of conventual life, it did not require solemn vows and permitted the women to go outside to teach in the Schools of Christian Doctrine.[124] As congregations gradually felt pressure to accept solemn vows and claustration, they continued their teaching vocation by taking girls as boarders within the cloister walls.[125]

The foundation of the Company at Avignon, perhaps as early as 1574, opened the way for the spread of the order to France.[126] By 1597, the Ursulines at Avignon accepted the Ferrarese version of the Rule—a melding of the Primitive Rule, the Reformed Brescian Rule, and the Milanese Rule. It included the brief of Gregory XIII, which gave the foundation the weight of recent papal authority, and a biography of Angela, which connected these newly formed congregations to both Angela's spiritual life and the vitality of religious renewal that had been the source of her ideal. This was important, because in the Milanese region Borromeo was popularly credited with the founding of the Ursulines.[127] The Avignonese Ursulines lived in their homes and taught young girls, but as the movement spread to France after 1592 a communal yet uncloistered form of life based on the Milanese Rule predominated. During the first quarter of the seventeenth century, however, either through their own requests or through the demands of bishops, French congregations were transformed into religious orders. Under social and religious pressure, claustration was imposed, teaching, even within the cloister walls, was discouraged, and the congregations gradually became aristocratic. Ultimately, they were forced to accept the Rule of St. Augustine. The idea of lay associations of women dedicated to an active apostolate or communities of uncloistered women flew in the face of political, ecclesiastical, and social pressure and the implementation of the Tridentine decrees.[128] Cloistered Ursulines prevailed over uncloistered ones until the latter disappeared entirely.

CONCLUSION

Like many of the other religious congregations founded during the Counter-Reformation, the Company of Ursulines had its source in the unusual vision of its founder and the strong appeal of a lay apostolate to women. Shaped by a vision realized by women in the early Church and by late medieval urban piety, Angela's ideals succumbed to the Church's vision of a renewed Christian society which demanded that female groups conform to episcopal supervision, claustration, and formal vows. With the loss of Angela's leadership, her Company yielded to internal strife and outside pressure to conform. Like other Counter-Reformation congregations for women, the original vision was subverted. Angela's ideal for an active apostolate for women lost its appeal by the end of the sixteenth century. Symbolically, when the Brescian notary Nazari took depositions for her canonization, no women spoke for her.

Select Bibliography

Documents relating to the life of Angela Merici and the history of the Ursulines in Italy are found in Brescia, Desenzano, Salò, Milan, Venice, the Vatican, and Brescia. There are two principal collections of documents. One is in Rome in the Archivio Segreto Vaticano, Sacred Congregation of Rites, *Processus*, especially numbers 340 and 341 which contain copies of the original documents pertaining to Angela's life drawn up at the time of the canonization proceedings in the eighteenth century, copies of the *Ricordi* and *Testamento* and the *Epistola confortatoria alle vergini della Compagnia di sant' Orsola composta* . . . , and the *Dichiarazione della Bolla*, of Gabriel Cozzano. Another major collection, located in the Archivio di Stato, Brescia, includes a large folio-size book called the *Secondo libro generale* which contains copies of the important documents of the early years including the writings dictated by Angela, the Nazari deposition, minutes of elections and meetings, lists of members, confessors, and agents, and new regulations made after Angela's death. In Brescia the Biblioteca Queriniana, MS D. VII. 8, contains Cozzano's important *Risposta contro quelli che persuadono la clausura alle Vergini di sant' Orsola*. The oldest known version of the Rule is located in Milan, Biblioteca Trivulziana, codex 367. In Milan, the Archivio Storico Diocesano, Sezione X, *Visita pastorale e documenti aggiunti*, Brescia, 1580, contains many documents pertaining to the visitation of Carlo Borromeo, including a version of the Rule in volume 13.

A list and the location of the known archival materials is found in Luciana Mariani, Elisa Tarolli, and Maria Seynaeve, *Angela Merici: Contributo per una biografia* (Milan: Ancora, 1986). This is the best modern study of the life of Angela and the history of the Company through the sixteenth century. It includes the location and a critical discussion of the sources including the early biographies, the Brescian documents, the writings of Gabriel Cozzano, the testimonies for canonization and the various versions of the Rule for the Italian Congregations. In addition, there are two hundred pages of the most important documents of the early Ursulines, the two earliest known Rules of 1546 and 1567. A two-volume study by Teresa Ledochowska, O.S.U., *Angela Merici and the Company of St. Ursula According to the Historical Documents*, translated from the French by Mary Teresa Neylan (Milan: Ancora, 1968), is useful and contains many documents, but the author did not know about the earliest version of the Rule and was not always critical in interpreting the documents, especially those regarding Carlo Borromeo. There are many other twentieth-century studies of the foundation and early history of the Ursulines, but all have made uncritical use of the sources and are unreliable.

Angela's followers and admirers began writing her biography in the sixteenth century: for example, that of the Capuchin and near-contemporary Mattis Bellintani, *Vita della Compagnia delle Vergini di S. Orsola* in *Monumenta Historica Ordinis Minorum Capuccinorum* 6 (Rome 1950), 77–94, which differs slightly from a manuscript version in Brescia, Biblioteca Queriniana. Less than twenty years after Angela's death Giovanni Battista Nazari, a Brescian notary, wrote a short biography based on sworn testimonies gathered from citizens of Brescia who knew Angela, *Libro della vita della riverenda e quasi beata madre Suor Angela fondatrice della Compagnia di S. Orsola di Brescia con le iustificationi di essa vita; et anco si contienne il voto delle Vergini di detta Regola*, found with all the canonization documents in the Archivio Segreto Vaticano, Sacred Congregation of Rites, *Processus* 341, fol. 927r-936v. In 1600, a Florentine Jesuit, Ottavio Gondi wrote the first biography to be printed, *Vita della beata Angela Bresciana, prima fondatrice della Compagnia di S. Orsola . . .* (Brescia, 1600). This went through many editions in the seventeenth century in French and Italian (some-times under the pseudonym Ottavio Fiorentino) and became the basis for a biography in the seventeenth century by the German author Herman Crombach, *St. Ursula vindicata* (Cologne, 1647). Bernardino Faino, a seventeenth-century Superior General of the Order, wrote *Vita della serva di Dio di b. memoria la Madre Angela Merici da Desenzano* . . . (Bologna: Ricaldini, 1672) based on some archival documents that disappeared after the suppression of reli-gious congregations in 1810. Carlo Doneda's *Vita della b. Angela Merici* . . . (Brescia: Bossini, 1768; 2nd ed., 1822) was also based on the early, and now lost, documents of the Company. Doneda was one of several promoters of Angela's canonization (under consideration at the time in Rome), an archivist of the Queriniana in Brescia, and an authority on Brescian history. Ten years later, a Jesuit scholar, Girolamo Lombardi, wrote *Vita della beata Angela Merici, fondatrice della Compagnia di S. Orsola* (Venice, 1778) which is based on the earlier biographies and documents which have since been lost. It is, nevertheless, a highly sentimentalized ac-count of her life.

Modern studies of the origins of the congregation include Paolo Guerrini's "La Compagnia di S. Orsola dalle origini alla soppres-sione napoleonica," in *S. Angela Merici e la Compagnia di S. Orsola nel IV centenario della fondazione* in Memorie storiche della diocesi di Brescia, 7th series (1936). Guerrini was a Brescian archivist who published frequently on topics related to the city in the sixteenth century, including a number of studies of Angela and the Ursulines.

For the relationship of the early Ursulines to ecclesiastical au-thority see Daniele Montanari, *Disciplinamento in terra veneta: La diocesi di Brescia nella seconda metà del XVI secolo,* Annali dell' isti-tuto storico italo-germanico 8 (Bologna: Mulino, 1987); Christo-pher Cairns, *Domenico Bollani, Bishop of Brescia: Devotion to Church and State in the Republic of Venice in the Sixteenth Century* (Nieuw-koop: De Graaf, 1976); Paolo Guerrini, "La visita pastorale di S. Carlo nella diocesi di Brescia," *Brixia Sacra*, 1 (1910), 261–96, 314–22; and Gualberto Vigotti, *San Carlo Borromeo e la Compagnia di S. Orsola* (Milan: Ancora, 1972).

The history of the spread of the Ursulines in seventeenth-century France was beyond the scope of this essay. The traditions and history were so different that the Italian heritage is seldom acknowledged in the histories of the French Ursuline Order. The place to begin is Mère Marie de Chantal Gueudré, o.s.u., *Histoire de l'Ordre des Ursulines en France* (Paris: Éditions St. Paul, 1960), and Marie-André Jegou, *Les Ursulines du Faubourg St. Jacques à Paris, 1607–1662*, Bibliothèque de l'École des Hautes Études, Section des Sciences Religieuses 82 (Paris: Presses Universitaires de France, 1981).

NOTES

1. Many women in sixteenth-century Italy wished to become part of the movement for new male religious orders that emphasized renewed piety and work in the world. Some corresponded with Loyola, urging him to found a female Jesuit order, and became his spiritual daughters. Charmarie J. Blaisdell, "Calvin's and Loyola's Letters to Women: Politics and Spiritual Counsel in the Sixteenth Century," in *Calviniana: Ideas and Influence of John Calvin*, ed. Robert V. Schnucker, Sixteenth-Century Essays and Studies 10 (Kirksville, Mo.: Sixteenth-Century Journal Publishers, 1989), pp. 235–55.

2. Many religious communities founded for an active apostolate called themselves companies or congregations to be distinguished from traditional religious communities. This terminology has created difficulties, especially for Catholic writers, who have viewed them as lay groups since they took private rather than public or solemn vows. See, for example, H. O. Evennett, "The New Orders," in *The New Cambridge Modern History* (Cambridge: Cambridge University, 1979), 2:289–90; and *The Spirit of the Counter Reformation* (Cambridge: Cambridge University Press, 1968), p. 85. Terese Ledochowska, o.s.u., "Conservatori," *Dizionario degli istituti di perfezione*, vol. 2 (Rome: Edizioni Paoline, 1975), col. 1627. Ruth P. Liebowitz, "Virgins in the Service of Christ: The Dispute over the Active Apostolate for Women During the Counter-Reformation," in Rosemary Ruether and Eleanor McLaughlin, *Women of Spirit: Female Leadership in the Jewish and Christian Traditions* (New York: Simon & Schuster, 1979), p. 152.

3. One modern study in particular has contributed to our understanding of the problems of identifying the origins of the ideal: Luciana Mariani, Elisa Tarolli, and Maria Seynaeve, *Angela Merici: Contributo per una biografia* (Milano: Ancora, 1986).

4. The earliest biographical information is (*a*) a letter written in 1566 by Fr. Francesco Landini, which was appended to editions of the Rule beginning in 1569 and published by Paolo Guerrini, "La Compa-

gnia di S. Orsola dalle origini alla soppressione napoleonica," in *S. Angela Merici e la Compagnia di S. Orsola nel IV centenario della fondazione* in Memorie storiche della diocesi di Brescia, 7th series (Brescia: Ancora, 1936), pp. 53–242; and (*b*) the official sworn testimonies of four witnesses (Giacomo Chizzola, Antonio Romano, Agostino Gallo, and Bertolino de Boscolo) collected by the Brescian notary Giovanni Battista Nazari and known as the *Processo Nazari*. The original of the *Processo Nazari* is apparently lost, but there is an authenticated copy in Brescia, Archivio di Stato (ASB), Cartella, "Compagnia di S. Orsola," *Secondo libro generale*. Another accurate copy is in Rome, Archivio Segreto Vaticano (ASV), Sacred Congregation of Rites (S.C.R.), *Processus 341*, fols. 927ff. Transcriptions will be found in Mariani et al., *Angela Merici*.

5. *Processus 341*; Giacomo Jacob Chizzola and Agostino Gallo (*Processo Nazari*, fol. 941r and fol. 944r–v, respectively) speak of Angela's ability to read but not write; Chizzola claimed that she knew Scripture well enough to discuss it with priests and learned men (fol. 944r–v).

6. Codex 367, Milano, Biblioteca Trivulziana (BTM) is the earliest-known version of the Rule. A slightly later version, known as the Turlino edition, is found in Cinquecentine, EE.1.m.1, Brescia, Biblioteca Queriniana (BQ); see Mariani et al., *Angela Merici*, pp. 443–58 and 459–90, respectively.

7. *Processus 341*, fols. 953–58; Mariani et al., *Angela Merici*, pp. 512–17.

8. *Processus 341*, fols. 946–53; Mariani et al., *Angela Merici*, pp. 507–12.

9. See his *Epistola confortatoria alle vergini della Compagnia di Sant'Orsola composta per il suo cancelgliere Gabriello Cozzano*, in *Processus 341*, fols. 958v–969r; his *Dichiarazione della Bolla del papa Paolo Terzo*, in ibid., fols. 969–83; and his *Risposta contro quelli persuadono la clausura alle Vergini di Sant'Orsola* in the BQ. All three have been included in Mariani et al., *Angela Merici*, pp. 556–94.

10. Angela's followers began writing her biography in the sixteenth century. For example, that of the Capuchin Mattis (Bellintini) a Salò, *Vita della Compagnia delle vergini di S. Orsola*, Monumenta Historica Ordinis Minorum Capuccinorum 6 (Rome, 1959), pp. 77–94, differs slightly from a manuscript version in Brescia, BQ. In 1568, Giovanni Battista Nazari, the Brescian notary who gathered testimony from witnesses, wrote *Libro della vita della riverenda e quasi beata madre Suor Angela fondatrice della Compagnia di S. Orsola di Brescia con le iustificationi di essa vita, et anco si contiene il voto delle vergini di detta Regola*, which was found with the canonization documents in the *Processus 341*, fols. 927r–936v. In 1600, a Florentine Jesuit, Ottavio Gondi, wrote the first biography to be published, *Vita della beata Angela bresciana, prima fondatrice della Com-*

pagnia di S. Orsola . . . (Brescia, 1600). This text went through many editions, in both French and Italian, in the seventeenth century (sometimes under the pseudonym Ottavio Fiorentino) and became the basis for a seventeenth-century biography by a German author, Herman Crombach. Bernardino Faino, a seventeenth-century superior-general of the Ursulines, wrote *Vita della serva di Dio di b. memoria la madre Angela Merici da Desenzano* . . . (Bologna: Ricaldini, 1672) based on archival materials that apparently disappeared after the suppression of religious congregations in the Napoleonic era. Carlo Doneda also based his biography *Vita della b. Angela Merici* . . . (Brescia: Bossini, 1768) on documents now lost. Doneda was one of the promoters of Angela's canonization. Ten years later, a Brescia scholar, Girolamao Lombardi, wrote *Vita della beata Angela Merici, fondatrice della Compagnia di S. Orsola* (Venezia, 1778) based on earlier biographies and lost documents. It is a highly sentimentalized account.

11. At a conference on "Dialogues with the Past," held at Boston University, November 15–17, 1990, in a paper entitled "The Confessional Urge: Holy Women and their Spiritual Directors in Early Modern Avila," Jodi Bilinkoff of the University of North Carolina, Greensboro, discussed the problems of studying holy women whose biographies were constructed for posterity by their male confessors and biographers to create models of how to lead a virtuous life.

12. For what follows see Mariani et al., *Angela Merici*, pp. 63–108. The authors have searched the archives of Desenzano and Salò, including communal registers, tax rolls, and notarial records, for information on the Merici and Bianacosi families.

13. *Processus* 341, *Processo Nazari,* fol. 937r; Mariani et al., *Angela Merici*, p. 533.

14. BQ, MS D.VII.20, *Testimonianza di Giacomo Tribesco* (one of Angela's spiritual sons), fol. 15v; Mariani et al., *Angela Merici*, p. 595.

15. Mariani et al., *Angela Merici*, p. 93.

16. Testimonies of Antonio Romano, Agostino Gallo, Giacomo Chizzola, in *Processus* 341, *Processo Nazari*, fols. 937v–942v, transcribed in Mariani et al., *Angela Merici*, p. 539; Nazari, *Vita*, fol. 929r.

17. Antonio Romano, *Processus* 341, *Processo Nazari*, fol. 937r–v; Mattis a Salò, *Vita della Compagnia*, p. 83; Mariani et al., *Angela Merici*, p. 533.

18. Milan, Archivio Storico Diocesano (ASDM), Sezione XIII, Vol. 61, *Regola della Compagnia di Santa Orsola*, Francesco Landini, *Estratto d'una lettera*, December 21, 1566; Teresa Ledochowska, o.s.u., *Angela Merici and the Company of St. Ursula According to the Historical Documents*, trans. Mary Teresa Neylan, 2 vols. (Milan: Ancora, 1968), 1:382–84; Mariani et al., *Angela Merici*, pp. 531–32.

19. *Processus* 341, *Processo Nazari*, fol. 954r; ASDM, Sezione III, vol. 61, Landini, *Estratto*; Mariani et al., *Angela Merici*, pp. 531–39.

20. Testimony of Agostino Gallo, *Processus* 341, *Processo Nazari*, fol. 944v; Mariani et al., *Angela Merici*, p. 539. *Processus* 341, Nazari, *Vita*, fol. 929r; Mariani et al., *Angela Merici*, p. 541.

21. *Processus* 341, fols. 656r–658v, 703v–706v; Mariani et al., *Angela Merici*, pp. 522–28.

22. Sister Mary Monica, o.s.u., *Angela Merici and Her Teaching Ideal* (New York: School of Brown County Ursulines, 1927); Alessandro Tamborini, *La Compagnia e le scuole della dottrina cristiana* (Milan: Daverio, 1939), pp. 40–42, is unreliable. Mattis (Bellintini) a Salò who knew Angela and wrote in detail about her life at Desenzano and Salò did not mention this. *Vita della Compagnia*, pp. 77–94.

23. For a discussion of adolescent conversions, see Michael Goodich, "Childhood and Adolescence Among Thirteenth-Century Saints," *History of Childhood Quarterly: Journal of Psychohistory*, 1, No. 2 (1973). Donald Weinstein and Rudolph Bell, in *Saints and Society: The Two Worlds of Western Christendom, 1000–1700* (Chicago: The University of Chicago Press, 1982), pp. 55–56, discuss the relationship between the death of a parent and religious conversion; see pp. 235–43 for the context in which female spirituality develops.

24. No evidence exists to document when and where she joined the Tertiaries. On Franciscan reform and the spirituality of the Observants at the time, see Mario Fois, "I papi e l'osservanza minoritica" in *Il rinnovamento del Francescanesimo-L'Osservanza: Atti dell' XI convegno internazionale di Studi Francescani, Assisi, October 20, 21, 22* (Perugia: Università degli Studi di Perugia, Centro di Studi francescani, 1983), pp. 31–105.

25. Pio Paschini, "I monasteri femminili in Italia nel '500," *Problemi di vita religiosa in Italia nel cinquecento: Atti del Convegno di Storia della Chiesa in Italia* (Padua: Antenore, 1960), pp. 31–60. Gabriella Zarri, "I monasteri femminili a Bologna tra il XII e il XVII secolo," *Atti e memorie della deputazione di storia patria per le provincie di Romagna*, n.s. 24 (1973), 133–224.

26. *Processus* 341, *Processo Nazari*, fol. 942r (Agostino Gallo); Mariani et al., *Angela Merici*, pp. 536–37. On the desire for frequent communion in the pre-Reformation period, see Pietro Tacchi Venturi, s.j., *Storia della Compagnia di Gesù narrata con sussidio di fonti inedite. I. La Vita religiosa in Italia durante la prima età della Compagnia di Gesù* (Rome: La Civiltà Cattolica, 1910), pp. 191ff. For a new perspective on the meaning of the Eucharist and food asceticism for women, see Caroline Bynum, *Holy Feast and Holy Fast: The Religious Significance of Food to Medieval Women* (Berkeley: University of California Press, 1987), pp. 73–112.

27. Bynum, *Holy Feast*, pp. 13–30, esp. pp. 18–19; Liebowitz, "Virgins in the Service of Christ," pp. 136–37; William Christian, Jr., *Local Religion in Sixteenth-Century Spain* (Princeton: Princeton University Press, 1981), p. 16; Jodi Bilinkoff, "The Holy Women in the Urban Community in Sixteenth-Century Avila," in *Women and the Structure of Society: Selected Research from the Fifth Berkshire Conference on the History of Women*, edd. Barbara J. Harris and JoAnn K. McNamara (Durham, N.C.: Duke University Press, 1984), pp. 74–80; Mary Elizabeth Perry, *Gender and Disorder in Early Modern Seville* (Princeton: Princeton University Press, 1990), pp. 97–104.

28. Sherrill Cohen, "Asylums for Women in Counter-Reformation Italy," in *Women in Reformation and Counter-Reformation Europe*, ed. Sherrin Marshall (Bloomington: Indiana University Press, 1989), pp. 166–89.

29. See, for example, Cartella, "Compagnia di S. Orsola," fol. 52; *Processus 341, Processo Nazari*, fol. 937r-v (Antonio Romano); 940v–942r (Agostino Gallo); Mariani et al., *Angela Merici*, pp. 533–40.

30. Paolo Guerrini, *Le cronache bresciane inedite dei secoli XV–XIX*, 4 vols. (Brescia: Ancora, 1925), 1:157; Carlo Pasero, "Il dominio Veneto fino all'incendio della Loggia," *Storia di Brescia*. II. *La dominazione Veneta (1426–1575)*, ed. Giovanni Treccanni degli Alfieri (Brescia: Morcelliana, 1963); see also *Storia di Brescia*. I. *La dominazione Francia, Spagna, Impero a Brescia* (Brescia: Morcelliana, 1958).

31. Antonio Cistellini, "La vita religiosa nei secoli XV e XVI, in *Storia di Brescia*. II. *La dominazione Veneta (1426–1575)*, ed. Giovanni Treccani degli Alfieri (Brescia: Morcelliana, 1962). Dermot Fenlon, *Heresy and Obedience in Tridentine Italy* (Cambridge, Mass.: Harvard University Press, 1972); Paolo Simoncelli, *Evangelismo italiano del Cinquecento* (Rome: Istituto Storico Italiano, 1979).

32. Cistellini, "Vita religiosa," passim; Guerrini, *Cronache bresciane inedite*, 1:157–58; Paolo Prodi, "Vita religiosa e crisi sociale nei tempi di Angela Merici," *Humanitas*, 29 N.S. (1974), 307–18.

33. Christopher Black, *Italian Confraternities in the Sixteenth Century* (Cambridge: Cambridge University Press, 1989); Brian Pullen, *Rich and Poor in Renaissance Venice* (Oxford: Blackwell, 1971).

34. Pio Paschini, *La beneficenza in Italia e le "Compagnie del Divino Amore" nei primi decenni del Cinquecento* (Rome: Editrice F.I.U.C., 1925); A. Cistellini, *Figure della riforma pretridentina* (Brescia: Morcelliana, 1948; repr., 1979); Pullen, *Rich and Poor*, pp. 203–205, 232–37.

35. Black, *Italian Confraternities*, pp. 206–207; Pullen, *Rich and Poor*, pp. 234, 258.

36. Guerrini, *Cronache bresciane inedite*, 1:157; Paschini, *La beneficenza in Italia*, pp. 47–48, 61–64; Cistellini, *Figure della riforma*, p. 93.

Ledochowska, *Angela Merici,* 1:56–80; Mariani et al., *Angela Merici,* pp. 109–89.

37. Black, *Italian Confraternities,* pp. 7, 207.

38. *Processus* 341, *Processo Nazari,* fols. 942v, 943r (Agostino Gallo); Mariani et al., *Angela Merici,* pp. 537–38.

39. *Processus* 341, *Processo Nazari,* fol. 944r–v; Mariani et al., *Angela Merici,* pp. 538–39.

40. Ibid.

41. *Processus* 341, *Processo Nazari,* fols. 938r–939r (Antonio Romano); Mariani et al., *Angela Merici,* pp. 533–34.

42. Ledochowska, *Angela Merici,* 1:66–68; Mariani et al., *Angela Merici* pp. 123–29.

43. There is no precise information on Barbara Fontana or on this period in Angela's life; Cozzano, *Processus* 341, *Dichiarazione della Bolla,* fol. 974r; Mariani et al., *Angela Merici,* pp. 197, 586.

44. The document of approval was appended to the Rule, after Angela's death. BQ, Cinquecentine, EE.1.m.1, *Regola* (Turlino); Mariani et al., *Angela Merici,* p. 488.

45. Ledochowska, *Angela Merici,* 1:103–105; Mariani et al., *Angela Merici,* pp. 226–30.

46. Cartella, "Compagnia di S. Orsola," fol. 100. Her cult became popular in Italy after the tenth century where she was adopted as patroness by a number of groups including virgins and philosophers. She was popularly portrayed with a book, crown, and wheel. *New Catholic Encyclopedia* (New York: McGraw Hill, 1967), 14:490.

47. Faino, *Vita della serva . . . Angela Merici,* pp. 49–50; Mariani et al., *Angela Merici,* pp. 215–20.

48. Ledochowska seemed to think so but without direct evidence; see *Angela Merici,* 1:103.

49. Black, *Italian Confraternities,* pp. 234–50.

50. Bernardino Faino, "Descrittione dell'Oratorio nel quale la Beata Madre Angela diede alla sua Compagnia di S. Orsola," *Miscellanea,* BQ, Ms.K.VI.1, fols. 35r–37r; Ledochowska, *Angela Merici,* 1:103–104; Mariani et al., *Angela Merici,* pp. 192–95.

51. Ledochowska, *Angela Merici,* 1:103–108.

52. The Milanese Codex 367 (note 6, above) of the *Regola* is believed to be the oldest version of the Rule in existence; see *Catalogo dei codici manoscritti della Trivulziana,* ed. Giulio Porro (Turin: Bocca, 1884), pp. 371–72. But there are several problems with this claim. See, for example, the discussion by Mariani et al., *Angela Merici,* pp. 370–73. The requirement in Chapter II of the Rule, "On dress," of a black cincture around the waist and a scarf around the neck suggests this version belongs to the period 1545–1546. The Turlino edition of the Rule was

printed in 1569. Two other copies of this version exist, in the Vatican Library and the British Museum. Both these early versions of the Rule are reproduced in facsimile in Mariani et al., *Angela Merici*, pp. 459–90. There are many modern critical editions of the Rule: for example, *Edizione anastatica della Regola della Compagnia di S. Orsola di Brescia istituta da S. Angela Merici nel 1535, approvata da S. Carlo nel 1581, con apparato critico e riferimento a tutti i testi precedenti e alle edizioni bresciane fino ad oggi* (Brescia: Ateneo, 1970); *Regola della Compagnia di S. Orsola di Brescia: Versione critica secondo lo spirito di S. Angela e la tradizione pubblicatia nella edizione anastatica della Regola del 1535–1581*, ed. Luigi Rinaldini (Brescia: Edizioni S. Orsola, 1971).

53. Gabriella Zarri, "Note su diffusione e circolazione di testi devoti (1520–1550)" in *Libri, idee, e sentimenti religiosi nel Cinquecento italiano*, edd. A. Prosperi and A. Biondi (Ferrara: Panini, 1986), pp. 143–44.

54. *Processus 341, Testamento*, fols. 953r–958v; Mariani et al., *Angela Merici*, pp. 512–20.

55. *Processus 341, Arricordi*, fols. 946v–953r; Mariani et al., *Angela Merici*, pp. 507–12.

56. *Processus 341, Testamento*, fol. 958r–v; Ledochowska, *Angela Merici*, 1:257–58; Mariani et al., *Angela Merici*, p. 512.

57. The concept of holy virginity was, of course, as old as the Church. St. Augustine commended the virgin life as best ensuring the growth and spiritual liberation of Christian women. George Tavard, *Women in the Christian Tradition* (Notre Dame: Notre Dame University Press, 1973), pp. 117–18. For the development of the ideal of the virgin as the bride of Christ, see John Bugge, *Virginitas: An Essay on the History of a Medieval Ideal* (The Hague: Nijhoff, 1975), Part I; JoAnn K. McNamara, "Sexual Equality and the Cult of Virginity in Early Christian Thought," *Feminist Studies*, 3 (1976), 145–58; Clarissa Atkinson, "Precious Balm in a Fragile Glass: The Ideology of Virginity in the Later Middle Ages, *Journal of Family History*, 8, No. 2 (Summer 1983) 131–43.

58. P. Chiminelli, *Terz'Ordine Francescano forza viva nella chiesa di ieri e di oggi* (Rome: Herder, 1952).

59. *Regola*, chap. 8, Codex 367 (Trivulziana); Mariani et al., *Angela Merici*, pp. 451–52, 501–502.

60. *Processus 341, Ricordi*, fol. 951v; Mariani et al., *Angela Merici*, p. 511.

61. *Processus 341, Testamento*, fol. 957r; Ledochowska, *Angela Merici*, 1:256–57; Mariani et al., *Angela Merici*, p. 516.

62. *Processus 341, Ricordi*, fol. 951v; Ledochowska, *Angela Merici*, 1:241–42; Mariani et al., *Angela Merici*, p. 511.

63. Mariani et al., *Angela Merici*, pp. 238–40.

64. Cartella, "Compagnia di S. Orsola," fols. 52ff.; Guerrini, "La

Compagnia di S. Orsola"; *Processus* 341, *Regola*, fols. 921v–924; Mariani et al., *Angela Merici*, pp. 231–56, 517–18.

65. Paschini, "I monasteri femminili"; Zarri, "I monasteri femminili a Bologna"; Gabriella Zarri, "I monasteri femminili benedettini nella diocesi di Bologna (secoli XII–XVII)," *Ravennatensia*, 9 (1981), 333–71.

66. Guerrini, "La Compagnia di S. Orsola," 7:132*n*1; Suzanne Wemple "S. Salvatore/S. Giulia: A Case Study in the Endowment and Patronage of a Major Female Monastery in Northern Italy," in Julius Kirshner and Suzanne F. Wemple, *Women of the Medieval World* (Oxford: Blackwell, 1985), pp. 85–102.

67. Richard Trexler, "Le célibat à la fin du moyen âge: Les religieuses de Florence," *Annales*, 17 (1972), 1338–45.

68. Milan, Archivio Arcivescovile, Sezione X, *Liber scriptarum Congregationis Virginum S. Ursulae et monasteriorum monialium Civitatis et Diocesis Brixiae scriptorum occasione visitationis apostolicae factae a sancto Carlo anno Dni 1580*, vol. 13:2; Ledochowska, *Angela Merici*, 2:50.

69. This analysis of the early membership is based on a list drawn up by Cozzano in Ledochowska, *Angela Merici*, 1:116–26; Mariani et al., *Angela Merici*, pp. 221–28.

70. Sr. Mary Monica, *Angela Merici and Her Teaching Ideal*, pp. 50–96, points out the numerous places in the *Ricordi* and *Testamento* that carry advice on pedagogy: for example, the second, fourth, seventh, and eighth *precetti* in the *Ricordi*, and the second, third, and fifth *legati* in the *Testamento*.

71. Giambattista Castiglione, *Istoria delle scuole della dottrina christiana fondate in Milano e da Milano nell'Italia ed altrove propagate* I (Milan: Malatesta, 1800); Miriam Turrini, "'Riformare il mondo a vera vita christiana': Le scuole di catechismo nell'Italia del Cinquecento," *Annali dell'Istituto storico italo-germanico in Trento*, 8 (1982), 407–89; Paul F. Grendler, *Schooling in Renaissance Italy* (Baltimore: The Johns Hopkins University Press, 1989), pp. 335–36; Paolo Guerrini, *Catechismi e scuole della dottrina cristiana della diocesi di Brescia* (Brescia: Pedrotti, 1940). L. Cajani, "Castellino da Castello," in *Dizionario biografico degli italiani*, 21 (1978), cols. 786–87; Paul Grendler, "Borromeo and the Schools of Christian Doctrine," in *San Carlo Borromeo: Catholic Reform and Ecclesia in the Second Half of the Sixteenth Century*, edd. John Headley and John Tomaro (Washington, D.C.: Folger Library, 1988), pp. 158–71, esp. 169*n*4.

72. ASDM, Sezione XIII, Vol. 61, "Regola della Compagnia santa Orsola (Per Pacifico Ponte nel mese d'ottobre, 1569)"; Francesco Landini, *Estratto*, pp. 27–32; Mariani et al., *Angela Merici*, p. 532.

73. *Processus* 341; Nazari, *Vita*, fol. 935v; Mariani et al., *Angela Merici*, p. 546.

74. It is not clear that the Church alone was responsible for support-

ing cloistering women. It has been suggested that in some parts of Europe the Church was responding to the secular needs of society and, especially, the demands of families. Roger Devos, *Vie religieuse féminine et société: L'origine sociale des Visitamdines d'Annecy aux XVII et XVIII siècles* (Annecy: Academie Salésienne, 1973), pp. 23–30.

75. Bull "Regimini universalis ecclesiae," esp. fol. 224r; Mariani et al., *Angela Merici*, pp. 547–49.

76. Ottavio Gondi, *Vita della beata Angela bresciana*, quoted in Ledochowska, *Angela Merici*, 2:11; *Processus* 341, fols. 958v–969r, Cozzano, *Epistola confortatoria*; Mariani et al., *Angela Merici*, p. 556.

77. Cozzano, *Risposta*, fol. 15r; Ledochowska, *Angela Merici*, 2:308–35; Mariani et al., *Angela Merici*, pp. 564–82.

78. Cozzano, *Risposta*, fols. 15r, 24r.

79. Ibid., fol. 19.

80. The documents reveal little about what follows except for a letter from Fr. Francesco Landini to Franceschino Visidomini in December 1566 (see note 3, above) and Cozzano's *Epistola confortatoria*, *Risposta*, and *Dichiarazione*. Mariani et al., *Angela Merici*, pp. 556–82. After the schism ended, some documents may have been deliberately destroyed; many were lost at the time of the suppression in the nineteenth century. The eighteenth-century biographers Doneda and Lombardi, who had access to the lost documents, mention the events. Ledochowska, *Angela Merici*, 2:2–66; Mariani et al., *Angela Merici*, pp. 259–307.

81. *Secondo libro generale*, fol. 53v; Ledochowska, *Angela Merici*, 2:7–8; Mariani et al., *Angela Merici*, pp. 247–48, 597–99.

82. *Processus* 341, fols. 958v–969; Ledochowska, *Angela Merici*, 2:308–335; Mariani et al., *Angela Merici*, pp. 556–64.

83. BQ, Ms D. VII. 8; Mariani et al., *Angela Merici*, pp. 564–82.

84. This may be surmised from the Confirmation added to the *Regola* in May 1545 by Gianpietro Ferretti when he became vicar-general of Brescia. Ledochowska suggests this was a political move to discourage further attempts by Lodrone to change the Rule. *Angela Merici*, 2:14–15. For the text of the confirmation see Mariani et al., *Angela Merici*, p. 489.

85. Lombardi, *Vita*, pp. 202–203.

86. The original order has disappeared, but it is referred to in a later document entitled *Ordinatione* of April 20, 1546, signed by Aurelio Duranti, archdeacon of Brescia, Donati Savallus, archpreacher of Brescia, and Lucrezia Lodrone, and included with the version of the *Regola* published in 1569 by Turlino. See Ledochowska, *Angela Merici*, 2:373; Mariani et al., *Angela Merici*, p. 490.

87. The circumstances under which the bull "Regimini universalis ecclesiae" was promulgated in 1546 are unclear and subject to interpretation. If Angela petitioned the pope for formal approval, her petition has

never been found. Cozzano refers to it, however, in his *Dichiarazione della Bolla*, *Processus* 341, fol. 973r. Evidence within the bull itself suggests that it was promulgated, not in response to Angela's petition, but in response to another. See ibid., fols. 972r, 978v of the bull; Ledochowska, *Angela Merici*, 2:355; and Mariani et al., *Angela Merici*, pp. 582–94.

88. Scholars differ on the interpretation of the documents related to this struggle: Ledochowska, *Angela Merici*, 2:7–30; 335–374; Mariani et al., *Angela Merici*, pp. 259–89.

89. See the *Ordinatione*, in Mariani et al., *Angela Merici*, p. 490.

90. *Processus* 341, *Dichiarazione della Bolla*, fol. 976r; Ledochowska, *Angela Merici*, 2:358; Mariani et al., *Angela Merici*, p. 588.

91. Ledochowska, *Angela Merici*, 2:369–70; Mariani et al., *Angela Merici*, pp. 547–49. Faino, *Miscellanea*, fols. 85r–95v; Mariani et al., *Angela Merici*, pp. 550–56. Ledochowska, *Angela Merici*, 2:16–31 and Mariani et al. disagree on the interpretation of these events, Mariani arguing that Duranti's execution of the bull exempted the vicar-general of Brescia from this threat.

92. *Ordinatione* appended to the *Regola*, 1569 (Turlino); Ledochowska, *Angela Merici*, 2:373; Mariani et al., *Angela Merici*, p. 490.

93. Cozzano, *Dichiarazione della Bolla*, *Processus* 341, fols. 973r–978r; Ledochowska, *Angela Merici*, 2:349–68; Mariani et al., *Angela Merici*, pp. 585–89.

94. *Processus* 341, Cozzano, *Dichiarazione della Bolla*, fols. 973r–978r; Mariani et al., *Angela Merici*, pp. 585–89.

95. Mariani et al., *Angela Merici*, p. 284.

96. Mariani et al., *Angela Merici*, pp. 291–305, have pieced together the only complete, critical account of these troubled years from a variety of sources, some recently uncovered.

97. Ledochowska, *Angela Merici*, 2:31–66; Mariani et al., *Angela Merici*, pp. 303–25.

98. *Dizionario biografico degli italiani*, vol. 15 (Rome: Istituto della Enciclopedia Italiana, 1972), cols. 736–738. Cabrini was born in Salò between 1510 and 1515, and he and Angela may have known each other, as Ledochowska, *Angela Merici*, 2:34, suggests.

99. Christopher Cairns, *Domenico Bollani, Bishop of Brescia: Devotion to Church and State in the Republic of Venice in the Sixteenth Century* (Nieuwkoop: De Graaf, 1976), pp. 149ff.; Daniele Montanari, *Disciplinamento in terra veneta: La diocesi di Brescia nella seconda metà del XVI secola*, Annali dell'Istituto storico italo-germanico 8 (Bologna: Mulino, 1987).

100. *Estratto*, in Mariani et al., *Angela Merici*, pp. 531–32.

101. *Regola* (Turlino); Ledochowska, *Angela Merici*, 2:265–75; Mariani et al., *Angela Merici*, pp. 459–87.

102. BQ, Ms.E.E.1.m.2, *Ordine et ceremonie*; for a précis, see Mariani et al., *Angela Merici*, pp. 311–17. These ceremonies were evidently based on medieval ceremonies for the consecration of virgins; see René Metz, *La Consécration des vierges dans l'Église romaine* (Paris: Presses Universitaires de France, 1954).

103. Faino, *Miscellanea*, fol. 16; passages quoted in Mariani et al., *Angela Merici*, p. 316. Luzzari, *Vite*, fols. 73–75, said that Cabrini made the decision because the virgins requested it.

104. Mariani et al., *Angela Merici*, pp. 308–11, refers to the pertinent notarial records.

105. *Secondo libro generale*, fols. 254r–256v; Ledochowska, *Angela Merici*, 2:20–47; Mariani et al., *Angela Merici*, pp. 320–24.

106. Ledochowska, 2:40–47; Mariani et al., *Angela Merici*, pp. 319–21.

107. Ledochowska, *Angela Merici*, 2:118–19, argues for a "drift" toward community.

108. Gualberto Vigotti, *S. Carlo Borromeo e la Compagnia di S. Orsola, nel centenario della ricostituzione in Milano della Compagnia di S. Orsola Figlie di S. Angela Merici (1872–1972)* (Milan: Ancora, 1972); Ledochowska, *Angela Merici*, 2:63–91; Mariani et al., *Angela Merici*, pp. 377–81, 417–20.

109. ASDM, Sezione XII, vol. 48, *Regola della Compagnia di Santa Orsola . . .* , fol. 6v; Mariani et al., *Angela Merici*, p. 316.

110. Borromeo, sermon to the people of Bellinzona, quoted in Ledochowska, *Angela Merici*, 2:388 from *S. Caroli Borromei Homiliae* III, ed. Joseph Anthony Saxx (Milan, 1747), p. 130.

111. Ledochowska, *Angela Merici*, 2:73–91.

112. Ibid., 85–86.

113. *Acta ecclesiae Mediolanensis ab eius initiis usque ad nostram aetatem*, 4 vols. (1892) (Acts of the Fourth Provincial Council, Milan, 1576), 2:493; Ledochowska, *Angela Merici*, 2:87, 387–88.

114. ASDM, Sezione XII, vol. 146; Ledochowska, *Angela Merici*, 2:102–20; Mariani et al., *Angela Merici*, pp. 420–21.

115. Teresa Ledochowska, "La regola del 1582 puó esprimere in maniera assoluta lo spirito originale della Compagnia di Sant'Orsola e il pensiero di Sant'Angela?" *Brixia Sacra*, 6, Nos. 5–6 (1971). Mariani et al., *Angela Merici*, pp. 377–81.

116. Ledochowska, "La Regola," 13.

117. Mariani et al., *Angela Merici*, p. 327.

118. Paolo Guerrini, "La visita pastorale di S. Carlo nella Diocesi di Brescia," *Brixia Sacra*, 1 (1910), 281; Ledochowska, *Angela Merici*, 2:95–102.

119. Lombardi, *Vita*, 203; Guerrini, "La Compagnia di S. Orsola," 7:163.

120. Ledochowska, *Angela Merici*, 2:143–52. For a list and summary of the various Rules, see Mariani et al., *Angela Merici*, pp. 369–428.

121. Ledochowska, *Angela Merici*, 2:147–53.

122. Ibid., 2:149; Mariani et al., *Angela Merici*, pp. 397–428.

123. Raymond Creytens, "La riforma dei monasteri femminili dopo i Decreti Tridentini," in *Il Concilio di Trento e la riforma tridentina: Atti del Convegno storico internazionale, Trent, September 2–6, 1963* (Rome: Herder, 1965), 1:46–49; and also his "La giurisprudenza della Sacra Congregazione del Concilio nella questione della clausura delle monache (1565–1576)," *Apollinaris*, 37 (1964), 251–81; Ledochowska, *Angela Merici*, 2:185–202; Liebowitz, "Virgins in the Service of Christ," 139–40, 143.

124. Ledochowska, *Angela Merici*, 2:102–43.

125. Ibid., 2:232–58; Liebowitz, "Virgins in the Service of Christ," 143.

126. Ledochowska, *Angela Merici*, 2:153–60.

127. Ibid., 89, 146.

128. Marie de Chantal Gueudré, o.s.u., *Histoire de L'Ordre des Ursulines en France*, 2 vols. (Paris: Éditions de St. Paul, 1957–1960). The history of the Ursulines in France parallels the history of other religious orders for women that tried to combine active and the contemplative life. For a new interpretation see Elizabeth Rapley, *The Dévotes: Women and the Church in Seventeenth-Century France* (Montreal: McGill-Queens University Press, 1990).

St. Ignatius de Loyola in 1556 by Jacopino del Conte. Jesuit Generalate, Rome.

5

The Society of Jesus

John W. O'Malley, S.J.

OF ALL THE RELIGIOUS ORDERS founded in the sixteenth century, none is more familiar to historians or has a fuller bibliography than the Society of Jesus.[1] Along with the Council of Trent, the Society is often presented as among the most powerful forces shaping Catholicism in the early modern period. Although recent studies have made us aware of how much richer and more complicated that phenomenon was, the Society still emerges with a special prominence among religious orders of the period.

Because of that prominence and because of the turbulent religious situation at the time the Society was officially approved by Pope Paul III on September 27, 1540, its historiography has been conditioned by both the polemics and the apologetics characteristic for centuries of writings concerning the religious issues of the period. Often taken as emblematic of all that was best or worst in Early Modern Catholicism, the Society emerged with an image that is ambivalent and at the same time misleadingly clear. Its historiography reflects this image, so that even today it is difficult to dispel misconceptions concerning its original inspiration, its goals, and its "way of proceeding," a favorite expression of the early Jesuits.[2]

IGNATIUS DE LOYOLA AND THE ORIGINS OF THE SOCIETY

Although, strictly speaking, the bull of approval of the Society was petitioned from Paul III by ten companions gathered in Rome, the unquestioned leader among them was the Basque nobleman Ignatius de Loyola, quite correctly regarded as the founder of the Society. Shortly after the papal approval, he was elected superior by his companions and continued to govern the Society until his death on July 31, 1556. Like all such founders, Ignatius had a determinative influence on the character of the Society, which was essentially the product of his vision of Christian spirituality and ministry.

Ignatius's influence was perhaps deeper and more abiding than that of some other founders, however, because of the literary heritage he left behind which was a touchstone to which Jesuits consistently recurred throughout the long history of the order.[3] While general of the order, he produced an immense correspondence with members of the Society and with others somehow associated with it. That correspondence today constitutes the largest published body of such literature from any sixteenth-century individual.[4] Important though it was for forming the nascent Society, it was not available in print until early in the present century. Until that time even Jesuits were familiar with only the minuscule portion of it that had been printed and circulated, principally within the Society.

Of more pervasive influence were three other documents that came exclusively or principally from him. The first and most important of these was the *Spiritual Exercises*, whose essential elements he had well in hand as early as 1525 and whose final version was published in 1548. That book not only set down the essential elements of the spirituality that would animate the Society, "the systematised, de-mysticized quintessence of the process of Ignatius's own conversion and purposeful change of life,"[5] but also established the basic goals and design for Jesuit ministry. It in effect also created a new instrument of ministry, the so-called retreat, which the Jesuits were the first to develop in an orderly way. No other religious order then or later had from its founder such a classic document for guidance.

While general, Ignatius was responsible for authoring the *Constitutions* of the Society, substantially completed by 1552, approved by the First General Congregation in 1558, and printed and circulated in 1560.[6] Although much aided in this task by others, especially his talented secretary, Juan de Polanco, he was clearly the inspiration for and final arbiter of their fundamental contents. The description of the *Constitutions* as an institutional embodiment of the religious vision of the *Exercises* is perhaps somewhat simplistic but not far off the mark. In any case, the *Constitutions* were notably different from the foundational documents of earlier orders in the psychological undergirding of their organization, in their attention to motivation and general principles, and in their insistence on flexible implementation of their provisions.

The third document that, at least indirectly, impressed Ignatius's vision on the Society in a special way was the relatively brief account he dictated in 1553–1555 of his life up to the time of the approval of the Society.[7] Although the text itself did not circulate widely in the Society, the basic facts recorded in it were employed by his contemporaries as a profile of the Jesuit vocation. Jerónimo Nadal, perhaps the most reliable interpreter of the Society in the first generation, visited on an official basis practically every Jesuit community in Western Europe during the twenty-year period beginning in 1552, explaining the *Constitutions* and telling the story about Ignatius's conversion, religious experiences, and ministry. Nadal taught that every Jesuit participated in an almost mystical way in what he called "the grace of the founder."[8]

Even aside from the paradigmatic role the early Jesuits attributed to Ignatius's story, there can be no doubt that the idea of the Society was generated in it. The story is well known, but too important to be bypassed here altogether.[9] Born in the castle of Loyola in northern Spain probably in 1491, Ignatius had the chivalric education of his class. His life gave no indication of any special religious sensibilities until he suffered severe wounds in the battle of Pamplona in 1521. During his long convalescence at Loyola he underwent a profound conversion occasioned by his reading Ludolph of Saxony's *Life of Christ* (ca. 1360) and Jacopo da Voragine's lives of the saints entitled *The Golden Legend* (ca. 1260). The notice he took of the peace and sense of spiritual satisfaction or "consolation" that these works engendered in him compared with the disquiet experienced when he dreamed of returning to his former ways would be the first basis of his later teaching of "discernment of spirits," a key element in his spirituality, explained in its fullest form in the *Exercises*.

He then spent a year in prayer and retirement at Manresa, outside Barcelona, 1522–1523, during which he had a number of mystical illuminations. The essence of the *Exercises* was conceived at this time. After a pilgrimage to the Holy Land, he returned to Spain in 1524 fully determined to spend his life in ministry or, to use his expression, in "helping souls." To do this more effectively, he decided he needed a better education. By 1526 he was ready to enter the University of Alcalá, where he remained for a year. While there he engaged in "helping souls" principally by teaching catechism and by guiding individuals through the *Exercises*. At Alcalá he had his first, but by no means last, brush with the Inquisition, and spent some forty-two days in jail awaiting sentence. He was acquitted, but the experience further convinced him of his need for study, which soon led him to the University of Paris, where he remained for seven years (1528–1535).

In Paris he gathered around him the other students at the University who would soon form the nucleus of the new order. Under his direction they all spent at different times about a month in prayer according to the *Exercises*, a program that would later be prescribed for all recruits to the order. The six included Francisco Xavier, another Basque nobleman who would eventually found the Society in India and Japan, and Diego Laínez, who would succeed Ignatius as superior general of the Society.

On August 15, 1534, these seven individuals, of whom only one was a priest, bound themselves to go on pilgrimage to Jerusalem in order to engage in ministry there, with the intention of possibly remaining for the rest of their lives. They further stipulated, however, that, if they were unable to obtain passage to the Holy Land within a year after their arrival in Venice, they would present themselves to the pope, so that he might send them on ministry wherever he thought best. Although the friends had not yet made any formal decision to bond themselves to one another in some lasting and more formal way, historians have correctly seen in this event the first foundations of what would become the Society of Jesus. Within a short while three other students joined the band with the same resolve to go to the Holy Land.

By early 1537 these ten graduates of the University of Paris had all arrived in Venice, where those who were not yet priests, including Ignatius, were soon ordained. While they tried to secure passage abroad, they spent their days in the area of the Veneto preaching, hearing confessions, teaching catechism, and caring for the sick in hospitals. Often asked to identify themselves, they decided they would tell inquirers they were members of the "company of Jesus," the *Compagnia di Gesù*. Schooled in the *Exercises*, they chose the name Jesus because they had no other superior but him.[10] *Compagnia*, widely used in Italy at the time to designate religious confraternities or brotherhoods, probably meant little more than that to them. (*Societas* was its Latin equivalent.) They were certainly not ready to say they were members of a religious order or on their way to becoming such.

Finally frustrated in their attempts to go to the Holy Land, they were all in Rome by early 1538 in accordance with their vow. Through the intervention of highly placed friends, they received a favorable welcome from Paul III. They continued their usual ministries, which included guiding individuals through the *Exercises*. Among these individuals, probably guided by Ignatius himself, was Cardinal Gasparo Contarini, leader of the Italian *spirituali* and the person soon responsible for persuading Paul III to approve the new *Compagnia*.

The ten companions in fact now had to face the question of their future. In the spring of 1539 they engaged in a long series of prayerful discussions on that issue, which eventuated in the decision to found a new order. To that end they drew up for papal approbation a short document outlining its nature and scope— called by them their *Formula vivendi*. With some minor changes this *Formula* constituted the substance of Paul III's bull *Regimini militantis ecclesiae* of September 27, 1540, the basic charter of the Society. The *Formula* was revised ten years later by Julius III.[11]

The bull of Paul III had not been easy to obtain. Sentiment ran strong at the papal court that there were already too many religious orders. Moreover, there were objections especially to two particulars of the *Formula*. First, the members of the Society did not want to be bound to celebrate the Liturgical Hours in common or in choir because it would interfere with their commitment to ministry. In the sixteenth century such celebration was considered the very essence of a religious order. Second, the members wanted to be bound by a special vow to God to travel anywhere in the world to do ministry when so ordered by the pope. It was difficult for members of the court to understand what this vow was meant to accomplish.

Both these provisions were in fact condensed symbols of the ultimate model upon which the first Jesuits wanted to fashion themselves. Certainly by 1540 under Ignatius's leadership they had begun consistently to think of themselves as imitating the ministry and itinerant style of life of Jesus and His disciples as presented in the synoptic gospels and of the evangelizing Paul in the Acts of the Apostles. Jesus' sending of the Twelve in the tenth

chapter of Matthew was especially meaningful to them as modeling the essence of their vocation: (1) to be sent, (2) in order to
preach the gospel (3) and to heal the sick, (4) without asking
for recompense.

The foreswearing of choir indicated the primacy they attached
to ministry, and the special vow indicated the worldwide scope
of those to whom they hoped to minister—as the *Formula* stated,
"whether among the Turks or any other infidels, even those who
live in the region called the Indies, or among any heretics whatever, or schismatics, or any of the faithful." It was the pope, they
believed, who would be best informed as to where in the world
they could most effectively be sent. In the *Constitutions*, however,
this quality was also attributed to the general of the Society, and
in a way that indicated that the purpose of the vow pertained to
him as much as to the pope.[12] In any case, the vow had to do
with ministry and "being sent," not with "loyalty to the pope,"
as it so often came to be described.[13]

After the companions had secured papal approval of the *Formula*, they proceeded about six months later to elect Ignatius as
their superior over his objections. For the remaining fifteen years
of his life, Ignatius directed the new order, dividing it as it expanded into smaller administrative units called provinces. There
were twelve of these by the time he died, including India and
Brazil, for about a thousand members. By the death in 1565 of his
successor, the membership had increased to over three thousand.

Ignatius and the early Jesuits ministered to women from all
ranks of society and especially through confraternities enlisted
them to assist them in many of their projects. Ignatius carried on
an extensive correspondence with women.[14] Nonetheless, he early
excluded the possibility of a female branch of the Society, possibly
because he could imagine it only according to the more contemplative models of the existing Second Orders that, among other
things, would require Jesuits as regular chaplains.

During his years as general, Ignatius continued to be admired
by those who knew him best for his gifts of prayer combined
with an ability "to find God in all things," which he in turn
constantly encouraged members of the Society to do.[15] Especially
important for the development of the Society, however, was his
ability to recognize others whose talents complemented his own
and to delegate to them appropriate tasks. Outstanding among

these were Nadal and Polanco, who continued to serve the two subsequent generals in much the same way. By the time Ignatius died, the Society had been equipped with its essential structure and ethos.

SPIRITUALITY AND MINISTRIES

In the *Exercises* the Jesuits possessed a general design for the spiritual journey, which they often characterized in classic terms as movement from purgation to enlightenment to union. This was the underlying design for what they hoped would happen in their own lives and what they hoped to foster in others to whom they ministered. Crucial to the *Exercises* was the conversion to deeper interiority in the First Week, symbolized and codified in a moral inventory of one's past life through a general confession.

The following three Weeks envisaged a further conversion to closer discipleship to Jesus in poverty and service to others. What was distinctive of the Jesuits was, of course, not the design itself but the clarity with which it was laid out and the agreed-upon presumption that to some degree it was meant for everybody. Although the Jesuits realized that the full course of the *Exercises* was not suitable for all, they tried to inculcate its basic lessons at every available opportunity and to insist that the Christian life was not static or a mechanical shuttle back and forth between habitual sins and sacramental absolution.

Besides the many teachings on the Christian life that were part of the common heritage of the late Middle Ages, the *Exercises* gave special emphasis to two that would become characteristic of the Jesuits. The first was the conviction that God spoke directly to every human being and that the authenticity of this word could be "discerned" within one's soul and then be taken as the basis for decision. "Consolation" of heart was the sign of the word and a test for the rightness of the decision. They hoped to live in a more or less abiding state of consolation and to help others do the same. It was this aspect of their teaching that most often brought them into conflict with Church authorities, who feared they were propagating the errors of the *Alumbrados* or other heretics.

The second teaching relates to the final meditation of the *Exer-*

cises, "The Contemplation to Obtain Love." In it the Christian is taught to contemplate the presence and action of God in all creatures and in all circumstances of life. The appropriate response is to commit oneself utterly to God's love and care, expressed in the prayer included in the meditation. Implicitly contained in it is a positive appreciation of "the world" as the locus in which one can "find God." Although the Jesuits subscribed to the usefulness or necessity of ascetical practices, insisting that they be appropriately moderated, they with their teaching on "finding God in all things" departed in a significant way from the tradition of "contempt of the world." With the Jesuits themselves, for instance, Nadal insisted again and again that "the world is our home."[16]

Besides being undergirded especially by these two features, the piety the Jesuits wanted to inculcate in themselves and others employed a number of particular practices. After definitive turning from one's habitual ways, it was sustained by daily meditation or contemplation, by daily examination of conscience, by daily assistance at Mass, by the hearing of sermons and the reading of Scripture or other devout literature. It was expressed by devoting as much of one's time and resources to the traditional spiritual and corporal works of mercy as appropriate to one's situation, generally through membership in a confraternity.

Special to the Jesuits was their insistence on more frequent reception of the sacraments of Penance and the Eucharist than was generally common at the time. By "more frequent" they meant monthly or weekly, or even slightly more often. They were motivated in this regard by their belief that this had been the practice of the early Church and, further, that these sacraments would be powerful in sustaining one on the journey now undertaken. For what they believed about the Eucharist in this latter regard, they were seemingly much influenced by the Fourth Book of the *Imitation of Christ*, a work whose reading they everywhere encouraged.

The ministries the Jesuits undertook were aimed at instilling the style of piety just described. In the beginning their ministries were to a great extent those developed by the mendicant orders in the Middle Ages, imbued, however, with the principles of their own spirituality and, especially after the founding of the schools, with a somewhat different culture. From the moment of entrance into the Society, every member was expected to engage in ministry, and in fact much of the ministry, except the direct administration of the sacraments, was done by Jesuits who were not ordained.

Moved by the conviction that they were called to "preach the gospel," the Jesuits gave special emphasis to various "ministries of the word." They were assiduous preachers, who gradually moved out of medieval modes of presentation into those favored by the humanist movement. Although they often preached in churches, occasionally several times a day, they also preached in the public squares, hospitals, shipyards, prisons, and similar places. They were among the first, or perhaps the first, to develop so-called "popular missions" of preaching and catechesis to hamlets and small villages in the countryside, later to the cities.[17]

Of special interest are the so-called "sacred lectures" that they delivered in conjunction with their preaching. Although such lectures were delivered by the mendicants before the Jesuits took them up, they have not been systematically studied and seem not to have been common.[18] Wherever the Jesuits preached over a period of time, they also instituted a series of lectures on a given topic, usually a book of Scripture. The series would run for two or three months, with lectures in the afternoon several days a week. Intended for a lay audience, these lectures have to be considered one of the first sustained experiments in "adult education."

Inspired by the early example of Ignatius, the Jesuits gave themselves wholeheartedly to the teaching of catechism to the young, at first using texts composed by others and then constructing their own. Of these latter, the catechisms by Peter Canisius that began to appear in 1554 were especially important, although they never became the exclusive texts. The Jesuits almost immediately discovered the exponential effects of having boys and girls teach catechism to each other, whether in Europe or in Brazil and India. They soon adopted almost everywhere the Spanish custom of setting the lesson to popular tunes, to the delight, it seems, of both the children and their parents. In their catechizing they wanted to teach *pietas* or *Christianitas*, not abstract verities, thus resisting to some extent the more cerebral turn such instruction began to take in the sixteenth century.[19]

Although the Jesuits were consistently encouraged by their superiors to guide individuals through the *Exercises*, they were often hindered by not being able to secure the physical situations of seclusion in which such a retreat could best be made. They some-

times set aside rooms in their own communities for this purpose
and later began to construct separate houses or parts of houses
for it. Women had to find other lodging, however, and received
their guidance from the Jesuits by visiting them in their churches.
Not all Jesuits were deemed suitable for this new and delicate
ministry, and those that were generally received their training
through an informal apprenticeship under someone more experienced, beginning with Ignatius himself.[20] The development of
such retreats helped move the art of spiritual direction into a new
phase by the early decades of the seventeenth century.

Since the Jesuits were not allowed by the *Constitutions* to accept
appointment as bishops or even as pastors of parishes, their sacramental ministry was for all practical purposes restricted to the
hearing of confessions and the administration of the Eucharist. As
we have seen, however, they attached great importance to these
two sacraments. They early began to give special care to the training of their members in "cases of conscience," i.e., in casuistry.
By 1564 they had instituted a course on this subject at the Roman
College, an innovation in the theological curriculum destined to
become normative within Roman Catholicism.[21] Among the first
books published by a Jesuit was Polanco's *Breve directorium ad
confessarii et confitentis munus rite obeundum* (1554), commissioned
by Ignatius himself for members of the Society but eventually
used by other priests in its many editions.

In the Jesuits' catechesis they placed much emphasis on the
traditional spiritual and corporal works of mercy, which they
regarded as among their most important ministries. They spent
a great deal of time in hospitals nursing the sick and in prisons
trying to better the condition of the inmates and especially win
release for debtors. They encouraged the laity with whom they
worked to form confraternities that would do the same and establish this kind of relief on a more stable basis.[22]

Though much of what they did in this regard was traditional,
in some instances they were innovators ahead of their times. The
best examples are the *Casa santa Marta* and the *Conservatorio delle
Vergini Miserabili* established in Rome by Ignatius in 1543 and
1546, respectively. The *Casa* was a kind of half-way house for
prostitutes who wanted to reform their lives. For the women who
entered the *Casa*, the Jesuits begged dowries so that they might
freely decide either to marry or to enter a convent. The Jesuits

also took it upon themselves to seek suitable husbands for those who wished to marry. The *Conservatorio* was an institution where prostitutes might place their daughters to save them from what was, even then, a family system. Both these institutions were soon committed to a confraternity for their governance and maintenance, and both found imitation in other cities where Jesuits ministered.

As the above examples suggest, the Jesuits' collaboration with what we might call the confraternity system was almost a hallmark of their ministry, little recognized by most historians. Better acknowledged has been the importance of the "Marian Congregation" (or Sodality of Our Lady), a confraternity for students founded in 1563 at the Roman College by the Belgian Jesuit Jan Leunis that was soon imitated in all the Jesuit schools throughout the world and then extended to the adult laity. Members of the Congregation were initiated into the Jesuit pattern of piety, which always included undertaking one or more of the works of mercy. These Congregations played a pivotal role within Catholicism in the seventeenth and eighteenth centuries and, in somewhat different form, into the twentieth.[23]

A decisive turn in their ministries occurred in 1548 when the Jesuits opened what was in effect their first school in Messina.[24] This possibility had not been foreseen by them up to that time and, in fact, seemed contrary to the itinerant terms in which they had originally conceived their ministry. Under the leadership of Nadal, the school at Messina with its basically humanistic program was an immediate success, and other Jesuits, including Ignatius, immediately saw the potential of this form of ministry which no other order had ever formally undertaken.

The very next year they opened a similar school in Palermo, and others followed in short order. By the time Ignatius died, the Jesuits were operating thirty-three schools in Europe, including the soon prestigious Roman College (later the Gregorian University), and plans were under way for opening more. By the turn of the century, they had around the globe some 240, and their educational program had been codified in their *Ratio studiorum* (1599). Although the vast majority of Jesuit schools were institutions of secondary education, some were full-fledged universities.

The significance of this development was revealed as early as 1560 in a circular letter from Polanco to all the superiors in the

Society in which he divided the Jesuits' instruments "for helping our neighbors" into two categories: (1) the schools, (2) everything else.[25] How did they come to attach such importance to the former category?

Two reasons are fundamental. First, they seem almost instinctively to have seen how compatible with their own goals was the *pietas* that humanistic educators envisaged as the goal of their educational program. Like so many of their contemporaries, they had long been convinced of the relationship between at least some degree of instruction and a properly Christian life, and the humanists provided them with a full articulation of what this might mean for youth.

Second, they also saw that the schools provided them with an excellent base for their other ministries. The distinction Polanco made in 1560 was not, therefore, as clear-cut as it sounded. Through the schools the Jesuits had immediate access to the parents of their students and an insertion into the public life of the city. Although the other ministries suffered some eclipse because of the importance attached to the schools, they continued to be diligently cultivated and in some ways were thereby enhanced.

Two other reasons for undertaking schooling, not so immediately or obviously religious, should not be underestimated. They saw the schools as part of their contribution to "the common good" of society at large. In a letter to Antonio Araoz in 1551 Polanco gave fifteen reasons why the Society was undertaking schools, many of which can be reduced to that concern. One of them, for instance, was so that parents could "satisfy their consciences in the obligation to educate their sons."[26] It perhaps needs be noted that the problem of heresy and heterodoxy is not mentioned among the fifteen.

Besides this social mission, the Jesuits also began to conceive of themselves as having through the schools a cultural mission. They introduced into Italy and other parts of the world where it was not known the pedagogy and principles of the so-called *modus parisiensis*, which among other things divided students into classes in which they progressed from elementary and foundational subjects to more advanced. As Polanco wrote to the superiors of the Society in 1553 about the Collegio Romano: "It will be a marvelous help to Italy, in whose schools two things are notably lacking—a graduated program of instruction and appropriate exercises to ensure assimilation of the materials. . . . Perhaps other schools will improve, inspired by our example."[27]

Although the impact the Jesuit schools had on Catholicism from this point forward has yet to be studied in a comprehensive way,[28] its importance is univerally acknowledged. Less clearly recognized is the impact the schools had on the Society itself. The schools conditioned the more evangelical character of the original inspiration and put limits on the "apostolic" mobility the Jesuits continued to prize—Ignatius soon learned that for many reasons teachers could not easily be moved to other assignments. They changed in practice the poverty at first envisaged, as most members of the Society began to reside in the endowed institutions that were the schools.

The schools also influenced the social classes to whom the Jesuits ministered. Striking in Jesuit documentation is the insistence that, along with an awareness that leaders in society had impact on others, Jesuit ministries were meant for all classes, for the rich and the poor, with a preference shown for those who were in greater spiritual, moral, or physical need. The Jesuits applied this same norm to their schools and would not undertake new ones unless they were endowed, thus ensuring the poor of equal access with the rich. In fact, however, the style of education they offered did not have as wide an appeal as they had hoped for the lower classes, and Ignatius's decision not to run primary schools tended unwittingly to preclude them from entering Jesuit secondary institutions. Historians have sometimes exaggerated the extent of this shift in clientele, but there is no denying that it occurred.

Perhaps most important, the schools gave the Society a somewhat unique relationship to culture. The schools committed the Society to a program of education for its own members that would qualify them to be teachers. The original ten companions were all university graduates and fully intended that future members of the *Compagnia* have a comparable education. But the schools notably heightened this persuasion and helped give it a systemic articulation that at the time was peculiar to the Jesuits.

More specially, Jesuits were called upon to teach "the humanities," not simply traditionally ecclesiastical disciplines like philosophy, theology, and canon law.[29] Some of their first books, for instance, were textbooks for their classrooms related to the pagan classics. This promoted an engagement with secular cul-

ture, modest enough at first, that would eventually become one
of the Jesuits' trademarks. It would lead them into drama, even
ballet.[30] Their teaching of "philosophy" made them scientists and
mathematicians.[31] When Nadal told the first two generations of
Jesuits that the world was their home, he perhaps did not realize
the full import of his statement.

REFORMATION AND COUNTER REFORMATION

The issues raised by the Reformation were within the purview of
Ignatius and his companions even at Paris but certainly not its
center. The destination they chose for themselves was Jerusalem,
not Wittenberg. About this time, it is true, Ignatius composed
his "Rules for Thinking with the Church," a kind of appendix
to the *Exercises*. The "Rules" looked as much, or more, to the
Alumbrados, and possibly the Erasmians, however, as to the Protestants. Once the companions arrived in Italy, some of them took
an aggressive attitude toward the infiltration of heresy there, but
this was one concern among many.

The familiar statement that the Society was founded to do battle
with Protestantism, therefore, badly distorts the truth. Nonetheless, while like many of their Catholic colleagues the Jesuits recognized the validity of much of the criticism "the Lutherans" leveled
against abuses in the Church, they had little sympathy with their
doctrine or disruptive tactics, as they understood them.[32]

After about 1550 the Reformation, especially in the Empire,
began to assume a larger role in their thinking. This was due to
a number of reasons. Among them was the ever more desperate
plight of the champion of the Catholic cause, Emperor Charles
V, and his final defeat, codified in the provisions of the Peace of
Augsburg, 1555. More pertinent, however, were developments
internal to the Society. Reports about the "collapsed" situation of
the Catholic Church had been received by Jesuit headquarters in
Rome since the early 1540s, but in 1549, after a brief sojourn in
Italy, Peter Canisius returned to the Empire, soon to head the
first Jesuit province there.

Canisius became the great catalyst for the Society's extensive
ministries in the Empire until his death in 1597.[33] Almost by defi-
nition those ministries dealt either directly or indirectly with Lu-

theranism. His insistent demands on Rome for reinforcements in manpower signaled a new alert. The establishment of the German College in Rome in 1552 and shortly thereafter of a chair of "controversialist theology" at the Roman College in view of the needs of the students at the Germanicum indicates that the Jesuits were not taking the situation lightly.[34] Moreover, in 1555 Nadal made his first trip to the Empire, where he was utterly appalled by what he saw. He would thereafter be an especially strong voice for assigning high priority to the German situation. Like many other Catholics, after about 1560 the Jesuits became more aware of Calvin and the dangers his followers posed to the Catholic Church in France.[35]

Nadal seems to have been the first person to propose in bold fashion—and with hindsight—the interpretation of the origins of the Society that linked it with the Protestant threat. By about 1563 he pitted Ignatius, the new David, against Luther, the Goliath.[36] Some Jesuits, like the young Antonio Possevino, took the battle against Protestantism as their specialty.[37]

There can be no doubt that the Society of Jesus would have been a much different organization and projected a much different image if it had not had to contend with Protestantism almost from its inception. Nonetheless, even in places where the struggle against the Reformation was its most acute, the Jesuits worked to a large extent with Catholics. The Society never defined itself primarily in terms of that struggle, as the *Constitutions* show. In many parts of the world, the direct impact of the Reformation on Jesuit ministries ranged from minimal to non-existent.

The indirect impact is another question altogether, and much more complex. The Reformation was the principal cause for a shift in mood, outlook, discipline, and doctrinal emphasis within the Catholic Church that would eventually influence almost every aspect of its life. Although under way earlier, the shift became clearly apparent by the middle of the century. It was symbolized by a more concerted rally around the slogan "reform of the Church," an historical phenomenon historians have categorized as the Counter Reformation or Catholic Reform.[38]

Sometimes wittingly, sometimes unwittingly, the Jesuits were profoundly influenced by these changes, which they often promoted or supported. Contrary to what is often said, however, they never arrogated to themselves "the reform of the Church" in those terms, and they continued to speak of their task simply as "helping souls." Although they undoubtedly had great impact on the "reform" of Catholicism, their origins are best understood as representing an independent burst of religious enthusiasm similar to the Franciscan movement in the thirteenth century.[39]

Several leading Jesuits, particularly Laínez and Alfonso Salmerón, played important roles in the Council of Trent.[40] The Jesuits as a body supported the Council and its general aims. Except for those few immediately involved, they nonetheless manifest a significant detachment about its specific determinations and rarely make reference to it in their voluminous correspondence.

The reasons for this attitude are doubtless many, but two seem especially pertinent. The doctrinal decrees of the Council, directed against the reformers, would seem to have little relevance to them, convinced as they were of their own orthodoxy. The disciplinary decrees perhaps had even less, since they concerned almost exclusively the episcopacy and pastorates, offices the Jesuits had foresworn. Except for confession, most of the ministries the Jesuits considered peculiarly their own received scant attention in the Council. Worrisome to them, in fact, was the tendency of the Council to emphasize episcopal authority over all ministries and to curtail the "privileges" of the religious orders in that regard.

In other words, the Jesuits as a body had somewhat different ways of meeting the generically common goals they shared with the Council and with others like Contarini and many churchmen who took the "reform of the Church" as their explicit task. The Council and the Society, like most other religious orders, were independent, occasionally intersecting, trajectories within Early Modern Catholicism.

DISTINCTIVENESS, ORGANIZATION, DEPLOYMENT

The Society bore many resemblances to the mendicant orders of the Middle Ages, but also differed from them in a number of particulars. Unlike them, the Jesuits did not recite or chant the Liturgical Hours in common, and the fully professed members pronounced a special vow about doing ministry everywhere, as we have seen. They had no obligatory fasts or penances. They retained both their baptismal and their family names. They kept no jails for recalcitrant members. They were forbidden to accept bishoprics or other prelacies. Those who were priests pronounced their final profession or its equivalent in the order several years after ordination.

They did not wear a religious habit. This "freedom in dress," as Nadal called it, was to allow Jesuits to work with all sorts of people, especially those who found religious habits repugnant. [41] Although this departure from custom provided that in general they would dress like respected secular priests in whatever region they found themselves, they soon began for the most part to follow the custom of the *casa professa* in Rome of wearing black cassocks unbuttoned in front, held together by a sash-like cincture. [42] In some parts of the world they thus became known as "the blackrobes." Their "freedom" in this regard, however, would at the turn of the century allow somebody like Matteo Ricci in China to don the traditional dress of the Mandarins. Jesuits elsewhere adapted accordingly.

They departed from the capitular style of government of the mendicants, according to which local chapters elected superiors and had greater authority in setting policy. Even General Congregations (the equivalent of general chapters) met on only an occasional basis, usually to elect the general. The General Congregations determined policy, however, of which the general was the executor. The general held office for life and appointed all other major superiors, who rejoined the ranks after their terms of office were completed. In practice and theory, the Jesuit general wielded more authority than the mendicant superiors.

Among the reasons given for this change was not to encumber the Jesuits' ministry with time-consuming chapters. More basic, however, was the desire to make it easier for superiors to move subjects as new pastoral needs arose, within the framework of the "apostolic" model of "being sent" or "missioned." Although Ignatius's temperament and background cannot be altogether dismissed as factors in what was surely a more authoritarian form of government, the other reasons were determinative.

Beginning about 1547 Ignatius put greater emphasis on the virtue of obedience in the Society than before, a development occasioned by some disturbing events in the province of Portugal, then under the unsteady leadership of one of his original companions from Paris, Simón Rodrigues. He came to see members of the Society distinguished from others in their prompt and full obedience, never however modeling it on the military pattern often attributed to it. Quite capable of issuing sharp orders, in his correspondence he more generally offered merely counsel and encouragement, insisting that those on the scene were better placed to make decisions about particulars than he.

In recruits to the Society, in fact, Ignatius and his colleagues looked for a certain flexibility in temperament that would make them capable of appropriate accommodation of general principles to local situations. Jesuit obedience was, in any case, conditioned by legislation that insisted on broad consultation by all superiors, including the general, and by a policy of frank communication between superiors and subjects that took full account of the needs, inclinations, and talents of the latter.

Ignatius was from the beginning enamored of Francis of Assisi's ideal of poverty, but realized that it would have to be much adapted to be practicable in the Society. In the end he came to insist especially on two things: first, that the Jesuits retain no property or money of their own but live exclusively off what the community held in common; second, that under no circumstances they accept direct remuneration for any of their ministries. This prohibition included even stipends for Masses. Regarding their diet, clothing, amount of sleep, and similar matters, however, Jesuits were simply to avoid extremes, and in case of doubt consult local doctors.[43]

The combined impact of all the aforementioned features, as well as others, helped convince the Jesuits that they were significantly different from previous religious orders, but they found that difference difficult to articulate for themselves and others in a way that would adequately convey its breadth and depth, especially as with time they appropriated more of the standard institutions of religious life like novitiates and regularized regimens in their communities. Perhaps the closest they came was in their persuasion of having their own "way of proceeding." That pregnant expression was meant to capture the pastoral and spiritual principles implied in the *Exercises*, the basic ideals of the *Constitutions*, the corporate wisdom of their ongoing experience of ministry, and the particular, sometimes mundane, regulations they laid down for themselves. It suggested that their identity was forged not so much by a collection of particularities that set them off from others as by a self-conscious style of going about things that was their own.

Be that as it may, the Society was able to attract large numbers of recruits, most of whom came from the middle social brackets. Except for the Capuchins, their growth exceeded by far the other orders founded about the same time to which they were most similar. This phenomenon was due to a number of factors, which included the international character of the Society reflected in the background of its first members, the impact of exciting news-letters from abroad by Xavier and others, possession of a manual like the *Exercises*, cultivation of new ministries like retreats and schools, the leadership gifts of the founder, his talent for choosing the right people to assist him, and the fact that he lived long enough after the founding to impress cohesion on the nascent organization. Moreover, although the early Society had some severe crises of government, it managed to deal with them reasonably effectively.[44] The development of its spirituality suffered from the fearful policies of Everard Mercurian, the fourth general (1573–1580).

By 1615, the Society counted about 13,000 members and thirty-two provinces. It had 372 schools and 123 residences spread throughout the globe but principally in Catholic areas of Europe. Some Jesuits were in England. They were especially important for the future of Catholicism in Germany and Poland. Heavy concentration of manpower in Italy and the Iberian peninsula continued, however, a pattern set during Ignatius's lifetime. As in the beginning, missionary activity remained a high priority, and relatively large numbers of talented Jesuits worked in India, Japan, China, the Philippines, South America, and, after 1632, present-day Canada.[45]

This distribution of membership reflected some generic priorities the Society set itself but was not the result of a master plan. In some places, notably Japan and China, the Jesuits worked out what can be properly described as a strategy to accomplish their purpose, but this was the exception rather than the rule.[46] While trying to guide their choices of where and how to commit themselves by applying criteria from the *Constitutions*, individually and corporately they often simply responded as needs and opportunities presented themselves. From 1581 to 1615 they had the good fortune to be led during this long term of office by Claudio Aquaviva, probably Ignatius's most able successor as general. Of the Jesuits of the first generation, four have been canonized: Loyola and Xavier in 1622, Francisco de Borja (successor to Laínez as the third general) in 1671, and Canisius in 1925.

Historiography

Issues and problems in recent historiography on the Society in the sixteenth century have been succinctly summarized by John Patrick Donnelly.[47] A few general observations on the subject will, therefore, suffice here. As Donnelly points out, the publication in this century of some 125 volumes of the *Monumenta Historica Societatis Jesu* that deal with early Jesuit history has provided scholars with an incomparable, but relatively unexploited, source for enlarging our understanding not only of the Society but also of Early Modern Catholicism in general. Social historians, for instance, have yet to discover the gold mine of the six massive volumes of Polanco's *Chronicon*, which details house by house, province by province, year by the year the doings of Jesuits up to 1556.

With some notable exceptions, in fact, the current resurgence of interest in Early Modern Catholicism has yet to turn to the Jesuits in a degree commensurate with their importance. The field is still largely plowed by scholars who are themselves Jesuits, with all the advantages and disadvantages such a phenomenon entails. In recent decades Jesuits have with good results been most intent on studying the spirituality of the early Society, at times with a focus limited to the *Exercises*.[48]

The series and other publications of the Jesuit Historical Institute in Rome are of high caliber and range over a variety of subjects. Most histories of the early Society and biographies, meanwhile, have continued to concentrate on narrative, generally failing to incorporate findings about Jesuit spirituality or to indicate the shifts in mission and self-understanding that took place among the Jesuits. Many tend to have a static, monolithic, and outdated understanding of the cultural context into which the Society was born and by which it was so much influenced. The ministries of the new order, almost its self-definition, have never been adequately analyzed. In general, research tends to be compartmentalized, usually within rather traditional categories.

We possess from Mario Scaduto a detailed and wide-ranging study of the generalate of Diego Laínez as it touches Italy.[49] The information Georg Schurhammer collected for his biography of Xavier was exhaustive.[50] The portrait of Ignatius painted by his first biographer and younger contemporary, Pedro de Ribadeneira, remains substantially unchallenged.[51] Aquaviva, among many other important Jesuits, has never been studied. Research has consistently tended to concentrate on the first generation.

The situation has improved even in the past decade. Especially useful in the future would be studies that analyze more precisely and frankly than heretofore the Jesuits' relationship to the many, complex, and often conflicting forces at work in the Catholic Church—those with which they were in concert, they with which they were not.

NOTES

1. See John Patrick Donnelly, s.j., "Religious Orders of Men, Especially the Society of Jesus," in *Catholicism in Early Modern History: A Guide to Research*, ed. John W. O'Malley, s.j. (St. Louis: Center for Reformation Research, 1988), pp. 147–62. For the period under consideration in this chapter, see especially the first volume of László Polgár, s.j., *Bibliographie sur l'histoire de la Compagnie de Jésus*, 3 vols. in 6 (Rome: Institutum Historicum Societatis Jesu, 1981–1990). Useful for that same period are *Répertoire de spiritualité ignatienne*, ed. Ignacio Iparraguirre, s.j. (Rome: Institutum Historicum Societatis Jesu, 1961), and Jean-François Gilmont, s.j., *Les Écrits spirituels des premiers jésuites: Inventaire commenté* (Rome: Institutum Historicum Societatis Jesu, 1961). See also the review of literature regularly published in the *Archivum Historicum Societatis Jesu* (henceforth AHSJ). For writings by Jesuits, see *Bibliothèque de la Compagnie de Jésus*, eds. Carlos Sommervogel, s.j., et al., 12 vols. (Brussels: Schepens; Paris: Picard, 1890–1960). The documentation from this early period has been edited and published in the *Monumenta Historica Societatis Jesu* (henceforth MHSJ) (Madrid and Rome: Institutum Historicum Societatis Jesu, 1894—).

2. For a more detailed treatment of the issues discussed in this chapter, see my *The First Jesuits* (Cambridge: Harvard University Press, 1993).

3. Critical editions of this corpus are found in the *Monumenta Ignati-*

ana of the MHSJ series. In English one can now consult, for example, *Ignatius of Loyola: The Spiritual Exercises and Selected Works*, edd. George E. Ganss, S.J., et al., The Classics of Western Spirituality 72 (New York: Paulist Press, 1991), and *The Complete Works of St. Ignatius of Loyola, With Two Hundred of His Selected Letters*, edd. George E. Ganss, S.J., et al. (St. Louis: The Institute of Jesuit Sources, forthcoming).

4. See Dominique Bertrand, S.J., *La Politique de s. Ignace de Loyola: L'analyse sociale* (Paris: Cerf, 1985), esp. p. 39.

5. H. Outram Evennett, *The Spirit of the Counter-Reformation* (Cambridge: Cambridge University Press, 1968), p. 45.

6. See the English translation, with able commentary and notes, by George E. Ganss, S.J., *The Constitutions of the Society of Jesus* (St. Louis: The Institute of Jesuit Sources, 1970). See also Antonio M. de Aldama, S.J., *The Constitutions of the Society of Jesus: An Introductory Commentary on the Constitutions*, trans. Aloysius J. Owen, S.J. (St. Louis: The Institute of Jesuit Sources, 1989).

7. There have been a number of English translations under different titles. Among the more recent is *A Pilgrim's Journey: The Autobiography of Ignatius of Loyola*, trans. Joseph N. Tylenda, S.J. (Wilmington, Del.: Glazier, 1985).

8. On Nadal, see especially Miguel Nicolau, S.J., *Jerónimo Nadal, S.I. (1507–1580): Sus obras y doctrinas espírituales* (Madrid: Consejo Superior de Investigaciones Científicas, 1949); Dennis Edmond Pate, *Jerónimo Nadal and the Early Development of the Society of Jesus, 1545–1573* (Ann Arbor: University Microfilms International, 1980); and William V. Bangert, S.J., *Jerome Nadal, S.J., 1507–1580: Tracking the First Generation of Jesuits* (Chicago: Loyola University Press, 1992).

9. The most compendious among recent biographies is Ricardo García-Villoslada, S.J., *San Ignacio de Loyola: Nueva biografía* (Madrid: Biblioteca de Autores Cristianos, 1986). J. Ignacio Tellechea Idigoras' *Ignacio de Loyola solo y a pie* (Madrid: Ediciones Cristianidad, 1986) is a sympathetic interpretation for a general readership. In English one may consult Cándido de Dalmases, S.J., *Ignatius of Loyola: Founder of the Jesuits*, trans. Jerome Aixala, S.J. (St. Louis: The Institute of Jesuit Sources, 1985), and Philip Caraman, S.J., *Ignatius Loyola: A Biography of the Founder of the Jesuits* (San Francisco: Harper & Row, 1990). Helpful for the last period of Ignatius's life is André Ravier, S.J., *Ignatius of Loyola and the Founding of the Society of Jesus*, trans. Maura Daly, Joan Daly, and Carson Daly (San Francisco: Ignatius Press, 1987).

10. See de Dalmases, *Ignatius*, pp. 149–53.

11. For an English translation of the revised version (1550) of the papal approbation, see Ganss, *Constitutions*, pp. 63–73. For the original Latin of both versions of the *Formula*, see Ignatius de Loyola, *Constituti-*

ones Societatis Jesu, Latinae et Hispanicae, cum earum declarationibus (Rome: Curia Praepositi Generalis, 1937), pp. xxii–xxxiii. See now Antonio M. de Aldama, S.J., *The Constitutions of the Society of Jesus, the Formula of the Institute: Notes for a Commentary* (St. Louis: The Institute of Jesuit Sources, 1990).

12. See Ganss, *Constitutions,* pp. 267–80 [603–32].

13. See my "The Fourth Vow in Its Ignatian Context: A Historical Study," *Studies in the Spirituality of Jesuits,* 15, No. 1 (St. Louis: American Assistancy Seminar on Jesuit Spirituality, 1983) and, in the same series, 16, No. 2 (1984), my "To Travel to Any Part of the World: Jerónimo Nadal and the Jesuit Vocation."

14. See *Saint Ignatius Loyola: Letters to Women,* ed. Hugo Rahner, S.J., trans. Kathleen Pond and S. A. H. Weetman (Edinburgh and London: Nelson, 1960).

15. Only a small portion of his spiritual journal has come down to us. See *Inigo: Discernment Log-Book: The Spiritual Diary of Saint Ignatius Loyola,* ed. and trans. Joseph A. Munitiz, S.J. (London: Inigo Enterprises, 1987).

16. See my "To Travel," pp. 6–13.

17. See my "Preaching," forthcoming in the encyclopedia of Jesuit history (Rome: Institutum Historicum Societatis Jesu). The most reliable and extensive treatment of Jesuit ministries during the sixteenth century is Mario Scaduto, S.J., *L'Epoca di Giacomo Laínez,* 2 vols. (Rome: La Civiltà Cattolica, 1964–1974) 2:469–650.

18. See Armando F. Verde, O.P., "Le Lezioni o i sermoni sull' 'Apocalisse' di Girolamo Savonarola (1490): 'Nova dicere et novo modo,'" *Memorie Domenicane,* N.S., 19 (1988), 5–109.

19. See, e.g., Jean-Claude Dhotel, S.J., *Les Origines du catéchisme moderne d'après les premiers manuels imprimés en France* (Paris: Aubier, 1967), and Gerald Strauss, *Luther's House of Learning: Indoctrination of the Young in the German Reformation* (Baltimore and London: The Johns Hopkins University Press, 1978).

20. See Ignacio Iparraguirre, S.J., *Historia de la práctica de los ejercicios espirituales de S. Ignacio de Loyola,* 3 vols. under slightly different titles (Rome and Bilbao: Institutum Historicum Societatis Jesu, 1946–1955).

21. See, e.g., Gian Carlo Angelozzi, "L'insegnamento dei casi di coscienza nella pratica educativa della Compagnia di Gesù," in *"Ratio Studiorum:" Modelli culturali e pratiche educative dei Gesuiti in Italia tra Cinque e Seicento,* ed. Gian Carlo Brizzi (Rome: Bulzoni, 1981), pp. 121–62, and Albert R. Jonsen and Stephen Toulmin, *The Abuses of Casuistry: A History of Moral Theology* (Berkeley, Los Angeles, and London: The University of California Press, 1988).

22. See, e.g., Vicenzo Paglia, *"La pietà dei carcerati:"* Confraternite e società a Roma nei secoli XVI–XVII (Rome: Storia e Letteratura, 1980).

23. See Louis Châtellier, *The Europe of the Devout: The Catholic Reformation and the Formation of a New Society*, trans. Jean Birrell (Cambridge: Cambridge University Press, 1989).

24. See, e.g., Gabriel Mir, S.J., *Aux sources de la pédagogie des jésuites: Le "modus parisiensis"* (Rome: Institutum Historicum Societatis Jesu, 1968); Aldo Scaglione, *The Liberal Arts and the Jesuit College System* (Amsterdam and Philadelphia: Benjamins, 1986); Paul F. Grendler, *Schooling in Italy: Literacy and Learning, 1300–1600* (Baltimore and London: The Johns Hopkins University Press, 1989), esp. pp. 363–82.

25. *Monumenta Paedagogica* (MHSJ), 3:305–306.

26. *Monumenta Ignatiana: Epistolae* (MHSJ), 4:7–9.

27. *Monumenta Paedagogica* (MHSJ), 1:425–26.

28. See, however, e.g., Marc Fumaroli, *L'Age de l'éloquence: Rhétorique et "res literaria" de la Renaissance au seuil de l'époque classique* (Geneva: Droz, 1980).

29. See, e.g., my "Renaissance Humanism and the Religious Culture of the First Jesuits," *Heythrop Journal*, 31 (1990), 471–87.

30. See e.g., Florencio Segura, S.J., "El teatro en los colegios de los jesuitas," *Miscellanea Comillas*, 43 (1985), 299–327; Jean-Marie Valentin, *Le Théâtre des jésuites dans les pays de langue allemande (1554–1680)*, 3 vols. (Bern, Frankfurt, Las Vegas: Lang, 1978); William H. McCabe, S.J., *An Introduction to Jesuit Theater: A Posthumous Work*, ed. Louis J. Oldani, S.J. (St. Louis: The Institute of Jesuit Sources, 1983).

31. See, e.g., William Wallace, O.P., *Galileo and His Sources: The Heritage of the Collegio Romano in Galileo's Science* (Princeton: Princeton University Press, 1984); Rivka Feldhay, "Knowledge and Salvation in Jesuit Culture," *Science in Context*, 1 (1987), 195–213; and Steven J. Harris, "Transposing the Merton Thesis: Apostolic Spirituality and the Establishment of the Jesuit Scientific Tradition," ibid., 3 (1989), 29–85.

32. See the still useful study by James Brodrick, S.J., *Peter Canisius* (London: Sheed & Ward, 1935). See also Engelbert Maximilian Buxbaum, *Petrus Canisius und die kirchliche Erneuerung des Herzogtums Bayern, 1549–1556* (Rome: Institutum Historicum Societatis Jesu, 1973).

33. See Peter Schmidt, *Das Collegium Germanicum in Rom und die Germaniker: Zur Funktion eines römischen Ausländerseminars, 1552–1914* (Tübingen: Niemeyer, 1984); Anita Mancia, "La controversia con i protestanti e i programmi degli studi teologici nella Compagnia di Gesù, 1547–1599," AHSJ, 54 (1985), 3–43, 209–66.

35. See, e.g., A. Lynn Martin, *Henry III and the Jesuit Politicians* (Geneva: Droz, 1973).

36. *Monumenta Nadal* (MHSJ) 5:607.

37. See, e.g., Mario Scaduto, s.j., "Le missioni di A. Possevino in Piemonte: Propaganda calvinistica e restaurazione cattolica," AHSJ, 28 (1959), 51–191.

38. See, e.g., Hubert Jedin, *Katholische Reformation oder Gegenreformation?* (Lucerne: Stocker, 1946).

39. See, e.g., my "Priesthood, Ministry, and Religious Life: Some Historical and Historiographical Considerations," *Theological Studies*, 49 (1988), 223–57, esp. 231–48; and "Was Ignatius Loyola a Church Reformer: How to Look at Early Modern Catholicism," *The Catholic Historical Review*, 77 (1991), 177–93.

40. See Scaduto, *Laínez*, 2:137–267.

41. *Scholia in Constitutiones S.J.*, ed. Manuel Ruiz Jurado, s.j. (Granada: Facultad de Teología, 1976), p. 434.

42. See Antonio Borras, s.j., "Entorno a la indumentaria de los jesuitas españoles en los siglos XVI y XVII," AHSJ, 36 (1967), 291–99.

43. See A. Lynn Martin, *The Jesuit Mind: The Mentality of an Elite in Early Modern France* (Ithaca and London: Cornell University Press, 1988).

44. See, e.g., Authur L. Fisher, "A Study in Early Jesuit Government: The Nature and Origins of the Dissent of Nicolás Bobadilla," *Viator*, 10 (1979), 397–431.

45. See William V. Bangert, s.j., *A History of the Society of Jesus* (St. Louis: The Institute of Jesuit Sources, 1972), pp. 46–175.

46. See Josef Franz Schütte, s.j., *Valignano's Mission Principles for Japan*, trans. John J. Coyne, s.j., 2 vols. (St. Louis: The Institute of Jesuit Sources, 1980, 1985).

47. "Religious Orders of Men" (note 1 above).

48. The classic, but now outdated, study is Joseph de Guibert, s.j., *The Jesuits, Their Doctrine and Practice: A Historical Study*, trans. William J. Young, s.j. (Chicago: Loyola University Press, 1964). See now, e.g., Evennett, *Counter-Reformation*, pp. 23–88; *Les Jésuites, spiritualité et activités: Jalons d'une histoire* (Paris: Beauchesne, 1974); my "Early Jesuit Spirituality: Spain and Italy," in *Christian Spirituality* III, edd. Louis Dupré and Don E. Saliers, World Spirituality: An Encyclopedic History of the Religious Quest 18 (New York: Crossroad, 1989), pp. 3–27; and my "Some Distinctive Characteristics of Jesuit Spirituality in the Sixteenth Century," in *Jesuit Spirituality: A Now and Future Resource* (Chicago: Loyola University Press, 1990), pp. 1–20.

49. See note 17 above.

50. *Francis Xavier: His Life, His Times*, trans. M. Joseph Costelloe, 4 vols. (Rome: Jesuit Historical Institute, 1973–1982).

51. See note 9 above.

St. John of the Cross by an anonymous artist in 1591. Museum of San Juan de la Cruz in Ubeda. Courtesy of the Institute of Carmelite Studies, Washington, D.C.

St. Teresa of Jesus by Fray Juan de la Miseria in 1576. Convent of San José, Seville. Courtesy of the Editorial de Espiritualidad, Madrid.

6

Teresa of Jesus and Carmelite Reform

Jodi Bilinkoff

CONVERSATIONS WITH WOMEN

IN HER AUTOBIOGRAPHY the future saint Teresa of Avila recalled the chain of events that led up to the foundation of the reformed Carmelite convent of St. Joseph's in her native city on August 24, 1562. Crucial to this process, as she reconstructed it, were two sets of conversations held with women. The first took place in September of 1560 among the coterie of nuns that met regularly in Teresa's living quarters in the convent of the Incarnation. Teresa, recently shaken by a terrifying vision of hell, had been wondering "what [she] could do for God" when her kinswoman María de Ocampo made an exciting proposal. Why not found a new convent along the lines of the reform movement then taking place among the Franciscans? Teresa reacted quickly and passionately to this suggestion, which promised to give concrete form to her many goals and desires for the Church.[1]

A second series of conversations took place in the spring of 1562 when Teresa was staying at the palace of Doña Luisa de la Cerda in Toledo. While involved in preparations for the new convent in Avila she met an extraordinary woman named María de Yepes. This illiterate but deeply pious *beata* from Granada had independently formulated a plan for Carmelite reform and was now walking barefoot to Rome to secure permission from the pope for her efforts. During many discussions María de Yepes persuaded Teresa to found St. Joseph's in complete poverty, with no fixed income, as required by the original Carmelite rule. This exchange, too, profoundly influenced the course of Teresa's reform program, as well as her own self-understanding.[2]

These two conversations are significant because they reveal how a number of issues fundamental to Teresa's concept of the renewed monastic life arose early in the reform process, and within the context of an apostolate of religious women. Even in this preliminary phase Teresa was forced to confront the problems of balancing the impulse for personal penance with a collective response to the needs of the Church, of interpreting and following the primitive Carmelite rule, with its call for strict enclosure, a small religious community and complete poverty, and of preserving the austerity, the quiet, and the freedom necessary for a communal life of prayer as she understood it. The two conversations with women also show the degree to which Teresa's program of Carmelite reform was linked to experiences in her own life.

From Doña Teresa to Teresa of Jesus

Teresa de Ahumada y Cepeda was born in the city of Avila, in central Castile, on March 28, 1515. Her family on her father's side were *conversos*, descendants of converted Jews. They belonged to Avila's then thriving merchant class, making their living primarily in the cloth trade. Like many *conversos* they aspired to the social prestige fully enjoyed only by Old Christians in early modern Spain.[3] Teresa's grandfather, father, and uncles all used their wealth and business connections to purchase luxurious homes and furnishings and to "buy" noble status, with its exemption from taxation and right to use the polite titles of "Don" and "Doña." Teresa would later identify the obsession with honor, particularly the concern for an aristocratic and ethnically "pure" pedigree, as an especially pernicious example of "attachment to the things of this world." Her rejection of these pervasive social values as incompatible with the true religious life probably stemmed, at least in part, from her own position as a member of an ethnically "tainted," parvenu family.[4]

At the age of twenty, moved by the "servile fear" of hell more than by the love of God, Doña Teresa entered Avila's Carmelite convent of the Incarnation. She made her formal profession as a nun the following year, in 1536. She would remain in this house for twenty-seven years.

If Teresa had sought to avoid the issues of class, caste, and honor by entering a convent, she was soon disappointed by life in the Incarnation. One of the largest of Avila's many religious houses, it held more than one hundred nuns at the time of her entrance. These were, for the most part, women of substance, daughters of the city's "honored and principal men," who maintained their privileges even while embracing the religious life. The nuns upheld distinctions of social rank, addressed one another by family names, and used, when appropriate, the title "Doña." Many elite nuns brought with them their own servants, or even slaves.[5]

Further, nuns took with them into the convent the aristocratic values by which they had been raised, especially the high regard for personal reputation. Teresa would later admit that she, too, enjoyed "things that are usually esteemed in the world" and hated to "suffer anything that seemed to be scorn."[6] She had assimilated her society's concern with prestige, although not completely, perhaps recognizing the shallowness of her claims to honor in the dynastic and ethnic senses.

Looking back years later, Teresa traced many of the Incarnation's problems to its adherence to a relaxed version of the original Carmelite rule. A Bull of Mitigation promulgated by Pope Eugenius IV in 1432 had moderated the thirteenth-century rule of strict poverty, chastity, and obedience. In retrospect, she voiced particular opposition to the lack of enclosure, but during her years at the Incarnation Teresa herself participated fully in this form of "laxity." Illness, family needs, and financial difficulties often kept her and other nuns away from the convent, sometimes for prolonged periods.[7]

In addition, monastic officials, recognizing the gifts of humor, tact, and verbal dexterity that Teresa had displayed since childhood, dispatched her on special assignments. "Some persons to whom the superiors could not say 'no' liked to have me in their company, and when urged the superiors urged me to go," she recalled in her autobiography.[8] We know from other sources as well that noblewomen in Avila and elsewhere frequently requested nuns as companions, especially in difficult times such as after the death of a husband or child. Monastic superiors had to accommodate these women, actual or potential financial benefactors of religious houses, and the charming Doña Teresa proved a particularly effective fundraiser. She thus found herself deep within the web of patronage and clientage relations that tied Avila's religious institutions to the city's powerful oligarchy and its aristocratic values.

The transformation of Doña Teresa de Ahumada to Teresa of Jesus occurred slowly, over a period of nearly twenty years. Eventually she came to reject the social and religious system by which she had lived for so long at the Incarnation.

Teresa's introduction to a meaningful life of prayer began in 1538, during one of her many visits outside the convent. On that occasion a pious uncle gave her a copy of Francisco de Osuna's *Third Spiritual Alphabet* (1527). This influential book acquainted her with the concept of recollection (*recogimiento*), a method of prayer based on a passive or quiet negation of self in order to receive God's communication without obstruction or distraction. A great lover of books since childhood, Teresa now began to devour the abundant devotional literature of her day.[9]

Her return to the Incarnation in 1540, far from aiding her in her new spiritual path, detoured her from it. She found herself once again forced to adhere to entrenched codes of social behavior with family members, nuns, and benefactors and to enhance her own reputation. "On the one hand, God was calling me," Teresa would later remember. "On the other hand, I was following the world."[10]

In the early 1540s the anguished Teresa began to receive her first divine revelations, most of which corresponded in some way to the guilt and discomfort she now felt with her way of life. Once, while talking with a nun who frequently engaged her in gossip and frivolous chatter, she saw "with the eyes of the soul" Christ watching her with stern disapproval. Later she saw this same nun accompanied by a hideous toad.[11] These experiences amazed and frightened her, but her attachment to the "things of the world" remained strong and kept her from being able to "resolve to give [herself] entirely to God."[12] For many years she continued to feel frustration and "aridity" in prayer.

Finally, around 1555, when she was some forty years old, Teresa de Ahumada began to have frequent and profound spiritual experiences. She saw visions, heard voices, and even arrived at the coveted state of mystical union with God. She came to recognize the connection between her lifestyle and the reception of these divine gifts: "Now then, when I began to avoid occasions [of sin] and to devote myself to prayer, the Lord started to grant me favors."[13]

Teresa's reading of devotional books, her interaction with a group of religious reformers then active in Avila,[14] and, especially, her continuing supernatural experiences completely transformed her life. The privileged nun, who for years had not dared to challenge the tenets of polite social convention, now found the strength to detach herself from worldly things and commit herself totally to the service of God. Of the origin of this power she had no doubt: "The Lord gave me the freedom and strength to perform the task. . . . He gave me the freedom that I with all the efforts of many years could not attain by myself."[15] She recognized, as did others, that her very identity had changed. As her friend Pedro Ibáñez later put it, "This lady is now known as Teresa of Jesus: formerly she was Doña Teresa de Ahumada."[16]

Around 1560 the dramatically altered Teresa received a vision that elicited for the first time a more than merely personal response to the question of how to serve God and save souls. It was a vision of hell, and in one horrifying moment she saw "the place the devils had prepared there" for her. For a fleeting instant she experienced the pain, the confinement, and the eternal despair awaiting her.[17]

Teresa's immediate reaction was missionary in nature. She pondered how to save from even greater torments the "Lutherans" (the name by which many Spaniards referred to the French Calvinist Huguenots). She then began to feel the "pleasant restlessness" that would characterize the rest of her life as a monastic reformer, mystic, and writer. "I was thinking about what I could do for God," she recalled; "and I thought that the first thing was to follow the call to the religious life, which His Majesty had given me, by keeping my rule as perfectly as I could."[18]

At this point Teresa began seeking an institutional way of fulfilling her new mission: to promote prayer as a source for personal renewal as well as a response to the collective needs of the Christian community. It was then that she discussed with María de Ocampo and other friends at the Incarnation plans for founding a convent of discalced, or barefoot, nuns (that is, wearing sandals as a sign of humility), an idea inspired by the reforms undertaken by Peter of Alcántara among the Franciscans. A few days after this conversation, Teresa received divine confirmation:

His Majesty earnestly commanded me to strive for this new monastery with all my powers, and He made great promises that it
would be founded and that He would be highly served in it. He
said that it should be called St. Joseph and that this saint would
watch over us at one door, and Our Lady at the other, that Christ
would remain with us, and that it would be a star shining with
great splendor.[19]

Compelled by God's decree, supported by like-minded religious
women, and aided by a group of sympathetic clerics and laypersons, Teresa of Jesus was at last ready to embark upon her
life's adventure: the reform of the Carmelite order.

Teresa's Vision of the Reformed Monastic Life

My purpose here is not to provide a detailed institutional history
of the Discalced Carmelites, as many competent accounts have
already been written (see bibliographic essay). Instead, I attempt
to call attention to some salient features of Teresa's reform program and to situate them in her response to life at the Incarnation
and exposure to contemporary currents of religious reform. I also
focus on Teresa's work among the Discalced Carmelite nuns,
rather than the friars, whose somewhat different history has also
been well documented.

Teresa of Jesus made strenuous efforts to eliminate all vestiges
of worldly honor in her convents. After many years of grappling
with this obsession, the reformer now worked hard to replace
honor with its reverse, humility, as the foundation on which to
build a renewed monastic life.

For example, she made the critical and risky decision to found
the convent of St. Joseph in strict poverty. In this she was profoundly influenced by Peter of Alcántara and the Franciscan tradition of mendicant poverty, as well as by the new understanding
of the primitive Carmelite rule awakened in her by María de
Yepes. Teresa came to reject the regular, fixed incomes (*rentas*),
usually tied to investments in land, which financially supported
most religious houses. She insisted, rather, that the nuns of St.
Joseph's rely entirely on the fruits of their own labor and on
God to move individuals to donate alms for their survival. This
decision, which dramatically affirmed her monastic vow of pov-

erty, also had important implications for her efforts to establish a principle of religious autonomy, as we shall see.[20]

Teresa undoubtedly realized that any policy other than one of strict poverty would jeopardize her plans for an egalitarian convent in which the social differences that divided the Incarnation would never take hold. She did not require that nuns enter St. Joseph's with dowries, although she gratefully accepted such offerings as alms. As time went on, many women of means would take the discalced habit, but Teresa could still proudly declare "I have never refused to accept anyone because of lack of money, provided I was satisfied with all the rest."[21]

She attacked even more vehemently distinctions based upon class and caste. "[The sister] who is from nobler lineage should be the one to speak last about her father. All the sisters must be equals," she stated flatly.[22] In sharp contrast to life at the Incarnation, Teresa saw to it that at St. Joseph's nuns used only the title Sister, or Mother in the case of the prioress. She abolished all forms of polite address and the use of family names. Even nuns of exalted pedigree adopted names in religion, deliberately obscuring their origins as they collectively dedicated their lives to God. In addition, Teresa never instituted statutes of *limpieza de sangre* (purity of blood), which would have required religious to prove pristine Old Christian extraction, without the "taint" of Jewish or Moorish blood. This feature distinguished Discalced Carmelites from virtually all other religious orders in sixteenth-century Spain.[23]

The nun who had spent more than twenty-five years living in private quarters at the Incarnation, surrounded by servants and family members, now insisted that the sisters at St. Joseph's hold their personal property and resources in common. The young Doña Teresa de Ahumada had resented being assigned menial tasks. The new woman, Teresa of Jesus, prescribed manual labor for all. She joyfully participated in the chores of the convent, even while serving as prioress and in times of illness. In her typically delightful way she reminded her nuns that the true religious life takes place in the kitchen as well as the choir: "The Lord walks among the pots and pans."[24]

Teresa envisioned a humble and ascetic lifestyle for Discalced Carmelites as appropriate for women who had chosen to imitate Christ. "The Houses must be poor and small in every way," she insisted. "Let us in some manner resemble our king, who had no house but the stable in Bethlehem where He was born and the cross where He died."[25] St. Joseph's was to hold a small but select group of women chosen for their virtues, indifference to worldly things, maturity, ability to read, and firm commitment to the religious life. These sisters would wear simple brown habits of the coarsest and cheapest cloth and sleep on mattresses made of straw-filled sacks. Teresa of Jesus fully understood the symbolic value of these ascetic measures. As Doña Teresa de Ahumada she had entered the Incarnation with a complete trousseau of fabrics, cushions, and hangings made from the cloth from which her family derived most of its wealth. Here, once again, she demonstrated her total rejection of her former life of comfort, worldliness, and honor.[26]

Teresa also struggled to break the ties that bound religious houses such as the Incarnation to secular institutions and, in particular, to individual aristocratic families. Her highly controversial decision to found St. Joseph's without fixed incomes must be understood in this socio-economic context, as well as in the religious tradition of voluntary poverty.

In Avila, as elsewhere, elites financially supported religious houses by establishing *capellanías* or chaplaincies. Typically, a patron would donate *rentas* in exchange for burial in a particular chapel. In a contractual agreement he would stipulate that the religious pray for his soul and for those of his family members and heirs in perpetuity. Accordingly, the residents of most religious houses in early modern Avila practiced a style of spirituality appropriate to the dynastic concerns of their benefactors. This included anniversary Masses and other vocally chanted commemorative and intercessory prayers.[27] Recall that superiors at the Incarnation, anxious to maintain this lucrative source of patronage, had sent the nun Teresa de Ahumada to comfort distressed noble ladies.

Teresa's refusal to accept fixed incomes for the convent of St. Joseph thus indicated not only her wish for monastic poverty but also her desire to establish a principle of religious autonomy. She and her nuns had taken vows to serve God, not to accommodate aristocratic families. "Don't think, my sisters, that because you do not strive to please those who are in the world you will lack food," she assured the nuns. "Leave this worrying to the One who can move all, for He is the Lord of money and of those who earn money."[28] Their liberation from the burden of pleasing "those who are in the world" gave Discalced Carmelites a form of freedom unknown to the socially bound nuns of the Incarnation. "True poverty brings with it overwhelming honor. Poverty that is chosen for God alone has no need of pleasing anyone but Him," Teresa explained. "It is clear that in having need of no one a person has many friends."[29]

Similarly, the reformer insisted upon strict enclosure for the nuns of St. Joseph's and severely limited their opportunities to receive family members or patrons as visitors to the convent. Although this policy may seem repressive or patriarchal, for Teresa voluntarily chosen enclosure, like poverty, had a potentially liberating effect. Her experience at the Incarnation convinced her that communication between nuns and secular society inevitably brought increased attachment to worldly things. More critically, "freedom" of movement and intercourse led to a loss of the more important type of "freedom," spiritual autonomy from social obligations and special interests. Therefore, the nuns of St. Joseph's, so strictly cloistered, were, paradoxically, more "free" than those who interacted with, but became enmeshed in the demands of the world.[30]

Teresa of Jesus also defended another important form of freedom for her nuns: the freedom to choose and change their spiritual directors. This decision too resulted from circumstances in her own life. Her experience with a long string of ignorant, indifferent, and even hostile confessors left deep emotional scars, as is evident in many of her writings. She deplored the excruciating situation that arose when nuns' "consciences tell them the opposite of what their confessor does." She continued, "And if they are restricted to only one confessor, they don't know what to do or how to be at peace." She concluded that nuns, authorized by their prioress and bishop or provincial, must have the "holy freedom" to bare their souls to confessors of their choosing, even if the priests belonged to other religious orders.[31] This painful issue would resurface after Teresa's death and cause difficulties for many of her spiritual daughters.

Finally, Teresa of Jesus sought ways of articulating a monastic life for religious women that also addressed the collective needs of the Church. As we have seen, she explained her decision to

found a new convent and to maintain a strict vow of poverty
in missionary terms. Anxious to counter the Calvinist religious
violence then engulfing France and the Low Countries, she
grasped at the means available to her as a woman and a contemplative; namely, prayer and penitence. If male clerics engaged in active apostolates, Discalced Carmelite nuns could exercise an
apostolate of prayer, which to Teresa was as powerful a weapon
against heresy as preaching, and more effective than the sword.

Long before she began her career as a monastic reformer, Teresa
had burned with a desire to save souls. She regarded with sadness
her Church, beleaguered not only by Protestant and Illuminist
"heretics" and Indian "heathens" from without, but also by apa-
thetic laypeople and corrupt and ignorant clergymen from within.
She cried out in her frustration. Sometimes, she exclaimed, "desires to serve God come upon me with impulses so strong I don't
know how to exaggerate them, and there is . . . pain in seeing of
what little use I am. . . . It seems to me this body and this state
[that is, being a woman and a nun] bind me. . . . If I [weren't]
so bound I would do very noble deeds. . . ." Hearing accounts
of Huguenot iconoclasm in France, she insisted "I would have
given a thousand lives to save one soul out of the many that were
being lost there."[32] Teresa's involvement with Carmelite reform
at last brought her a way of pursuing the apostolate for which she
had longed all her life.

Central to realizing this new mission was her understanding of
the meaning and function of prayer. Teresa envisioned St. Joseph's
as a community of committed women engaged in unceasing
prayer. But in a departure from other monastic traditions, including that of the Incarnation, she stressed interior, mental prayer, as
opposed to chanted vocal prayer. She instructed her daughters to
empty themselves of exterior distractions in order to transform
themselves into vessels for God's will. This powerful contemplative method, correctly implemented, she felt, would result in
genuine dialogue with God, not a one-way supplication.[33]

For Teresa, prayer practiced in this way *was* a form of action.
Anticipating the fears of her nuns that they would be unable to
bring souls to God because "[they] do not have the means, . . .
that not being teachers or preachers, as were the apostles, [they]
do not know how," she reassured them that "by prayer you will
be helping greatly." She urged the sisters to offer continual prayer

for the priests and prelates of the Church. If their devotions bolstered clerics in their struggles to resist worldly temptations and encouraged them in the service of God, then, she concluded, "we shall be fighting for Him even though we are very cloistered."[34]

Some scholars have suggested that Teresa of Jesus' unique contribution to the Christian tradition lies precisely in this fusion of the contemplative and the active. This vision was shared by her co-founder among the Discalced Carmelite friars, the brilliant mystic, poet, and theologian John of the Cross. He did participate in apostolic activities, delivering sermons, hearing confessions, and offering instruction in Christian doctrine on the local level. But he cautioned friars against becoming so involved in large-scale preaching tours, university careers, overseas missions, and the like that they neglected their call to quiet contemplation and prayer.[35] Perhaps one could say that Teresa of Jesus' program of Carmelite reform, with its stress on the rejection of honor, the achievement of spiritual autonomy, and the primacy of prayer in the service of the Church gave religious women the freedom to seek a truly apostolic life, while giving men the freedom to seek a truly contemplative one.

SUCCESSES AND SETBACKS

After many vicissitudes Teresa opened her reformed convent of St. Joseph in Avila in August of 1562 and settled down to what she hoped would be a peaceful and prayerful existence. But her life was once again dramatically changed by her encounter with the Carmelite Prior General Giovanni Battista Rossi (known to Spaniards as Rubeo) in the spring of 1567. Impressed with the contemplation and commitment displayed by the nuns of St. Joseph's, Rubeo ordered Teresa to found religious houses throughout Castile and what is now Andalusia. By her death in 1582, at the age of sixty-seven, she had personally founded fourteen more convents for women, directed another two at a distance, and played a critical role in the establishment of the first two Discalced Carmelite houses for men.[36]

Over the next forty years or so, the order achieved some notable successes, opening Discalced houses throughout Spain, as well as in France, the Low Countries, and elsewhere. But the movement also underwent fundamental (and, some would say, troubling) changes, leading many of Teresa's followers to wonder if her concept of the monastic life was not being abandoned.

Particularly disturbing were the incredibly complex and rather seamy power struggles carried out among the male leaders of the Discalced Carmelite hierarchy. The conflicts between such strong-willed individuals as Jerónimo Gración and Nicolás Doria had erupted even before Teresa's death, and had greatly saddened her last years. Now the unedifying spectacle of friars revealing themselves to be more competitive than contemplative threatened to undermine the entire movement for Carmelite reform.[37] In these turbulent early years the friars also opted for greater involvement in university education and began overseas missions to the Congo, departing from the eremitic vision of John of the Cross.[38]

In response to these developments many of her monastic daughters began an intense struggle to preserve *la herencia teresiana*, the legacy of Teresa of Jesus. An extraordinary second generation of Discalced Carmelite nuns, which included such highly articulate spokeswomen as Ana de Jesús, Ana de San Bartolomé, and María de San José, fought against considerable odds to establish religious houses that adhered to the values of humility, poverty, apostolic prayer, and religious freedom set down by the founding mother. In the increasingly conservative and hierarchical atmosphere of the early seventeenth century, all three became embroiled in conflicts with prelates and monastic superiors over the administration of convents and the right of nuns to choose their own spiritual directors. The gifted and headstrong María de San José in particular suffered disgrace and imprisonment over her unwillingness to surrender what she saw as basic Teresian principles.[39]

As religious institutions in Spain and elsewhere fell prey to worsening economic conditions and increasing concerns about upholding social norms, many features of Teresa's egalitarian ideal did indeed fall by the wayside. Even during the last part of her life the reformer was forced to compromise on the issue of monastic poverty. Reluctantly Teresa came to accept *rentas* as necessary for convents founded in rural locations. She acknowledged that these convents, remote from an urban population disposed to give alms or buy the articles spun or embroidered by the nuns, simply had to have a secure income or the sisters would starve. She also began to actively encourage prospective nuns to enter convents with dowries—the bigger the better—although she still refused to make this a requirement for acceptance into the order. In her last years she considered beginning even urban foundations with fixed incomes.[40]

But in 1587, only five years after Teresa's death, male Discalced Carmelite officials established a minimum dowry payment for female novices. This policy, of course, selected nuns from well-to-do families, "something very foreign to our Holy Mother," as María de San José bitterly complained. In an even more dramatic departure from the vision of Teresa of Jesus, the Discalced Carmelites in 1597 at last bowed to social pressure and instituted statutes of purity of blood. In an ironic twist, the order blocked entrance to the descendants of *conversos* extending back four generations, a policy that would have prevented Teresa de Ahumada from joining the order she founded.[41]

In 1614 the Roman Catholic Church beatified Teresa of Jesus; in 1622 she was canonized as Saint Teresa of Avila. While this recognition naturally validated her life and work, its meaning over time contained many ambiguities. She quickly attained a cultic prestige accorded few other female saints, but at the expense of losing her identity as a real-life woman of passion, intelligence, and a delicious sense of humor. In the baroque world of the seventeenth century, biographers and propagandists of the faith constructed a new Teresa, one that conformed to the agenda of the Counter-Reformation Church and the roles it assigned to women. Thus emerged the Saint Teresa of Bernini, the ecstatic mystic, the miraculous healer, the humble proponent of absolute orthodoxy and absolute obedience.[42] Virtually forgotten were her flesh-and-blood experiences in the world, especially those regarded as controversial. Hagiographers downplayed her insistence upon monastic poverty and autonomy and mental (as opposed to vocal) prayer, her struggles with inquisitors and censors over her writings and the odds against which she had to fight to establish her vision of the religious life. They were particularly effective at burying all references to Teresa's Jewish extraction. "Tainted" blood simply would not do for the "Seraphic Virgin" now elevated to the altars. To this day many Catholics know Teresa of Avila only as an otherworldly and somewhat saccharine mystic, and as *la Santa de la Raza*, a saint whose adherence to Christian doctrine was as pure as her blood.[43]

THE TERESIAN LEGACY

However, in the memorable words of Fray Luis de León, Teresa of Jesus bequeathed to future generations "two living images of herself," her writings and her daughters (and sons).[44] During the last twenty years of her life Teresa wrote prodigiously, producing four full-length books (*The Book of Her Life, The Way of Perfection, The Interior Castle,* and *The Book of Her Foundations*) and many shorter works: poetry, meditations, instructions for monastic administrators, personal recollections, and some five hundred letters. This extraordinary literary output attests to her strong vocation as a writer and to the importance she attached to helping souls through the written word.[45] Suppressed during her lifetime, censored and abridged for some three hundred years thereafter, the complete works of Teresa of Avila became available in reliable published editions only at the end of the nineteenth century.[46] Today her writings, in Spanish and in dozens of translations, attract the attention of innumerable literary scholars, theologians, and historians. She is regarded as one of the greatest writers of the Spanish Golden Age.

The tradition of reformed monasticism and literary expression for religious women was carried on after Teresa's death by many of her spiritual daughters. The Discalced Carmelite order continued to produce writing nuns and writings about nuns for at least a century after its inception.[47] Carmelite friars also helped to keep this legacy alive through their own writings (notably, those of John of the Cross), their biographies of nuns, their efforts to collect documents by and about Teresa, and their truly impressive record of historical scholarship (see bibliographic essay). And, of course, both the daughters and the sons of Mother Teresa have upheld, in their own ways, the founder's central vision of the apostolic power of prayer. Through their efforts the historical Teresa of Jesus, her message, and her mission have been preserved for posterity.

Bibliographic Essay

Teresa of Jesus and her reform of the Carmelite order have been studied extensively. Most of the documentation relevant to the foundation of the Discalced Carmelites has been published.

To understand this history better, one should begin with Teresa's own writings. *Santa Teresa de Jesús, Obras completas*, edd. Efrén de la Madre de Dios Montalva and Otger Steggink (Madrid: Editorial Católica, 1977) offers a critical edition of Teresa's complete works (including her letters) in one volume. The best English translation is *The Collected Works of St. Teresa of Avila*, trans. Kieran Kavanaugh and Otilio Rodríguez, 3 vols. (Washington, D.C.: Institute of Carmelite Studies, 1976–1985). This translation is historically accurate and rendered in an accessible American English. Unfortunately, these scholars have not yet translated Teresa's letters. Some prefer the more poetic, if more archaic style found in *The Complete Works*, trans. E. Allison Peers, 3 vols. (London: Sheed & Ward, 1946) and *The Letters of Saint Teresa of Jesus*, trans. E. Allison Peers, 2 vols. (London: Burns, Oates and Washbourne, 1951). For works of John of the Cross, see his *Obras completas*, ed. José Vicente Rodriguez, 3rd ed. (Madrid: Editorial de Espiritualidad, 1988); *The Collected Works of St. John of the Cross*, rev. ed., trans. Kieran Kavanaugh and Otilio Rodriguez (Washington, D.C.: Institute of Carmelite Studies, 1991) and *The Complete Works of Saint John of the Cross, Doctor of the Church*, trans. E. Allison Peers (Westminster, Md.: Newman, 1953).

There are several good documentary histories that trace the history of Teresa and her reform movement. Foremost among these is Silverio de Santa Teresa, *Historia del Carmen Descalzo en España, Portugal, y América*, 15 vols. (Burgos: El Monte Carmelo, 1935–1949), a magisterial, multi–volume compendium, offering a wealth of information. More manageable and up-to-date in terms of scholarly apparatus is Efrén de la Madre de Dios Montalva and Otger Steggink, *Santa Teresa y su tiempo*, 2 vols. (Salamanca: Universidad Pontificia, 1982, 1984). For English readers, E. Allison Peers's *Handbook to the Life and Times of St. Teresa and St. John of the Cross* (London: Burns, Oates, 1954), and the excellent introductory essays by Kieran Kavanaugh in *Collected Works* provide much helpful information.

Teresa of Jesus has been the subject of numerous biographies, most of them pious and uncritical. Fortunately, there are some noteworthy exceptions to this pattern. Stephen Clissold, *St. Teresa of Avila* (New York: Seabury, 1982), the best recent biography in English, combines a breezy journalistic style with careful archival research. For readers of Spanish, Rosa Rossi's *Teresa de Avila: Biografía de una escritora* (Barcelona: Icaria, 1984) offers stunning insights from a feminist literary scholar. (It is also available in the original Italian.) For a popular one-volume account by a noted Teresian scholar, see Efrén de la Madre de Dios Montalva, *Teresa de Jesús* (Madrid: Editorial Católica, 1981). Two older, but still useful biographies in English are Marcelle Auclair's *Teresa of Avila* (New York: Pantheon, 1953), translated from the French, and E. Allison Peers's, *Mother of Carmel: A Portrait of St. Teresa of Jesus* (London: S.C.M. Press, 1946). A classic biography of John of the Cross, now is its eleventh, updated edition, is Crisógono de Jesús' *Vida de San Juan de la Cruz* (Madrid: Editorial Católica, 1982). There is an English translation of an earlier, somewhat less reliable edition: *The Life of St. John of the Cross*, trans. Kathleen Pond (London: Longmans, 1958). See also Gerald Brenan's *St. John of the Cross: His Life and Poetry* (Cambridge: Cambridge University Press, 1973), and Ross Collings's *John of the Cross* (Collegeville, Minn.: Liturgical Press, 1990).

Much of the current scholarship on Teresa of Jesus and the early Discalced Carmelites has been published in the form of collected essays and anthologies. For example, Electa Arenal and Stacey Schlau, *Untold Sisters: Hispanic Nuns in Their Own Works* (Albuquerque: University of New Mexico Press, 1989), offers analysis and writings by the Carmelite authors Ana de San Bartolomé, María de San José, Cecilia del Nacimiento, and María de San Alberto. *Introducción a la lectura de Santa Teresa*, ed. Alberto Barrientos (Madrid: Editorial de Espiritualidad, 1978), brings together essays by excellent Carmelite scholars on Teresa's life, times, and spirituality and in-depth studies of her individual works. Many of these same scholars collaborated on a series of collected essays published by the Carmelite Editorial de Espiritualidad in Madrid: *Perfil histórico de Santa Teresa* (1981), *Hombre y mundo en Santa Teresa* (1981), and *Teresa de Jesús, mujer, cristiana, maestra* (1982). In English, two collections by E. Allison Peers are still useful, *Saint Teresa of Jesus and Other Essays and Addresses*

(London: Faber and Faber, 1953) and *Studies in the Spanish Mystics*, 2 vols. (London: Sheldon Press, 1927). A number of proceedings of conferences marking the fourth centenary of Teresa's death in 1982 have been published. Among the most comprehensive are *Centenary of Saint Teresa: Proceedings of The Catholic University Symposium, October 15–17, 1982*, ed. John Sullivan, Carmelite Studies 3 (Washington: Institute of Carmelite Studies, 1984); *Santa Teresa y la literature mística hispánica: Actas del I congreso internacional sobre Santa Teresa y la mística hispánica (1982)*, ed. Manuel Criado de Val (Madrid: EDI-6, 1984); and *Actas del congreso internacional teresiano (4–7 octubre, 1982)*, edd. Teófanes Egido Martínez et al., 2 vols. (Salamanca: Universidad de Salamanca, 1983). The fourth centenary of John's death in 1991 also caught the attention of scholars; see, for example: *Aspectos históricos de San Juan de la Cruz*, ed. Comisión Provincial del IV Centenario de la muerte de San Juan de la Cruz (Avila: Institución Gran Duque de Alba, 1990); *John of the Cross: Conferences and Essays by Members of the Institute of Carmelite Studies and Others*, ed. Steven Payne, Carmelite Studies 6 (Washington, D.C.: Institute of Carmelite Studies, 1992); and, most important, *God Speaks in the Night: The Life, Times, and Teaching of St. John of the Cross*, trans. by Kieran Kavanaugh (Washington, D.C.: Institute of Carmelite Studies, 1991), the collaborative effort of top Carmelite scholars from several countries; this is also available in Spanish and Italian.

There are dozens of books and articles that treat aspects of Teresian history, literature, and spirituality. Here are, listed in alphabetical order, some of the most helpful and thought-provoking published during the last thirty years: Tomás Alvarez, *Santa Teresa y la iglesia* (Burgos: El Monte Carmelo, 1980); Jodi Bilinkoff, *The Avila of Saint Teresa: Religious Reform in a Sixteenth-Century City* (Ithaca: Cornell University Press, 1989); Joseph Chorpenning, *The Divine Romance: Teresa of Avila's Narrative Theology* (Chicago: Loyola University Press, 1992); E. Trueman Dicken, *The Crucible of Love: A Study of the Mysticism of St. Teresa and St. John of the Cross* (New York: Sheed & Ward, 1963); Teófanes Egido, O.C.D., "The Historical Setting of St. Teresa's Life." *Carmelite Studies*, 1 (1980), 122–82 and "The Economic Concerns of Madre Teresa," *ibid.*, 4 (1987), 151–72. (This article, published in two parts, is the only one by this fine Carmelite historian that has been translated from Spanish into English); Victor García de la Concha, *El arte literario de Santa Teresa* (Barcelona: Ariel, 1978); José Gómez-Menor Fuentes, *El linaje familiar de Santa Teresa y de San Juan de la Cruz* (Salamanca: Gráficas Cervantes, 1970); Nicolás González y González, *El monasterio de la Encarnación de Avila,* 2 vols. (Avila: Caja Central de Ahorros y Préstamos, 1976); Francis L. Gross, Jr., with Toni P. Gross, *The Making of a Mystic: Seasons in the Life of Teresa of Avila* (Albany: State University of New York Press, 1993); Elizabeth Teresa Howe, *Mystical Imagery: Santa Teresa de Jesus and San Juan de la Cruz* (New York: Peter Lang, 1988), Enrique Llamas Martínez, *Santa Teresa de Jesús y la Inquisición española* (Madrid: Consejo Superior de Investigaciones Científicas, 1972); J. Mary Luti, "Teresa of Avila, Maestra espiritual," Ph.D. diss., Boston College, 1987; eadem, *Teresa of Avila's Way* (Collegeville, Minn.: Liturgical Press, 1991); Francisco Márquez Villanueva, "Santa Teresa y el linaje," in *Espiritualidad y literatura en el siglo XVI* (Madrid: Alfaguarra, 1968), pp. 141–205; Efrén de la Madre de Dios Montalva, "El ideal de Santa Teresa en la fundación de San José," *Carmelus,* 10 (1963), 219–30; Otger Steggink, *Experiencia y realismo en Santa Teresa y San Juan de la Cruz* (Madrid: Editorial de Espiritualidad, 1978); idem, *La reforma del Carmelo español: La visita canónica del general Rubeo y su encuentro con Santa Teresa (1566–1567)* (Rome: Institutum Carmelitarum, 1965); Catherine Swietlicki, *Spanish Christian Cabala: The Works of Luis de León, Santa Teresa de Jesús, and San Juan de la Cruz* (Columbia: University of Missouri Press, 1986); Alison Weber, "Teresa de Jesus," in *Spanish Women Writers: A Bio-Bibliographical Sourcebook,* edd. Linda Gould Levine et al. (Westport, Conn.: Greenwood, 1993), pp. 484–94; eadem, *Teresa of Avila and the Rhetoric of Femininity* (Princeton: Princeton University Press, 1990).

Notes

All English quotations are from the three-volume *Collected Works of St. Teresa of Avila,* trans. Kieran Kavanaugh and Otilio Rodríguez (Washington: Institute of Carmelite Studies, 1976–1985). For the original Spanish I have consulted Santa Teresa de Jesús, *Obras Completas* (Madrid: Editorial Católica, 1977). I use chapter and paragraph citations to facilitate reference to other editions. The following abbreviations are used throughout: *Life* = *The Book of Her Life; Way* = *The Way of Perfection* (Valladolid edition); *Interior* = *The Interior Castle*; *Foundations* = *The Book of Her Foundations*.

1. *Life* 32.9–10. Efrén de la Madre de Dios Montalva and Otger Steggink, *Santa Teresa y su tiempo*, 2 vols. (Salamanca: Universidad Pontificia, 1982), 1:384–88. Teresa's friend and patron Doña Guiomar de Ulloa also took part in these discussions.

2. *Life* 35.1–2. Montalva and Steggink, *Santa Teresa y su tiempo*, 1:411–13. For Teresa's interpretation of the Carmelite rule, see Efrén Montalva, "El ideal de Santa Teresa en la fundación de San José," *Carmelus*, 10 (1963), 219–30.

3. For these problems of class and caste, see Antonio Domínguez Ortiz, *Los judeoconversos en España y América* (Madrid: Istmo, 1978), and Albert A. Sicroff, *Los estatutos de limpieza de sangre: Controversias entre los siglos XV y XVII* (Madrid: Taurus, 1985).

4. Teófanes Egido, o.c.d., "The Historical Setting of St. Teresa's Life," *Carmelite Studies*, 1 (1980), 122–82. Idem, *El linaje judeo-converso de Santa Teresa (Pleito de hidalguía de los Cepeda)* (Madrid: Editorial de Espiritualidad, 1986).

5. Egido, "Historical Setting," 152ff. Nicolás González y González, *El monasterio de la Encarnación de Avila*, 2 vols. (Avila: Caja Central de Ahorros y Préstamos, 1976), 1:125–42. Otger Steggink, *La reforma del Carmelo español: La visita canónica del general Rubeo y su encuentro con Santa Teresa (1566–1567)* (Rome: Institutum Carmelitarum, 1965), pp. 289–311.

6. *Life* 7.2, 5.1.

7. González, *El monasterio de la Encarnación*, 1:143–75, 201. Montalva and Steggink, *Santa Teresa y su tiempo*, 1:239–68, 295–300, 311–17.

8. *Life* 32.9. Teresa came to stay with Doña Luisa de la Cerda after the death of the latter's husband. There she met María de Yepes. *Life* 34.1.

9. E. Allison Peers, *Studies in the Spanish Mystics*, 2 vols. (London: Sheldon, 1927), 1:79–131. Sara T. Nalle, "Literacy and Culture in Early Modern Castile," *Past and Present*, 125 (1989), 65–96.

10. *Life* 7.17.

11. *Life* 7.6–8.

12. *Life* 9.8.

13. *Life* 23.2.

14. Jodi Bilinkoff, *The Avila of Saint Teresa: Religious Reform in a Sixteenth-Century City* (Ithaca: Cornell University Press, 1989), pp. 78–107.

15. *Life* 24.7–10.

16. "Documents Illustrative of the Life, Works, and Virtues of Saint

Teresa," in *The Complete Works of Saint Teresa of Jesus*, trans. E. Allison Peers, 3 vols. (New York: Sheed & Ward, 1946), 3:313.

17. *Life* 32.1–5.

18. *Life* 32.9.

19. *Life* 32.11.

20. On Franciscan tradition see Lester K. Little, *Religious Poverty and the Profit Economy in Medieval Europe* (Ithaca: Cornell University Press, 1978); Teófanes Egido, O.C.D., "The Economic Concerns of Madre Teresa," *Carmelite Studies*, 4 (1987), 151–72.

21. *Foundations* 27.13.

22. *Way* 27.6. See also *Way* 12.4.

23. Egido, "Historical Setting," 169–82.

24. *Foundations* 5.8. Later the Discalced Carmelites accepted lay sisters to help with the manual labor, but no more than three per convent. See also *Foundations* 14.6; *Constitutions*, no. 22.

25. *Way* 2.9.

26. *Constitutions*, no. 28; "On Making the Visitation," no. 19. For Teresa de Ahumada's dowry at the Incarnation, see Silverio de Santa Teresa, *Historia del Carmen Descalzo en España, Portugal, y América*, 15 vols. (Burgos: El Monte Carmelo, 1935), 1:154–55. She later referred to unreformed Carmelites as religious "of the cloth" ("del paño").

27. Bilinkoff, *Avila*, pp. 49–50.

28. *Way* 2.1–2. This translation does not identify precisely, as does the original Spanish, the source of the money that usually supported religious houses: "Dejad ese ciudado al que los puede mover a todos, al que es *Señor de las rentas y de los renteros*" (emphasis added).

29. *Way* 2.6.

30. *Constitutions*, nos. 15–20. On questions of chastity and enclosure for women in this period, see Ruth P. Liebowitz, "Virgins in the Service of Christ: The Dispute over an Active Apostolate for Women During the Counter-Reformation," in *Women of Spirit: Female Leadership in the Jewish and Christian Traditions*, edd. Rosemary Ruether and Eleanor McLaughlin (New York: Simon & Schuster, 1979), pp. 131–52.

31. *Way* 4.16, 5.1–2. Jodi Bilinkoff, "Confessors, Penitents, and the Construction of Identities in Early Modern Avila," in *Culture and Identity in Early Modern Europe: Essays in Honor of Natalie Zemon Davis*, edd. Barbara Diefendorf and Carla Hesse (Ann Arbor: University of Michigan Press, 1993), pp. 83–100.

32. *Spiritual Testimonies* 1.4. *Way* 1.2. Jodi Bilinkoff, "Woman with a Mission: Teresa of Avila and the Apostolic Model," in *Atti del convegno internazionale "Modelli di comportamento e modelli di santità: Contrasti, intersezioni, complementarità"* (Turin: Rosenberg and Sellier, forthcoming).

33. *Life* 8.5: "For mental prayer in my opinion is nothing else than

an intimate sharing between friends." For controversy over mental prayer in early modern Spain, see Bilinkoff, *Avila*, pp. 140–45; J. Mary Luti, "Teresa of Avila, Maestra espiritual," Ph.D. diss., Boston College, 1987, pp. 94–157.

34. *Interior* 7.4.14. *Way* 3.5.

35. Gerald Brenan, *St. John of the Cross: His Life and Poetry* (Cambridge: Cambridge University Press, 1973), pp. 39–51, for example. See González, *El monasterio de la Encarnación*, 1:295–320, for John's activities in Avila in the years 1571–1577.

36. *Foundations* 2:1–6. Steggink, *La reforma*, pp. 341–56 and 380–422.

37. Brenan, *St. John of the Cross*, pp. 46–51, 59–65, 71–81, and 85–89. Kieran Kavanaugh, Introduction to *Foundations* (*Collected Works* III), pp. 58–73.

38. "'Let those who are great actives, who think to girdle the world with their outward works and their preachings, take note that they would bring far more profit to the Church and be far more pleasing to God . . . if they spent half as much time in abiding with Him in prayer'" (quoted in Brenan, *St. John of the Cross*, pp. 60–61).

39. Electa Arenal and Stacey Schlau, *Untold Sisters: Hispanic Nuns in Their Own Works* (Albuquerque: University of New Mexico Press, 1989), pp. 19–117, provides an overview of this history and excerpts of works by Ana de San Bartolomé and María de San José.

40. *Foundations* 9:2–3; 20:13. Kavanaugh, Introduction to *Foundations*, pp. 38–41. Egido, "Economic Concerns," 56–162.

41. Egido, "Economic Concerns," 156–58, and "Historical Setting," 169, 182n198.

42. Luti, "Teresa of Avila, Maestra espiritual," pp. 53–56.

43. Teófanes Egido, "El tratamiento historiográfico de Santa Teresa," in *Perfil histórico de Santa Teresa* (Madrid: Editorial de Espiritualidad, 1981), pp. 13–31.

44. "'I never knew, or saw, Mother Teresa of Jesus while she lived on earth; but now that she lives in Heaven I do know her, and I see her almost continuously in two living images of herself which she left us in her daughters and her books'" (quoted in Peers, *Complete Works*, 3:368–69. My thanks to Professor Joseph Chorpenning for this reference).

45. Rosa Rossi, *Teresa de Avila: Biografía de una escritora* (Barcelona: Icaria, 1984), pp. 48–49, for example. Francisco Márquez Villanueva, "La vocación literaria de Santa Teresa," *Nueva revista de filología hispánica*, 32 (1983), 355–79. Alison Weber, *Teresa of Avila and the Rhetoric of Femininity* (Princeton: Princeton University Press, 1990).

46. For publication histories of Teresa's works, see Enrique Llamas Martínez, *Santa Teresa de Jesús y la Inquisición española* (Madrid: Consejo

Superior de Investigaciones Científicas, 1972), pp. 221–488; and *Introducción a la lectura de Santa Teresa*, ed. Alberto Barrientos (Madrid: Editorial de Espiritualidad, 1978).

47. Arenal and Schlau, *Untold Sisters*, pp. 19–189. Darcy Donohue, "The Discourse of Sisterhood: Evidence from the Religious Houses of Early Modern Spain," paper presented at the Sixteenth-Century Studies Conference, St. Louis, October, 1988; idem, "Writing Lives: Nuns and Confessors as Auto/Biographers in Early Modern Spain," *Journal of Hispanic Philology*, 13, No. 3 (1989), 230–39. Luti, "Teresa of Avila, Maestra espiritual," pp. 370–90.

PHILIPPVS NERIVS FLORENTINVS ÆTATIS SVÆ ANN.LXXX OBIIT ROMÆ MDXCV R PATER

Longitudine dierum replebo eum, et oftendam illi falutare meum. Psalm. 90.

St. Filippo Neri by an anonymous sixteenth-century artist. Reproduced from Gabriele Cardinal Paleotti, *De bono senectutis* (Rome: Zanetti, 1595).

7

The Congregation of the Oratory

John Patrick Donnelly, S.J.

Introduction and Spirituality

THE CHURCH of the Counter Reformation is usually depicted as an institution that narrowed and regimented the teeming diversity of medieval piety and theology. The doctrinal decrees of the Council of Trent certainly did so, but during the same years there was striking vitality and experimentation in the formation of religious confraternities and congregations. Religious orders and congregations do not spring up at the *fiat* of the hierarchy; they grow from the experience of a few Christians who feel the need to give more permanent and structured form to their religious activity. The resulting congregations of men and women can be understood only in the context of that experience.

St. Filippo Neri, the founder of the Oratorians, unlike the founders of many religious orders, did not leave a significant corpus of writings as a spiritual legacy. He did not even write a rule for his followers. In the strict sense he did not found a religious order or congregation. What he left was a shining example and an apostolic thrust—an emphasis on the sacraments of Penance and the Eucharist and a peculiar set of devotional practices, the oratorio. The distinctive spirituality developed by the French Oratorians in the seventeenth century will be discussed later in this essay.

St. Filippo Neri

St. Filippo Neri, founder of the Oratorians, was born in Florence in 1515. During his youth he had many contacts with the Dominicans at San Marco, where the spirit of Savonarola remained strong. Filippo's father, an unsuccessful notary, sent him in 1533 to work with a cousin, a prosperous merchant near Naples; apprenticeship with relatives was common practice, but after several months young Neri left and trudged to Rome, uncertain about his future but certain that he was not cut out for business. At Rome a fellow Florentine, Galeotto del Caccia, gave him food and lodging, while Filippo undertook to tutor his two sons part-time. Mostly Filippo lived the life of an urban hermit, eating and sleeping sparsely and spending most of his time in prayer, visiting churches and the catacombs of San Sebastiano. During his first years Filippo walked the narrow streets in silence, usually by night, as he made the rounds of Rome's seven major pilgrimage churches, a journey of some twelve miles. In each he stopped for earnest prayer. Later in life he popularized this circuit, but the mood had changed to gaiety, song, and religious fellowship. After two years in Rome, Filippo recognized the need for more education in religious matters, so he acquired some books and attended lectures at the Sapienza, Rome's university, mostly in theology and philosophy. He was a quick student, but unlike Ignatius de Loyola at a similar stage, Neri continued to devote most of his time to prayer. He seems to have had no intention of taking a degree or becoming a priest.[1]

In 1538 he discontinued his studies and sold his books. Although he continued to devote most of his time to prayer, he began making wider contacts in Roman society, especially among young men who were attracted by his warm personality. He often sent them to confession as a first step toward personal reform. He steered many into the Jesuits and the Dominicans, but he himself made no step to enter a religious order. Neri made regular visits to the squalid public hospitals, bathing and encouraging the sick. In 1548 Neri and his confessor, Persiano Rosa, gave this work institutional form by setting up the Confraternity of the Most Holy Trinity, which differed little from thousands of confraternities throughout Catholic Europe. After a short period devoted to personal religious exercises, the confraternity brothers began helping the sick and pilgrims during the Jubilee of 1550. Neri, under strong pressure from Rosa, was ordained a priest on May 23, 1551, and took up residence at the church of San Girolamo della Carità, a hundred paces from the Palazzo Farnese, where he continued to live until 1583.[2]

It was also during the Jubilee of 1550 that Filippo and the Confraternity popularized at Rome the Devotion to the Forty Hours, which had begun two decades earlier in Milan. Gradually the Forty Hours (a public exposition of the Eucharist that commemorated Christ's forty hours in the tomb) came to play the major role it held in Catholic worship worldwide for the next four centuries. For Neri the Forty Hours was not a substitute for but an encouragement to frequent communion. Among his closest collaborators at San Girolamo was Buonsignore Cacciaguerra, who more than anyone in the sixteenth century deserves the title Apostle of Frequent Communion. A former merchant who was ordained at fifty-three, he settled in 1550 at San Girolamo, where he ministered to a circle of lay mystics; convinced that it was sinners who most needed the help of the sacraments, he began distributing communion daily to laymen and -women who crowded to San Girolamo—perhaps seventy on weekdays and 300 on Sundays.[3] Linked to frequent communion was frequent confession. During the Middle Ages Catholics received communion rarely—during the Easter season and perhaps at a few major feasts. Frequent communion deeply divided the priests at San Girolamo. Both Cacciaguerra and Neri were subject to petty persecution by the traditionalists—"if you only knew how much I had to suffer in that place," Neri once exclaimed in later years.[4] Cacciaguerra published a little book encouraging frequent communion which became a best seller.[5] The traditionalists at San Girolamo failed in efforts to enlist the hierarchy against Cacciaguerra and Neri. Supreme vindication came in 1579 when St. Carlo Borromeo visited the new Oratorian church of Vallicella and celebrated Mass there; so many came forward to receive the Eucharist from the hands of the "new St. Ambrose" that distribution took three hours.[6]

Important as the Eucharist was for Neri's ministry, it was in the confessional that he earned the title Apostle of Rome. His assigned duties at San Girolamo were minimal and left him

alone to follow his vocation and to transform the rather embryonic rite prescribed for the sacrament of Confession by the Fourth Lateran Council (1215) into an instrument of spiritual direction—one

that involved an ever closer relationship between a director and a
penitent and that came to constitute one of the most important
liturgical innovations of the Tridentine Church.[7]

In large measure the spirituality of the Counter Reformation grew
from the interchange between director and penitent. What actually
went on in the confessional between Neri and his penitents remains secret, of course; nor did he leave extensive letters of spiritual direction. But Neri served as confessor, director, and friend
to many young men who later became prominent churchmen; he
rarely served as director to women but many other Oratorians
did. Later in life Neri saw to it that priests at the Oratorian Chiesa
Nuova were available in the confessionals all morning on Sundays,
Wednesdays, Fridays, and feast days.[8]
    When Filippo arrived in Rome in 1533, Clement VII reigned
over a Renaissance city. Reforms began with Paul III (1534–1549),
not without some steps backward, but toward the end of St.
Filippo's life the religious atmosphere of Rome was radically different. Visitors to Rome in the 1570s, such as the English priest
Gregory Martin, the Spanish Jesuit Juan Maldonato, and Michel
de Montaigne, were struck by Roman piety.[9] Filippo Neri contributed to that transformation through both his example and his
influence with high churchmen, although his relations with the
popes were not always smooth. Like many others, he fell into
disfavor under Paul IV and Pius V; if nothing else, his merriment
and pranks must have jarred with their austere ideal of the priesthood.[10] In his later years he was generally regarded as a saint.
Gregory XIV and Clement VIII tried to make Neri a cardinal.[11]
Filippo declined because he had no taste or talent for administration, and the pomp and power of a red hat could only have hindered his ministry, which rested on his transparent sincerity, high
spirits, and goodness.
    Many stories circulated in Rome about Filippo's clairvoyance
and ability to read hearts. Today we are inclined to attribute his
success in analyzing people and events to psychological insight
and shrewdness where his contemporaries saw evidence that God
was working in and authenticating his Church through the mir-
acles of a living saint.[12] The recovery of Catholic self-confidence
in the later sixteenth century rested in good measure on such
convictions. Stories also circulated about Filippo's pranks and ec-

centricities. Famous was the old red shirt that he wore for years when at home; once he took to wearing fox fur in summer and parading about in a valuable fur cloak. He deliberately used homely and humorous language in speaking to the high and mighty, even to popes. Often he went about singing a ditty: "I am a dog chewing on a bone 'cause I can't have meat to chew on."[13] When stuffy, high-born guests came to the Oratorian community, Neri made one of the lay brothers dance a jig for them and once ordered Cesare Baronio, the famous church historian and later cardinal, to sing the *Miserere* at a wedding. He sometimes made penitents kiss the feet of a lay brother. For a time he went about with half of his beard shaved off. Once he went up to one of the Swiss guards in a solemn procession and pulled his beard. Such behavior was rooted in Neri's cheerful, playful disposition that can be traced back to childhood, but his eccentric behavior disarmed the cloying veneration in which he was held.[14] His antics reinforced one of Neri's maxims: "He who cannot bear the loss of his own honor and reputation will never advance in the spiritual life."[15] Sixteenth-century gentlemen were obsessed with their sense of honor and all too ready to fight duels to defend it. High churchmen were no less prickly about their honor. Once when ill, Neri asked Cardinal Ottavio Paravicini, who was visiting him, to fetch him a basin to spit in.[16] Filippo's "dishonorable" behavior was a silent but effective critique of a value system incompatible with the gospel.

The First Oratorians

Neri spent most of his weekday mornings hearing confessions. In the mid-afternoon friends used to gather in his room for a period of prayer and religious discussion, but as their numbers grew this was moved to a nearby refurbished loft or oratory—a chapel set up for prayer but not for Mass. Between 1554 and 1558 these services became more standardized, but remained informal. The Oratory became the name of the building, of the exercises, and of the nascent religious congregation that sponsored the exercises. These services often ran three hours, but people could come and go. Part of the time was devoted to silent prayer and vernacular hymns. The meetings began with a reading, often a devotional work or the life of a saint or even a letter from a Jesuit missionary. Anyone in attendance, including laymen, could be asked by St. Filippo to share his reflections on the subject. Another might then comment further, often in dialogue with the speaker. A prepared discourse followed, usually presented sitting down and without the rhetorical flourishes of Renaissance sermons.[17] The most important of these prepared discourses were those on church history presented by Cesare Baronio at Neri's request. On Sundays and feast days the meetings were open to women and children and often included an organized walk to various churches, singing, perhaps a sermonette by a child, and a visit to a hospital to distribute sweets. Sometimes as many as four thousand people joined the procession. Neri was the presiding spirit at these meetings but seldom seems to have made presentations.[18] During Filippo's last years improvisation and dialogue gave way to prepared presentations, usually four, but these at least avoided scholastic questions and stressed church history, the lives of the saints, and moral lessons. Older veterans lamented the lost spontaneity.[19]

In 1563–1564 the Florentine community in Rome asked Neri to take charge of their church, S. Giovanni dei Fiorentini. He sent them some of his closest companions, while he continued at San Girolamo; these provided the nucleus from which the Congregation of the Oratory grew. By 1567 there were eighteen members, living a community life but without vows or formal superior, although they looked to Filippo for leadership and were dubbed Filippini after him. When friction arose with the Florentines, the Filippini decided they needed a church of their own.[20] On July 15, 1575, Gregory XIII issued the bull *Copiosus in misericordia*, which recognized the Filippini as a congregation of priests and secular clergy and authorized them to draw up constitutions and rules which were then to be submitted to the pope for approval. The bull also put them in charge of the little church of Santa Maria in Vallicella. The old church of Santa Maria, just down the Corso from San Giovanni, was razed, and a vast new church, known as the Chiesa Nuova was begun in 1575; along with the Gesù of the Jesuits on the same street, the Chiesa Nuova was a pioneer in Baroque architecture. It has served as the mother-church of the Oratorians ever since the Filippini moved their quarters there in 1577.[21]

As early as 1565 the nucleus of what was to be the future Oratorian Congregation had already been formed around Neri. Most of these priests had been trained in law and had originally planned careers in the papal court system and curia before Neri drew them to his ideal of priestly service and community living. The most talented of the group were Cesare Baronio, Francesco Maria Tarugi, both future cardinals, and Giovanni Francesco Bordini. In August 1565 Pius IV granted them a series of privileges orally which were confirmed in writing by Gregory XIII on March 13, 1576, and by Sixtus V on September 5, 1586. The first attempt at a rule, drawn up in 1569, enjoined all those in the community or those who were to enter it to recognize Neri as "their superior and father" to whom they owed prompt obedience.[22] The growth of the final Constitutions of the Congregation of the Oratory was by slow stages. After nearly eight months of discussions twice weekly at which all the senior priests could express their views, Bordini drew up a set of Constitutions in 1583. Not all the Oratorians were satisfied with the 1583 Constitutions, but all signed a summary and accepted Neri as superior. There were later drafts of the Constitutions in 1588, 1595, and 1612; the last draft received papal approbation and served as the basic document governing the Oratorians until 1918.[23] Much of the Oratorian history has been a dialectic between the ideal of a free association of priests serving like ordinary diocesan priests but living in community and the tendency toward the more elaborate structures and rules of religious orders. Among the early Oratorians the chief spokesman for the second viewpoint was Antonio Talpa, who was able later to put some of his views into practice as superior of the large community in Naples.[24]

Neri himself was content with a few simple directives, but others were eager for a fuller set of laws.[25] Neri denied having begun the Congregation and seems to have distrusted its formal development. As he told a friend late in life, "I have not made this Congregation, God has made it, which I had never thought to make a Congregation."[26] Still, his contribution to the nascent congregation overshadowed that of his colleagues. It was he who had gathered and formed them and who gave them their goal. He exercised an informal veto on decisions regarding the Constitutions. He successfully opposed founding a new religious order: members of the Oratory were not to take the three vows of poverty, chastity, and obedience, and while they were to live in community, they retained their patrimonies. Some rules there must be, but these were to be minimal and look to the good ordering of the community. Superiors should rule by example. As Baronio put it later: "Our saint did not wish the government to belong to a single person, but that it should be a kind of well-ordered republic. That is why he took pains to suppress prerogatives generally exercised by superiors in other Congregations."[27] The 1583 Constitutions forbade priests to seek benefices or engage in secular affairs. The priests were to deal with one another as equals. All were expected to make mental prayer, but individuals were free to decide its time, place, and duration. Later redactions of the Constitutions tended to add specific recommendations, but these were light indeed compared to the rules of the religious orders. Thus, the Constitutions of 1612 state that meals were to be taken in common; after a reading at table one priest was to propose for formal discussion two problems, one dealing with Scripture, the other with moral theology. Curiously, the 1583 Constitutions said little about the priestly services which in Neri's view gave purpose and life to the Congregation. In fact, these services occupied most of the day. During the morning hours from dawn to noon one Mass followed another at the Chiesa Nuova, while the services and sermons of the oratory, already described, took most of the afternoon hours.[28]

The ambiguity of the Oratorian lifestyle and canonical status allowed the Oratorians to enjoy some advantages of both the diocesan and the regular clergy. They lived together as a community under a superior, which brought them a measure of discipline and the psychological support of companionship. By not claiming status as religious, they avoided the hostility toward religious communities found in many circles and their actions were not challenged, as were those of the Jesuits, when they did not perform all the practices traditionally associated with religious orders, such as wearing a distinctive habit and singing the Office in common.

Expansion Outside Rome

The friction with the Florentine community of Rome, whose church the Oratorians served before moving to the Chiesa Nuova, severely tempted San Filippo and his companions to take up an invitation from St. Carlo Borromeo to transfer their work to Milan in 1569; but several tasks imposed on his men by the pope and Neri's reluctance to see their apostolate in Rome dismantled scotched the transfer to Milan. In 1575 four Oratorians did establish a community in Milan, but difficulties soon developed, and Neri abruptly ordered them back to Rome the next year. St. Carlo founded a congregation of Oblates, partially modeled on the Oratorians but under his own strict control; one noteworthy difference was that the Oblates were bound to recite the Office in common. The imperious cardinal-archbishop and the gentle, genial San Filippo represent the polar opposites of Counter-Reformation sanctity.[29] Neri was reluctant to send his men out to form new communities. Their numbers barely sufficed for the oratory services and sermons among the people of Rome, which was always Neri's priority.[30] With the exception of Naples, the Oratorians spread to other Italian towns because local priests were inspired by what they saw and heard about the Philipine oratory, imitated its work, and requested affiliation. The first official affiliation came in 1579 with a community at San Severino in the Marches. Two groups of priests in Milan and other groups at Lucca, Bologna, and Fermo modeled themselves on the Roman community but without official links. Many churches—those at Naples, Montepulciano, and Verona, for instance—tried to imitate the oratory service of the Chiesa Nuova.[31]

It was at Naples in 1586 that the most important Oratorian community outside Rome was set up. Only reluctantly did Neri bow to the urging of Francesco Maria Tarugi and agree to send some of his best men there, including Tarugi and Antonio Talpa. The Naples community grew quickly and had nearly thirty members by 1588; many Neapolitans were attracted to its services, and generous benefactors came forward with financial support. Tarugi was the nominal superior from 1586 until his appointment by Clement VIII as archbishop of Avignon in 1592, but much of his time was spent in preaching, so that the actual direction of the community at Naples fell to Talpa.[32]

Tarugi and Talpa had a dream that the Oratorians could provide a model for reformed diocesan clergy throughout Europe; Neri entertained no such grand vision—he was concerned with and concentrated on providing priestly service to the people of

Rome—and opposed the expansion of the Congregation. At Naples the lifestyle of the Oratorians in many respects paralleled that of the religious orders, even though vows were not introduced. Partly the shift depended on minor touches: the cassocks in Naples were sewn up the middle, so that they were distinct from cassocks worn by diocesan priests; the Oratorians were addressed as *Padre*, the title given religious, and like religious they traveled outside the community with a companion. The priests were not to have personal possessions, their books, clothing, and furniture being furnished by the community.[33] Neri acquiesced reluctantly in these changes: "I accept and do not condemn your manner of life, even though it is more strict than ours here."[34]

More important were the number and the sort of young men that sought to join the Oratorians in Naples. In Rome recruits had been sparse; most of them were mature, and many were already priests so that they could be fitted into the community without much training or formation. In the first three years at Naples the Oratorians attracted twenty-five recruits, most of them quite young, boisterous, and lacking theological or spiritual training, and the drop-out rate was high. Tarugi and Talpa waived the requirement that recruits be at least eighteen. Since the recruits easily outnumbered the veterans, their formation could not be by mere assimilation into a large community where the veterans served as role models, as had been the Roman practice. Accordingly, a separate building was set up as a novitiate to train the young men, although they shared the community chapel and refectory. All these Neapolitan developments made the Roman Oratorians uneasy.

The main divergence, however, involved finances. At Rome the recruits usually had a patrimony or source of income, which they retained, but they were expected to make a regular contribution to the community's expenses. The young men entering at Naples had no financial security, and many came from a lower stratum of society than in Rome. Fortunately, outside benefactors provided for most of the community's expenses, although the community lived a leaner lifestyle than in Rome. Tarugi and Talpa felt that to require recruits to pay a regular sum to the community expenses would discourage or prevent many good recruits from entering. Recruits without money were welcome. Tarugi justified this to the Romans by observing that it would be cruel to turn away poor but zealous young men, and he invoked the parable of the man knocking on the door in the middle of the night for bread. Those recruits who did have money were asked to make a gift; they could keep their patrimony but were required to give an account of their income and were to spend it on charitable works. Tarugi also offered to send men to Rome after their training in Naples. In 1589 he also tried to get Filippo to come to Naples so he could see and judge the new community for himself, but the saint was old, infirm, and reluctant to leave Rome.[35]

Tarugi served as rector at Naples from 1586 to 1592, when Clement VIII made him archbishop of Avignon. There he did sterling service. In the same year the pope made Bordini bishop of Cavaillon. Later, Tarugi was appointed archbishop of Siena, and Bordini took his place in Avignon. In 1596 Clement VIII made both Tarugi and Baronio cardinals. These appointments no doubt gave great luster to the small Congregation of the Oratory, but it also robbed it of its best men at a time when Neri's own health was deteriorating and finding a successor as provost or superior general for the Congregation was a pressing concern. In 1587 Neri's health took a sharp turn for the worse. He tried to resign, but the community at Rome rejected his offer. There was no doubt that Tarugi was the obvious choice for provost in the mind of both the Roman community and Neri himself.[36] But Tarugi was absorbed in his new assignment in Naples, and gradually Neri's health recovered. At seventy-eight, Neri resigned in 1593. On July 21 two cardinals brought the community the name of Clement VIII's choice for his successor: Cesare Baronio. That evening the fathers in Rome went though an election and confirmed the pope's choice.[37] He continued in office until he was made a cardinal in 1596.

Baronio, or Baronius (1538–1607), was not Tarugi's equal as a preacher or administrator, but he was the greatest scholar among the Italian Oratorians and the only Oratorian who made a major contribution to the Counter Reformation (the effort to refute and repress Protestantism as distinct from the Catholic Reform understood as the theological, devotional, and moral reform and renewal of the Catholic Church). As has been seen, Neri urged Baronio to preach on church history at the oratory meetings and thereby encouraged his studies that made him the greatest church historian of the era. Reformation polemics involved arguments drawn from church history, an area largely neglected by medieval scholasticism, and both Protestants and Catholics developed conflicting ecclesiologies which they traced back to the early Church. The most important Protestant history was the *Centuries of Magdeburg* written by a group of Lutheran scholars who were encouraged by Matthias Flacius Illyricus. The work was in thirteen massive, learned volumes, one for each of the first thirteen centuries of Christianity, and was published in Magdeburg between 1559 and 1574. The work as a whole set out to prove how the Roman popes had progressively perverted apostolic Christianity.

Obviously, Catholics had to respond. Peter Canisius started the task, but it proved beyond his powers. Neri encouraged Baronio to devote his life to writing a systematic Catholic interpretation of church history. The result was the twelve large volumes of the *Annales ecclesiastici* (Rome, 1588–1607) which were based on a meticulous study of documents from the Roman libraries and archives and from materials sent to Baronio by scholars from throughout Catholic Europe. If both the *Centuries* and the *Annales* have a polemical slant, they nevertheless raised the level of historiography by building on a solid base of documents. Too much of Renaissance humanist historiography had neglected archival investigation in favor of rhetorical effects.[38]

Filippo Neri died on May 26, 1595 at age seventy-nine. The funeral ceremonies attracted an immense crowd, including many cardinals. After Neri's death the balance of power within the Congregation passed to the Naples community, which was supported by the two Oratorian cardinals, Baronio and Tarugi. In 1597 Clement VIII, urged on by Baronio, instructed the leaders of the Roman Oratory that they must consult with the Oratorian cardinals before making important decisions; he went on to forbid them from trying to force Naples to conform to Roman practices.

Meanwhile, the Neapolitans were trying to get the Romans to adopt two of their practices: first, that members were to make a promise (not a vow) to remain with the Congregation until death, and, second, that the Congregation should administer private property during the lifetime of an Oratorian and inherit it after his death. In 1601 the Roman community wrote to Naples and demanded that the Oratorians there cease acting contrary to the Constitutions. The Neapolitans replied by sending a delegate to Rome who proposed, after consulting with Baronio, that the two communities should split and go their own separate ways. The Romans backed away from this, claiming that they did not want to impose their views on another community or to split up the two communities that claimed Neri as their founder.[39]

In 1602, after long discussions and pressure from Baronio, Tarugi, and Talpa, the Roman Fathers agreed that the Naples community should be independent, as were the many smaller communities following the Oratorian pattern that were now springing up in many Italian cities. Talpa, supported by the two Oratorian cardinals, now conceived the plan for Naples to develop its own rule, which would become normative for the new communities. Meanwhile, the cardinals considered ways either to bring the Roman community into line with Neapolitan practice or to set up a second, Naples-style, community in Rome. In 1606 the two cardinals presented the Neapolitan rule to the pope for approval, but the Roman fathers objected to the Curia on a technicality: in 1602 the split between the two communities had not received papal ratification and hence the Naples community was still under the Roman provost or general and had no right to present a rule on its own. The cardinal in charge of the Segnatura della Giustizia was an old friend of Neri's and agreed with the Roman community. The Neapolitans had no recourse but to accept the reunion of the Congregation under the Roman provost.

Immediately after Neri's death the Romans had returned to redrafting the Constitutions. Following the saint's known wishes, they rejected the direction of convents, seminaries, and colleges; in this they were to differ sharply with the later French Oratorians, as will be seen. It was also decided that any Oratorians who spoke even privately in favor of introducing vows into the Congregation should be excluded *ipso facto* from it, even if their viewpoint enjoyed a majority among the membership. The government of the Roman Congregation was to be in the hands of the "Father," a superior elected for three years, but major decisions were to be submitted to a General Congregation. The Constitutions, redrafted yet again in 1610–1611, were finally ratified by Paul V on February 14, 1612. The next month a commission of cardinals decreed a second and permanent separation of the Rome and Naples Oratories. Henceforward, every Oratorian community was to be self-governing, including those already founded. Communities that later took the name of the Congregation of the Oratory were independent and under the jurisdiction of the local bishop but were expected to model their constitutions on those of the Roman Oratory in accord with a brief of Gregory XV of July 8, 1622.[40]

In the course of the seventeenth and eighteenth centuries some 150 Oratorian communities were set up after the Roman model. Here the overview of the expansion of the Philipine Oratory concentrates on the early seventeenth century since that is the focus of this volume. The early spread was largely confined to Italy. Already discussed were the communities set up at San Severino in 1579 and Naples in 1586. Between 1591 and 1650 thirty-five new Oratorian communities were established in Italy; those in large cities were at Palermo, 1593; Brescia, 1598; Perugia, 1615; Bologna, 1616; Padua, 1624; Florence, 1632; Genoa, 1644; and Turin, 1649. Venice and Milan are conspicuous for their absence, but there were communities in Venetian and Milanese territory. Ten of the new communities were south of Rome, with Sicily strongly represented; and twenty-five, north of Rome, with the Papal States strongly represented. Another twenty-nine communities were established between 1651 and 1700, and still another twenty-six between 1701 and 1774. Significantly, there were no new communities between 1775 and 1825—a pattern of decline paralleled to that of religious orders generally during the era of the French Revolution and Napoleon.[41]

The first Oratorian communities in Asia were in Portuguese India, at Goa in 1630, and at Banda in 1650; they antedated the first community in Portugal itself, set up at Lisbon in 1668. Four communities were established in northern Portugal between 1673 and 1686.[42] The only community in Brazil was set up in 1671.

The establishment of Oratorian communities in Spain began slowly. The first congregation was at Valencia in 1640, the second at Villena in 1650, and the third at Madrid in 1660. Then growth became rapid, with thirteen more communities by 1700. Oratorian houses were also established in Spanish America: four communities in Mexico between 1671 and 1697, one in Peru in 1689, and one in Guatemala in 1694.

The growth in northern Europe outside France was also slow in the seventeenth century. Two houses were founded in Belgium, both in 1620, at Montaigu and Apremont, with a third at Douai in 1629. There were two more in Poland, at Gostyn (1668) and

Sudzianna (1674). The two German houses were both at pilgrimage sites, at Kevelaer (1643) in the Rhineland and at Aufhausen
(1692) in Westphalia.

It was in France that the Oratorian ideal found its most influential expression during the seventeenth century, but developments
in France took a distinctive turn that require a more extended
examination. The first French community was at Cotignac in
Provence and had seven members when it received papal approval
in 1599. The same year St. François de Sales set up a community
at Thonon in Savoy. A Philipine community at Aix-en-Provence,
established in 1612 and approved three years later, set up eleven
daughter-houses within southern France during the next decade,
but only nine survived until 1619 when they and their mother-
community merged with the French Oratory of Jesus and Mary
Immaculate of Cardinal Bérulle.[43]

The Oratory of Pierre de Bérulle

Pierre de Bérulle (1575–1629, named a cardinal in 1627) was both
the founder of the French Oratory of Jesus and Mary Immaculate
and the most important spokesman of the distinctive spirituality
developed by the French Oratorians. Bérulle attended a Jesuit
college and made the *Spiritual Exercises* under a skilled Jesuit director. He was a friend of St. François de Sales's and confessor to
Carmelite nuns, yet his own spiritual writings were not deeply
influenced by Ignatian, Salesian, or Teresan spiritualities. The major influences on him were much older. He was steeped in the
writings of pseudo-Dionysius and especially of St. Augustine; together they formed the basis of his Neoplatonism. A secondary
influence were the Rheno-Flemish mystics, particularly Harphius.
The center of Bérulle's spirituality was Christ. The Jesus of the
synoptic gospels is overshadowed by the cosmic Christ of the
opening chapters of Ephesians and Colossians and the Word made
flesh of John's prologue. Bérulle's Christocentrism is not at the
expense of theocentrism. The Trinity is very prominent in his
thought and indeed enriches his approach to Christ, in whom he
sees a secondary trinitarian structure of Word, soul, and body.
Bérulle therefore easily overcomes the temptation of some mystics
to bypass Christ's humanity. If he dwells on the need for self-

annihilation, it is a prelude not to an empty nirvana but to an expansion of the soul's capacity for Christ. His spiritual writings are strongly oriented toward mysticism because he was writing for an audience more advanced than most readers of *The Introduction to the Devout Life* or retreatants making the *Spiritual Exercises*. For years he served as confessor to contemplative Carmelite nuns; his treatise on the vow of servitude to Jesus and Mary, written about 1612, attempted to win them over from the abstract school of mysticism to his own more Christocentric theology, but it raised a firestorm of protest from many nuns, Carmelite friars, and Jesuits. Bérulle's crowning work, *Discours de l'état et des grandeurs de Jésus* (1623, expanded in 1629) is his answer to his critics.[44]

The institutional relationship of the French Oratory to the Philipine Oratory defies easy characterization, especially since every Philipine community was canonically independent. Pierre de Bérulle, a model priest much esteemed at the French royal court, recognized as early as 1601 the need for a congregation of reformed priests who would set an example by their ministry to France, where standards were still very lax. France had just emerged from the wars of religion and was far behind Italy and Spain in beginning a sweeping Catholic reformation. Bérulle's own contacts with the Roman Oratory were mainly indirect. He knew of the work Neri had done in Rome, and two friends, St. François de Sales and Brûlard de Silly, described for him the work of the Oratorians in Italy and Savoy. He also made contacts with Père Romillion, superior of the Philipine Oratorians in Provence. Silly urged him to found a parallel organization.[45] On November 11, 1611, Bérulle founded the French Oratory with the encouragement of the archbishop at Paris, where its general continued to reside until the French Revolution suppressed the congregation. Paul V issued a bull of approbation in 1613. Two of Filippo Neri's closest associates, Tarugi and Bordini, served as successive archbishops of Avignon and encouraged the growth of the Philipine Oratorians in southern France.

Although the French Oratorians were closer to the Naples model cherished by Tarugi and Bordini than the Roman model that had triumphed in Italy, Neri and Bérulle shared a fundamental vision: devout priests living in community without vows but bound together by charity and by their work for God and his church. In both Italy and France the priests were incardinated in the diocese and worked under the bishop without the exemptions enjoyed by the religious orders. The model that Bérulle held up to his priests was Christ the Incarnate Word who through his priestly sacrifice reconciles man with God.[46] Priests of this sort, Bérulle was convinced, would be an inspiration for the French clergy generally and would blunt the attraction of Calvinism.[47]

The French Oratory differed from the Italian on many points. Bérulle and his successor as superior general, Charles de Condren (1588–1641), were gifted theologians and writers who developed the distinctive spirituality discussed earlier. Bérulle felt that French conditions demanded a tighter organization than in Italy; the communities were linked together under a general who served for life. The general, however, was under the authority of a General Assembly which was elected every three years and met to approve or reject his decisions. The General Assembly, moreover, elected his major subordinates. The general's power was then small indeed compared with that of the Jesuit general.[48] There were distinct novitiates and houses of formation for younger members at Paris, Lyons, and Aix.[49] The French seemed uninterested in developing the sort of oratory service that made the Chiesa Nuova so distinctive and was so beloved by Neri, but their singing of the Divine Office, often accompanied by musical instruments, was widely admired.[50] The French Oratorians, like the Jesuits, Capuchins, Vincentians, and Eudists, engaged in revival missions in country parishes.

Above all, the French Oratorians devoted themselves to teaching and running colleges, seminaries, and even military academies. Education played no more a part in Bérulle's original plans than in Neri's; the task was imposed by Paul V's bull of approbation.[51] The educational apostolate had two side effects, one good, one bad. The French developed a tradition of scholarship that far outstripped the Italians, Baronio excepted. But they also came into rivalry with the Jesuits, whose colleges dominated secondary education in seventeenth-century France. Bérulle foresaw the problem and instructed his men to avoid towns that possessed a Jesuit college. Many towns needed colleges, and when the city government could not get Jesuits or did not want them, the Oratorians were the obvious alternative. The curriculum at Oratorian colleges tended to be more modern and flexible, with less emphasis on classical languages and literature, than the Jesuit *Ratio Studiorum* allowed. Both sets of colleges were famous for their drama.

The rivalry progressively took on ideological dimensions. Bérulle was strongly attached to the papacy, and the early Oratorians faced opposition from the Sorbonne and the Parlement of Paris, but, later, Gallicanism became widespread among the French Oratorians. More important, so did Jansenism. Some generals—for instance, François de Bourgoing (general, 1641–1662)—opposed Jansenism strongly, but Abel Louis de Sainte-Marthe (general, 1672–1696) was sympathetic to it.[52] The most intransigent of the Oratorian Jansenists was Pasquier Quesnel (1634–1720), who fled to the Dutch Netherlands and set up a Jansenist church rather than submit to Louis XIV and the pope. Many young men from Jansenist families chose to join the Oratory precisely because they found there a tolerant or even congenial atmosphere.

In 1644 the fifth General Assembly decreed that the Congregation did not espouse any particular doctrinal option accepted among Catholics. Oratorians tended to scriptural and patristic studies, especially St. Augustine, more than scholasticism, to Plato more than Aristotle, and to spirituality more than dogmatics. This open atmosphere nurtured the attempts of Nicholas de Malebranche (1675–1715) and Bernard Lamy (1640–1715) at a synthesis of Descartes and St. Augustine. Louis Thomassin (1619–1695) pursued historical studies in theology, liturgy, and canon law. The greatest of the galaxy of French Oratorian scholars was Richard Simon (1638–1712), the father of the historical-critical study of the Bible.

Like the Philipine Oratory, its French sister was initially a community of priests. Although there were lay brothers in the Italian communities, they were few, and their main task, like that of the Jesuit brothers, was to serve the community. In addition to the traditional brothers, the French Oratorians developed a new category called confrères, who taught in the colleges. Since they took neither vows nor holy orders, the confrères could easily leave the Oratorians. The turnover rate among these young men steadily increased so that in the eighteenth century the Oratorian colleges often served to provide in-service training for young teachers before they moved on to better-paying jobs. This evolution certainly served the young men involved and education in France generally, but that was hardly how Neri and Bérulle saw the Oratorian vocation.[53]

The numerical growth of the French Oratory was rapid during Bérulle's generalate. In 1630, a year after his death, there were sixty-three communities, including thirteen colleges and four seminaries staffed by 400 priests, not counting lay brothers and young men in formation. During the next thirty years growth slowed, and education became still more the predominant ministry. By 1700 the Oratorians were operating twenty-two colleges and at least nineteen seminaries. In 1650 there were 480 priests. Growth peaked at 650 priests in 1714, after which a decline set in. By 1783 there were only 298 priests compared to 438 confrères; the latter made up 80 per cent of the teaching staff at the colleges. The French Revolution, which many Oratorians initially favored, abolished the Congregation. Since its re-establishment in 1852, its growth in France has been very slow. The French Oratorians also spread to the Spanish Netherlands, but in 1649 the Flemish houses became independent while the Walloon houses remained under the general in Paris. The age profile of entering novices changed gradually; from 1630 to 1679 the average age at entry was 23.3 years; from 1680 to 1759 it was 20.9. The fathers of the novices were almost without exception men of substance: 14 per cent were noblemen and 85 per cent were office holders, merchants, or professional men. Only 1 per cent were *laboureurs* or prosperous farmers. It seems that virtually none of the priests or confrères was recruited from the poorer peasants, who made up the majority of Frenchmen, although many of the lay brothers came from peasant backgrounds.[54] The location of Oratorian communities and the birthplace of the members was unevenly spread through France. While twelve provinces contributed less than 1 per cent each to the Congregation, in the period from 1611 to 1662 20 per cent came from Provence, 11 per cent from Normandy, and 9 per cent from the Ile de France.[55]

The French Oratorians had close links with three other religious communities. Before founding the French Oratory, Bérulle worked to establish Discalced Carmelite nuns in France and served as co-superior and confessor to many of them, including their leader Madame Acarie, Blessed Marie de l'Incarnation. His efforts to have the nuns take a vow of servitude to Jesus and Mary caused unquiet and resentment since many saw this vow as a confusing addition to the traditional religious vows. The Carmelite friars resented his role as co-superior and that of other Oratorians as confessors. His successor as general, Charles de Condren, was weary of the friction with the Carmelites, both male and female, and severed formal ties.[56]

Among Condren's penitents was Jean-Jacques Olier (1608–1657), whom he trained in Oratorian spirituality and inspired with the desire to establish Tridentine seminaries in France. In 1643 Olier, pastor of St. Sulpice in Paris, received approval for a society of priests who would devote themselves to staffing seminaries. By Olier's death the Sulpicians were directing seminaries in Paris, Nantes, Viviers, Le Puy, and Clement. Somewhat parallel is the story of St. Jean Eudes (1601–1680), who joined the Oratory in 1620 and was trained as a preacher by Condren. Later he enjoyed great success as a spiritual writer and in giving parish missions and conferences to parish priests. At Caen, where he was superior, he made plans for a seminary, but in 1641 Condren, who had encouraged his plans, died. His successor as general was François Bourgoing (1585–1662), who opposed the project. In 1643 Eudes left the Oratorians and set up the Congregation of Jesus and Mary, known as the Eudists, as a society of diocesan priests without vows dedicated to running seminaries and giving parish missions. By 1670 the Eudists were in charge of six seminaries in northern France. Both the Sulpicians and the Eudists were suppressed during the French Revolution but revived in the nineteenth century; today both outnumber the French Oratorians, who underwent the same fate.

BIBLIOGRAPHIC ESSAY

Only after this essay was completed did the most comprehensive and recent work on the Oratorians come to the author's attention: Antonio Cistellini's three-volume *San Filippo Neri: L'oratorio e la congregazione oratoriana, storia e spiritualità* (Brescia: Morcelliana, 1989). From 1970 to 1977 the journal *Oratorium: Archivum Historicum Oratorii Sancti Philippi Neri* was published semi-annually in Rome. Although devoted mainly to the Philipine Oratorians, it also carried articles on the French Oratory.

There are dozens of biographies of St. Filippo Neri. The most scholarly is that by Louis Ponnelle and Louis Bordet, *St. Philip Neri and the Roman Society of His Times (1515–1595)*, trans. R. F. Kerr (London: Sheed and Ward, 1932; repr. 1979), which builds on new archival research and discusses the sources for Neri's life (pp. 1–46). Less scholarly but very insightful is the biography by Meriol Trevor, *Apostle of Rome: A Life of Philip Neri, 1515–1595* (London: Macmillan, 1966), best known for her studies of John Henry Newman, the great English Oratorian. We know comparatively little about Neri's early life since he was a private person who left no autobiography or spiritual journal; only some thirty letters and a few sermons survive, largely because he burnt his papers shortly before his death. There is more information on his later years when he was regarded as a saint whose every action deserved watching. The process toward canonization began soon after his death in 1595, and many eyewitnesses left their recollections in writing. Their testimony, which early biographers drew upon, has been published in four volumes by Giovanni Incisa della Roccetta and Nello Vian, *Il primo processo per s. Filippo Neri* (Rome: Vatican Press, 1957–1963). Another fundamental source is the two-volume biography first published in 1622 by Neri's young friend and disciple Pier Giacomo Bacci, *The Life of Saint Philip Neri: Apostle of Rome and Founder of the Congregation of the Oratory*, trans. F. I. Antrobus (London: Kegan Paul, 1902). Specialized studies of Neri's life and works are mentioned in the notes to this essay.

Before 1650 the vast majority of Philipine Oratorians were Italians; the best recent studies are by Antonio Cistellini, "Oratoriani," *Dizionario degli Istituti di Perfezione* (vol. 7 [Rome: Edizione Paoline, 1979], cols. 770–71), who draws on Marciano's sprawling five-volume compilation, *Memorie historiche della Congregatione dell'Oratorio* (Naples, 1693–1702). On Baronio there is Pullapilly's study of his work as historian, *Caesar Baronius: Counter-Reformation Historian* (Notre Dame: Notre Dame University Press, 1967) and a massive collection of essays from a congress devoted to Baronio in 1979: *Baronio storico e la controriforma*, edd. Romeo di Maio et al. (Sora: Centro di Studi Sorani "Vincenzo Patriarca" [1982]).

The historiography dealing with the French Oratory in the seventeenth century is richer than for the Philipine Oratory. There are more than a dozen books on Bérulle. For his life before he founded the French Oratory, the best study is that by Jean Dagens, *Bérulle et les origines de la restauration catholique (1575–1611)* (Paris: Desclée de Brouwer, 1952), who also edited *Correspondance du Bérulle* in three volumes (Paris: Desclée de Brouwer, 1937–1939). In the 1870s Michel Houssaye published three volumes on aspects of Bérulle's life: *M. de Bérulle et les Carmélites de France, 1575–1611*; *Le Père Bérulle et l'Oratoire de Jésus, 1611–1625*; and *Le Cardinal de Bérulle et le Cardinal de Richelieu, 1625–1629* (Paris: Plon, 1872, 1874, 1875). Of the many studies of Bérulle's spirituality we note here only Jean Orcibal, *Le Cardinal de Bérulle: Évolution d'une spiritualité* (Paris: Cerf, 1965) and Michel Dupuy, *Bérulle: Une spiritualité de l'adoration* (Paris: Desclée de Brouwer, 1964). The third volume of Henri Brémond's classic *Histoire litéraire du sentiment religieux en France depuis la fin des guerres de religion jusqu'à nos jours* (Paris: Bloud et Gay, 1929) deals with Bérulle and his disciples Charles de Condren and Jean-Jacques Olier and quotes extensively from them. More recent is the anthology edited by William M. Thompson with a long introduction, *Bérulle and the French School: Selected Writings* (Mahwah, N.J.: Paulist, 1989).

A useful contemporary source for the first five generals of the French Oratorians (Bérulle, Condren, Bourgoing, Senault, and Sainte-Marthe), covering the years 1611–1690, are the three volumes of Père Charles Cloyseault (1645–1738), *Recueil des vies de quelques prêtres de l'Oratoire*, ed. R. P. Ingold (Paris: Poussielgue, 1882–1883). The most sophisticated study of the French Oratorians, strongly influenced by the *Annales* school and rich in statistics and graphs, is by Willem Frijhoff and Dominique Julia, "Les Oratoriens de France sous l'ancien régime: Premiers résultats d'une enquête," *Revue d'histoire de l'église de France*, 65 (1979), 225–65. More traditional is the survey by Hedwige de Polignac in *Une société de prêtres: l'Oratoire* (Paris: Éditions Émile-Paul, 1968). There are also several studies in English: notably, Charles E. Williams's *The French Oratorians and Absolutism, 1611–1641* (New York: Lang, 1989); Stephen John Wagley's "The Oratory of France, 1629–1672: A Social History," Ph.D. diss., University of Toronto, 1976; and H. G. Judge's "The Congregation of the Oratory in France in the Late Seventeenth Century," *The Journal of Ecclesiastical History*, 12 (1961), 46–55. Useful for Oratorian schools is a volume by Paul Lallemand, *Histoire de l'éducation dans l'ancien Oratoire de France* (Paris: Thorian, 1889; repr. Geneva:

Slatkine-Megariotis, 1976). A good study of an individual community is Jacques Maillard's *L'Oratoire à Angers aux XVIIe et XVIIe siècle* (Paris: Klincksieck, 1975). The literature on the great French Oratorian scholars, Bernard Lamy, Nicholas de Malebranche, Pasquier Quesnel, Richard Simon, and Louis Thomassin, is immense; a good starting point is the *Dictionnaire de théologie catholique*.

NOTES

1. Louis Ponnelle and Louis Bordet, *St. Philip Neri and the Roman Society of His Times (1515–1595)*, trans. R. F. Kerr (London: Sheed and Ward, 1932, reprinted 1979), pp. 65–112 for the hermit years; Meriol Trevor, *Apostle of Rome: A Life of Philip Neri, 1515–1595* (London: Macmillan, 1966), pp. 46–47.

2. Trevor, *Apostle of Rome*, pp. 66–68. Neri's work at San Girolamo is also discussed by G. L. Masetti Zannini, "San Filippo a San Girolamo della Carità," *Oratorium*, 6 (1975), 38–42.

3. Trevor, *Apostle of Rome*, pp. 75–80.

4. Ponnelle and Bordet, *St. Philip Neri and Roman Society*, pp. 182–86; Trevor, *Apostle of Rome*, p. 83.

5. On Cacciaguerra see Romeo De Maio, *Un mistico senese nella Napoli del Cinquecento* (Milan and Naples: Ricciardi, 1965).

6. Trevor, *Apostle of Rome*, pp. 80–85, 196; Ponnelle and Bordet, *St. Philip Neri and Roman Society*, p. 334. Later in life Neri recommended weekly communion to devout penitents. Ibid., p. 590. He insisted that all priests at the Roman Oratory celebrate Mass daily, so that up to twenty Masses were available each day for worshipers. Ibid., p. 338.

7. Eric Cochrane, *Italy, 1530–1630*, ed. Julius Kirshner (London and New York: Longman, 1988), p. 130.

8. Ponnelle and Bordet, *St. Philip Neri and Roman Society*, p. 388. Among Neri's penitents were eighteen future cardinals and three future popes: Clement VIII, Leo XI, and Gregory XIV.

9. Ibid., p. 16.

10. Trevor, *Apostle of Rome*, pp. 128–34, 172–73; Ponnelle and Bordet, *St. Philip Neri and Roman Society*, pp. 229–30, 268–70, 279–84.

11. Ponnelle and Bordet, *St. Philip Neri and Roman Society*, pp. 492, 514–16, 526, 529.

12. Ibid., pp. 113, 148–65.

13. Trevor, *Apostle of Rome*, pp. 144, 219, 280.

14. Ibid., pp. 213, 279, 258, 144; Ponnelle and Bordet, *St. Philip Neri and Roman Society*, pp. 423, 496.

15. Trevor, *Apostle of Rome*, p. 208.

16. Ibid., p. 266.

17. These Roman practices bear an interesting resemblance to prophesying among Elizabethan puritans. See Patrick Collinson, *The Elizabethan Puritan Movement* (Berkeley: University of California Press, 1967), pp. 168–76.

18. Ponnelle and Bordet, *St. Philip Neri and Roman Society*, pp. 263–65; Trevor, *Apostle of Rome*, pp. 117–22. Joseph Connors, *Borromini and the Roman Oratory: Style and Society* (Cambridge: The MIT Press, 1980), p. 6. Connors's work discusses the splendid Baroque oratory designed by Borromini next to the Oratorians' mother church of S. Maria in Vallicella that replaced Neri's humble oratory at San Girolamo. Scholars today no longer trace the development of the musical oratorio from the hymns or *laude* sung by Neri and his associates. See *The New Grove Dictionary of Music and Musicians*, s.v. "Oratorio," by Howard E. Smither, XIII:656–57, and Ponnelle and Bordet, *St. Philip Neri and Roman Society*, p. 265.

19. Ponnelle and Bordet, *St. Philip Neri and Roman Society*, pp. 389–97; Trevor, *Apostle of Rome*, p. 275.

20. Ponnelle and Bordet, *St. Philip Neri and Roman Society*, pp. 257–59. See also G. Incisa della Rocchetta, "I discepoli di San Filippo a San Giovanni dei Fiorentini," *Oratorium*, 6 (1976), 43–50.

21. Ponnelle and Bordet, *St. Philip Neri and Roman Society*, pp. 287–317; Connors, *Borromini and the Roman Oratory*, pp. 6–8. The text of the bull of institution is discussed and printed by Alfonso M. Stickler, "La bolla *Copiosus in Misericordia* di Papa Gregorio XIII," *Oratorium*, 6 (1975), 28–34. Antonio Cistellini also discusses the bull in his "Nascita della Congregazione Oratoriana," ibid., 22–25.

22. Connors, *Borromini and the Roman Oratory*, pp. 4–6.

23. Ponnelle and Bordet, *St. Philip Neri and Roman Society*, pp. 374–79, 386, 484–89; Thomas C. G. Glover, "The Juridical Development of the Oratory from 1612 to 1918," *Oratorium*, 3 (1972), 102–16.

24. Ponnelle and Bordet, *St. Philip and Roman Society*, pp. 374–75, 476–87. The status of the Oratorians in church law is discussed by Robert Lemoine, *Le Droit des religieux de Concile de Trente aux instituts séculiers* (Bruges: Desclée de Brouwer, 1956), pp. 88–97.

25. Ponnelle and Bordet, *St. Philip Neri and Roman Society*, p. 373.

26. Cistellini, "Nascita," 17; see also 18–21.

27. Quoted by Ponnelle and Bordet, *St. Philip Neri and Roman Society*, p. 374.

28. Ibid., pp. 385–88, 487, 325–26. In addition to the work at the Chiesa Nuova and the attached oratory, the Oratorians visited the sick and those in hospitals, taught catechism, and served as confessors to

prisoners of the Holy Office and as censors of books. Ibid., pp. 325–27 and 469–70. They were also involved in work of the many confraternities that flourished in Rome. Christopher Black, *Italian Confraternities in the Sixteenth Century* (Cambridge: Cambridge University Press, 1989), pp. 33, 46, 70, 190, 194, 196, 205, 208, 212, 275.

29. Ponnelle and Bordet, *St. Philip Neri and Roman Society*, pp. 307, 311–13, 329–38.

30. In 1567 there were eighteen men at the Roman Oratory, in 1575 there were twenty-six, and in 1578 there were thirty-three, of whom twenty-eight were Italians, with Piedmontese predominating. Ibid., pp. 295–97. Some members of the community were lay brothers who handled bookkeeping and the upkeep of the house. Unlike lay brothers in many religious communities, they were often literate and did not come from low social strata. Ibid., pp. 361–62.

31. Cistellini, "Nascita," 6–8, 13–16, 23, 25, 26; Ponnelle and Bordet, *St. Philip Neri and Roman Society*, pp. 372, 375, 382–83, 462, 474. There was some short-lived consideration given to merging the Oratorians with the Barnabites, and some members left the Oratorians to become Barnabites. Ibid., pp. 313, 474.

32. Trevor, *Apostle of Rome*, p. 274; Ponnelle and Bordet, *St. Philip Neri and Roman Society*, p. 483.

33. Ponnelle and Bordet, *St. Philip Neri and Roman Society*, pp. 476–78, 560.

34. Ibid., p. 479.

35. Trevor, *Apostle of Rome*, pp. 333–34; Ponnelle and Bordet, *St. Philip Neri and Roman Society*, pp. 481–84, 544–66. There was a considerable correspondence between the Roman fathers who were critical of the innovations in Naples and Tarugi and Talpa, who justified their actions as appropriate adaptations to different conditions. Ponnelle and Bordet, *St. Philip Neri and Roman Society*, pp. 479–84.

36. On Tarugi, see "Francesco Maria Tarugi, *Apostolicus Vir, omni laude praestantior,*" *Oratorium*, 6 (1975), 65–84.

37. Trevor, *Apostle of Rome*, pp. 274–86; Patrizio Dalos gives vital statistics on all the superiors general of the Congregation from Neri till 1975 in "I prepositi della Congregazione dell'Oratorio di Roma: I successori di S. Filippo Neri durante quattro secoli (1575–1975)," *Oratorium*, 6 (1975), 51–64. The usual term of office was three years, but most generals served several consecutive terms.

38. Cyriac K. Pullapilly, *Caesar Baronius: Counter-Reformation Historian* (Notre Dame: Notre Dame University Press, 1967).

39. Trevor, *Apostle of Rome*, pp. 332–36; Ponnelle and Bordet, *St. Philip Neri and Roman Society*, p. 562. Talpa's understanding of the Oratorian vocation is best seen in a document published with commentary

by Giovanni Incisa della Rocchetta, "Il trattato del P. Antonio Talpa sulle origini e sul significato dell'Istituto della Congregazione dell'Oratorio," *Oratorium*, 4 (1973), 3–41. The turbulent decade after Neri's death is reviewed by Marco Impagliazzo, "I padri dell'Oratorio nella Roma della Controriforma (1595–1605)," *Rivista di storia e letteratura religiosa*, 25 (1989), 285–307.

40. Trevor, *Apostle of Rome*, pp. 336–40; Ponnelle and Bordet, *St. Philip Neri and Roman Society*, pp. 558, 560, 562, 563. The Oratorian Constitutions also went through redrafting in 1588, but when some of the community developed second thoughts, the draft was not presented to the pope. Ibid., pp. 485–89. The Constitutions were printed in 1612 and 1630. Antonio Cistellini, "La redazione finale e le prime edizioni a stampa delle Costituzioni oratoriane," *Oratorium*, 2 (1971), 65–87.

41. Antonio Cistellini gives a list of all Italian foundations with dates and founders in his article "Oratoriani" in the *Dizionario degli Istititi di Perfezione*, vol. 7 (Rome: Edizione Paolini, 1979), cols. 770–71. His research is largely based on G. Marciano's massive *Memorie historiche della Congregatione dell'Oratorio* (Naples, 1693–1702), in 5 volumes. The most detailed recent study of one of these Italian communities is also by Cistellini, "I primordi dell'Oratorio filippino in Firenze," *Archivio storico italiano*, 126 (1968), 191–285. Cistellini also wrote the article "Oratoire philippin" in the *Dictionnaire de spiritualité*, 11:853–76, where he gives biographical data, with bibliography, on dozens of noteworthy Oratorians (869–875).

42. Eugénio dos Santos, *O Oratorio no Norte de Portugal: Contribuiçao para o estudo da história religiosa e social* (Oporto: History Center of the University of Oporto, 1982).

43. Cistellini, "Oratoriani," 771–73.

44. The classic work for Bérulle's spiritual ambiance is Louis Cognet's *La spiritualité moderne: 1500–1650* (Paris: Aubier, 1966); for Bérulle himself, see pp. 310–59; for his followers, pp. 360–410; for the Abstract School to which he was reacting, pp. 233–73.

45. Jean Dagens, *Bérulle et les origines de la restauration catholique (1575–1611)* (Paris: Desclée de Brouwer, 1952), pp. 90–91; Charles E. Williams, *The French Oratorians and Absolutism, 1611–1641* (New York: Lang, 1989), pp. 71, 84, 86; Hedwige de Polignac, *Une société de prêtres: l'Oratoire* (Paris: Éditions Émile-Paul, 1968), p. 62.

46. Williams, *French Oratorians*, pp. 74, 134–37. There were some French Oratorians who wanted to add vows but they were outvoted. Ibid., pp. 256–61.

47. Ibid., pp. 71, 80.

48. H. G. Judge, "The Congregation of the Oratory in France in

the Late Seventeenth Century," *The Journal of Ecclesiastical History*, 12 (1961), 47.

49. Paul Lallemand, *Histoire de l'éducation dans l'ancien Oratoire de France* (Paris: Thorian, 1889; repr. Geneva: Slatkine-Megariotis, 1976), pp. 208–10.

50. Polignac, *Une société de prêtres*, p. 69.

51. Paul Auvray, "L'Oratoire de France," *Oratorium*, 3 (1972), 60, 61.

52. Judge, "Congregation of the Oratory," 46–57; Lellemand, *Histoire de l'éducation*, pp. 140–82.

53. Auvray, "L'Oratoire de France," 61–62; Willem Frijhoff and Dominique Julia, "Les Oratoriens de France sous l'ancien régime: Premiers résultats d'une enquête," *Revue d'Histoire de l'Église de France*, 65 (1979), 244–49.

54. These statistics are based on Frijhoff and Julia, "Les Oratoriens de France," 227–58. They give four maps of Oratorian communities at various times (pp. 228–31); page 250 has six maps indicating the geographical origins of the Oratorians, 1641–1790; there are also five graphs and five tables illustrating Oratorian demographics (pp. 236–60). Williams also provides tables and graphs based on different manuscript sources. *French Oratorians*, pp. 338–43. His material largely confirms Frijhoff and Julia.

55. Williams, *French Oratorians*, pp. 336–37.

56. Ibid., pp. 99–172, esp. 136–39, 261–65; Polignac, *Une société de prêtres*, pp. 73–79. Carmelite convents and Oratorian communities tended to be in the same towns. Ibid., p. 67.

St. François de Sales in 1618, attributed to
Jean-Baptiste Castaz. Visitation Monastery,
Turin.

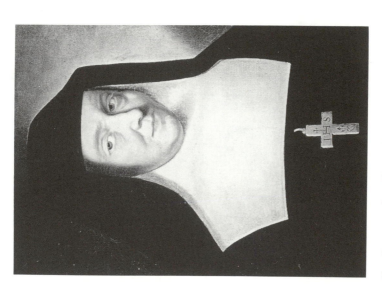

St. Jeanne de Chantal by an anonymous
seventeenth-century artist. Maison de la Galerie, Annecy.

8

The Visitation of Holy Mary: The First Years
(1610–1618)

Wendy M. Wright

IT WAS AN ERA of upheaval and of innovation. Christendom in the sixteenth and early seventeenth centuries felt the revolutionary impact of humanist thought and the religious reforming zeal that had sought to purge yet finally split Christian Europe in two. Everywhere new definitions of the Christian life were being proposed; everywhere new experiments in discipleship were being tried. Among those in the Christian world that looked to Rome for authority, adventurous new communities, arising in response to the perceived needs of the time, were emerging. One of these fledgling communities was the Visitation of Holy Mary founded in 1610 by François de Sales (1567–1622) and Jeanne de Chantal (1572–1641). Bishop de Sales and Madame de Chantal's lives spanned the turn of the seventeenth century. They also spanned and, for a moment, harmonized the turbulent currents of Catholic religiosity of the time. The two aristocrats first established their little women's congregation at Annecy in Savoy, a tiny duchy perched midway on the Alpine crest between France and Italy.

The date and place of its foundation situated the Visitation at a precarious moment in the history of women's communities in the Church. Like their male counterparts, women of the Roman communion had been experimenting with new forms of discipleship for some time. Extending the medieval monastic model of the life of "perfection" (that is, a life shaped by the vows of poverty, chastity, and obedience), Christians had felt the need for more flexible forms of community life that could accommodate more active or "apostolic" vocations and provide serious Christians with new options in the way they chose to live out their baptismal call. But while their male contemporaries were able to realize their plans rather quickly through the establishment of new canonically recognized or ecclesially sanctioned forms of life, such as communities of clerics regular, it took women's communities more than a century effectively to break in practice with the monastic model. It would take a good deal longer for the Church to formally recognize a "state" of life for women midway between the monastic and lay states.[1]

The Visitation was created midway in this process. Though, clearly, it shared the fate of many other women's congregations that were unable to institutionalize new ideals, it was not simply a group that was active in orientation and thwarted in its purpose. It was a community, I will argue, that was in its inception neither classically "contemplative" nor "active" in its vocation, but, rather, representative of a wider view of the Christian life that its founders espoused.

THE CONTEXT OF CONTEMPORARY COMMUNITIES

In both vision and form the Visitation of Holy Mary was founded and then reshaped in the turbulent and often conflicting currents coursing through Catholicism in this era of reform. On the one hand, there was a restraining current of thought that had its roots in traditional practice and was reaffirmed in the decrees of the Council of Trent. It held that to be perfect (or to embody the ideal Christ-life) one must be separated from the world in locale and dress, live in common, and vow oneself to the evangelical counsels of poverty, chastity, and obedience. In terms of positive legislation that established canons by which such a state of perfection (i.e., lifestyle) was to be officially recognized, an individual could be deemed to be in the "religious" life (perfect) when he or she belonged to a community which (*a*) had the approbation of the Holy See, (*b*) required solemn vows, and (*c*) observed cloister.[2]

Since the high Middle Ages, the Roman Church had been in the process of formulating this legislation and had frowned upon the establishment of any new religious orders. The canonical seal upon this restraining current was set in the Tridentine era when in the decade of the 1560s Pius V published his *Lubricum genus* which specified that all professed religious *must* take solemn (and thus perpetually binding) vows and his *Circa pastoralis* which imposed strict enclosure on all women religious with solemn vows and on all tertiaries and non-tertiaries living in common (with or without solemn vows). By the latter, any women's group professing itself dedicated to the evangelical counsels and to a life of Christian discipleship was obligated to accept the enclosure and solemnity of vows that defined the monastic state. The ancient form of Christian perfection, in this restraining current of thought, was to remain predominant in the Catholic world.[3]

On the other hand, the era of reform that was the sixteenth and early seventeenth centuries also witnessed an innovative current, one that addressed the need to respond to a changing world. A growing sense of call to active apostolic work among the increasing masses of urban poor, the need for evangelization among a religiously ignorant population, the desire to create supportive faith communities among men and women, laity and clergy—all these and other factors lay behind this innovative Catholic current.

To respond to these rapidly emerging issues, new groups in fact did sprout up throughout Catholic Europe. They emerged because the spirit of the times prompted it and because until Trent, and even after it, there was a lack of clarity within the Church about the status of some of those new Christian communities, which was reflected in local practice.[4] These groups were often loosely referred to as "congregations," and they often chose to constitute themselves with "simple vows" or "private vows" or without any vow at all. Frequently they functioned without cloister. The congregations were commonly regarded as legal when instituted with the consent of the local ordinary. The practice was for individual groups to seek approval at the diocesan level, and bishops were generally understood to be free to allow such associations to function within their jurisdictions. In other words, the law governing the foundation of new associations, strictly interpreted, and common practice did not always coincide.

WOMEN'S COMMUNITIES

Certainly, the Middle Ages had witnessed attempts to form women's associations that stretched the notion of the life of perfection well beyond the monastic model. The Beguines of the thirteenth century are the most noteworthy example. Originating in northern Europe, groups of Christian women, sometimes living in common, sometimes in family homes, lived chastely, simply, and did good works. The Beguine movement was eventually suppressed, primarily because of its unregulated status.[5] But the historical annals continue to provide examples of these extra-regular women's movements. The *beatas* or holy women of mid-fifteenth-century Spain are an outstanding example.[6] Likewise, the establishment in the medieval world of third orders and the formal regulation of anchorholds for solitaries might be seen as attempts on the part of ecclesial authorities to regulate to some extent the religious enthusiasm of women who were not, in their own minds, called either to cenobitic monastic life or to marriage.

Within the era of our concern, the period of Catholic reform, there is abundant evidence of innovation among women feeling themselves called to the Christ-life. Many groups managed to forge, and some occasionally to retain, an ambiguous status somewhere between the monastic and the secular states. In many ways, women's communities challenged tradition even more than their male counterparts. This was mainly because canonical legislation covering female associations as well as popular sentiment tended to be more restrictive, less amenable to granting exemptions, and less friendly toward unregulated forms of community. The popular adage, expressive of the line of thought from which this legislation flowed, was *aut maritus aut murus*, indicating that, ideally, women should have "either husbands or [cloister] walls."

Despite the widespread sentiment that discouraged options beyond marriage or enclosed religious life, women all over Europe in the sixteenth and seventeenth centuries responded to the irresistible call to band together and experiment with new forms of Christian community.[7] They showed themselves especially generous in hearing the cries of the poor and marginalized. Hospital work and providing for the needs of the destitute, the orphan, and the young girl in need of education or training most concerned them.[8] But the history of women's communities, especially in the several decades on both sides of the turn of the century, exhibits a distinctive oscillating pattern of innovative foundation and restriction.

Several of these communities were offsprings of the newly created societies of priests. The Theatines engendered a female counterpart in Italy in 1583 but, unlike its male branch, it never spread outside of its country of origin. Similarly, Antonio Zaccaria, founder of the Barnabites, had earlier breathed life into an experimental community of women, the Angelic Sisters of St. Paul, established in Milan in 1535 and in Cremona in 1549. These women gave religious instruction, organized groups of charitable women, reformed convents, and cared for orphans and the sick in cooperation with their Barnabite brothers in northern Italy. Their apostolic work was finally curtailed in 1552 with the imposition of cloister on their communities.

More successful in maintaining its non-monastic character (and in this it is unusual for its time), the earlier community of Frances of Rome, the Oblates of St. Benedict of Tor de' Specchi founded in 1425, was a society of pious women, not under formal vows, whose charism was service to the poor. Frances's name and work were famous throughout Italy, and her reputation continued to inspire Christian imitation into the period of our concern. François de Sales himself claimed her association as a model during the founding of the Visitation.[9]

There is also the slightly earlier case of Bernardina Sedazzari, a Ferrara native who founded a community of devout laywomen in 1406 under the name of Corpus Domini who maintained an unvowed lay community independent of ecclesiastical control for twenty years. Her association, due to conflicts of leadership within the group after her death, was transformed into a monastic community following the Rule of St. Augustine. Bernardina's example is part of a larger movement of pious laywomen's communities—the *penitenti* or *pinzochere*—that existed contemporaneously on the Italian peninsula during the fifteenth century.[10] All over Europe, non-monastic and unregulated women's societies continued to develop in the sixteenth century. Nearly all suffered the same fate, moving from innovation to monastic enclosure, solemn vows, and formal "religious" status by the early decades of the seventeenth century.

The Ursulines are the most well known of the associations that emerged from the innovative current surging through Christendom. Founded in 1535 at Brescia by Angela Merici as a society of virgins living without formal vows in their own homes, they dedicated themselves to the Christian education of young women.

Over time, the Ursulines underwent a number of significant transmutations. At the instigation of Bishop Carlo Borromeo, they were introduced into Milan where they were allowed to retain their flexible status midway between the secular and the technically religious state but were gathered into group-living situations. But after the community had moved onto French soil, partly because of the pressure of the restraining current made enforceable by the decrees of Trent and partly at the initiative of the Paris Ursulines themselves, in 1612 the community in France became a cloistered one observing solemn vows and the modified rule of St. Augustine.[11]

Across the English channel, a young Catholic Yorkshire woman named Mary Ward and her followers planned to open a school in The Netherlands, with the long-range plan of returning to their native England to work for the Counter-Reform. In 1614 they began this work. Referred to as the "English Jesuitesses," the English Ladies modeled themselves on the militant Society of Jesus. The story of their evangelical zeal, their early successes, and the subsequent condemnation of their efforts mainly because "they went freely everywhere, without submitting to the laws of clausura [and] exercised works unsuitable to their sex, capacity, their feminine modesty . . ." is a sad one. In 1631 a Bull of Suppression formally ended their work.[12]

On the continent numerous women's teaching congregations like the Ursulines sprouted up. Stretching the limits of contemporary ecclesial and social convention, most of these groups of vowed women experimented with forms of discipleship that challenged the traditional monastic model. The Compagnie des Filles de Notre-Dame was the inspiration of Jesuit fathers who sought to establish schools for women as counterparts to their own colleges in order to combat the force of Protestant persuasion among the female population of a religiously divided France. The Compagnie's first leader was Jeanne de Lestonnac, who, beginning in 1609, vigorously instilled in her charges the Jesuit *ratio studiorum* and the fruits of the Ignatian *Spiritual Exercises*. In structure this group was midway between the monastic model—enclosure was preserved—and the Jesuit "mixed" life of action and contemplation. To enable the women to perform their educational tasks, much of the praxis of monastic life such as the saying of the Divine Office and severe penances and fasts was lifted.[13]

About the same time as the Ursulines were being imported into Avignon, another teaching community, the Congregation de Notre Dame, was being established in Lorraine. Its founding father, Pierre de Fourier, was dedicated to the idea that religious women could work actively in the Church without giving up monastic standards by observing a modified clausura which would allow them to leave the house when necessary and to accept day students into their classrooms. Committed to the education of poor girls especially, Fourier's congregation struggled for several decades to achieve official sanction. Along the way, severe modification of the original plan occurred, including the transformation of the communities into full monastic status, which resulted in the shrinking of their central mission, the education of the poor. Similarly, the intended unity of the congregation's various houses ran awry of canonical legislations about subordination of congregations to the local bishop.[14]

These and other experiments in Christian life were taking place as the Visitation was in the process of its foundation. The Visitation was the product of an era in which flexible forms of cloister, vows, and approbation were not easily initiated. It would take a few more years for these anomalous women's groups to gain acceptance. Vincent de Paul and Louise de Marillac are generally credited with effecting this breakthrough with their Filles de la Charité, but in fact the transition was more gradual and sociologically subtle than this.[15] Before them, women's groups had mainly attempted a modification of traditional monastic life. The Filles de la Charité denied all claim to the status of "religion." Instead, they were *filles séculières*, practicing a modification of the secular life, adapting it to be more devout, more ordered. Moreover, most of the recruits for Vincent and Louise's frankly apostolic foundation, which had service to the poor, sick, and needy as its raison d'être, were drawn mainly from peasant and working classes, unlike the entrants to many monastic foundations, who were aristocratic or wealthy young women. The social and financial questions surrounding these women's entry into a form of life other than marriage were quite different.

Nonetheless, by the middle of the seventeenth century the *filles séculières* had become a respectable part of Christian society and gradually mutated into secular feminine institutes providing staffing for innumerable schools, orphanages, hospitals, and asylums:

Little by little these groups, born in response to pressing needs, broke the ancient bond between clausura and the feminine religious life. These pious women, known also as *filles dévotes* (since they were not bound by solemn vows) did not receive the name of religious, which at that time was reserved exclusively for cloistered nuns. But they existed, they endured, and they made themselves known. They received their consecration through the good works they did.[16]

THE VISITATION: FRANÇOIS DE SALES

It was in the midst of these innovative and restraining cross-currents that the Visitation of Holy Mary was born. It was the offspring of two extraordinary people, François de Sales, re-forming bishop of Geneva, eloquent preacher and noted writer, and Jeanne de Chantal, a fervent young widow of Dijon eager to dedicate her life to her God. The remarkable story of their meeting, their intense friendship, and the spiritual vision that they shared can only be alluded to here.[17] Suffice it to say that the two of them—he, filled with desire to be part of the renovation of Catholic society, and she, his directee and later his friend and colleague who experienced a call to a life of special intimacy with God—saw their desires converge in the creation of a new women's community. It was their dreams, prompted by the Spirit they believed to be behind them, that gradually gave flesh to and animated their offspring.

Before he met his future friend Jeanne, François was deeply involved in the work of the Catholic reform. Born the eldest child of a Savoyard nobleman and his young wife in 1567, de Sales fell heir to the religious controversies of his time.[18] Annecy, the Alpine city nearest to his family's estates, had been, since the 1540s, the temporary refuge of the Catholic bishop of Geneva. Roman loyalists had long been banned from the Swiss capital, the cradle of Calvinist reform, and so Catholic forces had been pushed south and were concentrated in the nearby duchy of Savoy. François grew up well aware of the controversies seething in Christendom. They were played out, as it were, on his own doorstep. As a youth he was sent to the Jesuit college of Clermont in Paris and there was introduced to the humanist curriculum that characterized Jesuit education and to the assertive spirit of renewal that motivated the Society of Jesus. The techniques of education practiced in the Jesuit schools were those proposed by humanist thinkers of the time: encouragement rather than punishment and persuasion rather than compulsion. Young François avidly absorbed much of what was offered him.

Firmly undergirding all Jesuit educational philosophy (as well as their other apostolic work) was their central principle: all for the greater glory of God. The Jesuits were engaged in the long-range task of renewing society, of nurturing a Christendom toward its full religious flowering. François as a student imbibed this principle and continued to live it for the rest of his life. He joined the local branch of the Marian Sodality, the Congregation of Mary (La Belle Dame). The Society of Jesus had overseen a veritable pan-European network of devotion in their Marian congregations.[19] Originally established in Europe's Jesuit colleges in the 1570s in order to foster a life of piety among students, these latter congregations, whose members consecrated their lives to the Virgin Mary, grew to include mature men in all walks of life and from all classes, in town and country village. Part of the Jesuit vision of the construction of a revitalized Catholic society, the Marian congregations promoted methodical meditation on the life and passion of Christ, a life of purity, the use of the imagination to transform each daily moment and event into a Christian reflection, daily examination of conscience, frequent communion, and evangelical zeal to leaven a decadent society with the yeast of fervent devotion.

Even after he left Clermont for further studies in Padua, François carried with him the spirit of Jesuit evangelization. The Jesuits were interested in the total reform of society, from workingman to housewife to merchant, aristocrat, and king. They were involved in empowering laity as well as clergy and promoted groups like the Marian congregations in pursuit of this ideal.

At Padua, where he was sent next, the young de Sales studied law, because his father wanted it, and theology, because he wanted it. Under the spiritual direction of Jesuit Father Possevin he was confirmed in his future vocation. At the university he found himself caught up in the intellectual excitement of the Neoplatonic revival. He was steeped in an atmosphere that bristled with the dialectics of divine love. He encountered the Italian Christian Re-

naissance head on and was entranced by it. Especially did he ad-
mire the legacy of Carlo Borromeo, recently deceased bishop of
Milan, whose austere sanctity and prodigious reforming activity
in his diocese were to serve as a model for the young man, particularly with regard to the creation of his own women's community.

The young Savoyard was exposed to the reputation of Frances
of Rome's congregation, actually visiting the community, and he
was introduced to the primitive Ursulines that Borromeo had
introduced into his diocese. Everywhere creative forms of Christian life were evident and caught his attention. The lingering spirit
of Filippo Neri, promulgator of a joyous and optimistic spirituality, was present in the Italian religious atmosphere and in this way
became part of François's own spirit.

When François the student left Padua in 1592, he carried away
with him an appreciation for the ferment and innovation that
characterized Italian Christianity of the late sixteenth century. He
went on to become co-adjutor to the bishop of Geneva and finally
bishop of that refugee diocese, which thrust him fully into the
religious controversies that beset the French-speaking world during the era of reform.[20] To his episcopal task François brought,
among many other gifts and perspectives, a long-range vision that
saw clearly that all works should be directed to the establishment
of a renewed Christendom, a belief that the devout life could and
must be lived at all levels of society and in all circumstances, and
an appreciation for the new possibilities that presented themselves
in pursuit of the life of perfection and the establishment of the
standard of Christ in the world.

JEANNE DE CHANTAL

It was in 1604, when he was thirty-five years old and gaining a
widespread reputation for his preaching and reforming zeal, that
François de Sales met Jeanne de Chantal. She was a young widow
of thirty-two with four young children who sought him out as
spiritual guide.[21] It was natural that she should do so for the charismatic Savoyard directed many women. Indeed, his voluminous
correspondence shows de Sales as a perceptive and insightful guide
for lay and religious women alike. He seems almost to have spe-

cialized in their spiritual care, a vocation many churchmen of his day deemed no vocation at all but a waste of time.[22]

Jeanne, a Dijonese native, came to him with a spirituality formed in the contest of the French wars of religion in which her father had been a loyalist for the Catholic cause. She brought an enthusiasm, then gaining momentum among the French Catholic population, for the life of devotion. She also brought her unique interior gifts: an unfolding capacity for deep contemplative prayer, a thirst for the life of withdrawal, a facility for nurturing others, and a passionate loyalty to all she held dear.[23]

Over a period of six years during which time she became François' directee, they entered into a process of mutual discernment about Jeanne's future. She seemed distinctly called to some formal type of religious life, although during these years of discernment, François counseled his friend not to yearn too much beyond the state of widowhood in which she found herself. Devotion, he admonished her, could be practiced in any state of life. Gradually a vision began to emerge.

Working with as many women as he did and having a high regard for their religiosity, François had for some time noted that there were unmet spiritual needs among those to whom he ministered. So many women were inflamed with the love of God and yet the avenues open to them to live out that love explicitly were few. There was either the cloister or the married state. But in French and Savoyard society, women's monastic life was either in a state of unacceptable decadence or undergoing reform.[24] And reformed monastic life was rigorous, both physically and mentally. Chief among the popular reformed orders was Teresa of Avila's Discalced Carmelites, exported from Spain and imported to France under the prestigious protection of Pierre de Bérulle and the noted Parisian devout, Madame Acarie. Austere, penitential, and demanding, the Teresan Carmel could offer a spiritual home only to those women hardy enough to withstand its rigors. What about women of more delicate constitution or with physical handicaps or with little taste for physical mortification? Where else might they go if they wished to give themselves wholly to God?

Similarly there was little provision for widows who might still be called upon to discharge their familial responsibilities. The absolute cloister imposed on female religious made any sort of semi-withdrawal from secular society impossible. Finally, one more unmet need had caught the Genevan bishop's attention. Married women often expressed a desire for a place of retreat, a refuge from the busy demands of the household where they might be refreshed by silence and prayer. The impenetrable walls of enclosure could not open to let them in, even for a brief period of renewal.

Jeanne, the young widow with parental responsibilities restraining her ability to give herself completely to a life of prayer, was a prime example of the type of woman with whom François frequently came in contact. Slowly the vision of a new community began to emerge. An unobtrusive band of women, some frail, some handicapped (as long as the disability did not hinder them from a minimal observance of the rule), some widowed, some tender in their youth, some in old age, would live a hidden life of great devotion. They would be daughters of prayer. But their asceticism would be entirely interior, for their external life would be, while simple, not physically austere. And they would offer a place of retreat for a limited number of laywomen for brief periods of time. In addition, they would engage in the activities common to women all over Europe, the care of others. Responding to the particular needs of the poor or sick in the surrounding community would be part of their life of devotion.

This life matched the needs and established religiosity of women like Jeanne, a mother and daughter who fulfilled her familial duties, routinely nursed the poor and sick in her neighborhood, and yet experienced a radical call to a life of interior prayer. Together the two friends set out to make their emergent vision a reality.[25] Carefully, Jeanne arranged her own affairs, settling her estates, planning for the schooling of her son away from home, the marriage of her elder daughter, and the boarding of her two youngest in the community she would enter.[26] François on his part began the process of drawing up a rule, looking for an appropriate site and encouraging vocations.

It was decided that Annecy itself would be the best location for the foundation because, as events fell into place, Jeanne's daughter married François's brother, which necessitated that the mother be near the young bride to help her manage her household. Moreover, Annecy (our "dear Nessy" they called it) suited the unobtrusive spirit of the new congregation. Hidden in the Swiss Alps, far from the glamour of Parisian society or the bustle of mercantile Dijon, the village provided a perfect place for these daughters of prayer to respond to the love of God through charity exercised among themselves extending into the nearby population.

EARLY DESIGN OF THE VISITATION

Obviously, François remembered his contact with the new women's forms of life being tested in Italy. The flexibility of their simple vows or the absence of vows, the lack of cloister, and the local nature of these Italian models gave him a precedent to work with. Certainly, he was well aware of the technical requirements for a recognized religious life: solemn vows, absolute cloister, and the approbation of the Holy See. But he was not founding a formal order. Instead, he was interested in a flexible community— he used the terms congregation, institute, houses, monastery, daughters, and sisters interchangeably—which could meet the needs of the women to whom he ministered. Beyond this, the Visitation can be seen as a part of François's long-range vision of a renewed world, in which devout persons from all walks of life, in all states and conditions, would be raised up to leaven the whole loaf of Christendom.[27] They could be women, even widows, even the handicapped. All had hearts formed to respond lovingly to God. The Church must recognize and create a place for such as these.

The history of vows within the Visitation is murky. For example, it is not known whether actual vows were taken by all members in the earliest years. The 1613 Constitution makes it clear that all members must take a vow of chastity but that novices would be permitted to make vows of poverty and obedience only with the permission of the superior. It does seem certain that by 1615 the sisters took simple vows of poverty, chastity, and obedience renewable each year, which in no way bound them canonically.[28]

As for cloister, while a life of seclusion was emphasized, primarily for the maintenance of an atmosphere of prayer, the walls which separated the entrants from "the world" were supple. Widows could be allowed exit when the demands of family were pressing. After the novitiate year, which was spent entirely within the house, the women were able to go out in groups of two or more to minister to the neighboring needy. The outings were strictly regulated to avoid conflict with the prayer rhythm of the community. The particular ministry was to be tailored to the specific needs of the region and could be varied or suspended if necessary. Finally, the cloister could be entered by lay retreatants for only a few days at a time.

The community was to be approved by and under the jurisdiction of the ordinary of the diocese, in the case of the founding house in Annecy, François de Sales himself. This stipulation was essential. On the one hand, the supervision of the local ordinary was expected for a congregation. The decrees of Trent had insisted on this. Further, the Visitation in its founders' eyes was to remain juridically independent of any male order. Its spirit was to be its own. Certainly, chaplains and confessors were needed, but both François and Jeanne insisted that Jesuits would best understand their charism. The liberty of spirit, the radical call to "live Jesus," the firmly rooted humanist assumptions of Salesian spirituality, were compatible with the Ignatian perspective. Further, its diocesan nature kept the congregation free from outside regulation, thus allowing it to be adapted to local and internal needs.[29]

Clearly, the primitive plan of the Visitation fell well outside the canons of religious life as technically defined. But François de Sales brought a broad notion of the life of perfection to his work as founder. In a famous passage penned in 1614 he revealed his unique views on the "state of perfection." Monseigneur de Sales's "Preface for the Instruction of Devout Souls on the Dignity, Antiquity, and Variety of Congregations of Women and Girls Dedicated to God" describes six rungs or states of perfection beginning with bishops and "religious" as formally designated, moving through those who take simple vows but are deemed "religious" (i.e., Jesuit scholastics), those in papal orders, congregations binding themselves with simple vows, oblation, or public declaration, and, finally, those outside any community who make any kind of vow or declare their intent to live devoutly. A broad span of lifestyles is included in the Genevan bishop's notion of the perfect life. His focus is more upon the goal or intention of the life than upon the outward form that life might take.[30]

SALESIAN SPIRITUALITY

The Salesian spirit that animated the Visitation was one born of the collaboration of the two friends.[31] François was the chief architect of the new community; Jeanne, its first builder. It was she, along with a handful of other women, who embodied its spirit and put into practice the Salesian way of realizing the Christian life. But this spirituality was larger than the Visitation and could be lived out in many different forms of life. The community drew upon the central insights of the Salesian vision and nuanced or developed them to conform to the particularities of its own life.

The motto of the institute reflects its raison d'être: *Vive Jésus!* To let Jesus live, to have the vital center of being, the heart, surrendered to Him so that "I no longer live but Christ lives in me": this was the core of the Salesian spirit. Specifically, the Jesus to be lived was the humble Jesus of Matthew 11:25–30 who invited all who are burdened to come to learn from Him. What one learns, in the Salesian perspective, is the heart of the Savior. One's own heart is to conform to the One Who could proclaim Himself "gentle and lowly of heart."

Salesian spirituality drew inspiration from the Christian humanism that flourished in Europe in the sixteenth century.[32] Profoundly optimistic in the sense that it imaged a God desirous of intimacy with humankind and a humankind responding to the divine initiative, Salesian spirituality celebrated human talents, invention, arts, and efforts in things religious.[33] It was likewise a very "human" devotion, its principles sometimes referred to as "inspired common sense."[34] Practical and psychologically perceptive, the Salesian spirit taught that the devout life should enhance everyday human experience and that human experience should ground and inform devotion. In becoming fully human, one uncovered the divine life that shapes humankind. In going to God one plumbed what is deepest and most personal in the human heart.

In keeping with its humanist perspective the Salesian tradition focused attention upon the discernment of the will of God as experienced in daily life. François de Sales and Madame de Chantal taught that the will of God is found between what they called "the signified will of God"—God's will to *be* done—and "the will of God's good pleasure"—God's will done. Thus, the totality of God's will, which is ultimately unknowable in this life, is known partially through individual efforts of discernment (prayer, Scripture-reading, consulting tradition, and persons of holiness) and partially through the events that happen independently of human consent. Somewhere between doing what one feels called to do and adapting oneself to circumstances lie wisdom and true devotion.[35]

The devotion that makes Jesus live could, in François' and Jeanne's eyes, be lived out in any vocation. The Christian life need not be confined by monastery walls. It could be practiced anywhere, in the midst of family life, in the marketplace, at court, or in the country. Similarly, Jesus was lived not only in the solitary encounter between God and the individual but also in the midst of human relationships as well. Relationships were seen to be central to one's love of God. Friendship especially, when it was based on mutual aspiration for the divine, was the vehicle through which one lived Jesus.[36] Mutual regard, gentleness, attentiveness, each caring relational gesture was understood to be the embodiment of the Christ-life in the world.

Thus, devotion had to do with living the gentle, humble Jesus in the particular situation in which one found oneself rather than in any specific lifestyle or through any regulated form of prayer or practice. The Salesian spirit was one of great freedom. It emphasized the liberty of the children of God to choose to love for self-serving ends or to love with a "pure love" modeled on the unconditional love of God. It also emphasized that there were a myriad of ways that the Spirit leads God's children. Therefore, many ways of praying, both meditative or contemplative, were acknowledged.[37] Spiritual direction in a Salesian context focused on following the unique movement of the Spirit rather than upon rigidly legislating formal exercises or prayers.

A spirituality adaptable to any situation, the Salesian tradition focused upon interiority. While pointedly concerned with the renovation of the whole person, it affirmed that renovation began within, not without.[38] Devotion occurs primarily in the heart;

secondarily (but not unimportantly), it makes itself known in a visible way. Devotion should not, in François's and Jeanne's view, interfere with the rightful fulfillment of one's duties in life. It was not intrusive. To "engrave" the name of Jesus on the heart, as de Sales enjoined, was to engage both intellect and will, to become involved in an integrative, dynamic process that transformed a person into what he or she most loved, Jesus, the child whose heart, of all hearts, was most attuned to and responsive to the loving heart of God. Heart language is thus abundant in Salesian literature. Preaching, spiritual direction, formation, and friendship—all were carried on "heart to heart" at the deepest center of the person where the movements of God's own heart came to be perceived.[39]

The life of God was hidden in the heart. From this axiom flowed the characteristic Salesian appreciation for the little and the hidden in everyday life. The characteristic Salesian virtues were the "little ones": simplicity, gentleness, humility, patience, kindness, and so on.[40] Rather then focus upon the "heroic" and remarkable virtues of the Christian life, the instinct was to give attention to those unobtrusive yet very trying disciplines that attract little public attention. Most characteristic of the little Salesian virtues is gentleness or *douceur*. Often translated as "sweetness," *douceur* was more than sentiment. *Douceur* is a quality of person that corresponds to the light burden offered by the Matthean Jesus. It suggests a sense of being grace-filled, graceful in the broadest sense of the term. This gracefulness extends from external demeanor to the very quality of a person's heart.[41]

The rich tapestry of Salesian spirituality was woven from the lives and experiences of the two founders of the congregation of the Visitation of Holy Mary. The Visitation was one experiment, one form of life, that drew upon and (subsequently shaped) the ideals Bishop de Sales and Madame de Chantal shared, ideals which others sought to realize within marriage, in the marketplace, in the episcopal entourage, or at the court of kings.

LIFE WITHIN THE COMMUNITY

The intent that guided and sustained the early Visitation was that of its motto *Vive Jésus*. It was as simple as that. Yet the outward manifestation of this living was to be shaped by the particulars of the lives of its earliest members. When the community opened its doors in 1610, it had merely four members, Madame de Chantal, Charlotte de Bréchard (a de Chantal family friend), Jacqueline Favre (whom François had known since she was a girl), and Anne-Jacqueline Coste (a serving woman the bishop had met during his missionary years in Geneva, who was to serve as out-sister for the house). Within the first few years their numbers had so outgrown their building, the Maison de la Galerie, that they were forced to move to a new facility. By the time of Jeanne's death in 1641 the Visitation included more than eighty houses scattered throughout France.[42]

But by that time the little congregation had seen itself transfigured into something much more formal than one could have imagined from its primitive beginnings. In the early years their life was to be very, very simple but not austere. The daily rhythm was monastic in orientation, prayer punctuating the day at regular intervals. To conform to the gentler needs of the women, the traditional and demanding monastic Office was to be replaced by the Little Office of Our Lady, a briefer and less taxing prayer form. Nor, once membership grew, were all the women required to recite the entire Office. Sisters were to be ordered into three ranks with varied but overlapping duties, some being occupied more with liturgy, others focused more upon the domestic maintenance of the house.[43]

The spirit of the place was one of gentleness, of winning the heart for God, not subduing the body. Food was simple but ample. Fasting was moderate and limited to specific liturgical periods. Physical mortifications, so popular in reformed monastic communities, were discouraged or forbidden. The Visitandines wore a habit which they had designed to express the simplicity of their lives. By seventeenth-century aristocratic standards, it did just that.

Modeled on the widows' garb of the day, the Visitandine habit was made of simple black fabric, set in loose pleats at the waist falling to the floor. The habit's bodice was likewise loosely pleated from the yoke. A girdle of black corded fabric circled the waist and hung down in small flaps in front. Over the bodice lay the white barbette, its square front being recognizably unique among religious women's habits. A snug white cap hugged the head down to the forehead and was held in place by a black strip of binding (this too was a unique feature of the order's dress). The long veil, of a lighter fabric than the habit, draped down six inches below the girdle, the front and side parts of it folded back and pinned to the binding and shoulders. The sleeves of the habit were full and folded up to the wrists or down over the hands depending on whether one was working or in choir. Folded up, the sleeves revealed little black sleeves that fitted to the elbow and, beneath that, the white edge of an under chemise. For work the entire habit could be hitched up to the waist, front and back, allowing freedom of movement in a loose black tunic that was worn beneath. Community members wore a distinctive cross modeled on François de Sales' own pectoral cross of sterling silver; it was about two-and one-half inches long, one-half inch wide, and one-fourth inch thick. Each opened and housed a relic. On one side of the cross was engraved a double-barred cross and a flame with the initials M A (for *mons amoris*, the mountain of Calvary which in Salesian literature is the mount of love). On the reverse side were engraved I H S, the double cross, three nails, and three drops of blood.

Simplicity and gentleness were evident as well in the style of direction and formation practiced in the house: persuasion, not force, attention to individual difference, winning hearts to the love of God by tender love of one another.[44] Segments of the day were given over to prayer, eating, simple work (done mainly in silence), assembly (for the ongoing formation of community), obedience (a formal opportunity for personal growth), spiritual reading, and recreation. All the daily rounds were to be observed in a spirit of silence and reflection. When the sisters went out on their missions of mercy (which they did only after the year of novitiate), they did so within the time frames allotted for work. The prayer rhythm was the constant that directed their day. It is clear that the group was never intended to be primarily apostolic in orientation. The care of others was seen as an outflowing of their essential vocation, to become daughters of prayer. Jeanne, speaking to the sisters, recalled the words of their founding father:

[the aim of the congregation] is to give God daughters of prayer and souls so interior that they will be found worthy to serve His infinite Majesty and adore Him in spirit and truth. Let the great

established orders of the Church honor Our Lord with heroic practices and striking virtues.

I would like my daughters to have no other intention than to
glorify Him with their lowliness, and this little Institute of the
Visitation to be like a humble dovecote of innocent doves whose
concern and energy is directed to meditating on the law of the
Lord without being seen nor understood by the world.[45]

THE TRANSFORMATION OF 1618

The primitive form of the Visitation of Holy Mary, like many
contemporary women's congregations, did not survive un-
changed in the conflicting currents of reform surging through
Christendom.[46] The change came as the community grew beyond
the borders of Savoy and ventured into France. In 1613, three
French women filled with admiration for the work Monseigneur
de Sales and Madame de Chantal had undertaken, presented themselves and proposed to make a new foundation in Lyons under
the jurisdiction of the archbishop, Denis-Simon de Marquemont.
In 1615, after a rather confusing beginning, the new group invited
Jeanne and two other Visitandines to come to establish a Visitation
house.[47] The archbishop had overseen their entry into France but
soon began to express reservations about the existence of an informal congregation with a mitigated cloister, simple vows, and a
private constitution as opposed to an officially sanctioned rule.
De Marquemont's objections were several.[48] The lack of strict
enclosure would cause scandal. For French women of the classes
from which the Visitation would recruit, the outside visiting of
the sick as well as the freedom of widows to come and go would
be an unacceptable practice. Similarly, the lack of formal, perpetual vows would cause social havoc. When women entered traditional religious life, they became legally dead. They could not
inherit property or enter into any other binding vows such as
those of marriage. What family could with conscience allow a
daughter to enter a community she might at some time leave?
What about dowries, what about inheritance, what about a marriage contracted after she had left? Further, what young woman
would want to belong to a foundation in which she would have
essentially none of the status, the merit, the perfection, or the

indulgences of true religious? The Lyons bishop, being French, was opposed to such innovations. French society of the time equated committed Christian life with austerity and enclosure. The new congregation hardly qualified. Finally, de Marquemont was a strict interpreter of ecclesial pronouncements, and this was the time in France when Tridentine regulations were beginning to be accepted and enforced.[49] His eventual "victory" over François de Sales in the matter of the Visitation has been termed a "triumph of French legalism."[50]

The Genevan bishop mounted a vigorous defense of the plan he had proposed. It was not innovation, he claimed, but a harkening back to ancient Christian practice. He pointed out the success of Frances of Rome's Oblates. He argued eloquently for a broader view of the life of perfection than the one that supported his fellow bishop's view of the religious life. A surviving correspondence informs us of the vigor of the debate.[51] But the Frenchman was insistent, and, after all, he as the local ordinary had jurisdiction over any congregation founded in his diocese. First, visitation to the sick and the breach of cloister for families' sake by widows could not be tolerated. Next, he offered his colleague two choices: either the Visitation should be established as a congregation with perpetual cloister or it should become a formally approved religious order observing cloister and solemn vows. He indicated that he could not see why the former option should be chosen, as the women themselves would object to having the obligations of true religious but not having the status of such.[52]

The years 1616 to 1617 were crucial in the transition. For a brief while, it appeared as though a creative compromise might be reached. De Sales agreed to establishing the community as a congregation with enclosure as long as certain exceptions could be made. In 1616, he wrote to Cardinal Bellarmine in Italy asking for an exemption permitting widows to take the habit and allowing laywomen entry into the cloister for brief periods of retreat. The reply confirmed the viability of the overall project, citing the existence of informal congregations in Italy which were under the control of the ordinary and even applauding their sanctity. But the cardinal agreed that to make exceptions like the ones requested for a group that could call itself religious was outside the bounds of canonical legislation.[53]

The French bishop's persuasiveness and the austere spirit of the

Church in that country won the day. For the Visitation to grow beyond its mountain home and extend into France, it would have to become an approved order. And approval by the Holy See meant no exception to enclosure. Experiments were not acceptable there, because of the proximity to the Huguenots, although they might be tolerated farther south. So in 1618 the entire congregation became a formal order acknowledged by Rome observing the Rule of St. Augustine, practicing complete enclosure, and bound by perpetual vows. François de Sales, in his typical fashion of "living between the two wills of God," graciously accepted the transformation once it was clear to him that change was inevitable. His correspondence with his Lyons colleague suggests that he felt that the principal end of the Visitation had been maintained in the transition (although contemporary sources quote him secondhand as feeling that the change was not altogether to his liking).[54] As for Jeanne de Chantal and the community itself, the surviving documents testify to the sisters' amenability to the altered routine. "All at once we found ourselves changed, with a desire for the cloister," they are recorded as remarking.[55]

Some unique features of the original design were retained. The gentle, interior asceticism of Salesian spirituality was still to be cultivated. The handicapped, frail, elderly, and widows were to be accepted if their disabilities did not make it impossible for them minimally to observe the rule. The brief Little Office of Our Lady replaced the usual great monastic office. Physical mortifications were kept to a bare minimum, and a moderate physical regime was observed. Lost were the possibilities of going in and coming out: by widows for the management of family business, by the sisters for the ministry to the neighboring sick and poor, by laywomen for spiritual refreshment.

Was the founders' original intent for the congregation essentially subverted or was it essentially fulfilled? Scholars have argued both ways. Their arguments revolve around the question: Was the Visitation of Holy Mary intended to be a contemplative community or an active one?[56] Was the Christian heart of this little band prayer or service? What has frequently been suggested is that the Visitation was intended to be similar to Vincent de Paul's seventeenth-century Filles de la Charité, who would become an active community, but this, clearly, is not true. Apostolic work was never their primary end. Visiting the sick was always a sec-

ondary work of the sisters, and was minutely regulated so as
not to interfere with the rhythm of prayer which dominated the
women's day. These visits were undertaken only by the older
sisters, and they were not of a specified nature. The community's
charism was not associated with a specific work or apostolate. The
Visitation spirit was more classically contemplative; their vision of
themselves was of women living the life of the gentle, humble
Jesus. Mother de Chantal wrote to her spiritual daughters at Annecy with words that expressed the community's charism.

> Live Jesus! Yes my beloved sisters and daughters, I say the words
> with intense delight: LIVE JESUS in our memory, in our will, in
> all our actions! Have in your thoughts only Jesus, in your will only
> the longing for His love, and in your actions have only obedience
> and submission to His good pleasure by an exact observance of
> the Rule, not only in externals but, much more, on your interior
> spirit; a spirit of gentle cordiality toward one another, a spirit of
> recollection of your whole being before our divine Master and that
> true sincere humility which makes us gentle and simple as lambs.
> Finally, strive for that loving union of hearts which brings about
> a holy peace and the kind of blessing we should desire to have in
> the house of God and His Holy Mother.[57]

Yet the Visitandines were clearly not intended to be a traditional
monastic order. For in another, structural, sense the primitive
form of the Visitation *was* a forerunner of the Filles de la Charité.
In its attempt to create a new structure of community life that lay
between the extremes of the religious and the secular states, it can
be viewed as part of an energetic, long-term movement within
Christendom to adapt to new societal challenges. In particular, it
must be seen within the history of women's communities engaged
in that task. From the Beguines to Frances of Rome's Oblates,
from the various Italian communities to Mary Ward's English
Virgins, from the Filles de la Charité and beyond, women's
groups experimented with simple vows, no vows, mitigated
cloister, no cloister, modified habit, and no habit. Eventually new
forms of life emerged, giving women new options. By the end
of the seventeenth century, as we have seen, this finally became
possible.[58]

But perhaps the question "Was the Visitation meant to be contemplative or apostolic?" is not the right question. In its primitive
form the Visitation of Holy Mary did not fit neatly into either

category.[59] For François de Sales and Jeanne de Chantal the devout life was not exhausted by entering into a particular lifestyle. Devotion was everyone's call. Whatever institutional structures there are ought to reflect the special needs of the devout. Thus there ought to be a community suited to women drawn to lives of deep prayer yet needing adequate facilities to care for their health and well-being, an environment conducive to pursuing lives of reflection and providing enough mobility to go out to fulfill their familial and neighborly duties (if they lived within the community) or to come inside to refresh themselves in the springs of silence and solitude (if they lived outside). Was this the active or the contemplative life? It was neither and both. It was devotion lived out by the women François knew. It was devotion for women like Jeanne de Chantal.

Undergirded by an expansive vision of a renewed Christendom constituted by persons of devotion from all walks and stations in life, the Visitation was created to fill an existing need. What was needed was a place, a dovecote, for women whose lives were not contained by medieval categories of the states of perfection, who broke the boundaries of expectation when, as laywomen, married, widows, handicapped, and aged they sought God as fiercely and deeply as "professional" religious. Neither disposed to the rigors of external asceticism nor called to lives of apostolic service, these women and their early community were the products of the fervent Christian imagination of the Catholic world during the era of reform.

Select Bibliography

An indefatigable writer and faithful chronicler of the Visitation's early years, Françoise-Madeleine de Chaugy is our chief source for much that occurred in the order during the first years of its existence. Mère de Chaugy was Jeanne de Chantal's own personal secretary as well as her niece. Her familiarity with the foundress's own history and personality make her reminiscences and contemporary records an invaluable historical resource. Her major works, published in printed form for the first time in the nineteenth century, are *Mémoires sur la vie et les vertus de sainte Jeanne-Françoise de Chantal*, first edited by l'Abbé Boulange in four volumes (Paris, 1842) and later published by Les Religieuses du monastère de la Visitation d'Annecy in eight volumes (Paris: Plon, 1874), a text which still serves as the sourcebook for much Salesian and Visitandine scholarship; *Les Vies de quatre des premières mères de l'Ordre Sainte Marie* (Annecy: Clerc, 1659), corrected and augmented version by M. Louis Veuillot (Paris, 1852), reissued by the sisters of the first monastery (Paris, 1892); *Les Vies de sept religieuses de l'Ordre de La Visitation Sainte Marie*, 2nd ed. (Annecy: Clerc, 1659), ed. Charles d'Hericault (Paris, 1860); *Vies de neuf religieuses de l'Ordre de La Visitation Sainte Marie* (Annecy: Clerc, 1659); *Les Vies de plusieurs superieures de l'Ordre de la Visitation Sainte Marie* (Annecy: Fonteine, 1693).

Our most accurate source for the Constitutions and early documents associated with the founding as well as the critically edited collected works of the bishop of Geneva is *Oeuvres de saint François de Sales, évêque et prince de Genève et docteur de l'Église*, 27 vols. (Annecy: 1892–1964). Further important source documents are *Coustumier et directoire pour les Soeurs religieuses de la Visitation Sainte Marie* (Lyons: de Coeursilly, 1628), which is composed of notes left by St. François and put in order by Jeanne and other early superiors.

Madame de Chantal's collected works do not all exist in a critical edition. The best collection is *Jeanne-Françoise Fremyot de Chantal: Sa Vie et ses oeuvres*, 8 vols. (Paris: Plon, 1874–1879). Recently, her letters have undergone critical evaluation and are available as *Sainte Jeanne de Chantal: Correspondance*, ed. Sister Marie Patricia Burns, 4 vols. (Paris: Cerf, Centre d'Études Franco-Italien, 1986–1993). English editions of her letters include *Francis de Sales and Jane de Chantal: Letters of Spiritual Direction*, translated by Péronne Maris Thibert, v.h.m, and selected and introduced by Wendy M. Wright and Joseph F. Power, o.s.f.s. (Mahwah, N.J.: Paulist, 1988). Also of importance are her *Responses de nostre tres-honorée et digne Mère Jeanne-Françoise Frémyoit sur les règles, constitutions et coustumiers de nostre Ordre de la Visitation* (Paris, 1632, 1665, 1756; and Annecy, 1849).

Classic and more recent treatments of the community's origins include Émile Bougaud, *Histoire de sainte Chantal et des origines de la Visitation*, 2 vols. (Paris: Bloud et Gay, 1921), English translation (New York: Macmillan, 1930); Ernestine Le Couturier, *La Visitation* (Paris: Grasset, 1935) and the same author's *Françoise-*

Madeleine de Chaugy et la tradition salesienne au XVIIe siècle (Paris: E. Vitte, 1933); Abbé M. Descarques, "Aux origines de la Visitation," *Nouvelle Revue Théologique*, 73 (1951), 483–513; Roger Devos, "Le Salesianisme et la société au XVIIe siècle in *Saint François de Sales: Témoignages et mélanges,* Mémoires et documents de l'Académie Salesienne 80 (Annecy: l'Académie Salesienne, 1969), pp. 211–44; idem, *Les Visitandines d'Annecy aux XVIIe et XVIIIe siècles,* Mémoires et documents de l'Académie Salesienne 84 (Annecy: l'Académie Salesienne, 1973).

Biographies of the two founders include Michael de la Bedoyère, *François de Sales* (New York: Harper, 1960); Jean-Pierre Camus (Bishop of Belley), *The Spirit of Saint François de Sales*, trans. C. F. Kelley (New York: Harper and Bros, 1952), an early work penned by a contemporary of François's; E.-M. Lajeunie, *Saint François de Sales: L'Homme, la pensée, l'action,* 2 vols. (Paris: Victor, 1964); this work is available in English as *Saint Francis de Sales: The Man, the Thinker, His Influence,* 2 vols. (Bangalore, India: S.F.S. Publications, 1986–1987); André Ravier, *Un Sage et un saint: François de Sales* (Paris: Nouvelle Cité, 1985); this work in available in English as *Francis de Sales, Sage and Saint* (San Francisco: Ignatius Press, 1988); Henri Bremond, *Sainte Chantal* (Paris, 1912); Elisabeth Stopp, *Madame de Chantal: Portrait of a Saint* (London: Faber and Faber, 1962; Westminster, Md: Newman, 1963); Wendy Wright, *Bond of Perfection: Jeanne de Chantal and François de Sales* (New York and Mahwah, N.J.: Paulist, 1985); André Ravier, *Jeanne-Françoise Frémyot, Baronne de Chantal: Sa Race et sa grace* (Paris: Labat, 1983); the English translation is entitled *Saint Jeanne de Chantal: Noble Lady, Holy Woman* (San Francisco: Ignatius Press, 1989).

Notes

1. On this long-term transition from the monastic to the apostolic models of Christian life, see Robert Lemoine, *Les Droits des religieux du Concile de Trente aux instituts séculiers* (Paris: Desclée de Brouwer, 1955) especially for its canonical point of view. Elizabeth Rapley's *The Dévotes: Women and Church in Seventeenth-Century France* (Montreal: McGill-Queen's University Press, 1990) focuses especially upon this transition among women's groups. Though she aptly places the Visitation (espe-

cially as an institution) in this ongoing process, she nonetheless misunderstands the original charism of that congregation and so perpetuates the notion that it became what it was never intended to be. But I will argue this below.

2. On the technical aspects of the perfect life as an exterior state as defined in this era, see Lemoine, *Droits des religieux*, pp. 13ff.

3. The Lateran Council of 1215 had forbidden new "religions," and Gregory X's promulgations at the Council of Lyons in the latter part of the century confirmed this. Pius V rejected any intermediate form of religious life between seculars and regulars, and he fixed the regular state with solemn vows.

4. Gradual tolerance by bishops, legates, and pontiffs themselves, as well as grassroots activity, eventually undermined the authority of *Circa pastoralis* and *Lubricum genus*.

5. On the Beguines, see E. W. McDonnell, *The Beguines and Beghards in Medieval Culture* (New Brunswick, N.J.: Rutgers University Press, 1954); *Beguine Spirituality*, ed. Fiona Bowie, trans. Oliver Davies (New York: Crossroad, 1990). Carol Neil's "The Origins of the Beguines," *Signs: Journal of Women in Culture and Society*, 14, No. 21 (1989), 321–41, speaks to the close relationship between late-medieval women's monasticism and the beginnings of the Beguines. From Flanders and Belgian Brabant to Northern France, the Rhineland, Bavaria, and Italy (where they were called *bizoche*), these women were known. The movement was important enough to be recognized as a unified phenomenon with articulate spokespersons, to provoke suspicion, and, eventually, to be suppressed.

6. *The Book of Prayer of Sor Maria of Santo Domingo: A Study and Translation*, ed. Mary Giles (Albany: State University of New York Press, 1990) is an interesting study of a *beata* with a discussion of the circumstances surrounding her way of life. Like many unregulated women, she was suspected of heretical or immoral leanings, getting caught up in the controversy about the *alumbrados*.

7. Rapley, *Dévotes*, pp. 10–23, gives a concise overview of the social and the political forces that made a "feminine invasion" into the religious or the devout life possible.

8. It is interesting to note the way that concerns that were traditionally seen to be women's concerns—caring for the sick, guiding and instructing the young (especially girls), providing for children, providing food—became Christian ministries in the period under attention.

9. One of the major differences between Frances of Rome's group and many other congregations was that hers remained small and diocesan. Associations that grew and crossed regional or national boundaries had a difficult time gaining approbation.

10. Mary Martin McLaughlin, "Creating and Recreating Communities of Women: The Case of Corpus Domini, Ferrara, 1406–1452" in *Signs: A Journal of Women in Culture and Society*, 14, No. 2 (1989), 293–320.

11. A good discussion of the various factors involved in the transformation of the Ursulines is found in Rapley, *Dévotes*, pp. 48–60. Interesting to note, it was the Paris women themselves who campaigned for enclosure, indicating how strong the high status and respectability of the cloistered life was in French Catholic circles, especially among the upper classes. See also Marie de Chantal Gueudre, *Histoire de l'Ordre des Ursulines en France*, 3 vols. (Paris: Editions St. Paul, 1957).

12. M. C. E. Chambers, *The Life of Mary Ward*, 2 vols. (London, 1882), and Rapley, *Dévotes*, pp. 28–34. See also Henriette Peters, *Mary Ward: Ihre Persönlichkeit und ihr Institut* (Innsbruck and Vienna: Tyrolia Verlag, 1991).

13. Rapley, *Dévotes*, pp. 43–48.

14. Fourier's teaching community is featured in Paul Rousselot, *Histoire de l'éducation des femmes en France* (New York: Lenox Hill, 1971; reprint of 1883 original). See also Rapley, *Dévotes*, pp. 61–73.

15. See Rapley, *Dévotes*, pp. 74–141.

16. Robert Lemoine, *Le Monde des religieux: L'époque moderne 1563–1789* (Paris: Éditions Cujas, 1976), p. 15; this work is the second part of *Histoire du droit et des institutions de l'Église en Occident*, edited by Gabriel Le Bras and Jean Gaudemet. A fascinating sidelight: one of the new non-monastic teaching communities that was able to establish itself in mid-century was the Filles de la Croix. This group of secular schoolmistresses, observing simple vows, was the first in France to succeed in this. They followed the original rule of the Visitation, which had been given to their foundress, Madame de Villeneuve, by François de Sales himself after the design of the early Visitation had been altered.

17. On their friendship see Wendy M. Wright, *Bond of Perfection: Jeanne de Chantal and François de Sales* (New York: Paulist, 1985).

18. For thorough biographical treatments of St. François see E. M. Lajeunie, *Saint François de Sales: L'homme, la pensée, l'action*, 2 vols. (Paris: Victor, 1964), which has been translated into English as *Saint Francis de Sales: The Man, the Thinker, His Influence* by Rory O'Sullivan, O.S.F.S., 2 vols. (Bangalore, India: S.F.S.F. Publications, 1986, 1987); Michael de la Bedoyère, *François de Sales* (New York: Harper, 1960); or André Ravier, *Un Sage et un saint: François de Sales* (Paris: Nouvelle Cité, 1985).

19. On the Marian communities consult Louis Chatellier, *The Europe of the Devout: The Catholic Reformation and the Formation of a New Society* (Cambridge: Cambridge University Press, 1989). It was particularly through the writings of Francis Coster, S.J., that this life of devotion

was disseminated. The German Jesuit's *Book of the Confraternity* and his *Five Meditations on the Life and Prayer of the Virgin Mary, Mother of God* initiated confraternity members from Naples to Cologne, to Paris, to Toulouse into the reforming spirit generated by their Jesuit sponsors. Members were to become "interior men," leading exemplary lives formed in the image of Christ. Their efforts were directed not toward self-serving ends but toward the revitalization of society. Thus, many congregations were actively involved in works of charity and education. Care of the poor and orphans, the sick and invalid, instruction in moral and doctrinal theology, the revitalization of the family and marriage as an arena of Christian action—all these occupied the devouts.

20. Among his early episcopal efforts was the reconversion of the Chablais region.

21. The finest biography of Jeanne in English, and perhaps in any language, is Elisabeth Stopp's *Madame de Chantal: Portrait of a Saint* (London: Faber and Faber, 1962, Westminster, Md.: Newman, 1963).

22. Cf. Theophiler Schueller, O.S.F.S., *La Femme et le saint: La Femme et ses problèmes d'après Saint François de Sales* (Paris: Les Editions Ouvrières, 1970).

23. On the shaping of Jeanne's religiosity see Wendy M. Wright, "Two Faces of Christ: Jeanne de Chantal" in *Peace Weavers: Medieval Religious Women* II (Kalamazoo, Mich.: Cistercian Publications, 1987), pp. 353–64.

24. On the entire sweep of religious renewal in France during this era see Henri Bremond's classic *Histoire littéraire du sentiment religieux en France depuis la fin des guerres de religion jusqu'à nos jours*, 3 vols. (Paris: Bloud et Gay, 1921).

25. The process by which the discernment of Jeanne's vocation occurred was not as straightforward as it appears here. Jeanne herself spent hours in the parlor of the Carmel in Dijon receiving advice from the superiors there. Had she not had the care of her children and larger familial responsibilities she no doubt would have chosen a traditional monastic life. That the Visitation from the beginning had such a strongly contemplative aura is due, in great part, to its Mother Superior's own bent.

26. Her youngest daughter, Charlotte, died before she entered the community. Her next youngest, Françoise, spent a considerable part of her youth within the confines of the community. On Jeanne's surviving daughters see Alexandre de Menthon, *Les Deux Filles de Ste Chantal* (Annecy: Monastère de la Visitation, 1913).

27. See André Ravier's preface in *St François de Sales: Oeuvres*, Bibliothèque de la Pléiade (Paris: Gallimard, 1969), pp. xxxvii-lx.

28. Abbé M. Descarques, "Aux origines de la Visitation" in *Nouvelle Revue Théologique*, 73 (1951), 500ff.

29. The positive side of local diocesan control is shown here. The negative side was discovered when a community wanted to extend itself beyond local borders and to maintain a unity that transcended local jurisdiction. The plan of Pierre Fourier's Canonesses was subverted when it outgrew its diocesan origins. See Rapley, *Dévotes*, pp. 61–72.

30. *Oeuvres de Saint François de Sales, évêque et prince de Genève et docteur de l'Église*, 27 vols. (Annecy: 1892–1964), 25:291ff. His ideals reveal his Ignatian formation, for the Jesuit mission in many ways involved the recreation of Christian society. Although it was not explicitly intended to challenge social structures, nonetheless, in its insistence on empowering the laity, Jesuit ideology sowed the seeds for a new kind of Church where ancient distinctions like monastic and secular would break down.

31. The approach taken here, that Salesian spirituality is the collaborative issue of de Sales and de Chantal, goes somewhat against the grain of traditional scholarship, which has seen Bishop de Sales as the sole originator of the Salesian tradition. Instead, I have tried to delineate the characteristics of that tradition by drawing upon the perspectives of both these saints. The brief summary of Salesian spirituality presented in this introductory section is a result of that process. The position is more fully elaborated in *Francis de Sales, Jane de Chantal: Letters of Spiritual Direction*, ed. Wendy M. Wright and Joseph F. Power, o.s.f.s., trans. Péronne Marie Thibert, v.h.m., Classics of Western Spirituality Series (Mahwah: N.J.: Paulist, 1988), pp. 9–86.

To give Madame de Chantal credit for her formative role is likewise somewhat at odds with her own wishes. In her lifetime, Jeanne de Chantal consistently refused the title of foundress of the Visitation, modestly insisting (as recorded in the *Life* by Mère de Chaugy) that she was simply the eldest daughter among sisters who had somewhat more access to the father (de Sales) than her siblings.

32. For two views of de Sales's place in the currents of Christian humanism consult Julien-Eymard d'Angers, *L'Humanisme chrétien au XVIIe siècle: St François de Sales et Yves de Paris* (The Hague: Nijhoff, 1970), and Bremond, *Histoire littéraire* I.

33. On Salesian optimism see Henri Lemaire, *François de Sales: Docteur de la confiance et de la paix* (Paris: Beauchesne, 1963), pp. 19–30, and William Marceau, c.s.b., *Optimism in the Works of St. Francis de Sales* (Visakhapatnam, India: S.F.S Publications, 1983).

34. The phrase was coined by Elisabeth Stopp in her introduction to *St. Francis de Sales: Selected Letters* (New York: Harper & Bros., 1960), pp. 33–34.

35. See *Letters of Spiritual Direction*, edd. Wright and Power, pp. 40–43.

36. On friendship see especially *François de Sales, Correspondance: Les Lettres d'amitié spirituelle*, ed. André Ravier, Bibliothèque Européenne (Paris: Desclée de Brouwer, 1980). An account of the friendship between François and Jeanne is found in Wright, *Bond of Perfection*.

37. This statement must be understood in the context of early seventeenth-century Roman Catholicism, which tended to emphasize methodical forms of meditation on the life and passion of Christ. Like Ignatian spirituality, Salesian spirituality participates in this trend. François de Sales's *Introduction à la vie dévote* is an especially good example of this. There are several English translations available of this text, including John K. Ryan's *Introduction to the Devout Life* (Garden City, N.Y.: Doubleday Image, 1966) and a new version by the Missionaries of St. Francis de Sales (Malleswaram, Bangalore: S.F.S.F. Publications, 1990).

38. The shift to interiority as the primary locus of spiritual growth is a particular feature of Christian spirituality in the period between the medieval and the modern worlds. Margaret Miles in her *Practicing Christianity: Critical Perspectives for an Embodied Spirituality* (New York: Crossroad, 1988), pp. 89–90, writes that in our present era there is a widespread assumption that "change in behavior follows, rather than precedes insight. . . . most historical people thought it obvious that insight follows change; changed behavior—changed activity—produce insight."

39. On the image of the heart in Salesian writing see John A. Abbruzzese, *The Theology of Hearts in the Writings of St. Francis de Sales* (Rome: Institute of Spirituality, Pontifical University of St. Thomas Aquinas, 1983) and Wendy M. Wright, "That is What It Is Made For: The Image of the Heart in the Spirituality of Francis de Sales and Jane de Chantal" in *Spiritualities of the Heart*, ed. Annice Callahan, R.S.C.J. (Mahwah, N.J.: Paulist, 1990), pp. 143–58.

40. See Thomas A. McHugh, "The Distinctive Salesian Virtues, Humility and Gentleness," *Salesian Studies* (October 1963), 45–74.

41. On the Visitandine incorporation of the little virtues, see Wendy M. Wright, "The Hidden Life of the Gentle, Humble Jesus: The Visitation of Holy Mary as Ideal Women's Community," *Vox Benedictina*, 7, No. 3 (July 1990), 281–300.

42. Seminal books on the Visitation's early years include Ernestine LeCouturier, *La Visitation* (Paris: Grasset, 1935); Roger Devos, *L'Origine sociale des Visitandines d'Annecy aux XVIIe et XVIIIe siècles* (Annecy: Académie Salesienne, 1973); Émile Bougaud, *Histoire de Sainte Chantal et les origines de la Visitation*, 2 vols. (Paris, 1879).

43. Devos, *L'Origine sociale* is especially good from a sociological per-spective on the organization of the early congregation.

44. On formation practices see Wendy M. Wright, "St. Jane de Chan-tal's Guidance of Women," in *Salesian Living Heritage*, 1, No. 1 (Spring 1986), 16–28. A somewhat condensed version of this, in French, is found in *L'Univers salésien: Saint François de Sales hier et aujourd'hui*, Actes du Colloque International de Metz, 1992, ed. Hélène Bordes and Jacques Hennequin (Paris: Diffusion Champion-Slatkine, 1994), pp. 307–19.

45. *Oeuvres*, 17:16–17, contains de Sales's own letter. It is quoted by Jeanne in the second volume (*Oeuvres diverses I*) of *Jeanne Françoise Frém-yot de Chantal: Sa Vie et ses oeuvres*, 8 vols. (Paris: Plon, 1874–1879), p. 186.

46. Rapley, *Dévotes*, places the transition in the context of other women's communities, which is helpful. But, as suggested, she miscon-strues the charism, seeing it as essentially apostolic.

47. The women first organized something of a rival community, la Congrégation de la Présentation, which was modeled on Annecy. But the existence of factions and cross-purposes made it imperative that the members of the model, the Visitation, be called in to make a firm foundation.

48. The complete correspondence between Denis de Marquemont and Bishop de Sales on the matter of the Visitation is found in *Oeu-vres*, 25:322–42.

49. It had taken over fifty years for the regulations of Trent to be officially adopted by the French church. The differences in opinion and perspective of the two bishops indicates how complex the process of adoption really was.

50. Descarques, "Aux origines," 510.

51. Ibid.

52. This was, in fact, an accurate depiction of the climate of French spirituality, women included. It will be remembered that it was in France that the Ursulines became a formal order. The transition was initiated by the Paris Ursulines themselves.

53. *Oeuvres*, 17:418.

54. "This congregation has been established so that the weak and infirm might never be prevented from pursuing the perfection of divine love because of the great austerities or harshness of the life." This is the "end" of the Visitation as articulated in the Constitutions of 1618 (ibid., 25:51–52).

In 1616 de Sales had written that "The visits to the sick were added as an exercise that conformed to the existing devotion of those who began the congregation and to the practices of the place where they were, not as its primary end." That same year he had listed as its "ends" the retirement of the infirm or aged, widows with family responsibilities, and laywomen for brief periods of time (ibid., 338). Obviously, in the intervening years François had honed his original expectations considerably. Descarques's "Aux origines" chronicles the entire process well.

But there are other contemporary quotes to suggest the bishop's disappointment rather than his acquiescence. J. P. Camus records him as saying "'Now I shall be their godfather, rather than their founder, since my institution has been undone'" (quoted in Lemoine, *Droit des religieux*, pp. 185–86). Apparently he also told Madame de Villeneuve, foundress of the Filles de la Croix, that the sisters had been cloistered "against his original design" (see Rapley, *Dévotes*, p. 215n70).

55. This rather simple quote is, I think, surprisingly suggestive. It points to the Salesian teaching on living between the two wills of God. In short, this teaching suggests that one pursue with full vigor what one has discerned the will of God to be. Then, when circumstances continually seem to thwart one's plan of action, one should gracefully let go of the original discernment. Certainly, the sisters would live this spirit concretely.

Jeanne herself was plainly drawn to the contemplative life. Whatever flexible design had been intended, she would certainly have seen prayer and the love of God as the core of the community life. By the time the formal change of 1618 came, she had disposed of virtually all her civil obligations. Both father and father-in-law had died, and the family estates been taken care of. Her young married daughter, whom she was overseeing, had died in childbirth. Her remaining older childrens' marriages she was able to arrange from within the cloister.

56. Henri Bremond and more recently Elisabeth Stopp and André Ravier have held that the contemplative charism was central from the beginning. They thus make little of the change, holding that the spirit of the congregation was not greatly altered. This is the approach taken by most scholars working within the Salesian tradition. On the other hand, Émile Bougaud, l'Abbé Descarques (to a certain extent), and, most recently, Elizabeth Rapley have emphasized the discontinuity of the transition. Their reading of the events remains fixed in both the popular and the non-specialist imaginations.

57. *Sa Vie*, pp. 290–91.

58. See especially Lemoine, *Droits des religieux*, for the canonical point of view and Rapley, *Dévotes*, from the standpoint of women's history, on this development.

59. One might think that the name of the institute, the Visitation of Holy Mary, might give some clue as to the original charism. But the name only underscores the complexity of the issue. François originally

planned to name the group after St. Martha, clearly the image of the "active" life in Christian tradition. Jeanne preferred dedication to the Virgin Mary, since she had been her own special protectress since childhood. The Visitation was taken as the model for the group when François, approving its "hiddenness" (it was not a solemn feast in the church calendar), realized that it showed Mary (the type of the contemplative life) filled with the divine mystery going about the ordinary work of caring for others.

Certainly the Virgin had been the model of the contemplative life throughout the medieval period, she being the patroness of many contemplative communities, and she, at the Annunciation, the image of the contemplative soul receiving the spirit. But in the mid-seventeenth century, Mary became the principal patroness of the new congregations. The extra-canonical tradition of the Presentation of Mary in the Temple became important to schoolmistresses. And the Visitation was invoked by Vincent de Paul for his women's charities as well as a mandate for missionary activity throughout the Church (Rapley, *Dévotes*, pp. 170–73).

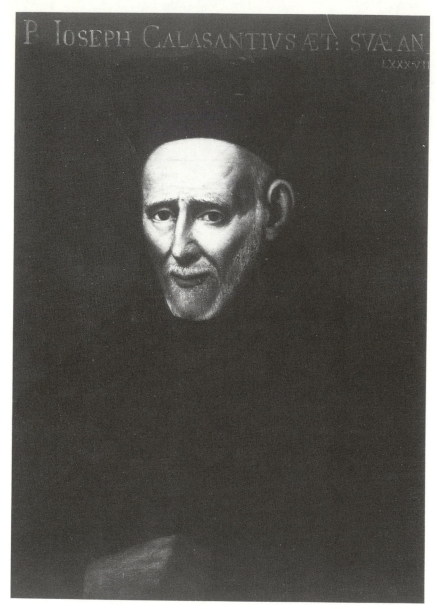

St. José de Calasanz at eighty-seven years of age by
an anonymous artist in 1644. Reproduced from an
1864 copy in the Piarist Generalate, Rome.

9

The Piarists of the Pious Schools

Paul F. Grendler

THE NEW religious orders of the Catholic Reformation may have devoted more energy to spiritual and intellectual instruction than to any other activity. But only one of them devoted itself exclusively to education, indeed, to the schooling of poor boys. This was the Poor Clerks Regular of the Mother of God of the Pious Schools, founded by José de Calasanz (1557–1648). The Piarists, as they are usually called outside of Italy and Spain, established their first school in Rome, 1597, and became a religious order in 1617. But they had a difficult first half-century, because offering universal free education for boys elicited contradictory responses in a hierarchical age.

JOSÉ DE CALASANZ

Calasanz (Calasanctius in Latin, Calasanzio in Italian) was born in the village of Peralta de la Sal in the Kingdom of Aragon in the hills close to the border with Catalonia, approximately sixty kilometers north of Lérida, on July 31, 1557.[1] He was the second brother in a family of seven surviving children, two boys and five girls. His father earned his living as a blacksmith and also served as mayor of the village. Given his father's modest occupation, the debate in the older biographies about whether or not he was a noble *hidalgo* seems irrelevant. Although not affluent, the family had enough income to enable the second son to learn Latin and to undertake university studies. Calasanz studied canon and civil law at the University of Lérida from 1570 or 1571 until 1577. The older biographies assert that Calasanz received a doctorate in law, but the place and date are unknown. He received the tonsure, the first step toward becoming a priest, in 1575, and began to study theology in 1577 at Alcalá de Henares, a better-known university. When his elder brother died in 1579, his father sought to dissuade him from a clerical career so that he might continue the family line. But Calasanz persevered; his vow to become a priest at the time of a life-threatening illness may have eased his father's opposition. He was ordained a diocesan priest in Sanahuja in his home diocese of Urgel in 1583.

Calasanz began a career as a clerical administrator performing diocesan and local duties in the service of several bishops. He became the pastor of a church in the diocese of Urgel, receiving the income from its accompanying benefice. Calasanz was called a doctor of theology in 1589, but the institution conferring the degree is unknown. At this time he resembled hundreds, probably thousands, of intelligent, ambitious young priests from the provinces climbing the ladder of ecclesiastical preferment. The next step on this career path was to harvest more lucrative benefices from the ultimate dispenser of ecclesiastical patronage, the pope. So in September 1591 Calasanz renounced his pastorate and benefice in order to go to Rome to obtain a Spanish prebend, a benefice conferring cathedral chapter revenues on the holder. He was in Rome in February 1592.

THE POOR OF ROME

Rome had a decisive impact on Calasanz, but in a manner very different from what he expected. The young priest from the provinces cooling his heels in the anterooms of curial officials was increasingly drawn into the teeming life of Rome. A census of 1591 counted 117,000 inhabitants, many of them sick, needy, and ignorant.[2] Ministering to their needs were numerous charitable confraternities, i.e., voluntary associations of clergy and/or laymen. In or about 1596 Calasanz joined the *Arciconfraternità dei XII Apostoli*. This Archconfraternity of the Twelve Apostles had been founded through the efforts of Ignatius de Loyola in the 1540s, and its twelve members twice a week visited the sick in order to comfort them and to distribute alms. In the process Calasanz became acquainted with the range and extent of the needs of the

poor throughout the city.[3] Sometime between 1594 and 1597 Calasanz also joined the *Confraternità della Dottrina Cristiana* (Confraternity of Christian Doctrine). This confraternity may have best
expressed the dual educational and charitable impulses of the
Catholic Reformation, and perhaps it launched Calasanz on his
future career as educator.

Castellino da Castello (1470/1480–1566), a secular priest from
Como, founded the first School of Christian Doctrine in Milan
in the autumn of 1536.[4] These schools taught religion and elementary reading and writing for one to three hours every Sunday
and religious holiday, approximately eighty days a year. They
provided catechisms, paper, pen, ink, and cool water on hot days,
while their teachers developed imaginative techniques for teaching
large numbers of pupils at an elementary level. Every Sunday and
religious holiday, laymen taught boys in one church, and women
taught girls in another. In order to expand the schools, Castellino
and his lay helpers founded lay confraternities to carry on the
mission. Thus, the Schools of Christian Doctrine became a mass
catechetical and literacy movement spreading to cities, towns,
and, to some extent, the countryside throughout Italy. They
taught tens of thousands, perhaps more, boys and girls. The instruction was necessarily limited to basic religion, reading, and
writing, because the Schools of Christian Doctrine taught only
one day in four or five.

However inadequate the rudimentary schooling of the Schools
of Christian Doctrine, it was the only education available to the
bulk of Italian children. Free universal education did not exist
anywhere in Italy and in only a few towns in Europe. Italy had no
educational system in the modern meaning of the term; instead,
numerous private masters, a limited number of municipal teachers, and a tiny handful of clergymen in church schools taught
Italian boys and a few girls. But almost all these schools charged
fees that parents had to pay. Even with the addition of the irregular
schooling provided by the Schools of Christian Doctrine, probably only about one-third of Italian boys and about 12 per cent
of Italian girls received schooling and became literate in the sixteenth century.[5]

At an unknown date, Calasanz began to teach catechism classes
in Rome. Marco Antonio Arcangeli, another member of the Confraternity of Christian Doctrine, had for several years taught cate-

chism classes in a room or two at the church of Santa Dorotea in Trastevere, the poorest district of Rome. Arcangeli needed help, which Calasanz gave. This teaching experience seems to have catalyzed in Calasanz' mind an idea: why not provide free regular daily education in both religious doctrine and academic subjects to poor boys throughout Rome? If they could receive elementary schooling as well as religious instruction, they might both save their souls and escape from poverty.

Filled with the desire to educate the poor, Calasanz asked various authorities to provide free schooling to the poor boys of Rome.[6] The only free education that the city of Rome offered was through the *rioni* teachers, one for each of the fourteen administrative districts (*rioni*) of the city. Their salaries were paid by the city government, in return for which these municipal teachers were required to teach for free the poor boys of the *rione*. All other pupils had to pay supplementary fees based on the level of Latin instruction received. Unfortunately, the *rioni* schoolmasters consistently evaded their obligation to teach the poor in favor of teaching more fee-paying students. At best, possibly four or five poor boys studied for free alongside twenty-five or thirty paying pupils in each school.[7] Calasanz asked the *rioni* masters to teach all the poor in their districts. The *rioni* teachers responded that they would need higher salaries to compensate for the loss of fee-paying students if they were to teach more poor students. Calasanz then asked the Roman city government either to increase the salaries of the *rioni* teachers or to open new schools for the poor. But the city leaders responded that they lacked funds to do anything.

Calasanz next tried the religious orders. He went to the rector of the Jesuit Collegio Romano, the famous Jesuit school in the heart of Rome, to ask that it accept poor, illiterate pupils. Like most Jesuit schools, the Collegio Romano did not charge fees, but a boy had to learn reading, writing, and some Latin grammar elsewhere before entering the Collegio Romano at the age of ten to twelve. This was the standard policy of Jesuit schools, and it had the effect of excluding the lower classes throughout Europe.[8] The rector reiterated Jesuit policy: the Collegio Romano would not take beginners. Calasanz next asked the Dominican Order to instruct poor boys. The master-general replied that the Dominicans were already so occupied with preaching, missions, hearing confessions, praying the Divine Office, and other activities that they could not teach the poor.

THE FIRST PIOUS SCHOOL

Unable to persuade existing institutions to teach the poor, Calasanz took matters into his own hands. In the autumn of 1597 Calasanz, Arcangeli, and two others from the Confraternity of Christian Doctrine transformed the Santa Dorotea catechism school into an everyday free school for poor boys. This was the first Pious School.[9] Classes met in two or three rooms in or contiguous with the church of Santa Dorotea. Since no other free schooling existed in Rome, the school attracted an enrollment of more than a hundred in the first week.

The teachers had to find additional help and support for the school, which soon had about 500 pupils. When the parish priest at Santa Dorotea died in early February 1600, Calasanz, who had emerged as the leader of the small band of teachers, decided to move the school across the Tiber into the center of the city. Indeed, the lack of institutional support seems to have strengthened Calasanz' resolve to establish his own school. Calasanz began to call his group of teachers "The Congregation of the Pious Schools." They, in turn, elected him rector of the school. Initial financial aid for the new venture came from some Roman prelates whom he had possibly met during several years of residence in the household of Cardinal Marc'Antonio Colonna.[10]

This is the traditional account of events through 1600. Even though some dates are lacking and Arcangeli's role is unclear, the progress of events is evident. Calasanz' dolorous experience working with the poor of Rome awakened him to the desperate need for schooling. The masses of illiterate poor had been there for centuries, but only Calasanz seemed to see them. He first taught in the catechism school at Santa Dorotea, then developed a larger vision: free daily schooling for all poor boys. Calasanz apparently never considered establishing a school for poor girls, and the notion of boys and girls sharing a classroom was unimaginable at this time. The Spanish careerist clergyman had become schoolmaster to the Roman poor.

The earliest description of the school comes from a letter of

Calasanz written between 1602 and 1605.[11] The school was now located in a rented building near Sant'Andrea della Valle in the center of Rome. It taught poor boys who presented certificates from parish priests testifying to their poverty. The boys studied "reading, writing, commercial arithmetic, Latin, Christian doctrine, and good habits." This free school had an enrollment of 500 poor boys, the majority of them from the parish of San Lorenzo in Damaso, whose church was located approximately 250 meters distant from Sant'Andrea della Valle. Financial support came from wealthy Roman prelates. Calasanz thanked the addressee, a cardinal, for his gift of 20 *scudi* at Christmas and another 20 *scudi* at Easter. These semi-annual donations had come "for several years."

Another document from the period 1604 to 1610, anonymous but likely written by Calasanz, described the instruction and pedagogical methods of the Pious School of Rome.[12] Now enrolling 700 pupils, the school met for two and one-half hours in the morning and another two and one-half hours in the afternoon except during the hottest days of the year. Like other Italian schools, it met throughout the calendar year, with the exception of various holidays and a vacation of fifteen to thirty days during the hottest part of the summer.[13]

Bells dividing the schoolday into quarter-hour segments moved teachers and students briskly from one exercise to another in the lower classes. Boys learned the alphabet and how to read syllables in the ninth or lowest class. Because the teacher could not possibly hear individual recitations from the sixty or seventy boys in his class, he wrote the letters of the alphabet on large sheets of paper attached to the wall, and touched the letters and syllables with a stick while the students spoke them in unison. Upon learning a few words, the boys graduated to the eighth class. Here another group of sixty or more boys read a primer in a similarly regimented fashion. The teacher examined individual students throughout the day; a student who had mastered the primer moved up to the seventh class.

In the seventh and sixth classes (really one class of about 130 boys divided into an advanced and a slower section) boys learned to read vernacular religious books. Here and throughout the school, the teachers encouraged better performance through contests and rewards. The Pious School had taken to heart the advice of Italian Renaissance humanistic pedagogues who recommended the use of rewards and condemned punishment. Calasanz also copied the example of the Schools of Christian Doctrine and Jesuit schools, both of which used competitions extensively in order to encourage excellence.

In the fifth class, two teachers instructed about 140 boys in both vocational and higher academic subjects. In the morning one part of the class studied abbaco, i.e., Italian commercial arithmetic needed for merchant or shopkeeping careers, while the other part memorized Latin nouns. In the afternoon, all students learned to write. This class marked a finishing point for some boys who left the school for an apprenticeship or employment upon finishing abbaco instruction at about the age of twelve. The Pious School had prepared them to earn a living, a goal that Calasanz always kept in mind.

Those who continued in school now studied a standard Latin humanistic curriculum to be found in all Latin schools of the period.[14] The fourth class made an intensive study of Latin grammar and memorized the catechism. The third class studied verbs and read the *Colloquia sive linguae Latinae exercitatio* (published 1538) of the Spanish humanist Juan Luis Vives (1492–1540). This was a beginning Latin reader comprising amusing short dialogues. The second class continued to study verbal syntax; it also read a few letters from Cicero's *Epistulae ad familiares*, another text used throughout Europe to teach classical Latin prose. Students who had reached this level of learning might also audit classes at the Jesuit Collegio Romano. The first or highest class in the Pious School studied Latin gerunds and supines, read parts of Cicero's *De officiis*, and Virgil, presumably the *Aeneid*. All future Pious Schools followed the above curriculum with limited deviation.[15] The Pious School ended at this point. Some boys, who were probably thirteen to fifteen years of age, would continue their education at the Collegio Romano. Others would find employment or enter the religious life.

Like all the schools of the Catholic Reformation, the Pious School of Calasanz made religious instruction and practices an integral part of the curriculum. Inculcating good morals and saving souls were as important as learning academic subjects. The school day began with attendance at Mass and recitation of the Litany of the Blessed Virgin Mary. Students confessed and received Holy Communion at least once a month. On Sundays and holidays students had to come to the school for a short session of prayers and catechetical instruction. Classes ended half an hour early on Tuesdays and Saturdays so that students might give ear to spiritual exhortation. Finally, the Pious School engaged in perpetual prayer throughout the day. A priest and nine students knelt and prayed in the school chapel for fifteen to thirty minutes until relieved by the next group.

Calasanz borrowed curricular content and pedagogical techniques from several sources but harnessed them to his own vision of teaching the poor. The idea of an intellectual and spiritual mission to teach rudimentary education and religious instruction to the poor probably came from the Schools of Christian Doctrine; the highly structured system of classes came from the Jesuits. Some of the techniques for handling very large classes were earlier found in both catechetical and Jesuit schools.

The Pious School was unique because it was a free school exclusively intended for large numbers of the poor. Barefoot, rag-clad boys were welcomed in the school, which provided the books, paper, pens, ink, and, on occasion, food that the boys lacked.[16] Calasanz very strongly insisted that his schools must be absolutely free of charge. Calasanz did not want pupils to bring firewood to school or mothers to wash the teachers' clothes, although this was occasionally allowed. He even discouraged gifts to the teachers, an endemic Italian practice then and now.

Some of the problems that the schools faced demonstrated that the Piarists certainly did serve the poor. For example, the Piarists discovered that pupils came to school accompanied by younger siblings. Mothers probably sent these toddlers to school so that they could go outside the home to work. The pedagogical consequences were predictable: the little tagalongs were not mature enough to learn, but succeeded in disrupting the concentration of their older brothers. Calasanz had to order his schools to send them home again.[17]

A school offering students an opportunity both to learn reading, writing, and commercial arithmetic in the vernacular, and to study the Latin humanities curriculum, was unique. Every other school in Italy (and possibly throughout Europe) taught either the Latin curriculum that prepared boys for leadership roles in society, or the vernacular curriculum that trained boys for the world of work. None taught both simultaneously, so far as is known. Hence, other schools, whether private, municipal, or operated by religious orders, reinforced social divisions: pupils from the upper ranks of society attended Latin schools, while the rest attended vernacular schools. But Calasanz created a free school that enabled students to cross the economic divide between rich and poor. Once enrolled, boys from poor and modest families could leave poverty behind and advance in society through education. Calasanz also fervently hoped that the religious training of his school would enable students to save their souls.

ESTABLISHMENT OF THE ORDER

The small band of clerical and lay teachers began to act like a religious community. On July 14, 1604, Pope Clement VIII authorized the group of about twenty, now calling themselves "Operari delle Scuole Pie" (Workers of the Pious Schools), to live in common. They contributed to their joint expenses according to their means, began to eat in common in September 1604, and may have shared living quarters before long. Priests were called "padri" (fathers) and laymen "fratelli" (brothers), even though the members had not sworn the vows of a religious order. Calasanz' informal pious association of persons united to teach the poor fluctuated from a maximum of thirty-four to a low of eight in the next eight years. Turnover was high, as only about a quarter of those who joined the group remained.[18]

Calasanz wanted to establish a congregation of priests with solemn vows, and he needed more teachers. In order to achieve both goals, he asked Pope Paul V to join his small group to an established order, the Congregation of the Clerks Regular of the Mother of God, founded by Saint Giovanni Leonardi (1541–1609) and recognized by the papacy in 1595. The "Matritani," as they were sometimes called, were a tiny order of priests devoted to pastoral activities; they had the church of Santa Maria in Campitelli in central Rome, not far from the Pious School. The pope ordered the two to unite in 1614, and the Matritani to lend thirteen of their number to teach in the Pious School. The Matritani lacked Calasanz' single-minded commitment to schooling, however, and would not accept such a rigorous vow of poverty as Calasanz desired. The union foundered on these differences.[19]

Paul V separated the two and authorized the establishment of an autonomous religious congregation for Calasanz' group in a papal brief of March 17, 1617. This date is taken to be the official establishment of the order. The key provision was that every house of the new congregation would have a school, except the novitiate. The new congregation elected Calasanz their superior. In a papal brief of November 23, 1621, Pope Gregory XV approved a full congregation whose title was "Chierici Regolari Poveri della Madre di Dio delle Scuole Pie" (Poor Clerks Regular of the Mother of God of the Pious Schools). They were usually called "Scolopi" in Italian (an untranslatable contraction of Scuole Pie), and "Escolapios" in Spanish. The pope then approved the constitutions of the new order, written by Calasanz, on January 31, 1622. To the normal three solemn vows of poverty, chastity, and obedience, he added a fourth vow: to teach.[20]

The Piarists were the only Catholic Reformation order exclusively devoted to teaching. Whatever their original purpose, other orders broadened their scope to undertake several ministries. Calasanz stubbornly refused to do this. The schools were so important, and teachers in such short supply, that he refused to permit his order to undertake any other religious ministry, such as preaching. He did not even want his priests to go out at night to comfort the sick. Calasanz acknowledged this to be a great work of charity, but those who engaged in it would be unable to teach the following day.[21] Many times he refused to permit his priests to become confessors to laymen. He feared that those who became confessors would be drawn away from teaching, the sole mission of the order. He also believed that the post of confessor was an excuse for laziness: some priests heard confessions, then did nothing the rest of the week, in his view.[22]

As enrollment at the Roman Pious School grew, the Piarists moved several times in order to find adequate space at a rent they could afford, or to take advantage of a building offered to them. The most important move occurred in November 1605 when they moved into a building in Piazza San Pantaleo in the heart of Rome. In 1612 the Piarists bought the building contiguous to the church of San Pantaleo; the papacy then ceded the church to the Piarists. The church and building are located just off what is now the Corso Vittorio Emanuele II, about 150 meters west of Sant'Andrea della Valle. The *palazzo* at San Pantaleo housed the Roman Pious School and the headquarters of the order for the next 150 years.

Financial support for the Roman Pious School came from donations from the popes and prelates of Rome. Clement VIII (1592–1605) and Paul V (1605–1621) gave the Pious School annual subsidies. Various cardinals, including the scholars Cesare Baronio and Silvio Antoniano, also helped. Cardinal Lodovico de Torres was the first cardinal-protector of the Piarists, from 1607 to 1613; Cardinal Michelangelo Tonti (1566–1622) was another major supporter.

The Piarists also begged for their needs, calling their begging expeditions "searches" (*cerche*). They went door-to-door "in search of" grain, wine, and olive oil to feed the teachers, wood to heat the school, and so on. So far as is known, the Jesuits, Barnabites, and other new religious orders of the Catholic Reformation did not make door-to-door begging an integral part of their fund-raising. Calasanz embraced begging, not only because of the needs of the schools and the order, but also because he wished to emphasize the spiritual benefits of living an existence similar to the poor to be served. Begging was controversial. For this reason Calasanz advised the members of his congregation to beg only when the need was great. In 1619 he told the Piarist community at Frascati not to beg bread if they had any wheat on hand. Begging under these circumstances would produce unfavorable gossip, and rightly so, in his view. We must not go out begging unless driven by necessity, he wrote. But if you need cooking oil, you may go "searching" for it.[23]

Once the Piarist order was established, Calasanz eagerly expanded his schools to other towns. The Piarists founded schools in Frascati (near Rome) in 1617; Narni (in Umbria in central Italy) in 1618; Carcare (in Liguria near Genoa in northeast Italy), Fanano (near Modena in northern Italy), and Norcia (in Umbria in central Italy) in 1621; Savona (in Liguria) in 1623; Genoa in 1624; Messina (Sicily) in 1625; Naples in 1626; Florence in 1630; Ancona (on the Adriatic Sea) and Cosenza (south of Naples) in 1631; and Palermo in 1634. Other schools followed in Nikolsburg (in Moravia) in 1631 and elsewhere in northern Europe, including Warsaw in 1642. In almost every case the schools enrolled several hundred students. In 1637 the Piarists had six provinces (Rome, Liguria, Naples, Tuscany, Sicily, and "Germany," i.e., northern Europe) with a total of 27 houses, all but the novice house with a school. The order had 432 members in 1637.[24] By 1646 the Piarists had 37 houses and 500 members in Italy and abroad.[25]

As the Piarists expanded their schools into other towns, they relied on the same mix of benefactors as the other new religious orders did. Princes, nobles, prelates, and some clergymen contributed funds, while numerous legacies collected in return for celebrating Masses for the souls of the departed provided the rest.[26] Inevitably the Piarists competed for funds with other religious orders, and this generated some friction. Occasionally, the Piarists took direction of a municipal school in exchange for annual subsidies from the town government. Norcia in Umbria and Volterra in southern Tuscany were examples.[27]

SPIRITUALITY

The Piarists did not evince an original spirituality; nor did they have a unique system of meditation. They emphasized devotion to the Blessed Sacrament through perpetual prayer and to Mary, the Mother of God. To some extent they followed Ignatius de Loyola's meditative approach. However, the spirituality of the order was, in a sense, translated into action in the world. The teaching vow, an emphasis on their own poverty, and service to the poor through education were the bases of their spirituality.

Calasanz was the quintessential doer. A letter of 1644 urging another member of the order to give good example expressed his view. At least once every day the Piarist should go into the school and spend some time teaching reading or writing to the younger pupils, Calasanz wrote. If done solely for love, this act will win greater merit with God than prayer. For, as St. Augustine said, he who prays does well, but he who assists others does better. Even in my old age (nearly eighty-seven) I often go into the classroom to help.[28]

SUPPRESSION

In February 1622 Pope Gregory XV named Calasanz Superior General for a nine-year term. Upon its expiration, Urban VIII in

January 1632 made Calasanz (now 74 years of age) Superior General for life.[29] All must have expected that the dedicated old man, who had already lived far beyond normal life expectancy, would soon die. He, in turn, must have felt that his order was securely established. Neither came to pass; Calasanz lived another sixteen and one-half years, during which time he saw his order suppressed.

Despite the seeming success of their mission, dissent festered in the ranks of the order. As early as 1625 a Piarist attacked Calasanz' policies and leadership. In his desperate search for more teachers, Calasanz had accepted poorly educated men unsuited for the religious life, the critic charged. Moreover, he had shortened the two-year probationary period for novices and had dispatched ill-prepared lay brothers to the classroom. Calasanz was giving lay brothers too much responsibility for tasks that should be done by priests. This internal critic blamed these problems on Calasanz' frenetic desire to open more schools. The papacy nominated a visitor who made some recommendations, but no substantial change ensued.[30]

The critic brought to the surface a contentious issue, the question of the duties and position of the lay brothers, called "fratelli operari" (brother workers). Like nearly all male religious orders, the Piarists were divided into priests and brothers. Piarist priests were better educated, performed more important tasks, and led the order. Brothers had less education, might perform domestic duties, and did not rise to positions of authority.

Piarist priests and brothers also taught different subjects. Lacking Latin, the brothers taught the elementary reading and writing classes, and commercial arithmetic.[31] Priests who needed Latin to be ordained taught the higher, more prestigious subjects. They did not want to teach the lowest classes full of sixty squirming little boys. On the other side, lower clerical status and elementary teaching made some *fratelli operari* unhappy: they wanted to be priests. Students would respect them more, and their teaching would be easier, if they wore the priest's biretta, they believed.

Calasanz decided that the *fratelli operari* should be elevated to the priesthood. Despite his two doctorates, Calasanz did not link educational achievement to privilege and was remarkably unpretentious. Believing strongly in the spiritual importance of teaching survival literacy to the poor, Calasanz saw no difficulty in raising the brothers who taught the primary classes to the status of the better-educated priests. Hence, the general congregation meeting of October 1627 authorized the elevation of *fratelli operari* to the priesthood. Moreover, everyone in the order beyond the novice stage was permitted to wear the biretta of the priest. These measures would, in the words of the decree of the general congregation, promote concord, unity, and fraternal charity within the order. By 1631 or 1632, the Piarists had fewer then twenty *fratelli operari* in an order of three hundred.

Equality did not work well. Whatever the pedagogical benefits and satisfaction for the brothers, the decision to advance them to the priesthood probably meant the promotion to leadership roles of men lacking adequate preparation, education, and spiritual formation. Piarist historians believe that this decree led some ambitious men lacking spiritual ardor to enter the order in the expectation of quick advancement. Indeed, some Piarists who later became Calasanz' enemies became priests through the decree.[32] And an unknown number of older, better-prepared priests must have resented the leveling decree.

Equal clerical status did not yield harmony, partly because the educational gap among members was widening. Calasanz encouraged the Piarists to study more, and he wanted them to learn from the age's most innovative scholars, however controversial they might be. On Calasanz' invitation, Tommaso Campanella (1568–1639) taught philosophy to a group of Piarists at the house in Frascati in 1631. The novitiate was becoming a center for higher education, and the Piarists were becoming a learned order.[33]

The celebrated association of some Florentine Piarists with Galileo Galilei began in 1634 if not earlier. The Roman Congregation of the Holy Office had condemned Galileo for holding Copernican views in June 1633. It punished him with perpetual imprisonment, which was commuted to house arrest at his home in Arcetri on the outskirts of Florence. Always interested in mathematics and science, Calasanz had probably already established preliminary contacts between members of his order and the eminent scientist. In October 1634 Calasanz approved of closer association between some of the Florentine Piarists and Galileo. In April 1639 Calasanz granted permission to one of the Piarists to stay overnight at Galileo's house in order to assist the nearly-blind scientist.[34] Several Florentine Piarists worked with Galileo in these years, and one of them taught Galilean mathematics at the Medici court in Florence.

Since the attempt of 1627 to deny differences in learning and status failed to heal the rift, Calasanz and other leaders of the order changed direction at the next general meeting of the order in 1637. They revoked the decree of 1627; in the future lay brothers might not teach, they could not advance to the priesthood, and were forbidden to wear clerical dress, including the biretta. Only priests could teach, and all teachers were to be tested for competency, an obvious move to raise the educational level of the order.[35] The policy reversal tacitly recognized that the attempt to treat all equally was not working. But again the change must have provoked controversy.

A final cause for dissension was unhappiness concerning Calasanz' leadership. As early as 1625 a Piarist had criticized Calasanz for refusing to consult the assistant generals of the order and for governing like an "absolute prince."[36] Indeed, from the beginning Calasanz had made practically all the decisions. As the order expanded, he continued to insist on being consulted on everything, making his wishes known by means of a stream of letters from Rome. To cite one example among many, in 1627 he chastised both the provincial of the Neapolitan province and the head of the Naples house over the dress of the novices there. The job of the general of an order is to govern, Calasanz wrote. Since I am not in the Indies, I must be consulted.[37] An authoritarian personality accompanied his steadfast dedication to the mission of teaching the poor. Nor did Calasanz shrink from ordering harsh punishments for erring Piarists. For example, he ordered a lay brother at Norcia to be put into legirons and fed only bread and water every other day of the week until further notice as punishment for his *pazzia e scandolo* ("craziness and scandal").[38] The number of letters ordering punishment seemed to increase over the decades. At this distance it is not possible to determine if Calasanz became increasingly severe as he aged or whether members of the order, especially the lay brothers, misbehaved more often.

The internal dissension exploded into rebellion in 1641. In the spring of that year, a Piarist in Florence named Mario Sozzi denounced four of his colleagues to the Florentine Inquisition for holding Galilean views.[39] He specifically accused the Galilean Piarists of believing that the earth moved around a stationary sun;

that all matter was composed of atoms, a view contrary to Aristotle's doctrine of form and matter; and that the world had no beginning or Creator. Even though Sozzi was a known schemer and troublemaker, the charges could not be completely rejected. Some Piarists did hold Galilean views, and there certainly were difficulties within the order. The accusation of Galileanism was guaranteed to provoke a hostile reaction from the papacy of Urban VIII whose Holy Office had forced Galileo to abjure. Even worse, the denunciation gave rivals and enemies an opportunity to attack the order.

The first group of enemies were rival teaching orders, that is, the Barnabites, the Somascans, and especially the Jesuits, with whom the Piarists had been on bad terms for years. The other orders competed with the Piarists for donations. And they believed that the Piarists were attracting some upper- and middle-class pupils who would otherwise attend their schools. Indeed, the Piarists had modified their rules a little. Either under papal pressure, or because the need for a certificate of poverty from a parish priest discouraged some parents from sending their sons to school at all, the Pious Schools had dropped the certificate as a condition for enrollment in 1617.[40] The Piarists had also opened a tiny boarding school requiring fees in Rome in 1630 and a small class for nobles within the larger Piarist school in Florence in 1638.[41] But the number of upper-class pupils enrolled in Piarist schools was extremely small. The overwhelming majority of students continued to come from the lower ranks of society.[42] Nevertheless, the other orders feared greater competition for upper- and middle-class schoolboys. In order to check Piarist educational expansion, the Jesuits demanded that they drop the humanistic Latin curriculum and teach only vernacular reading, writing, and arithmetic. But Calasanz consistently refused to restrict the educational scope of his schools.

The second group of external enemies were social conservatives, which meant almost all members of the ruling class. They had from the beginning criticized the Pious Schools for teaching the working class inappropriate skills. Free schools for the poor undermined the social order in their view. Society consisted of different orders, each with its unique function. Patricians ruled, the clergy performed sacred duties, and artisans, farmers, servants, and soldiers worked. Educating the lower classes deprived society of the services of workers. It might be acceptable to teach working-class boys elementary vernacular reading and writing skills as a Christian work of charity. But the conservatives strenuously objected to giving free Latin instruction to working-class boys. If poor boys learned Latin, they would try to become clergymen and university graduates, thus depriving the commonwealth of their useful labor.[43]

Campanella, a friend and supporter of the Pious Schools, had brilliantly answered these charges in an unpublished defense of the Piarists written in 1631 or 1632.[44] Calasanz answered again in 1645 with a memorandum presented to the commission of cardinals investigating the order. Far from damaging the social order, the Pious Schools contributed to society by teaching all who came, he argued. The poor should not be excluded because of their inability to pay; rather, the poor should be taught because God sometimes raised up learned philosophers and theologians from their ranks. Society need not fear the loss of the work skills of the lower classes, because only a few students from their group had the capacity to rise. Even more important, those who remained artisans after studying in the Pious Schools would carry on their craft in a better way to the benefit of society as a whole. In addition, eliminating Latin instruction would make it impossible for poor boys to become priests. Calasanz pointed out that various papal bulls had encouraged the clergy to operate schools and seminaries for this purpose.[45]

The papacy appointed a commission of cardinals to investigate the Piarists. Enemies, including a Jesuit, took leading roles in the investigation, which went very badly for the Piarists.[46] The Roman Inquisition even came to arrest Calasanz on August 9, 1642, and the eighty-five-year-old Calasanz was marched off to the Holy Office prison! Cooler heads prevailed, and he returned to San Pantaleo by the end of the day.[47] This demonstrated more clearly than anything else that enemies had the upper hand.

The commission ruled against the Piarists. Upon its recommendation the papacy reduced the order to the status of a congregation without vows on March 16, 1646. Individual Piarists were removed from the direction of Calasanz and returned to the authority of local bishops. Moreover, the order could no longer accept new members; those who had already professed vows were permitted to leave for other religious orders. About two hundred left, some for other orders, some for lay status.[48] The other three hundred Piarists stayed with the order, and the mother school at Rome continued to function. That the majority remained testified to their dedication to the schools and their loyalty to Calasanz. But the prohibition against adding new members would slowly strangle the order.

Calasanz exhibited remarkable equanimity through the troubles. When news of the suppression of the order came, he replied with the words of Job: "The Lord gave, the Lord has taken away. Blessed be the name of the Lord" (1:21).[49] He counseled patience. Calasanz died in Rome on August 25, 1648, at the age of ninety-one, convinced that his order would be vindicated.

RESTORATION

Calasanz was correct. In response to the repeated requests of the remaining Piarists and their supporters in the hierarchy, the papacy restored the Piarists to the status of a congregation with simple vows in 1656 and to a full religious order with solemn vows and tighter rules in 1669. With the restoration, the order rebuilt its numbers. The Piarists counted 16 houses and 442 members in Italy alone in 1676.[50]

The Piarist order grew to a European total of 94 houses and 950 members in 1706. The Piarists then expanded considerably in the eighteenth century, probably reaching the highest membership in their history at that time.[51] Considerable expansion occurred in northern Europe, as the Piarists founded houses and schools in Baden, Budapest, Vilna, and Prague. After the order was introduced into the land of its founder in 1683, Spain also became a stronghold, with houses in Madrid, Zaragoza, Valencia, and elsewhere. In time the Piarists developed a great reputation for learning, especially in the sciences. This led Pope Clement XII to authorize the Piarists to accept university appointments in the 1730s. Some did. The order continued to expand through the eighteenth century at a time when other Catholic Reformation teaching orders stagnated or were suppressed; the Piarists had 218 houses and about 3,000 members in 1784. And they received complete papal vindication and endorsement for Calasanz' vision when he was beatified in 1748 and canonized in 1767.

CONCLUSION

Catholic Reformation religious orders manifested two distinguishing characteristics at inception. They owed their existence to the genius of a dedicated founder, and they vowed to serve in the world. The Piarists exhibited these two characteristics perhaps more intensely than any other order. After establishment, Catholic Reform orders had to negotiate a transition period in which they needed to surmount three hurdles. Leadership had to pass smoothly from the founder to his successors. The order had to develop the structure and procedures enabling it to continue and expand. And it needed to design and implement a training program for new members. Some orders, especially the Jesuits, had notable success in this transitional phase. The Society of Jesus inculcated new members with a specific spirituality, which gave them a strong sense of the order's identity and mission, and trained them well for the order's worldly tasks.

The Piarists negotiated this transition with great difficulty. Nearly fifty years of strong leadership under Calasanz set the direction of the order but produced serious strains. The Piarists initially failed to develop a good training program for new members, possibly because they lacked a specific spiritual program and seemingly had only a brief, inadequate novitiate for new members. Only after Calasanz' death and a good deal of travail were the problems surmounted. Then the order fully realized Calasanz' vision: that all boys regardless of their economic circumstances might be educated and their souls saved.

SELECT BIBLIOGRAPHY

This is a select bibliography of basic works on Calasanz and the Piarists in their first half-century. The Archivio Generale of the order is located at San Pantaleo in Rome. A brief printed list of some of the archival materials, especially those dealing with Calasanz, is found in György Sántha, César Aguilera, and Julián

Centelles, *San José de Calasanz: Su obra, escritos* (Madrid: Biblioteca de Autores Cristianos, 1956; repr. by the same publisher 1984), pp. xxvii–xliii. This is the largest and most important biography of Calasanz. It includes extensive discussion of the educational content and techniques of the Pious Schools and more than one hundred pages of documents translated into Spanish. The earliest comprehensive biography of Calasanz is Vincenzo Talenti, *Vita del B. Giuseppe Calasanzio della Madre di Dio, Fondatore delle Scuole Pie* (Rome: Zempel, 1753; 2nd ed., Florence: Scuola Tipografica Calasanziana, 1917). Other biographies include Urbano Tosetti, *Compendio storico della vita di S. Giuseppe Calasanzio, fondatore delle Scuole Pie* (Florence: Stamperia Calasanziana, 1824), first published by Zempel in Rome in 1767, with numerous editions; Joseph Timon-David, *Vie de Saint Joseph Calasanct, fondateur des Écoles Pies*, 2 vols. (Marseilles: Blanc & Bernard, 1884); Valentin Caballero, *Orientaciones pedagogicas de San José de Calasanz, el gran pedagogo y su obra cooperadores de la verdad*, 2nd ed. (Madrid, no publisher, 1945); Quirino Santoloci, *Giuseppe Calasanzio, educatore e santo, 1648–1948* (Rome: Istituto Grafico Tiberino, 1948); and Francesco Giordano, *Il Calasanzio e l'origine della scuola popolare* (Genoa: A.G.I.S., 1960). A short summary biography with comprehensive bibliography is G. Cianfrocca, "Giuseppe Calasanzio (José de Calasanz)," *Dizionario degli istituti di perfezione*, vol. 4 (Rome: Edizioni Paoline, 1977), cols. 1343–51.

The *Epistolario di San Giuseppe Calasanzio*, ed. Leodegario Picanyol, 9 vols. (Rome: Edizioni di Storia e Letteratura, 1950–1956) contains 4,578 letters, written between 1588 and 1648, along with useful historical commentary. Letters to Calasanz are not included. A tenth volume contains 281 additional letters and occasional pieces by Calasanz which have come to light since 1956, plus useful indices: *Epistolario di San Giuseppe Calasanzio*. Vol. 10: *Scritti apparsi posteriormente e raccolti*, ed. Claudio Vilá Palá (Rome: Editiones Calasanctianae, 1988). Other collections of letters are *Epistolarium Coaetaneorum S. Iosephi Calasanctii, 1600–1648*, ed. György Sántha and Claudio Vilá Palá, 7 vols. (Rome: Editiones Calasanctianae, 1977–1982); and *Epistulae ad S. Iosephum Calasanctium ex Europa Centrali, 1625–1648*, ed. György Sántha (Rome: Editiones Calasanctianae, 1969). *Il pensiero pedagogico della Controriforma*, ed. Luigi Volpicelli (Florence: Giuntine-Sansoni, 1960), pp. 561–85, provides Italian translations of three key documents:

the "Breve relazione" of 1604–1610, the Constitutions of the order drafted by Calasanz, and Campanella's "Liber apologeticus."

Several series of Piarist publications devoted to the publication of documents and monographs on the history of the order began in the 1930s. Unfortunately, they have not always continued and are very difficult to locate in North America. The *Ephemerides calasanctianae* produced at least 36 volumes from 1932 through 1967, but apparently no longer is issued. The *Monumenta Historica Scholarum Piarum* series is still active. The journal *Archivum Scholarum Piarum* issued 15 fascicules, from 1936 through 1956, but then stopped. It came back to life as a biannual in 1977, publishing twenty-four issues through 1988, although the volumes from 1977 onward do not indicate that this is a "new series." It is published at the order's historical institute located at Piazza de' Massimi 4, 00186 Rome. The *Archivum* and additional Piarist materials can be found in the library of The Catholic University of America, Washington, D.C.

A good brief history of the order is Giovanni A. Ausenda, "Chierici Regolari Poveri della Madre di Dio delle Scuole Pie," *Dizionario degli istituti di perfezione*, vol. 2 (Rome: Edizione Paoline, 1975), cols. 927–45. Leodegario Picanyol has written several monographs on different aspects of the order. See in particular *Brevis conspectus historico-statisticus Ordinis Scholarum Piarum* (Rome: Mantero, 1932); and *Le Scuole Pie e Galileo Galilei* (Rome, 1942), not seen.

For individual Piarist schools, see Pasquale Vannucci, *Il Collegio Nazareno, MDCXXX–MCMXXX* (Rome: Tipografica Italo-Orientale "St. Nilo," 1930); Leodegario Picanyol, *Le Scuole Pie di Fanano* (Rome: Padri Scolopi di S. Pantaleo, 1941); Angelo Sindoni, "Le Scuole Pie in Sicilia: Note sulla storia dell'ordine Scolopico dalle origini al secolo XIX," *Rivista di storia della Chiesa in Italia*, 25 (1971), 375–421; and Romano Cordella and Eusebio Severini, "I primi tempi delle scuole pie a Norcia," *Archivum Scholarum Piarum*, 6, No. 12 (1982), 205–56.

Tosetti, *Compendio storico* (1824 ed.), pp. 317–340, offers biographies of twelve early Piarists. On a major early Piarist author of textbooks, see A. Dolci, "Apa, Giovanni Francesco (1612–56)," *Dizionario biografico degli Italiani*, vol. 3 (Rome: Istituto della Enciclopedia Italiana, 1961), p. 601.

A. K. Liebreich has written several important studies on the

Piarists: "The Contribution of the Piarist Order to Popular Education in the Seventeenth Century," Ph.D. diss., Cambridge University, 1986 (not seen); "The Florentine Piarists," *Archivum Scholarum Piarum*, 6, no. 12 (1982), 273–304; and "Piarist Education in the Seventeenth Century," *Studi secenteschi*, 26 (1985), 225–77, and 27 (1986), 57–88. For Tommaso Campanella's defense of the Piarists, see K. Jensen and A. K. Liebreich, "Liber apologeticus contra impugnantes Institutum Scholarum Piarum with introduction and English translation," *Archivum Scholarum Piarum*, 8, No. 15 (1984), 29–76.

Finally, for a comprehensive bibliography of the writings of Piarists over the centuries plus works about the order, see Leodegario Picanyol, *La biblioteca scolopica di S. Pantaleo di Roma*, 2 vols. (Rome: Editiones Calasanctianae, 1952, 1955).

I wish to thank Professor Nelson Minnich for his assistance.

NOTES

1. This is the date given by the most recent biography, G. Cianfrocca's "Giuseppe Calasanzio (José de Calasanz)," *Dizionario degli istituti di perfezione*, vol. 4 (Rome: Edizioni Paoline, 1977), col. 1343. For the details of his birth, family, and Spanish career, I also follow György Sántha, César Aguilera, and Julián Centelles, *San José de Calasanz: Su obra, escritos* (Madrid: Biblioteca de Autores Cristianos, 1956; repr. 1984), pp. 4–5; and the detailed commentary accompanying the first few letters in *Epistolario di San Giuseppe Calasanzio*, ed. Leodegario Picanyol, 9 vols. (Rome: Edizioni di Storia e Letteratura, 1950–1956), 2:13–36. Because of the paucity of information, the biographies differ a little about his birth, early life, and Spanish career.

2. Pio Pecchiai, *Roma nel Cinquecento* (Bologna: Licinio Cappelli, 1948), p. 447.

3. Guerrino Pelliccia, *La scuola primaria a Roma dal secolo XVI al XIX* (Rome: Edizioni dell'Ateneo, 1985), p. 178.

4. On the Schools of Christian Doctrine, see Alessandro Tamborini, *La compagnia e le scuole della dottrina cristiana* (Milan: Tipografia Arcivescovile, 1939); Miriam Turrini, "'Riformare il mondo a vera vita cristiana': Le scuole di catechismo nell'Italia del Cinquecento," *Annali dell'Istituto storico italo-germanico di Trento*, 8 (1982), 407–89; Paul F. Grendler, *Schooling in Renaissance Italy: Literacy and Learning, 1300–1600* (Baltimore and London: The Johns Hopkins University Press, 1989), pp. 333–62; and Pelliccia, *La scuola primaria*, pp. 29–42, for Rome.

5. Grendler, *Schooling in Renaissance Italy*, chaps. 1, 2, and pp. 102–108.

6. Vincenzo Talenti, *Vita del B. Giuseppe Calasanzio della Madre di Dio, Fondatore delle Scuole Pie*, 2nd ed. (Florence: Scuola Tipografica Calasanziana, 1917), pp. 48–52; and Urbano Tosetti, *Compendio storico della vita di S. Giuseppe Calasanzio, fondatore delle Scuole Pie* (Florence: Stamperia Calasanziana, 1824), pp. 51–52, for the following.

7. Grendler, *Schooling in Renaissance Italy*, pp. 78–82.

8. Ibid., pp. 373–74.

9. Quirino Santoloci, *Giuseppe Calasanzio, educatore e santo, 1648–1948* (Rome: Istituto Grafico Tiberino, 1948), p. 51; Tosetti, *Compendio storico*, pp. 57–58; and Pelliccia, *La scuola primaria*, p. 179. The exact opening date of the school is not known. Sántha, Aguillera, and Centelles, *San José de Calasanz*, p. 21, suggest late October 1597.

10. Pelliccia, *La scuola primaria*, pp. 180–81.

11. It is printed in *Epistolario*, ed. Picanyol, 2:47–48.

12. This "Breve relazione sul modo usato nelle scuole pie per insegnare agli alunni poveri che d'ordinario sono più di settecento non solo le lettere ma sopratutto il santo timor di Dio" is attributed to Calasanz and printed in Santoloci, *Giuseppe Calasanzio*, pp. 89–96; and in *Il pensiero pedagogico della Controriforma*, ed. Luigi Volpicelli (Florence: Giuntine-Sansoni, 1960), pp. 561–65. As A. K. Liebreich points out, in "Piarist Education in the Seventeenth Century," *Studi secenteschi*, 26 (1985), 226 n. 1, Piarist scholars now question the traditional date of 1610 and suggest that it might be as early as 1604.

13. A. K. Liebreich, "Piarist Education in the Seventeenth Century," *Studi secenteschi*, 27 (1986), 57–59; and Grendler, *Schooling in Renaissance Italy*, pp. 34–35, on the normal academic calendar.

14. For the standard Latin curriculum, see Grendler, *Schooling in Renaissance Italy*, chaps. 7–9.

15. See Liebreich, "Piarist Education," who offers a great deal of information on the curriculum of the Florentine school later in the century.

16. Liebreich, "Piarist Education," (1986), 73–74. See also Letter 1292 of January 10, 1630, and Letter 1713 of November 12, 1631, in *Epistolario*, ed. Picanyol, 4:149, 433; and Letter 4138 of October 10, 1643, in ibid., 8:211.

17. "Scrissi la posta passata, che in quanto alla Scuola dei piccolini faccia quanto gli ordinarà il Sig. Vicario al quale scrivo, che consideri che molte madri per levarsi via il fastidio di casa causatoli dai fanciullini piccoli li mandano alla scuola in compagnia di un altro maggiore, et ne segue, che né il piccolo impara per non essere capace, né lascia imparare al grande. . . ." Letter 77 of Calasanz to Pellegrino Tencani in Norcia,

August 13, 1621, Rome, in *Epistolario*, ed. Picanyol, 2:131. "Scuola" here means an individual class, not the entire school.

18. Pelliccia, *La scuola primaria*, pp. 181–82.

19. *Epistolario*, ed. Picanyol, 2:49–55. V. Pascucci, "San Giovanni Leonardi," *Dizionario degli istituti di perfezione*, vol. 4 (Rome: Edizioni Paoline, 1977), cols. 1276–80; V. Pascucci, "Chierici Regolari della Madre di Dio delle Scuole Pie," ibid., vol. 2 (Rome: Edizioni Paoline, 1975), cols. 909–12; and (no author) *Vita del Beato Giovanni Leonardi fondatore della Congregazione dei Chierici Regolari della Madre di Dio scritta da un sacerdote della medesima congregazione* (Rome: S. Congregazione de Propaganda Fide, 1861). See pp. 62, 148–50, of the last work for evidence of lingering resentment against Calasanz for his alleged attempt to use the Matritani for his own purposes.

20. For key parts of the Constitutions in Italian translation, see *Il pensiero pedagogico*, ed. Volpicelli, pp. 566–70; see also Pelliccia, *La scuola primaria*, p. 183.

21. "Quanto all'andar de notti all'infermi sebene è opera di charità grande non possono li nostri che insegnano tutto il giorno andarvi la notte, perchè mancaranno all'opera il giorno seguente. . . ." Letter 2276 of September 23, 1634, in *Epistolario*, ed. Picanyol, 5:426.

22. See Letter 1334 of March 2, 1630; and Letter 1419 of June 16, 1630, in *Epistolario*, ed. Picanyol, 4:178, 236. See Letter 3112 of July 2, 1639, in ibid., 7:89; and Letter 3871 of January 11, 1642, in ibid., 8:54. For the accusation that confessors were lazy, see Letter 2849 of April 24, 1638, in ibid., 6:333. See also Calasanz' memorandum of 1625 in which he worried greatly about a slackness in dedication to teaching by members of his order because of the attraction of other activities. Letter 380a, in ibid., 2:344–46, with commentary by Picanyol.

23. "Quanto all'andare accattando per la città il pane non mi pare conveniente mentre havete del grano perciò che saria dar a mormorar et con ragione et non dovemo noi andar accattando senza necessità. Però potrete mandar a cercar oglio fuori quando haverete bisogno. . . ." Letter 32, January 4, 1619, in *Epistolario*, ed. Picanyol, 2:80–81.

24. The figure comes from the first full count made by the Piarists themselves at the time of their general meeting in 1637. Pelliccia, *La scuola primaria*, p. 193.

25. Joseph Timon-David, *Vie de saint Joseph Calasanct, fondateur des Écoles Pies*, 2 vols. (Marseilles: Blanc & Bernard, 1884), 1:382–419 (chap. 17), gives a good summary of the founding of new schools. See also Giovanni A. Ausenda, "Chierici Regolari Poveri della Madre di Dio delle Scuole Pie," *Dizionario degli istituti di perfezione*, vol. 2 (Rome: Edizioni Paolini, 1975), cols. 929–30, for a brief list.

26. See the analysis of the income of the Florentine school in Lie-

breich, "The Florentine Piarists," *Archivum Scholarum Piarum*, 6, No. 12 (1982), 295–98. A study of the finances of Catholic Reformation religious orders is badly needed. As the Piarist example demonstrates, there was a significant transfer of funds from wealthy laymen and prelates to the new religious orders. The latter, in turn, used the donations and legacies to finance charitable and educational activities that benefited the poorer segments of society. But the story, which should include an assessment of the impact on society of this transfer of funds, awaits its historian.

27. Romano Cordella and Eusebio Severini, "I primi tempi delle scuole pie a Norcia," *Archivum Scholarum Piarum*, 6, No. 12 (1982), 205–56; Mario Battistini, *Il pubblico insegnamento in Volterra dal secolo XIV al secolo XVIII* (Volterra, 1919), p. 54.

28. "Vengo con la presente ad essortar V. R. ad un atto di perfettione et di buon essempio per tutti li altri di casa et anco per li secolari fuori et è che ogni giorno almeno una volta vada nelle scuole et reciti quatro o sei scolari hor siano dello scrivere hor siano del leggere et di piccolini che così darà buon nome alle scuole et col suo essempio incitarà li altri Padri et fratelli a far l'istesso essercitio et le assicuro che facendo questo per sola charità acquistarebbero maggior merito appresso Iddio che se facessero oratione, essendo vero quel detto che non mi ricordo di che santo sia seben mi pare sia di S. Agostino che dice qui orat bene facit sed qui juvat melius facit et questo che io ancora vecchio come sono vado spesse volte per le scuole ad agiutar." Letter 4204 of June 28, 1644, in *Epistolario*, ed. Picanyol, 8:240–41.

29. Pelliccia, *La scuola primaria*, p. 193.

30. Ibid., pp. 187–91.

31. The following two paragraphs are based on Sántha, Aguilera, and Centelles, *San José de Calasanz*, pp. 132–36.

32. Santoluci, *Giuseppe Calasanzio*, pp. 126–27.

33. Sántha, Aguilera, and Centelles, *San José de Calasanz*, pp. 148, 235–39, 266–67; K. Jensen and A. K. Liebreich, "Liber apologeticus contra impugnantes Institutum Scholarum Piarum with Introduction and English Translation" *Archivum Scholarum Piarum*, 8, No. 15 (1984), 30–33, 35–38.

34. Letter 3074 of April 16, 1639, in *Epistolario*, ed. Picanyol, 7:65. For the association with Galileo, see Liebreich, "Florentine Piarists," 288–92.

35. Sántha, Aguilera, and Centelles, *San José de Calasanz*, pp. 136, 266 n. 11.

36. Pelliccia, *La scuola primaria*, p. 187.

37. Letter 732, November 20, 1627, in *Epistolario*, ed. Picanyol, 3:191–93, including Picanyol's comment. See also Sántha, Aguilera, and Centelles, *San José de Calasanz*, p. 11.

38. Letter 3788, November 27, 1641, in *Epistolario*, ed. Picanyol, 7:465.

39. See Sántha, Aguilera, and Centelles, *San José de Calasanz*, pp. 165–68 and notes, for the text of the denunciation and information on the Galilean Piarists; the short summary of Picanyol in *Epistolario*, 7:347–51; and Liebreich, "Florentine Piarists," 288–94.

40. Tosetti, *Compendio storico*, p. 97, offers the first explanation; Liebreich, "Piarist Education," (1986), 74–75, the second.

41. See Pasquale Vannucci, *Il Collegio Nazareno, MDCXXX-MCMXXX* (Rome: Tipografica Italo-Orientale "S. Nilo," 1930); and Liebreich, "Florentine Piarists," respectively.

42. The only analysis of the social backgrounds of Piarist pupils known to me is found in Liebreich, "Florentine Piarists," 284–88; it is largely repeated in "Piarist Education," (1986), 78–81. Her sampling from 1680 to 1703 in the Florentine Pious School reveals that 70 per cent to 90 per cent of the pupils came from artisan families.

43. The first part of Campanella's defense of the Piarists (see next note) summarized well the social conservatives' arguments against the Piarist schools.

44. See Jensen and Liebreich, "Liber apologeticus," for the Latin original and an English translation; and *Il pensiero pedagogico*, ed. Volpicelli, pp. 571–85, for an Italian translation of Campanella's treatise.

45. For a Spanish translation of Calasanz' defense, see Sántha, Aguilera, and Centelles, *San José de Calasanz*, pp. 710–16. Pelliccia, *La scuola primaria*, pp. 195–97, presents a summary.

46. Pelliccia, *La scuola primaria*, p. 194. All the biographies of Calasanz give detailed accounts of the long and complicated proceedings.

47. Tosetti, *Compendio storico*, pp. 195–204; Santoloci, *Giuseppe Calasanzio*, pp. 141–43.

48. The figures come from Ausenda, "Chierici Regolari Poveri . . . delle Scuole Pie," col. 930.

49. Santoloci, *Giuseppe Calasanzio*, p. 160.

50. Pelliccia, *La scuola primaria*, p. 207.

51. The following survey with its statistics is based on Ausenda, "Chierici Regolari Poveri . . . delle Scuole Pie," cols. 932–44.

Contributors

JODI BILINKOFF was awarded a Ph.D. in history from Princeton University in 1983. She is an associate professor of history at the University of North Carolina at Greensboro and the author of *The Avila of St. Teresa: Religious Reform in a Sixteenth-Century City* (Ithaca: Cornell University Press, 1989).

CHARMARIE J. BLAISDELL, who is an associate professor of history at Northeastern University, received her Ph.D. in history from Tufts University in 1970.

Richard L. DeMolen earned his Ph.D. in history from the University of Michigan in 1970. He served as the editor of the *Erasmus of Rotterdam Society Yearbook* from 1981 to 1993 and is the author of *The Spirituality of Erasmus of Rotterdam* (Nieuwkoop: De Graaf, 1987) and *Richard Mulcaster and Educational Reform in the Renaissance* (Nieuwkoop: De Graaf, 1991).

JOHN PATRICK DONNELLY, S.J., received his Ph.D. in history from the University of Wisconsin in 1972, and is professor of history at Marquette University. He is the author of *Calvinism and Scholasticism in Vermigli's Doctrine of Man and Grace* (Leiden: Brill, 1976) and *Reform and Renewal* (Wilmington, N.C.: Consortium Books, 1977); the co-editor and co-translator of *Robert Bellarmine: Spiritual Writings* (Mahwah, N.J.: Paulist, 1989); and editor and translator of *Girolamo Savonarola: Prison Meditations on Psalms 51 and 31* (Milwaukee: Marquette University Press, 1994). He has served as president of both the Sixteenth Century Studies Conference (1977) and the Society for Reformation Research (1990–1991).

ELISABETH G. GLEASON, who is professor of history at the University of San Francisco, earned her Ph.D. in history from the University of California at Berkeley in 1963. She wrote *Reform Thought in Sixteenth-Century Italy* (Chico, Ca.: Scholars Press,

1981) and *Gasparo Contarini: Venice, Rome, and Reform* (Berkeley, Los Angeles, and London: University of California Press, 1993).

PAUL F. GRENDLER was awarded his Ph.D. from the University of Wisconsin in 1964 and is professor of history at the University of Toronto. He is the author of four books and has edited two others. His most recent book is *Schooling in Renaissance Italy: Literacy and Learning, 1300–1600* (Baltimore: The Johns Hopkins University Press, 1989). He has won two Marraro prizes and has been president of the American Catholic Historical Association (1984) and The Renaissance Society of America (1992–1994).

KENNETH J. JORGENSEN, S.J., who is an assistant professor of history at Albertus Magnus College (New Haven), received his Ph.D. in history from Columbia University in 1989.

JOHN W. O'MALLEY, S.J., professor of church history at the Weston School of Theology (Cambridge, Massachusetts), received his doctorate in history from Harvard University in 1966. Among his books are *Giles of Viterbo on Church and Reform* (Leiden: Brill, 1968), *Praise and Blame in Renaissance Rome* (Durham, N.C.: Duke University Press, 1979), and *The First Jesuits* (Cambridge, Mass.: Harvard University Press, 1993).

ROGER A. WINES, who is professor of history at Fordham University, was awarded his Ph.D. in history from Columbia University in 1961. He is the author of *Enlightened Despotism* (Boston: Heath, 1967).

WENDY M. WRIGHT received her Ph.D. in religious studies from the University of California at Santa Barbara in 1983. She is an associate professor of theology at Creighton University and is the author of *Bond of Perfection: Jeanne de Chantal and François de Sales* (New York: Paulist, 1985), *Francis de Sales: Introduction to the Devout Life and Treatise on the Love of God* (New York: Crossroad, 1993), and co-author and editor, with Joseph F. Power, O.S.F.S., pf *Francis de Sales, Jane de Chantal: Letters of Spiritual Direction* (Mahwah, N.J.: Paulist 1988).

Index